THE STRUGGLE FOR IRAQ'S FUTURE

THE
STRUGGLE FOR
IRAQ'S FUTURE

HOW CORRUPTION,
INCOMPETENCE AND SECTARIANISM
HAVE UNDERMINED DEMOCRACY

ZAID AL-ALI

YALE UNIVERSITY PRESS
NEW HAVEN AND LONDON

For information about this and other Yale University Press publications, please contact:

U.S. Office: sales.press@yale.edu   yalebooks.com
Europe Office: sales@yaleup.co.uk   www.yalebooks.co.uk

Set in Sabon MT by IDSUK (DataConnection) Ltd
Printed in Great Britain by CPI Group (UK) Ltd, Croydon, CRO 4YY

A catalog record for this book is available from the Library of Congress and from the British Library.

ISBN 978-0-300-18726-7

10 9 8 7 6 5 4 3 2 1

2018 2017 2016 2015 2014

To my brother Omar, who never knew Iraq, and to my son Joud, for whom I wish a better future than the past we have known.

CONTENTS

Map — viii

Introduction — 1

1   A legacy of oppression and violence   17

2   On the origins of Iraq's new political elites   39

3   Creating a new political order   75

4   A country back from the dead   103

5   Defective politics   125

6   A country left to languish   161

7   The ravages of corruption: The second insurgency   189

8   The third insurgency: Environmental disaster   219

9   What is to be done?   243

Endnotes — 257

Bibliography — 281

Index — 289

TURKEY

DAHUK

Lake Urmia

Mosul

Erbil

NINAWA

ERBIL

KURDISTAN

SYRIA

Kirkuk

SULAYMANIYA

Sulaymaniya

TAMIN

Tigris

Euphrates

IRAN

Tikrit

SALAHUDDIN

Samara

DIYALA

Fallujah

Baghdad

Ramadi

JORDAN

ANBAR

Karbala

Kut

BABIL

WASIT

KARBALA

Hilla

Najaf

Diwaniya

Amara

QADISIYA

MAYSAN

Euphrates

Tigris

DHIQAR

NAJAF

Samawa

Shatt al-Arab

Nasiriya

SAUDI

Basra

ARABIA

BASRA

MUTHANNA

KUWAIT

– – – – border of Kurdistan region

Kuwait City

Persian

———— provincial boundaries

Gulf

0   50   100   150   200 miles

0   50   100   150   200 km

INTRODUCTION

In 2013, politics in Iraq reached a new low. Apart from the usual depressing failures in terms of services, corruption, security and the environment, a number of other developments finally revealed the full extent of the government's incompetence.

For several years, the security services have used a small handheld device to detect explosives, known as the Advanced Detection Equipment (ADE) 651. These devices were purchased at a desperate time: car bombs had already claimed the lives of thousands of people, and there was an urgent need to improve security measures. Physical searches were effective but were far too time consuming and could cause traffic jams of epic proportions, bringing life to a grinding halt.

ATSC Limited, a UK company that was founded by Jim McCormick, a former police officer with no previous experience in electronics, programming or engineering, claimed that the ADE 651 was 'a revolutionary tool in the effective detection and location of Narcotics (drugs), Explosives, and specific substances at long-range distances' and that it functioned according to a principle that the company referred to as 'Electro-Magnetic Attraction'.[1] The ADE 651 and similar devices had been used in other countries, including Afghanistan and Lebanon.[2] The Iraqi government purchased an unknown (but large) number of the ADE 651 from ATSC for approximately US$85 million.[3] It required so many government departments and institutions to use the device that there were not enough to go around. A market sprang up overnight, with government departments buying and selling the devices to each other at a profit. One department in the ministry of justice obtained one for $50,000 (even though each device cost just a few dollars to manufacture). The department's staff was so terrified of losing or damaging it that they placed it in their building's safe – out of harm's way – and never put it to use.[4]

Even to the casual observer it is clear that the devices are useless. Yet for years they have been employed by security forces at checkpoints throughout the country and at the entrance to ministries and other institutions. The device consists of a small plastic handle with a horizontal antenna attached. When a vehicle approaches a checkpoint, the driver has to wait while a soldier holds the device so that the antenna is level horizontally. He then walks parallel to the car, bobbing from left to right. If, during the soldier's dance, the antenna tilts towards the vehicle, the suggestion is that the car may contain explosives.

Like anyone who has spent any time in Iraq outside the Green Zone, I have been through thousands of checkpoints where the ADE is employed. On occasion, during particularly long trips, I have been through more than a hundred checkpoints in a single day while travelling in the same car. Although the car's contents were always the same (empty apart from passengers and some computers), the ADE would sometimes tilt towards the vehicle and sometimes not. There was no clear pattern; it was pure chance. Even when it did tilt, we were never searched anyway. The troops manning the checkpoint would always ask if we had any perfume with us. An answer in the affirmative guaranteed that we would be politely waved through with a smile.

Years after the ADE was first deployed, explosions were still taking place with alarming frequency. The attackers' weapon of choice was the car bomb, and sometimes several of these would go off in a dozen locations throughout the country within just a few hours. Clearly the terrorists were transporting significant amounts of explosives about with relative ease. Certainly the presence of army and police checkpoints every few hundred metres, and their heavy reliance on the ADE 651, did not appear to impede their movements. Many Iraqis and international observers began to question the device's effectiveness.

Since ATSC was a UK company, and as its founder was based not far from London, the BBC took it upon itself to investigate the issue in 2010. In the presence of a BBC reporter, researchers from Cambridge University took one of the devices apart, the better to understand the technology and how it was supposed to work. The supplier would provide the purchaser with a number of cards, each of which was designed to detect a particular type of explosive. The cards fitted into a holder that was attached to the antenna. In front of the BBC's cameras, university researchers took some of the cards apart and analysed their contents: they were empty. They contained no digital or electronic information whatsoever. There was no way that the ADE 651 could be used to detect anything. A number of other investigations were also carried out on the device, including by the US military. The conclusion was always the same. Some of the world's leading scientists therefore confirmed what just about any Iraqi who has been through a checkpoint had known for years.[5]

Following the BBC's investigation, UK law enforcement officials banned the ADE 651's export to Iraq and Afghanistan. The affair led to criminal investigations and prosecutions in both Iraq and the UK. On 10 February 2011, al-Rasafa court of appeal in east Baghdad issued an arrest warrant against General Jihad al-Jabiri, who at the time was head of the counter-explosives department at the ministry of the interior and who had been responsible for purchasing the ADE 651 on the government's behalf. On 4 June 2012, al-Jabiri was sentenced to four years in prison. The court's spokesman said that the decision was motivated by the fact that the devices were overpriced and based on bogus technology.[6]

In July 2012, the UK Crown Prosecution Service charged six people, including James McCormick, with the 'alleged manufacture, promotion and sale of a range of fraudulent substance detector devices', including the ADE 651, to countries such as Iraq.[7] During the course of the investigation, it was discovered that the ADE 651 had been modelled on failed golf-ball detectors that were on sale in the US. In May 2013, the court sentenced McCormick to ten years in prison and confiscated the property that he had accumulated, courtesy of his contracts with the Iraqi government, including several homes and a yacht. In his sentencing remarks, the judge addressed McCormick: 'The device was useless, the profit outrageous and your culpability as a fraudster has to be placed in the highest category . . . [H]otel security staff and many other users trusted their lives to the overpriced devices sold by you, which were no more than crude plastic components with a disconnected antenna and a capability of detecting explosives no better than random chance.'[8]

News of these developments spread far and wide in Iraq, and many wondered how the government would react. Clearly, there were few available options – and none of them attractive. Prime Minister Nouri al-Maliki had cultivated a public persona as someone who was strong on security. He had largely taken credit for the reduction in violence in 2007 and 2008 and, following the March 2010 parliamentary elections, he had assumed control of the security services, including the ministries of the interior and defence. Security was unquestionably his responsibility, and there were significant grounds for holding him personally accountable for the use of the device (among other failures). It is unheard of for senior officials in Iraq to hold up their hands and admit 'mea culpa', so nobody expected the government to apologize. Given the weight of evidence against the ADE 651, however, no one believed that it would keep them in use. It was most likely that the devices would be quietly withdrawn and the matter downplayed by senior officials.

On 21 May 2013, two weeks after the UK court decision, several explosions ripped through the capital, killing dozens of people. The devices were still in use. The prime minister organized a press conference a few hours later with a large part of his cabinet. He solemnly condemned the violence. The first question from the packed hall of journalists was about the ADE 651: how could it be that it was still in use, given the recent court ruling in the UK?

The prime minister's reply left me and others dumbfounded. Despite international consensus on the issue, he stood before his audience and insisted that the devices did in fact work:

> We formed committees the day the claims [of corruption] and rumours took place. We formed three committees: a science and technology committee, a defence committee, and a mixed committee. The results were that the devices detect between 20 and 54 per cent under ideal conditions. 'Ideal conditions' means that the soldier has to have been trained in the use of the device, and that he knows how to use the cards, given that the card that is used to detect bombs does not detect arms, and the one that is used to detect arms does not detect bombs . . . Some Iraqi MPs are talking about corruption. The relevant people were taken to court and are now in prison. A court case was filed in Britain, and the person responsible for the forgery [is also in prison]. But what is the truth? *The truth is that some of the devices were real and those devices do detect bombs, while the devices which the court case was about were fake. The problem lies with those that were fake. As for the devices that are real, their problem is that using them correctly requires experience.*[9]

For al-Maliki, the problem was that some of the devices were fake and others were not. This was a distinction that no one else had made or recognized and was purely of his own creation. One wonders what the deputy prime minister, Hussein al-Shahristani thought of the comments: he has a PhD in chemical engineering from the University of Toronto and throughout the press conference was standing with a poker face immediately to the left of the prime minister.

Officials in Thi Qar, one of the country's poorest areas, did not have the benefit of an advanced western education in science, but nevertheless they saw through the ruse and banned the ADE 651, committing themselves to purchase dozens of sniffer dogs instead.[10] Meanwhile, in Baghdad, car bombs continued to rip apart the lives of the people that the government pretended to protect with a piece of plastic that was worse than useless. July 2013 witnessed more than a thousand security-related deaths. Still more people were maimed. Yet not a single senior official accepted any responsibility. I learned from a friend that an acquaintance of mine was among those killed. A few years back, he had lost his brother in another explosion and had taken in his brother's children, who had nowhere else to go. Following this new wave of attacks, they were left fatherless for a second time.

There were only two ways of interpreting the prime minister's comments: either he believed what he was saying (which would mean that he was incapable of understanding what was painfully obvious to just about everyone else) or he was deliberately twisting the truth (which would mean that the security and wellbeing of Iraqis was for him secondary to protecting his own reputation). It was a perfect illustration of how Iraqis' problems were caused not by religion and race, but by misgovernment. The question, for me and for many others, was how we had reached this point in our country's history and what solutions existed.

* * *

Iraq is a personal matter for me. Having been exiled from my country at a very early age, I did my utmost to reintegrate back into society shortly after the 2003 invasion. I was involved in the effort to rebuild the state – not for professional or financial reasons, academic interest or curiosity, not as a stepping stone to other opportunities, nor to kill time while I waited for something else to do. I left a promising career elsewhere in the hope of rediscovering a country that I could call home without feeling out of place, and of putting the experience that I had gained in my professional capacity to some useful social purpose. However, after years of negotiations, meetings, agreement, and drafting sessions with counterparts in the Iraqi state and the international community, I finally wrapped up my involvement, frustrated by the impossibility of life in Baghdad and the absence of progress at every level.

Iraq's recent history is full of tragedy, and large sections of our population have suffered terribly. By comparison, my story prior to 2003 was relatively uneventful. But it serves as a contextual backdrop for my involvement in the country after the 2003 war and informs my sense of priorities and attachment to the people that I had been separated from for so long.

My family had already left Iraq prior to my birth. After having been purged and exiled in 1970, and having returned to Iraq following the national reconciliation process that for a time allowed dissidents to resume their activities, my father had accepted a position with the foreign service, and was posted first to Sweden and then to Spain, where I was born in 1977. By the time Iraq invaded Iran in September 1980, he had been transferred to Iraq's permanent mission to the United Nations. Months after the invasion, he returned to Baghdad to seek clarification of the causes behind the war and of the government's future plans. On his return to New York, he resigned from his position in protest at what he concluded had been unjustified aggression. From that day until 2003, I could not set foot in Iraq and had almost no contact with those elements of my extended family that had remained in the country. We later learned that after 1990, when my father took on a more active role in the opposition, our family back home was made to suffer: some were fired from their positions in the civil service, while others were regularly harassed by the security services. In 1987, we had to move to London, where my family remained until 2003. During the following sixteen years, I accompanied my father to meetings with the exile community, including with senior political leaders. Although I rarely participated in any of the discussions, the experience gave me important insights into many of the individuals who would later collaborate with the US occupation after the 2003 war.

By September 2001, I had accumulated three degrees in law, was developing a specialization in commercial litigation and arbitration, and had just moved to New York to continue what was looking like a promising career. The 9/11 attacks took place on my second day in my new office. I was based in the mid-town area, far away from Ground Zero, but the day of the attack and the weeks that followed were an awful time. Matters took a turn for the worse when the Bush administration's attention centred on Iraq. My family and I were conflicted: a new war would probably mean that we would be able to reconnect with our relatives; however, we had come to distrust US foreign policy in Iraq, particularly as it fell under the control of the Republican party, and even more so once neo-conservatives acquired so much influence. We could draw little comfort from the administration's allies in the exile community, with whom we were all too familiar.

By the time the war started in March 2003, I had moved to Paris, where I practised commercial arbitration with some of the world's leading experts. Shortly after the US started bombing Baghdad, my father travelled to the Syria–Iraq border: he wanted to be in his country as the US army completed the invasion, as he felt he could not simply stand on the sidelines and wait for news from afar. At one point, we lost contact with him and were unsure if he had made it in (there were no mobile phones in Iraq at the time and no internet access). Later we learned that he had reached his hometown and was carried through the streets by our relatives, many of whom had not seen him for decades (and the vast majority of whom I had never seen). Back in Paris, when the US army swept into Baghdad and assisted a small group of Iraqis to pull down a statue of Saddam Hussein in Firdos Square on 9 April 2003, I stood and watched the statue fall and could not stop thinking that it was just a matter of time before my life changed irrevocably.

Despite the early warning signs and increasing levels of violence, and despite the fact that most formerly exiled Iraqis shrank from the prospect of returning to their country, the atmosphere in 2003 and 2004 was optimistic. Many Iraqis were planning their futures in the expectation that the US occupation would wind down within a few years, that the violence would recede, and that life in Baghdad would soon settle into a state of normality. Within that context, I spent a year deciding what would be the best way of contributing to the transition process. I considered many possibilities, but in the end I was offered a position as a legal adviser to the United Nations, initially to work on drafting the constitution, and later on issues relating to parliamentary and judicial reform. I resigned from my position in Paris and moved to the Middle East, hoping that Iraq would quickly emerge from the wreckage of the war and occupation as a modern and prosperous country, and that I would shortly move from the United Nations to work directly for the state. With this in mind, I contacted the ministry of higher education to ask for a teaching position, and I prepared a syllabus for a course on European law that I hoped to teach to undergraduate students. I was concerned that my many years away would mean that I would never be able to integrate fully, and so I had plans to throw myself in at the deep end and study for a PhD in law at the University of Baghdad.

Around a year after I arrived, the team of jurists and experts that I was working with at the UN essentially disbanded, each of my former colleagues moving on to pursue opportunities in other countries. Because of my commitment to my country, I continued working with the United Nations on various projects for another five years. During that time, I kept a low profile, mainly out of a concern to maintain my integrity and to avoid endangering my family; working too closely with the ruling elites would have been problematic. As a result, I was involved in a number of important technical projects which did not attract the interest of senior politicians, but which were designed to circumvent their authority without them realizing. Among other things, this included an effort to develop the parliament, the judiciary and oversight agencies into functioning institutions that would allow some form of oversight of government. Although my counterparts and I made significant progress towards that goal, in the end parliament was completely sidelined and the courts co-opted, while the government functioned as if there was no one watching and no one to answer to.

My decision to leave Paris and to focus all my efforts on Iraq allowed me to satisfy a number of objectives: I reconnected with my family and my country; I became familiar with customs that I had only read about; and I gained intimate knowledge of the workings of the new state. My Arabic improved, as did my sense of belonging. I made friends from all over the country, many of whom I visited regularly in their homes in the countryside or in Iraq's small towns, where we would spend days and nights debating what might have been, what was and what possibly could be. I heard incredible stories of poverty, hardship and forgiveness, and saw with my own eyes what the consequences of poor policy can be. My colleagues, friends and relatives shared their principal grievances and fears with me; and from them I discovered imaginative ways of cursing politicians. I learned to complain about the poor electricity supply and to yearn for rain during a dust storm.

To my immense regret, all of this happened against the backdrop of a country falling apart. As soon as I started in my new position in early 2005, the conflict worsened and eventually brought the state and society to the brink of collapse. Instead of taking on the teaching position that I was hoping for, I spent close to six years in my post with the United Nations. And rather than settling in Baghdad, as I had planned, I was forced to constantly shuttle between Baghdad, Erbil, Beirut, Amman, Cairo, Istanbul and other cities.

My father was one of the few who returned in 2003 without seeking to profit from the new order. During the summer of 2006, after receiving numerous threats, he finally decided that he could stay no longer. The thought of him packing his bags after just three years back home, possibly never to return, was particularly distressing. As many as 4 million others were similarly driven from their homes, including relatives and friends. Misery was all around, and my resentment towards the people who were responsible for this crisis grew in proportion to the tragedies that I witnessed.

By the end of 2010, it had been clear to me for some time that the state's development agenda was a hoax, and that (my own personal development aside) I was essentially wasting my time trying to assist a state that was led by the worst elements in society. What was the point of negotiating anti-corruption frameworks with mid-level officials, when ministers and other high-ranking officials were robbing the state in broad daylight? What good could come of reforming a government department, when all our work could be reversed in the blink of an eye if someone so desired? Who were we fooling in thinking that anything that we were doing would make any difference?

In the 1970s, Iraqis generally eschewed corruption and theft, largely because they believed (rightly or wrongly) that the state's revenue was being put to good use and should be protected. By the time Nouri al-Maliki's second government was formed in November 2010, moral standards had plummeted, in large part because of an understanding that anything that was not stolen would just be wasted or gobbled up by the political parties anyway.

In that context, the prospects of 'making a difference' seemed at best remote, and I started looking around for other options. In January 2011, I was in Baghdad when the Tunisian dictator was deposed by a popular revolution. My uncle wept as he considered the prospect of the first genuinely free and democratic Arab state. Over the coming few years, one Arab country after another would be rewriting its constitution, and my experience in Iraq could be helpful, particularly as a warning of what not to do. A few months later, I started participating in conferences and meetings on constitutional reform in Tunisia and Egypt, and eventually wound down my professional involvement in Iraq altogether, although I continued to pursue a number of personal initiatives.

*   *   *

By 2013, ten years after the 2003 invasion that was supposed to bring an end to despotism and usher in a period of unparalleled prosperity for the country, Iraq was in an uncomfortable position. The government, individual ministries, the parliament, political parties, the courts, the provinces, academics, civil society and the media were all stuck in a terrible morass: although they all complained that the state was failing the people, there was no dynamic in play that could possibly bring about change. There was no initiative on the table to solve any of the problems that the state was suffering from. The most troubling aspect of this was that all the issues that officials and citizens were complaining of in late 2013 were almost precisely the same issues that had first been placed on the table in 2003. Despite a new constitution that had been approved by a referendum in 2005, there was so much disagreement on almost all of its content that the state was paralysed.

The lack of progress at every level has had a terrible impact on the general population. In many countries, when politics break down, essential services continue functioning normally, though progress on key issues is delayed or suspended until the crisis is resolved. In Iraq, there were virtually no services to speak of post-2003, and so a frozen state left the average Iraqi in a difficult, dangerous and precarious position. Among other things, the ruling parties could not agree what the country's political system should be – or even whether it should be centralized, decentralized or should become a federation. One consequence was that complete stalemate ensued over which level of government should control natural resources such as oil, gas and water. Another consequence was that oil production (and therefore exports) only barely increased from 2003 to 2013, despite the auctioning off of the country's most precious assets to international corporations.

The politicians were in deep disagreement over what role the security services should play and under whose control they should be. The constitution's ambiguous provisions were exploited by the prime minister, who took over both the police and the army, leading to accusations by his rivals that both had become heavily politicized and were committing crimes throughout the country. Both institutions saw their legitimacy tarnished as a result. There was no agreement on what development plan the state should follow, so public services barely improved after 2003. Electricity production was (and to this day remains) terrible, so that large swathes of the country do not receive any power whatsoever for days on end, particularly during the summer. Although corruption was identified as a major impediment to progress as early as 2005, the state has not passed any notable reforms to curb graft. The result is that for years Iraq has ranked as one of the most corrupt countries in the world, including in 2013. The decades-long decline in the education sector has not been reversed, and the country's best teachers and thinkers have left.

The private sector has barely recorded any growth since 2003, and has not generated any significant employment opportunities for the hundreds of thousands of young Iraqis who swell the ranks of the unemployed every year. Finally, there has been almost no public discussion of the state's identity, what its underlying philosophy is and what role religion should play in forming policy.

For the average Iraqi family today, life is very difficult. If a family member has access to a government job, and if the family is lucky enough to own its home, one salary is probably enough to cover the very basic essentials, including food and clothing – but is probably not enough to pay for heating and gas. There is a strong incentive to find additional employment. Because of the lack of opportunities, the absence of oversight and the prevalence of corruption, most families end up paying bribes to governmental officials whenever positions are advertised. And needless to say, the investment usually does not pay off. Those families that do manage to supplement their income with a second or third salary use the funds to pay for private schools, private health care and perhaps even trips abroad.

A large proportion of the population, particularly in the south, is left without a regular income to speak of, which means that they have to fend completely for themselves, with precious little assistance from the state. Millions are not connected to the electricity or water networks and eke out a living as if the state did not exist. Many have been pushed even further to the margins of society, and have been reduced to living in informal garbage dumps, raising their children in the midst of open sewers.

Regardless of income, however, no Iraqi, no matter how wealthy or privileged, can isolate him or herself completely from the disaster surrounding them. Aside from the never-ending terrorist attacks, the failing services and the garbage-strewn streets, the environment has been deteriorating at an alarming rate, and hundreds of dust storms are recorded every year. The storms make life unbearable for everyone and are a clear warning that something drastic needs to change urgently.

The purpose of this book is to explain how this situation has come about. It particularly seeks to do this through an analysis of the current ruling elite's rise to power and of the decisions it has taken since 2003. I also explore what solutions exist for the country in its efforts to rescue itself and to establish a successful democratic system of government. Many analysts have blamed the United States for having imposed on Iraq a group of former exiles with no professional skills, and for having rigged the system of government in their favour. Others have noted that it is the Iraqis themselves who are to blame for their woes, pointing out the poor performance of their elected representatives since 2005. The argument is that if Iraqi society as a whole could not produce a better crop of politicians, then it has only itself to blame. I explore both of these perspectives, based on my own observations from before the war and my professional dealings with the new ruling elites since 2003.

Chapter 1 provides a brief review of Iraq's modern history, with particular emphasis on how specific policy decisions – from the period of the monarchy all the way to the Baathist era – have affected standards of living. In particular, I explore the impact that the absence of democracy and the concentration of power and wealth have had on the country and its blatant inequities.

Chapter 2 explores the origins of Iraq's new ruling elites. It provides some background on the years that they spent away from Iraq and looks at the impact that time had on their psychology, their capacity to administer a country and their ability to cooperate in what was supposed to be a multiparty democratic environment.

Chapter 3 sets out my understanding of what went wrong during the first two or three years of US occupation, particularly as the new elites worked to design the framework of their new state. First of all, I ask whether the process by which the constitution was conceived was truly democratic, particularly in light of all the available evidence; second, I explain the system of government that the constitution imposes, and ask what the consequences have been – and whether they could have been foreseen.

Chapter 4 describes the chaos and violence that ensued after the new constitution came into force and Nouri al-Maliki's first government was formed in mid-2006. Thousands were killed each month, millions were forced from their homes, and the state essentially collapsed, as state employees kept their heads down and tried to evade the attention of the militias. As violence receded in 2008, however, a new social environment was created by a population that had grown weary of sectarianism, corruption and inefficiency, and by a number of new political alliances that sought to capitalize on that sentiment by campaigning on nationalist platforms (i.e. in favour of a united Iraqi nation). I describe the unique political opportunity that was created by the 2009 and 2010 elections to unite the country behind a single programme focusing on reconciliation and reconstruction.

Chapter 5 explores how the ruling elites responded to that call. It questions the decision to create governments of national unity and looks at the impact it had on governance. Al-Maliki for years complained that those arrangements limited his capacity to govern, and many have accused him of seeking to monopolize the state by capturing its most essential institutions from within. I ask whether or not he has been successful in this, and also question what impact that strategy and the constitutional framework are likely to have on the state in the long run, particularly on federalism, decentralization and service delivery.

Chapters 6, 7 and 8 set out in detail the impact that Iraq's system of government has had on governance. Chapter 6 focuses on a number of vital issues, including basic services, the oil and gas sector, economic policy and the failure to engage in legal reform, particularly the framework for protecting fundamental rights. Among other things, these failures have contributed to an ever-growing refugee crisis, and have led to the exodus of entire communities, including the Christian community. Chapter 7 explores how Iraq's constitutional and political system has created a huge space in which corruption can thrive. In particular, it describes the gaping loopholes that have existed for years and asks why the government and parliament have done virtually nothing to close those loopholes. Chapter 8 focuses on an area that is often overlooked by analysts and other interested parties. I have been trying for some time to draw attention to the speed at which Iraq's environment is deteriorating, and this chapter reflects my thoughts on and knowledge of the issue. I describe in some detail the transformations that have been taking place in Iraq's environment over recent decades, and explore how the ruling elites have exacerbated that crisis.

Chapter 9 rounds things off by asking whether there is any common political ground in Iraq on which a new, truly representative and accountable government can be created. I conclude by proposing a road map for reform, focusing on the kind of substantive changes that can and must be embarked upon to repair the state, and I discuss the type of process that can be followed to have that vision implemented peacefully and through democratic means.

*   *   *

The contents of this volume are the product of close to ten years' work. The events that I describe and the opinions that I express are based on information that is publicly available, but they also draw significantly on my own personal involvement in Iraq from 2005 onwards. A large number of people have greatly exaggerated the roles that they played in Iraq after 2003. Considering how disappointing the entire venture has been, the idea of boasting about supposed accomplishments in Iraq has always struck me as an odd one. In my case, I can honestly say that, although I was involved at some critical junctures, I cannot take responsibility for any of the decisions that were made. During the drafting of the 2005 constitution, I was one legal adviser in a large team of dedicated individuals at the United Nations. Although I had strong opinions about the process and about the shape that the constitution was taking, I was never in a position to influence the outcome of discussions on the key issues that the state's future depended on. The same applies to all the projects that I was involved in after the constitution came into force in 2005: although my colleagues, counterparts and I tried to make a difference, we were frustrated at every turn by the ruling elites.

*　*　*

This book would never have been possible without the assistance of a number of former colleagues, including in the Iraqi judiciary, the ministry of justice, the parliament and the Kurdistan regional government. Many of these individuals have become very close friends, with whom I have had frank, protracted and repeated conversations about the state of our country over a period of years. Their contribution has been invaluable, but they must remain nameless out of a concern for their privacy. Aside from those of my friends and colleagues who continue to be based in Iraq, a number of individuals deserve special mention.

My father's humanity and his commitment to his country and to its people have been an inspiration throughout my life. The decisions that he made, the positions that he adopted and the compromises that he entered into inform the way I choose to live my own life. I do not know how conscious he is of the impact that he has had, but his path has provided me with an understanding of the world that is grounded in a desire for equity and fairness for all, without discrimination.

Nour Bejjani, a former colleague at the United Nations and an excellent jurist, carried out much of the legal and factual research that forms the backbone of this book. Her contribution was invaluable and is greatly appreciated. A number of others, including Justin Alexander, Alia al-Dalli, Ziad Daoud, Andrew Hammel, Nicholas Haysom, Joost Hiltermann, Raed Jarrar, Hayder al-Khoie, Greg Muttitt, Khalil Nahas, Harith al-Qarawee, Mani Radjai, Yahia Said, Cheryl Saunders, Paulos Tesfagiorgis and Reidar Visser provided me with feedback, insight and criticism at various points in the process. I am also indebted to Phoebe Clapham at Yale University Press for her support, her guidance and her excellent advice.

Lastly, and most importantly, anyone who benefits from this book should thank my wife, Rouba Beydoun, who ensured that I was given enough time and space to draft the manuscript, who assisted in carrying out some of the research and who reviewed many of the chapters. As an unreasonable author who was also juggling several other commitments simultaneously, I regularly tested – but never reached – the limits of her patience, and for that I shall always be grateful.

As regards those in Iraq or abroad who helped me learn and understand more of the world around me, I have nothing but gratitude for their generosity, kindness and patience. Anything positive that I may have achieved in my life is owed entirely to them. Only the mistakes have been mine.

CHAPTER ONE

A LEGACY OF OPPRESSION AND VIOLENCE

A thousand years ago, Baghdad, the capital of Iraq, was the world's most important centre of knowledge and learning. It was home to scientists, physicians, translators and philosophers, some of whom travelled from the far reaches of a vast empire to participate in the most advanced intellectual discussions that were taking place at the time. The city was established in the year 762 as the Abbasid caliphate's capital, from which it ruled over the entire Middle East, including the whole of modern-day Iraq, much of North Africa and large parts of Asia.

With over a million inhabitants, it was said to have been the world's most populous city for several hundred years. Its citizens were served by the world's first public hospitals, some of which are supposed to have been as large as palaces. All this was made possible by knowledge that had been developed in previous eras by the Greeks (meticulously translated into Arabic) and Persians, but it also owed much to the city's cultural and linguistic diversity.[1] It was in antiquity that a country referred to as 'Iraq' came into existence; it was generally acknowledged to cover the area between Mosul and Basra and to stretch from west of the Euphrates to east of the Tigris.[2] It all came to an end in 1258, when Baghdad and much of what remained of the empire were destroyed by the Mongols. Subsequently, the city and the territory that makes up modern-day Iraq were invaded and incorporated into a number of larger territories, most notably the Ottoman Empire, which administered the country almost uninterrupted for five centuries, from the sixteenth century until the First World War.

At the beginning of the twenty-first century, most interested observers believed that the Ottomans had divided Iraq into three separate provinces (the *vilayets* of Mosul, Baghdad and Basra), and that those provinces roughly corresponded to the areas where Iraq's three major ethno-sectarian groups (Kurds, Sunni Arabs and Shia Arabs) lived. In fact, the country's internal boundaries shifted on a number of occasions during Ottoman rule and never corresponded to the generally accepted divisions. For example, although Basra province did exist between 1550 and 1690, it was integrated into Baghdad province for most of the following two hundred years. It re-emerged once, between 1850 and 1862, but was again absorbed into Baghdad, making a final appearance in 1884. And even when it did exist, it only covered a small corner of Iraq's south-eastern territory; the bulk of the country's Sunni and Shia Arabs, as well as the Shia shrine cities of Najaf and Karbala, were always grouped together in Baghdad province. In addition, while the country was under Ottoman control, Baghdad was long considered to be the administrative centre of the area that today constitutes Iraq and was never regarded as merely another province.[3]

By the time the British Empire managed to wrest the country from the Ottoman Empire at the end of the First World War, the local population had fallen on hard times. The country still enjoyed great diversity – the majority had a very distinct dialect of Arabic as its mother tongue (as well as a number of regional variants), but significant minorities spoke various dialects of Kurdish and Turkish, as well as Chaldean, Farsi and others. And although most people were Muslim, both the majority Shia and the minority Sunni groups were home to various schools of thought, while the rest of the population included assorted groups of Christians, Jews, Mandeans and Yazidis.

At the same time, however, by the end of the First World War, Iraqi society had suffered the consequences of the collapsing Ottoman state. The country was very underdeveloped and suffered gross economic disparities. Rates of illiteracy, poverty and disease were high everywhere, but especially so in rural areas. Outside the major cities, tribal and traditional rules were often still in force, meaning that the government's authority was not recognized, and farmers and labourers were often forced into a state of virtual serfdom. Iraq was also still prone to disasters, such as floods, famine and outbreaks of such debilitating diseases as malaria. Society was deeply stratified, so that power, money and influence were concentrated in the hands of a small – and very exclusive – group of individuals.

THE MONARCHY PERIOD

When it took control over the whole of Iraq in 1918, the British government promised the locals self-determination and prosperity. Over the next two years, however, British officials subjected Iraqis to brutal treatment, burdensome taxation and arbitrary justice, and also made clear their intention of curbing Iraqi sovereignty and of exerting direct influence over the country's governance. In response, Iraqis became increasingly determined to prevent one occupier merely replacing another.

At a meeting in Damascus in 1919, a group of Iraqi officers issued a declaration, according to which they sought 'the independence of Iraq . . . within its natural borders which are . . . from the line of the Euphrates north of Dayr al-Zor and the Tigris River Bank near northern Diyar Bakr to the Gulf of Basra. It also includes the banks of the Tigris and the Euphrates east and west, as confined by the natural barriers.'[4] The Great Iraqi Revolution broke out in May 1920 and brought together nationalists from different backgrounds and confessions who worked together against British rule. Armed fighters, mainly from tribal areas, attacked and gained control of several areas that had previously been under British control and there attempted to establish an independent Iraqi authority. Although the uprising was crushed in November 1920, it caused the occupation forces so much trouble that they felt compelled to shift their strategy in favour of ruling indirectly, through a weak Iraqi administration.

In March 1921, the British authorities decided that the future Iraqi state should be a constitutional monarchy and selected Faisal bin Hussein as their candidate for king. Bin Hussein was a wartime ally who was originally from the Hijaz area of present-day Saudi Arabia and who had very little connection to Iraq and its people. He and the British authorities based his claim for legitimacy on the fact that he was a descendant of the Prophet Mohamed (the same rationale that has been used to prop up regimes in Jordan and Morocco) and had played a leading role in the Arab revolt against the Ottoman Empire. Shortly after he settled in the country and found that a large proportion of his subjects did not recognize his authority, he was contemptuous enough to write: 'This government rules over a Kurdish part, most of which consists of a majority of ignorant people . . . and an ignorant Shi'a majority that belongs to the same [ethnicity as] the government. But the oppression they had under the Turkish rule did not enable them to participate in the governance or give them the training to do so.'[5]

A plebiscite was organized by the British authorities in Iraq in July 1921 to confirm the future monarch's position: 96 per cent of the population voted in favour of the British candidate (the only one on offer).[6] The British high commissioner in Iraq then negotiated a treaty of alliance with the provisional Iraqi authorities, which was signed in October 1922 (the Anglo-Iraqi Treaty) and which significantly influenced Iraq's future constitutional framework. This treaty provided for a draft constitution to be prepared by the king and presented to a constituent assembly, and indicated that the new constitution 'shall contain nothing contrary to the provisions of the present Treaty'. This included the requirement that King Faisal should 'fully consult the High Commissioner on what is conducive to a sound financial and fiscal policy'. The British government was also given free access to air bases, and it could place civilian and military 'advisers' throughout the state. Iraq's sovereignty was being curbed for all to see.

A new constitution was drafted by British and Iraqi officials, in consultation with the UK's colonial office,[7] and was eventually approved by an indirectly elected constituent assembly.[8] The constitution officially established Iraq as a liberal democracy, which promoted modernism and development and which would hold regular elections. However, enormous constitutional authority was granted to the king and the small retinue of advisers and politicians that surrounded him. The king had unrestricted power to appoint the prime minister and could convene, adjourn and dissolve parliament at will. That power was used to appoint Nuri Pasha Said (one of the king's wartime companions) as prime minister on fourteen separate occasions, even though he was among the most hated figures in the country. The king was also responsible for appointing the entire upper chamber of parliament – the only condition being that appointees must have 'secured the confidence and esteem of the public', which effectively meant that the king could appoint anyone he wanted.

The monarch likewise held both executive and regulatory power and could simply refuse to ratify laws passed by parliament. Similarly, all members of the judiciary were appointed by royal decree. Most importantly, perhaps, although the new state was ostensibly a democracy and was required to hold regular elections, the electoral laws and the system of government denied the vast majority of the population effective political representation. The monarchy and the government were so closely intertwined with the moneyed classes that pro-poor policies were hardly ever considered or seriously applied. Iraq's government and democracy were designed to allow for power

transfers within a small coterie of wealthy Iraqis, while the rest of the population looked on.

Having connived with the British Empire in constructing a kleptocracy
that was dominated by an ethno-sectarian minority, Faisal discovered that he
was unloved by his subjects and that his stature as their monarch did not
inspire any significant social movements in his favour. In 1933 – more than
ten years after he ascended to the throne and thirteen years after the 1920
revolution, which had sought to establish an independent state free from
British occupation – he was moved to write:

> There is still – and I say this with a heart full of sorrow – no Iraqi people
> but unimaginable masses of human beings, devoid of any patriotic idea,
> imbued with religious traditions and absurdities, connected by no common
> tie, giving ear to evil, prone to anarchy, and perpetually ready to rise
> against any government whatever.[9]

Thus, rather than admit his own failures and reform the state to make
it more representative and accountable for its actions, Faisal blamed Iraq's
divisions on the population's inability to rally to him.[10] In truth, despite
its difficulties and the lamentable state of education, Iraq's population was
well aware of the inequity of the situation, which was the real reason why the
people were so 'ready to rise against any government whatever'. Not only
was Faisal's statement one of the first instances of senior government officials (in this case, the head of state) politicizing sectarianism to obfuscate the
state's failures, but it also did enormous damage to international perceptions
of Iraq's people – and sometimes even to Iraqis' appreciation of themselves.

The monarchy period was marked by a failure to respect community
rights, a contentious issue for such a diverse country. The vast majority of
the monarch's new ruling elite consisted of Sunni Arabs, and very little provision or effort was made to improve democratic representation for the rest
of the population. Early on, the Kurdish population sought some form of
autonomy on educational, linguistic, cultural and other matters, but was
generally ignored. A number of uprisings and rebellions took place as a
result, and these were put down by the UK's Royal Air Force. The first
bombing raids took place in 1919, when aircraft were dispatched to the
north, where they left death and destruction in their wake. Arthur Harris,
who would later hold the rank of air chief marshal during the Second World
War, commanded squadrons of bombers in Iraq during the 1920s, and wrote

in 1924 that: '[The Arabs and Kurds] now know what real bombing means, in casualties and damage; they now know that within 45 minutes a full sized village can be practically wiped out and a third of its inhabitants killed or injured.'[11]

Another British official put the matter in the following terms:

> I think it may surprise people at home to know generally [how] we have been bombing these people. Mind you, I don't say it is not necessary. There is no other way of making them do as they are told. At the same time bombing is becoming almost as common as patrolling a disorderly area with military police. On October 14 there were seven distinct bombing attacks in various districts. Hardly a day has passed without the aeroplanes going to some disaffected district and dropping explosives.[12]

For the following seven decades, community rights were systematically either ignored or denied by the state, which sought to quell dissent using the methods that the British had pioneered, leading to a recurring Kurdish guerrilla war in the north and successive uprisings and rebellions in the rest of the country.

Finally, the monarchy period was tainted by its subservience to the interests of a foreign military occupation.[13] The best illustration of this came in 1925, when the Iraq Petroleum Company (headquartered in London and with the British government as its largest shareholder) managed to obtain from the Iraqi state a concession to explore and exploit oil resources without having to pay any royalties for the first twenty years. The Iraqi state would therefore not receive anything in exchange for its most precious resource, despite the deplorable levels of poverty in the country.

By the 1950s, after thirty years of British-sponsored rule, the monarchy was in serious trouble. King Faisal had died in 1933 and had been succeeded by his son Ghazi, who died in 1939 in a mysterious car accident. After a period of regency, Faisal II, who had been only three when his father died, ascended to the throne in 1953. In the meantime, although the royal family was not originally Iraqi and had arrived in the country with virtually nothing, its personal property had grown immeasurably, even though Iraq's economy had hardly advanced. Per capita income and human development had essentially remained stagnant for decades. The king had favoured former Ottoman elites, tribal sheikhs and his wartime companions over the interests of the masses of poor. Thus, while most of the population remained rural throughout the monarchy and as far as possible lived off agriculture, farmers seldom owned their land and had no prospect of doing so. Cultivable areas were concentrated in the hands of great landowners. The state provided hardly any material assistance to farmers, whether in the form of equipment, medical facilities, housing, credit facilities or otherwise. Thousands of Iraq's poor fled the countryside at this time in the hope of a better existence in the major cities.

On arrival there, they found that the government would do little to accommodate them. This led to the emergence of slums throughout the capital and elsewhere (many of which still stand today). While the monarchy paid lip service to social justice and land reform, the few measures that were passed were never seriously applied. Tax collectors, for example, would simply be turned away by wealthy Iraqis. In addition, successive governments pursued inept economic policies that caused sudden spikes in inflation, which were always followed by popular uprisings.[14] The state made only a superficial effort to redress these injustices, while ensuring that the moneyed classes were allowed to prosper and benefit from not having to pay their armies of servants and manual labourers decent compensation. In a 1952 mission report, the World Bank summarized the depressed conditions that the population had to endure:

> [The] economic potential is in sharp contrast to the poverty prevailing in Iraq. The standard of living of the people is extremely low ... Almost 90 percent of the population are illiterate and many are subject to debilitating diseases such as malaria, hookworm and bilharzia. Housing and sanitation are for the most part primitive. The fundamental reasons for these conditions are low output and low productivity. Most of the manpower on the land is underemployed for a large part of the year, and considerable unemployment exists in the major cities. Vast tracts of land await reclamation and irrigation before they can be used. Much of the available water is wasted owing to lack of storage and regulation of flow. In the spring disastrous floods often inundate large areas; and in the fall water is acutely short. Agricultural output is hampered not only by the inadequate and irregular supply of water, but also by the progressive salination of the soil in the irrigated areas. Agricultural techniques are primitive, the number and quality of draft animals are inadequate and there is insufficient equipment. Industry is little developed. Although perhaps as many as 60,000 people are engaged in industrial production

(other than oil), virtually all of these are employed in small undertakings where the work is largely done by hand and productivity is accordingly quite low. Probably only about 2,000 are working in what might be characterized as modern industrial plants.[15]

Furthermore, the monarchy was seriously out of touch with Iraqi popular opinion on a number of foreign policy issues. Despite promises of support from Arab regimes, including the Iraqi monarchy, hundreds of thousands of Palestinians were exiled from their homes following the 1948 war and the establishment of the state of Israel, thereby exposing the incompetence and disregard of governments across the region. One of the first responses came in the form of the 1952 overthrow of the Egyptian monarchy by the Free Officers, led by Gamal Abdel Nasser. Following his successful expropriation of the Suez Canal in 1956, Nasser's popularity soared across the region, eventually leading to the establishment of the United Arab Republic, by which Egypt and Syria formally merged into a single country under Nasser's leadership. In that context, the Iraqi monarchy's pro-British tendencies and its hostility towards Egypt's rise were increasingly problematic for its prospects of survival.

Inevitably, revolutionary ideologies spread throughout Iraq, spearheaded by the Communist party, which at the time was the only organized political party in the country, even though it was officially banned. It operated in secret, but its ideology spread as Iraqis became increasingly aware of the crude form of oppression that they were being subjected to. It attracted adherents from among students, workers, farmers, officers and even prisoners – in large part due to 'a gross maldistribution of the benefits deriving from the oil wealth of the country, but also to a transfer of real income from the many to the few'.[16]

Partly in response to the situation, in 1952 the government renegotiated its concession agreement with the Iraq Petroleum Company to raise the amount of royalties that it would receive. It also sought to implement a number of long-standing policies to redress certain of the country's more glaring inequalities. Despite the additional oil revenue, the state was already in a deadlock of its own making; the wheels of insurrection were in motion, and the state was in no position to resist.

REPUBLICAN INSTABILITY

The monarchy was deposed in a military coup led by General Abed al-Karim Qasim and Abdul Salam Arif on 14 July 1958. The events were marked by significant violence, partly as a result of the resentment felt towards the former ruling regime. King Faisal II, who was only twenty-three at the time, and most of his family members were executed that day, and several members of the former political elite (including Nuri Pasha Said) were killed in the days that followed. Many of the survivors fled during the coming weeks and months (a few of them finally making a return in 2003).

Qasim and his Free Officers established Iraq as a republic, a form of government that the country maintains today. It was radical and revolutionary, in the sense that it intended to completely overhaul society through social, legislative and economic reform. As the monarchy's tired and ineffectual cast of characters (some of whom had been in and out of power for decades) were eliminated, they were replaced by a younger generation that was full of hope and dynamism. They sought legitimacy by curbing corruption and serving the interests of Iraq's poor. After decades of activism by radical groups, most notably the Communist party, large sections of society were impatient for change and showed their support by participating in their hundreds of thousands in mass rallies, at a time when traditional religious gatherings could attract no more than a few hundred believers.

In fact, change had started prior to 1958: the increased oil revenues from 1952 onwards and some of the reforms that had been undertaken by the monarchy (including some limited advances in education) had already set Iraq on the path of development. The country also had a number of comparative advantages to draw on, including a relatively small population, ample natural resources (including abundant surface water), a rich cultural history and significant momentum towards reform. From 1958 onwards, as investments were made in education, infrastructure, manufacturing and health care, the country applauded. New roads, dams and bridges were constructed, salaries were raised, an educated middle class was created and then sustained for close to three decades. These were the individuals who eventually formed the backbone of the Iraqi state and who kept it together, despite a never-ending series of challenges.

Socially and economically progressive policies were formulated and implemented, although not always successfully. During the monarchy's final years, a number of pro-poor laws had been introduced, including a social security law and a series of income measures. However, the former elites had become adept at ensuring that they would never compromise their privileges and worked to ensure that the legislation was never applied. One of the revolution's objectives was to enforce the measures for the first time and to introduce a number of others, in particular a series of land reform laws. Tribal courts were abolished and judges were forbidden to refer to tribal customs in deciding cases. A monarchy-era law that capped the rent that tenant farmers had to pay (at 50 per cent of their crop) was enforced for the first time. A new revolutionary law imposed limitations on the size of landholdings, which led to the expropriation of a third of Iraq's cultivable land, to be redistributed in small parcels. Across the country, the poor and peasants felt empowered, and many looted their former landowners' properties. The revolution also provided significant relief for women, who had previously suffered from a web of regressive laws that had placed them on a distinctly unequal footing vis-à-vis men.

The 14 July revolution marked the beginning of a period of forty-five years of autocratic rule. Inevitably, revolutionary fervour was tempered by a total absence of democracy, which meant that the only form of political competition was the elimination of rivals, until only one party (or one individual) held a monopoly on government.

Twelve days after the previous order was overthrown, a new constitution was adopted without even the pretence of public debate. It allocated both legislative and executive power to the government, and made no provision for a parliament of any kind. Naturally, Qasim dominated the government, which meant that he was effectively the only decision-maker in the country. Although it was termed an 'interim' text, in order to convey the impression that it would soon be replaced by a more permanent and legitimate document, the constitution remained in force until Qasim was killed five years later.

Many new parties were formed and many existing parties came out of hiding during the early days of the republican period. The Baath party was first established in Syria in the 1940s, and it formed an Iraqi branch in 1952. Its all-encompassing ideology was based on unity (for the Arab people), freedom (for the nation to determine its path, but not necessarily for the individual to engage in free expression) and socialism (as a means to achieve greater economic equality within the nation).[17] At the time of the 1958 revolution, the party had a few hundred members, but it quickly gained traction, particularly in the military, parts of which were already imbued with pan-Arab ideology. A number of Islamist parties were also formed, including some that would come to dominate Iraq in the post-2003 era.

Dismayed at how attracted Iraqis were to radical and left-wing ideologies, traditional and religious groups decided to organize political parties of their own, consciously modelling themselves on the Communist party's formation. Secret cells were set up, an ideology was formulated, and propaganda materials were produced and distributed. Most prominent among these movements was the Islamic Dawa Party, which was formed in 1959 with Ayatollah Mohamed Baqr al-Sadr as one of its leading members. Reputedly a gifted theologian who (unlike many of his contemporaries) understood and sympathized with the plight of the poor, he developed the party's ideology through a series of writings, including a major work on Islamic economics.[18]

Like their predecessors, the new ruling elites sought to convince the people of their openness through a series of half measures, while never conceding any real power. Political party activity and press freedom were liberalized – but only cosmetically and only if they posed no threat to the new elites' hold on power. A mechanism for registering political parties was established, but the authorities used the discretion they had awarded themselves to reject applications from any party that could attract widespread popular support. The Communist party was one of the first to seek registration; but, though it had mobilized its members to defend Qasim's administration (on the grounds that it was Iraq's first progressive government), its application was turned down. Shortly thereafter, the revolutionary government undermined the Communist party's influence over the unions and farmers, and cracked down on any press outlets that deviated from the officially sanctioned line. An election law was promised but never delivered, and in time all ministers who were affiliated to political parties or ideologies were dismissed from government, firmly depoliticizing the cabinet altogether. The result was that policy formation and implementation were monopolized by Qasim, leading to an inevitable decline in vitality and activity, and eventually to complete breakdown.

After a number of unsuccessful attempts, Qasim was eventually deposed and executed in a coup in February 1963 that was organized by the Baath party's military wing, which was itself deposed by pro-Nasserist military officers that November. On both occasions, the coups were led not by a single individual, but by groups of officers and activists who decided that they had to find some way to share power. They took their cue from Egypt's 1952 coup, which had led to the establishment of a 'revolutionary command council' (RCC), an institution that was officially intended to propel the country towards modernization at a pace that the ordinary political process could not match. The problem, however, was that Arab 'revolutionary' governments were always good at defining what they were against, but were much less willing to state exactly what they favoured. Given that the new officer elites were inherently undemocratic in their outlook and methods, the people could not be involved in deciding how the RCC should be established and who its members should be. A related problem was that, given how narrowly the RCC defined itself, policy formation and implementation was concentrated in the hands of a very small number of individuals.

In 1963, Iraq's new Baathist rulers followed Egypt's lead and established an RCC – an unelected and unaccountable group of individuals who were defined in the new constitution merely as 'the revolutionary body that led the people and the national armed forces on 8 February 1963 to overthrow the regime of Abed al-Karim Qasim and which adopted revolutionary power in the name of and for the benefit of the people. Its membership will not exceed twenty members.' The RCC granted itself executive and legislative authority, and was itself the only body that could appoint or remove one of its own members.

When the Baath party was deposed a few months later, a new law was issued that reformed the RCC's membership and functioning. In its final provision it blamed political parties for 'deviating from the July 1958 revolution' and stated that 'a great change took place on 18 November 1963 which allowed for the glorious revolution to emerge. After having carried out the revolution, the armed forces placed their confidence in the Revolutionary Command Council's new and proper formation, which answered the call and carried the responsibility.' The same law also provided for the president of the republic to be granted full legislative and executive authority for a one-year period, with the possibility of renewal. In retrospect, it is difficult to believe that these laws and statements were issued without a sense of irony.

THE BAATHIST ERA

In July 1968, the Baath party took power for a second time. Ahmed Hassan al-Bakr (who had previously been appointed prime minister after the February 1968 coup) assumed the presidency; his relative, Saddam Hussein, was appointed vice president, and a new RCC was constituted. The Baath party's 1970 constitution redefined the body as the 'supreme institution in the State, which on 17 July 1968 assumed responsibility for implementing the will of the people by removing authority from the reactionary, individualistic and corrupt regime and returning it to the people'. The people, however, were never intended to be part of the equation; the RCC retained many of its former characteristics, including the lack of term limits and the non-democratic and unaccountable nature of its membership.[19] All subsequent administrations until 2003 were led by an RCC, although in its final incarnation it was completely under the control of Saddam Hussein.

In many respects, the Baath party was the same as its republican predecessors. It shared with them a contempt for democracy, which meant that the same pattern of fierce rivalry and elimination was destined to continue, within both the party and the entire political class. The new Baathist constitution provided for a parliament to be established, but it explicitly curbed that parliament's powers by preventing it from legislating on military, financial and public-security matters, and in any event did not allow elections to take place for the first twelve years of Baathist rule.

Given the lack of democracy, the Baathists had to develop a plan that would reduce the likelihood of a coup. In the first few years of their rule, this involved reconciliation with their long-standing adversaries. They worked to bring an end to the Kurdish guerrilla war by negotiating a comprehensive agreement that supposedly sought to integrate Kurds into the Iraqi state, while at the same time protecting their community rights. An agreement was reached and signed by the Iraqi authorities and the Kurdistan Democratic Party, Iraq's largest Kurdish political party, on 28 March 1970. It recognized past discrimination against Iraq's Kurdish population and provided for a number of practical measures to reverse that trend. Government offices and the military had to ensure that Kurds had equal access to employment, that schools were constructed in Kurdish areas in order to raise the standard of education, and that local administration offices were staffed with Kurds (or at least Kurdish-speaking officials). The agreement also provided for the suffering that had been caused by the conflict to be redressed, so that displaced villagers were allowed to return to their homes. Where the government had appropriated land for 'public utility purposes' (generally understood to refer to the oil and gas sector, particularly in Kirkuk province), the agreement provided for villagers to be resettled elsewhere and to be 'properly compensated'.

Finally, and perhaps most importantly, the accord called for a constitutional amendment that would recognize the Kurdish population as one of the main components of the Iraqi nation and that would allow for the Kurdish language to be recognized as an official language, alongside Arabic. Thus, the 1970 interim constitution was the first to acknowledge the Kurdish language as one of the country's official languages in areas where Kurds were in a majority. It also established the principle of decentralization, although it did not provide any practical guidance as to what specifically should be administered locally and what should remain under the control of the central authorities. This was followed by a 1974 law that provided for the establishment of an autonomous region in areas with a majority Kurdish population.

Predictably, however, the Baathists drafted the agreements and the subsequent legal reforms in a way that ensured that they would not have to concede any of their authority. For example, although the 1974 law provided for the establishment of a legislature and an executive authority in the Kurdish region, and although there were detailed provisions on how the autonomous region's budget was to be financed, the new local authorities remained clearly and firmly under the control of the central government in Baghdad. Among other things, the law stated that all legislation emanating from the region had to exist within 'the state's general policy', which was left undefined. It required the region's budget to be approved by the central authorities in Baghdad, all security-related forces to be answerable to the central ministry of the interior, and all regional departments to report regularly to the relevant central ministries. It also allowed the president of the republic to dissolve the regional legislature. This flawed and limited concept of decentralization lasted only as long as the military ceasefire. When hostilities resumed in the 1980s, the central authorities lost control over significant geographical areas in the north.

A similar strategy was pursued with respect to the Communist party. Although the party's leadership was not at its strongest, its ideology still attracted a strong following throughout Iraq, including in the armed forces, and this made it a potent force and a threat to the Baathists' monopoly on power. After a few trust-building measures, in 1971 two government portfolios were allocated to communists. In July 1973, the Nationalist Progressive Front was established, and this was nominally chaired jointly by the Baath party and the Communist party. In the ensuing years, communist publications were circulated more or less freely, and the party held its first open congress. It was only a matter of time, however, before the Baath party felt sufficiently secure to move against the communists throughout the country. That moment came in 1977, when arrests were made in the military. These were followed by executions. For the next two years, one action after another was taken against the communists, until the alliance was formally dissolved in 1979. The party's publications were again banned and the full weight of the state's repressive institutions descended on its leaders, most of whom had by then already fled to Beirut.[20] This was the official end of any pretence at political plurality, and it set the stage for an even darker period in Iraqi history.

The final act came in August 1979 with the now infamous purge of the Baath party by Saddam Hussein. Born in al-Awja, a poor and isolated village on the outskirts of Tikrit, Hussein had endured class-based discrimination that he never forgot. He joined the Baath party, plotted against the state, was shot, exiled and imprisoned all before he reached the age of thirty. During the 1970s, he steadily acquired significant power, particularly in the security services. He started to snap at the heels of President al-Bakr, who not only was his relative, but was also far older. In July 1979, al-Bakr stepped down on health grounds and Hussein formally took over.

One of his first moves was to convene a party congress in August 1979, specifically to purge the party's leadership of any potential enemies. It was a grotesque display: Hussein stood before several hundred Baathists and presided over the proceedings with cigar in hand. He explained that a conspiracy to overturn the party and his own rule had been uncovered. A visibly petrified party cadre was forced to stand at the podium and describe the plot's objectives and plans. Alleged traitors were led out of the hall, to be either executed or imprisoned. The session reached its nadir, however, when Ali Hassan al-Majid, one of Hussein's relatives (later tasked with overseeing the Anfal campaign against Kurdish villages), stepped up to address the gathering. Abdel Khaleq al-Samarai had been one of the Baath party's leading and most popular figures, but had been imprisoned in July 1973 after calling for the working class to be given a leading role in the party. Now, in front of what was left of the congress participants, al-Majid called for al-Samarai to be dragged from his lonely cell and executed. Hussein readily assented.

It was thus that the Baathists under Saddam Hussein abandoned any pretence of legitimacy, favouring undisguised oppression instead. Spying, intimidation, torture and threats by the state had always been routine in Iraq, but under Hussein's rule they grew to alarming levels. A number of security agencies were either created or reformed to monitor the thought, speech and activity of every Iraqi citizen. The Jihaz al-Amn al-Khaass (the Special Security Organization) was the most powerful of these agencies; its network of spies kept a close watch on the people who surrounded Hussein and on potential enemies. It was headed by family – first by the president's cousin and then by his son.

Everyone was considered a potential threat, and so everyone was monitored and repressed. Entire groups of people were targeted because of their
religious or ethnic background, or because of their political affiliation. Tens
of thousands of Fayli Kurds were expelled to Iran on the pretext that they
were originally from that country. Members of the Communist party, Dawa
and many others were either arrested or forced out of the country en masse.
Even minor officials were continually monitored to pre-empt security lapses.
The president himself would review detailed reports on those individuals
who surrounded him, including his chef's wife, who was a gambling addict
and was therefore judged to be a security risk.[21] A scientist who was involved
in the nuclear programme had expressed a desire to educate his children
abroad; Hussein penned a note in red ink in his file that he should never be
allowed anywhere near the border.[22]

The Mukhabarat's (the standard Arabic term for 'secret police') modus
operandi was particularly inhumane, encouraging Iraqis to spy and report
on each other. People were so terrified that they were even careful not to
speak disparagingly of the president in front of their own family or in the
comfort of their own homes. Relatives abroad who were suspected of
belonging to opposition groups were never spoken of: an entire generation of
children reached adulthood without ever hearing the names of uncles or
aunts who had taken a stand against the regime.[23] The security services even
encouraged people to denounce their parents, their children, other members
of their family or anyone who was close to them and who might be a threat
to the regime. In the early 1980s, when one of my relatives tried to discipline
her five-year-old grandson, he threatened to tell the police that she despised
the president (so terrified was she that she was reduced to embracing pictures
of Hussein in front of the boy in an effort to convince him otherwise).

It was also in the 1980s that Saeed, a ministerial clerk in Baghdad, received
a letter from his brother who had emigrated to the US some time before.
With it came news of his life abroad: he had completed a degree, had secured
employment and was now living comfortably with good prospects of
remaining in America. In the final paragraph he questioned his brother's
decision to remain in Iraq: the Baath party was increasingly repressive, he
wrote, and this unfortunate trend was certain to continue. He ended by
imploring his brother to follow his example and emigrate to America. Saeed
took off his reading glasses, placed the letter on his knee and stared straight
ahead. He had done nothing wrong – the contents of the letter had not been
written by him, so there was no reason for concern. He placed the letter in a

drawer in his bedroom with some other papers and tried to forget the entire episode. A week later, he was called to a meeting with the Mukhabarat.

The discussion started politely enough: the officer asked Saeed about his work and life in his neighbourhood. But soon the conversation took a sharp turn: the officer asked whether Saeed had received any mail recently. Saeed responded that he could not remember anything of importance. The officer opened a file and placed a letter on the desk. He turned it so that it faced Saeed. Had he forgotten the letter that he had received from his brother? Saeed felt the blood drain from his face. His lower lip quivered as he asked: 'You kept a copy of the letter?' 'No,' replied the officer coolly, 'you have a copy.' He placed his hand on the letter: 'This is the original.' Saeed was sentenced to five years and one month in prison for not informing on his brother.[24]

The repression became almost unbearable when Baath party ideology was effectively ditched in favour of a cult of personality, with the president as its focus. It was forbidden to question anything that Hussein said or did, even when his decisions were foolish and selfish in their motivations and disastrous in their consequences. The intellectual elite was already inclined to emigrate, but now its rate of flight accelerated.

The radical expansion of the security police's activities was, of course, financed by Iraq's increasing oil wealth. In 1972, the government completely nationalized the Iraq Petroleum Company, which had been established under the British occupation to exploit Iraq's oil resources. Its continued operation after the fall of the monarchy had long been considered an affront by an increasingly radicalized country. The decision to completely take over its operations was immensely popular, and it also provided the government with levels of finance that its predecessors could only have dreamt of. Spurred on by the 1973 oil crisis (which caused international oil prices to quadruple) and by an increase in national oil production, Iraq's national income grew almost tenfold from 1973 to 1979, while GDP per capita rose by almost six times. This new revenue was used to fund salary increases, investment in industry, agriculture and education, and significant expansion of the government workforce. It was a period of unparalleled economic prosperity for Iraq, and the country emerged as a major economic power with a skilled workforce. To some, the potential was exciting; to others it was frightening. But ultimately it was unsustainable, given that power was concentrated in the hands of a single individual, particularly when that person was as foolhardy as Saddam Hussein. As a result of a never-ending series of misguided decisions, the whole of Iraq's potential was squandered. The poor were eventually completely downtrodden by Hussein, who suffocated public discourse as never before and whose disastrous military adventures brought ruin to the country and to the wider region.

As if to illustrate that point, in the 1980 elections – the first to be organized since the Baath party took power – only those individuals who were 'believers in the principles of the national socialist revolution' could be officially registered as candidates. In 1995, the conditions for eligibility were tightened even further and bordered on the surreal: candidates were required to have 'contributed to the Iraq–Iran war and the 1991 Gulf War either by having participated directly, or through the provision of financial and intellectual support'. Needless to say, parliament was completely depoliticized and was reduced to the status of yet another bureaucratic institution.

The first major reversal of the Baathists' fortunes came in September 1980, when Saddam Hussein ordered the armed forces to invade Iran, against the counsel of his own advisers. Relations with Iraq's eastern neighbour had been tense for some time. Aside from historical and chauvinistic rivalries between Arabs and Persians, the shah of Iran had for decades provided support to Kurdish rebels in northern Iraq, only to abandon them to be crushed by Iraqi forces whenever it suited him. In February 1979, the shah was deposed by a revolutionary uprising that brought with it significant volatility. At times this spilled over into Iraq.

Saddam Hussein, though terrified that he could be swept aside by the same revolutionary fervour, also perceived a number of opportunities. The chaos in Iran and the purges that were taking place within the military there meant that the armed forces would be unable to resist an assault by Iraq, so there was territory available for the taking. Secondly, the shah had been one of the West's staunchest allies in a vital geopolitical area, but he was now being replaced by a revolutionary regime that had already taken American diplomats hostage. The Baathists could therefore prop up their regime by replacing Iran as the West's enforcer in the area. In September 1980, Iraqi forces swept into south-west Iran, an area that had a sizeable Arab population and that was rich in natural resources.

Despite Iran's isolation and the support that Iraq received from the region and from the West (and partly because of Hussein's insistence on involving himself in the details of the war), Iraq's military suffered a number of setbacks. By 1982, the Iraqis were forced to retreat from Iran and to defend themselves from within their own territory. In desperation, they decided to deploy chemical weapons to stem the Iranian tide. This caused horrific injuries and pollution to the atmosphere, the effects of which are still being felt today. Moreover, the Iranians allied themselves with Kurdish fighters to invade from the north, prompting violent reprisals by the Iraqi military against Kurdish civilians. These reprisals sometimes involved chemical weapons. They culminated in the Anfal campaign, a series of military assaults with chemical weapons that led to over a hundred thousand deaths. Over a million people were displaced and thousands of villages were razed to the ground.

After the war ended in 1988, those Iraqis who hoped that their lives might improve were sorely disappointed. The country's war debt ushered in an economic crisis that was exacerbated by declining oil prices. Saddam Hussein accused Kuwait and the United Arab Emirates of conspiring against Iraq by exceeding the quotas that had been set by the Organization of the Petroleum Exporting Countries, and he also alleged that Kuwait was actually drilling and extracting oil on Iraqi territory. The negotiations were acrimonious and ultimately fruitless.

On 2 August 1990, the Iraqi army invaded and annexed Kuwait. Five and a half months later, an international coalition of armies, led by the United States military, did exactly as they had promised and launched a bombing campaign that destroyed much of Iraq's civilian and military infrastructure. One month later, ground troops drove Iraq's forces into headlong retreat. Tens of thousands were killed as they fled. Some of the surviving officers were furious with their leadership and launched an uprising in southern Iraq that spread rapidly to Kurdistan. Protesters seized control of large tracts of the country and held them until what remained of Saddam Hussein's special forces descended on them with the acquiescence of US forces.

When the dust cleared, Saddam Hussein was still indisputably in power over the entire country – aside from Iraq's three northern provinces, which from 1991 to 2003 administered themselves as the semi-independent region of Kurdistan and had virtually no contact with the rest of Iraq. This area was not recognized as an independent country, but to all intents and purposes that is what it was: it adopted a different currency from the rest of Iraq, it maintained its own foreign relations and trade with surrounding nations (although much of that trade consisted of cross-border smuggling), and it was separated from the rest of the country by a military front. Although the region was supposed to be democratic (and indeed elections were organized and resulted in the formation of a parliament and government), tribal land disputes eventually spiralled into a full-scale internal civil war. Eventually, in

1996, this led to the formation of an internal border that remained in existence until 2003. Despite these (and many other) problems, the region nevertheless managed to improve the standard of living considerably, in particular by comparison with the rest of the country. International organizations were given a much freer hand to operate in the area, and the political atmosphere was far more open than in the rest of Iraq.

Beyond the Kurdistan region, the rest of the country languished: after the initial invasion of August 1990, the United Nations Security Council imposed the most comprehensive sanctions regime ever devised to coerce Iraq into withdrawing from Kuwait. After the war ended, the sanctions were kept in place, though now they were intended to compel the state to destroy whatever might be left of its weapons of mass destruction. The rules were simple: Iraq could not import or export anything for any reason. The effect on Iraq's economy – which was heavily dependent on food imports and on international revenues generated by its oil industry – was debilitating. In March 2013, Dr Safa al-Sheikh Hussein, who was then Iraq's deputy national security adviser but who, prior to 2003, had been a brigadier general in the Iraqi air force, summarized the impact of sanctions thus: 'I was in the military and I witnessed three wars . . . More than [1 million] people were killed during these wars. The infrastructure was destroyed. The army was destroyed. But I can sincerely say it is nothing compared with the sanctions.'[25] By the time the sanctions were lifted, the country's collective psyche had been transformed. Once renowned throughout the region and internationally for their intellectual advances, their fierce commitment to honesty, their activism and their pride, Iraqis were now hungry, sick and out of touch.

The sanctions reduced the country as a whole to beggar status, while leaving its senior leadership virtually unscathed: government salaries were cut to around $2 a month, and this pittance was supplemented by inadequate food rations. Poverty rates soared, basic medicines ceased to be available and malnutrition ballooned. Virtually no funds were allocated to education, transportation, housing or infrastructure. By and large, the middle classes managed not to starve; but anything more than survival was out of the question. For the overwhelming majority, there could be no thought of buying a new car or even a basic household appliance; of obtaining adequate medical care; or of securing a decent education. Denis Halliday, the UN humanitarian coordinator in Iraq for a year during the 1990s, resigned in protest over the sanctions programme, which he described as 'genocide' and which he said was responsible for 'the deaths of thousands every month in Iraq'.[26]

The entire sanctions programme appeared to be designed to inflict the maximum amount of pain on those most in need. Shortly after it was imposed, Iraq's oil infrastructure had been devastated by bombing. The sanctions, however, did not allow any spare parts to be imported. So repairs could not be carried out and production levels could not be restored.

In 1996, the Oil for Food Programme was launched. This was supposedly to alleviate suffering, but in fact it only prolonged it. The programme allowed the government to sell a limited amount of oil in order to purchase basic necessities for the population. Not only did the decision come years too late for the hundreds of thousands who had already died, but the programme was wholly inadequate to meet the population's needs. Spare parts still could not be imported, and nor could anything else that was even remotely technical in nature. To add insult to injury, even though every dollar counted, the salaries of senior UN officials were deducted from the oil revenues, rather than being paid by the countries that had imposed the programme in the first place. To make matters still worse, there was no let-up in Baathist repression during this period: in 1999, the government replaced the usual dial tone that Iraqis would hear when they picked up the telephone with a recorded message congratulating them on having re-elected Saddam Hussein in a referendum on his rule.[27] Aside from the usual daily humiliations, new rules were introduced that any individual found guilty of abandoning military service should have an ear amputated and should be branded with a cross on his forehead.

THE 2003 WAR

After the attacks on the United States of 11 September 2001 – carried out by a small group of al-Qaida extremists who were totally unconnected to Iraq – the Bush administration set its sights on Baghdad. Throughout the 1990s, many neo-conservative politicians had openly called for the US to go to war in Iraq, nominally to change the regime, but mostly just to project American power once more. By 2001, they were back in government and determined to see their policy through to the end.

They argued that, despite the wars and the sanctions, Saddam Hussein had miraculously retained his capacity to develop and deploy weapons of mass destruction. They also contended, rather implausibly, that he could send some of those weapons to al-Qaida – even though the two were ideological opposites. Despite the unconvincing nature of all the evidence presented by the Bush administration to support its plans, despite international consensus against the conflict and in the absence of a United Nations Security Council Resolution authorizing the use of force, the US and the UK invaded Iraq in March 2003 and swept through the entire country in just a few weeks.

By April 2003, US and British troops, together with a handful of allies (the 'Coalition'), had managed to occupy the entire territory previously controlled by the Iraqi state. Though significant publicity was given to early attacks against the Coalition by what were presumed to be Iraqi special forces, there was little resistance in the capital itself. The state now belonged to the occupying forces and it was their responsibility to secure the peace.

It was in this context that, after a lifetime spent in exile, I was able to visit Iraq for only the second time and to see the effects of war, despotism and sanctions with my own eyes. As I stood at the border crossing between Jordan and Iraq, I caught my first glimpse of Iraqis who had lived through it all (as opposed to the comfortable members of the diaspora that I had become so accustomed to). I instantly felt completely out of place. Each of them – all of those who were there waiting, as I was, to be allowed across the border – seemed physically ill. Their clothes were dirty, threadbare and ill-fitting. Their beards were soiled and untrimmed. They all looked tired and distressed as they shifted nervously from one desk to another, waiting to be granted permission to enter Iraq. Several had had their ears amputated; two had serious deformities; one dragged his leg behind him as he walked; a few had facial blemishes. We were from the same country, but their skin was considerably darker than mine because of the long hours spent under the blazing sun, waiting. If any of them had bothered to look at me, I have no doubt that he would have considered me foreign.

It felt more like the waiting room of a provincial health clinic in one of the poorer countries of the world than the border of what should, by all rights, have been a wealthy country. These people seemed to be clinging onto life only because they were forced to, and not – as is the case in the western world that I was accustomed to – because they enjoyed it. Over the following weeks, I saw the extent of the dilapidation everywhere and also picked up early signs that the new ruling authorities were in no hurry to bring relief to those who needed it most. Anyone who hoped that better days were ahead was about to be sorely disappointed – just as they had been so often in the past.

CHAPTER TWO

ON THE ORIGINS OF IRAQ'S NEW POLITICAL ELITES

Before we look in depth at how the new Iraqi state was constructed after 2003, the principal actors must be properly introduced. Aside from the various individuals that the Bush and Blair governments placed on the ground to steer and implement policy in Iraq, a number of former exiles played a key role both before and after the invasion.

For decades the US and the UK had been cultivating allies among the Iraqi exile and opposition groups. As they prepared to invade Iraq, they called on those groups, realizing full well that, if they were going to occupy the country, they would need assistance on a number of fronts, both political and logistical.

Politically, they could be very useful: the occupation could not last forever, and the US would early on need to impose an Iraqi face on its presence – above all to burnish the entire operation's legitimacy locally. The US was also keen to ensure that criticism of the occupation was kept to a minimum, and so efforts were made to co-opt as many political forces as possible. Logistically, the opposition groups were needed to act as an interface with Iraqi society if and when sensitive agreements with the locals had to be negotiated. They could also be useful sources of information, either on general matters or in response to specific intelligence requirements. Finally, if there was a shortage of manpower, opposition groups could provide 'boots on the ground', particularly given that many maintained their own militias.

The US and the UK had not always shared the same attitude towards exile and opposition groups. The UK had been hostile to republican Iraq from the outset – not just because the monarchy that it had installed had been over-thrown and brutally murdered, but also because its oil interests had been gradually nationalized, culminating in the UK's expulsion from the market in 1972. Although there was little that it could do on its own, Britain had started nurturing relationships with Iraqi dissidents and had recruited informants from among the Baath party's own ranks. The US, meanwhile, had adopted a more ambivalent attitude, particularly after Iraq launched its war against Iran's new anti-American regime in 1980. By the time that conflict ended, the US's relationship with Baghdad had become so close that it had even taken to expelling Iraqi dissidents from its territory simply to please Saddam Hussein. It was only after the invasion of Kuwait in 1990, when Iraq officially and very firmly acquired international pariah status, that the positions of the US and the UK became aligned. For the next thirteen years, funding and logistical support were provided to a number of groups, while regular contact was maintained with others.

Some of the exiles contended that they represented large swathes of Iraqis; but since free elections and reliable polling had never taken place in Iraq, it was impossible to gauge accurately the extent of the exile groups' popularity. In any event, everyone understood that, regardless of what the Iraqis wanted, a select few from within the exile community would receive preferential treatment and would be imposed on Iraq if ever the Baathist regime was brought down. Some would be plucked from obscurity to become part of the new political elite; others would be placed at the helm of large bureaucracies, with massive budgets at their disposal. The question was therefore how the chosen few would be selected, and what type of experience they would bring to the table.

The US and UK used various criteria to choose their allies from within Iraq's opposition camp. Some parties were considered, rightly or wrongly, to be essential partners – either because it was thought they had a broad social base in Iraq or because they enjoyed the support of other nations that had an interest in the country (most notably Iran). Other groups did not have much support within or outside Iraq, but were nevertheless identified by the US and UK as useful allies, either because their ideologies were deemed compat-ible or because they were considered pliant.

The Supreme Council for the Islamic Revolution in Iraq (SCIRI)[1] fell into the first category. SCIRI was founded in Tehran in 1982 to rally Iraqi Shia Islamists to the cause of a post-Baathist, religiously inspired Iraq. Its well-oiled public relations machine conveyed an air of confidence and dominance, and this led to SCIRI being granted unprecedented access to various plat-forms both nationally and internationally. In practice, this meant that its leaders were regularly called upon by the US and the UK to participate in high-level meetings. After the 2003 war – well before its real electoral weight could be properly gauged – SCIRI's members were allowed to heavily influ-ence the new state's trajectory, not least by taking on leadership of the committee that was responsible for drafting the constitution. In December 2006, its then leader Abdel Aziz al-Hakim was invited to the White House, where he made a public statement in the Oval Office as President Bush sat beside him.[2]

One of the main reasons for SCIRI's importance within the international community was the close relationship that it enjoyed with Iran, from which country it received training and other forms of material support. Iran mainly supported Shia Islamist parties that were ideologically aligned with Tehran's leadership (in particular, it required that they comply with *wilayah al-faqih*, according to which tenet the state should be led by clerics). Nevertheless, Iran deployed its influence to achieve a number of objectives – not least that the Iraqi state and military should never again be used to threaten Iranian interests. It threw its weight behind SCIRI by promoting its leaders and their attempt to gain control over the state. But SCIRI's Iranian ties were something of a liability within Iraq: during the Iran–Iraq war, the organization had formed military brigades (the Badr Corps) which fought on the Iranian side; thus it had often carried out acts of violence against fellow Iraqis on Iran's behalf – something that many have not forgotten. SCIRI's excessively sectarian policies were also particu-larly unpopular. Iraqis were to punish the party heavily in the 2009 local elections and the 2010 parliamentary elections. It made a partial comeback in 2013, but only after it shed its sectarian outlook and distanced itself from Iran.

The US and the UK also maintained relations with the two main Kurdish parties, mainly because they were considered to represent a large section of Iraq's population. For decades, the Kurdistan Democratic Party (KDP) and the Patriotic Union of Kurdistan (PUK) were involved in a guerrilla war to improve the status of their Kurdish brethren, who had long suffered from discrimination by the state. The KDP and the PUK established their own quasi-independent state in Iraq's three northern provinces (see Chapter 1) in 1991, and although they clashed frequently during the 1990s (and at one point brought the region to a state of civil war), they also acquired a certain amount of experience in dealing with western interests and interlocutors. By 2003, they had managed to restore relative stability and cohesion to the region, and had recruited a number of international advisers to guide them through the transition phase. They had also clearly identified both their negotiating positions and the end result they would seek in any post-war negotiations.

By the time the US occupation got off the ground, this Kurdish alliance was the most sophisticated and organized political group in the entire country. Its concerns included ensuring that the structure of the Kurdish region, its lopsided relationship with the central government in Baghdad and its security forces were all maintained. It also insisted that a fair proportion of the revenues raised from the national oil sector should be invested in the region, and that there should be a process whereby Kirkuk province and a number of districts in other provinces with large Kurdish populations could be integrated into Kurdistan.[3]

The second category of US allies in Iraq included the Iraqi National Accord (Wifaq) and the Iraqi National Congress (INC). Neither had any following to speak of in Iraq prior to 2003, but they were picked up by the US and the UK for various reasons.

Wifaq was established in London in the early 1990s as a secular, nationalist grouping of exiled former Baathists, dissident military officers and professionals. Ayad Allawi emerged early on as its leader, a position that he has used to rally support from liberal, secular Iraqis. His family was part of Baghdad's privileged elite; he joined the Baath party early in his youth and was rumoured to have used his status to complete his university studies. He defected after moving to the UK, and in 1978 survived an assassination attempt by unidentified assailants at his London home. Throughout the 1990s, Allawi received significant material support from the US and Gulf countries, and became one of the US's privileged partners when the 2003 war broke out.

Like Wifaq, the INC has long been dependent on the leadership of one person, in this case Ahmed al-Chalabi, the scion of a wealthy family of Baghdadi traders. Up until 1958, al-Chalabi's family had benefited from its close relationship to the monarchy to accumulate impressive wealth. After 1958 and the revolution, the family fled, leaving its properties behind. Ahmed and his relatives worked from Europe and various Arab capitals to develop their banking business. He was responsible for running the Jordan-based Petra Bank, but was forced to flee the country in disgrace in the late 1980s, after the bank failed to satisfy the Jordanian central bank's capitalization requirements. A subsequent audit by Arthur Andersen revealed the extent of Petra's irregularities and insider dealings.

Al-Chalabi went on to reinvent himself as a leader of the Iraqi political opposition and to found the INC. Throughout the 1990s he enjoyed a close relationship with US and UK policy makers. His group managed to obtain millions of dollars of funding, despite repeated complaints by auditors that its accounts were 'questionable' or 'unsupported'.[4] In spite of the significant support offered to him from abroad, al-Chalabi became Iraq's perennial loser, never able to win a single seat in parliament in his own right. During its time in exile, the INC generally adopted liberal and secular positions, but as its fortunes waned after 2003 it shifted towards a more explicitly Shia Islamist politics.

A further category of organizations maintained relations with western and regional interests, but did not officially receive any material support from the US or the UK prior to 2003. The Shiite Islamic Dawa Party, which from 2005 came to play a dominant role, was one such. In the late 1950s, with the number of people attending Communist party rallies dwarfing the number of religious pilgrims, Dawa was formed to promote religious values. Over the coming decades, it operated largely in clandestine fashion, and was eventually accused of several assassination attempts against senior Baath party officials, including Saddam Hussein. Its leadership was pursued, imprisoned, murdered and exiled to neighbouring countries. By 2003, the party was led by Ibrahim al-Jaafari, a medical doctor who had been in exile in the UK, and its membership was mostly middle class. Because the party did not enjoy any privileged relationships with foreign nations, and because of a number of schisms that significantly reduced its membership, it was generally considered to be a second-tier player in the post-2003 political spectrum. This subsequently worked in Dawa's favour: in 2005, al-Jaafari, the party's secretary general, was chosen as prime minister, after the refusal of the country's major parties to allow any of their rivals to hold the position had led to stalemate. For the same reason, he was followed in 2006 by Nouri al-Maliki, his successor as the party's secretary general. Dawa's fortunes rose as a consequence.

The Iraqi Islamic Party (IIP), which was affiliated to the Muslim Brotherhood, was in a similar position. Its leaders were exiled by the Baath regime, and most of them settled in the UK or in the Gulf monarchies. The party did not feature among the US's or the UK's officially privileged partners prior to the war, although relations were maintained with it. Following the 2003 war, the IIP's leadership was invited by the US occupation forces to participate in the country's new governance structure. It accepted without hesitation, and for a time was an essential part of the political equation, although its fortunes have ebbed since 2009.

*   *   *

Generally speaking, prior to 2003 most Iraqis living outside the country wanted nothing to do with the opposition. It was widely perceived within the diaspora as undemocratic, since most opposition groups did not adhere to any form of internal democracy – they demanded allegiance to a narrow set of individuals rather than to a clear ideology. The issue of foreign funding was also difficult for many to accept.

Those individuals who actively collaborated with the opposition parties did so for a variety of reasons: a few had family ties to politics or to specific political movements; some were true believers in the cause; others had been promised senior positions in post-Saddam Iraq. For some of the remainder, it was simply the best professional and financial opportunity that was open to them. Many of these individuals simply followed the wave of exiles back to Iraq after the 2003 war, hence the spectacle of grossly unqualified individuals taking on senior positions in the state and overseeing major projects.

*   *   *

Here it is worth introducing the Sadrist movement, which was in a category entirely of its own. Prior to the 2003 war, very few (if any) of Iraq's exiled politicians had made any allowance for the possible emergence of a major domestic political movement. The Sadrists were led by Muqtada al-Sadr, the scion of a family of Shia clerics who focused primarily on the needs of the millions of disenfranchised poor. Despite having been violently repressed by the Baathists prior to 2003, what was left of the family had remained firmly anchored in Iraq. Largely for this reason, the Sadrists are possibly the only political movement outside the Kurdistan region that has a genuine social base and that can rely on the consistent support of a core group of the population. It is the only major political movement outside Kurdistan not to have significant numbers of exiles within its ranks, and it is also the only mainstream group to have actively opposed the US occupation and to have rejected any form of collaboration. The movement established its own militia, the Mahdi Army, which played an active role in the 2005–07 civil conflict.

COLLABORATION IN A SORDID INTERNATIONAL ENVIRONMENT

For all their different backgrounds, the former exiles had much in common. They were the product of a very particular upbringing and history that essentially catapulted them into power, even though they were grossly unqualified for the job. They reached the highest echelons of government, but would often become lost in a web of bureaucracy of which they had no previous knowledge and which they struggled to understand even several years after their return to Iraq.

Predictably, many reacted by erecting emotional barriers to protect themselves from humiliation. This situation was compounded by the fact that they were conspiratorially minded to begin with: they were far more comfortable in an atmosphere of distrust, where they could intrigue and conspire against their opponents. Inevitably they spent far more time engaging in pointless argument than in tackling the many problems that plagued daily life in Iraq. Moreover, those exiles who went into government after 2003 were those most willing to collaborate with the occupation, which required a degree of moral compromise (to say the least). Instead of being inspired by a new Mandela-like figure, ordinary Iraqis found a cohort of incompetent operators foisted on them from without.

The first and perhaps most important attribute of the former exiles was a willingness to make profound moral concessions to gain power: each of the former exiles had to decide whether and to what extent he was willing to collaborate with foreign governments that for decades had wrought havoc in Iraq. Although many countries had maintained relationships with Iraqi political parties in an effort to influence how the country's natural resources might be managed, after 2003 the US and the UK would be the gatekeepers to the upper echelons of power. Only the actors that they allowed would have any role in government – at least in the early period of the occupation. Being part of the new ruling order from the start would guarantee a high public profile, which would almost certainly translate into votes.[5] There was therefore an important incentive to seek out and win the favour of key US and UK officials prior to the invasion.

The decision to do so was a fraught one, for the US was not just any random occupying force. By 2003, it had accumulated a significant amount of baggage: it had previously supported Saddam Hussein in his war against Iran, even though it was well aware that the Iraqi military was responsible for a series of nerve-gas attacks (which the US then sought to downplay);[6] and it had unnecessarily destroyed Iraq's civilian infrastructure in 1991 and had kept an inhumane sanctions regime in place for twelve years to force the government to give up weapons it did not have at the time. The UK, meanwhile, had previously granted export licences to supply the Iraqi military with specialized equipment.

When the US and the UK turned their sights once again on Iraq and argued that they had to address real and immediate security concerns caused by supposed weapons of mass destruction (WMDs), right from the start it looked like another chapter in a long history of deceit. Both countries strenuously denied that Iraq's vast oil reserves were relevant to their policies and claimed that the issue had not even been discussed prior to the war. But in the run-up to the invasion, public opinion in both the US and the UK was very sceptical of the reasons for going to war. In September 2002 the British government published the most detailed case yet for war. This came in a document entitled *Iraq's Weapons of Mass Destruction: The assessment of the British government* (the 'Dossier'), which supported the government position with specific allegations about Iraq's WMDs.[7] Shortly after its publication, it became obvious that the Dossier's contents were flawed. All the supposed weapons factories that it described as being 'of concern' had in fact recently been visited by inspectors and the media and had been found to be in a state of total disrepair, often festooned with cobwebs.

Following a meeting in Camp David in September 2002, President Bush referred to a report by the International Atomic Energy Agency (IAEA), according to which Iraq was 'six months' away from building a nuclear weapon. He concluded by saying: 'I don't know what more evidence we need.'[8] In fact, the IAEA made clear immediately afterwards that it had never issued such a report, and did not support the allegation that Iraq was anywhere near developing a nuclear weapon. This meant that the president of the United States was fabricating evidence on live TV.[9]

Even worse was the fact that the US and UK governments were relying as one of their main sources of information on an Iraqi defector named Khidhir Hamza, who was allegedly involved in Iraq's nuclear programme.[10] What the US and the UK did not reveal was that Mr Hamza had been kicked out of Iraq's nuclear design team in 1987 after he was caught stealing three air-conditioning units. Thus any information that he had was woefully out of date.[11] The man had been outed as a fraud by his former colleagues and international experts who were familiar with Iraq's defunct nuclear programme, but that was not enough for the US and the UK to stop relying on him for 'evidence'.

After the 2003 war, the US expended significant resources in an effort to locate Iraq's elusive WMDs. As expected, nothing was ever found.[12] Not only did the US never apologize for this failure, but it even refused to acknowledge that any mistake had been made – first by arguing that WMDs had, in fact, been found, and later by blaming the intelligence community.[13] To make matters worse, it later transpired that, despite their claims to the contrary, the US and the UK had had many meetings with western oil companies prior to the 2003 war on how Iraq's resources would be carved up afterwards.[14]

Some members of the exile community argued that none of this mattered. Their only concern was to bring an end to Baathist rule, not whether the US or the UK actually believed that there were WMDs. My perspective – and that of many others in the exile community – was that one could not possibly hope to achieve an honest result if the objective was dishonest. If the US and the UK were guilty of constructing an artificial rationale for war, of distracting world attention for close to a year, and of wasting inordinate amounts of time and effort – and of doing so in a way that was transparently dishonest – then I could not bring myself to trust them on any of their other stated objectives, including their supposed desire to bring democracy to Iraq. The entire episode made me question both their intentions and their capacity to achieve anything worthwhile in the country. Taken together with their sordid history of involvement in Iraq, it was clear to me that the occupation was unlikely to have any positive outcome.

The practical impact of these developments should not be underestimated. The failure to locate any WMDs cast a cloud over the entire mission, affecting morale and credibility. The US invasion of Germany during the Second World War and the subsequent Marshall Plan had been motivated by a clear humanitarian and political purpose. But once it was established that there were no WMDs in Iraq, many Americans and Iraqis were left wondering what the point of the 2003 invasion had actually been. As a result, many upright and hard-working Americans of integrity were deterred from serving in Iraq. Conversely, the administration's blatant dishonesty and incompetence attracted ideologically driven and corrupt officials.

The moral quandary only worsened as reports of killings at checkpoints and of collective punishment and torture by US forces on the ground increased in frequency. Although on the outside it may have seemed sporadic, the flow of such reports within Iraq was steady and lasted for years. Stories of abuse were ever present, and torture survivors formed support groups to obtain redress. Apart from the Kurdish north, virtually all areas and all communities were affected, and this made it impossible to dismiss the reports.

Years later, in April 2013, a bipartisan report by former senior US officials found that it was 'indisputable' that the US had engaged in torture. It provided details of the systematic abuse of detainees in a number of countries, including Iraq.[15] The actions were sometimes so inhumane that several of the perpetrators have suffered mental illness, and some have been driven to commit suicide.[16] Thus, even for those Iraqis who were willing to forgive or forget all that had been done in the past and to focus on constructing a better future for the country, there were almost daily reminders of the occupation's inhumanity. This would cause all thinking people to question their involvement.

*　　*　　*

Any Iraqi faced with collaborating with the US occupation had to make a number of decisions, whether consciously or not. First, collaboration would require them to ignore the fact that the entire basis for the war was flawed. That the arguments in favour of war were so blatantly unfounded strongly suggested that the US was getting ready to administer Iraq with the same degree of ideologically driven incompetence and with the same contempt for facts and analysis. Secondly, collaboration would require forgiveness for a number of unnecessarily brutal policies that had been inflicted on Iraq over the years: US support for Saddam Hussein in his war against Iran; the 1991 destruction of Iraq's civilian infrastructure; and the untold suffering and misery that had been imposed by the international sanctions (based on poor policy and analysis by incompetent and uncaring US and UK officials). This was made all the more difficult, since no acknowledgement of a mistake had ever been forthcoming. Thirdly, ongoing repression, violence and other crimes by US forces on the ground meant that potential collaborators would have to constantly justify their decision to collaborate not only to themselves but also to their communities.

This was a lot to swallow, and most Iraqis were unwilling and unable to work in government in that context. Some of those who initially accepted the challenge resigned early on because of the rising death toll and the reports of abuse. Others argued that a refusal to collaborate would mean the US occupation would be allied only with the most cynical and selfish elements of society. Although this rationale was broadly understandable, and although a number of principled people did join the political process, they were all eventually sidelined. Instead, there was a marriage of convenience between those individuals who were most willing to engage in moral compromise and unre-pentant and ideologically driven US officials who were responsible for untold suffering in Iraq. These two groups supported one another through the years, so that by the time of the elections in 2005 (and again in 2010), formerly unheard-of exiles were benefiting from having been thrust into the limelight by the US and from the fact that all domestic opposition (save ethnic and religious organizations) had been eradicated by the Baathists.

One example was Ayad Allawi, who was a complete nonentity in Iraq prior to 2003. In that year he was appointed to the Governing Council by the US, and was then made interim prime minister in 2004. In January 2005, his electoral alliance (which was little more than a self-promotion vehicle) obtained 14 per cent of the vote. Clearly there is no way that Allawi would have been able to accomplish any such feat without US support both prior to the 2003 war and after it.[17] We will also never know what would have become of SCIRI or its founding members without unwavering Iranian support.

AN ATTEMPT AT PRE-WAR PLANNING

By 2002, as the wheels of war were starting to turn, the US and the UK made a major attempt to bring various Iraqi parties together to negotiate a common vision for the future of their country. The effort was known as the Future of Iraq Project, and it culminated in a meeting in Washington in September 2002. A series of thematic working groups were established, including a 'Democratic Principles Work Group' which considered how Iraq should transition to democracy, human rights, the rule of law, civil society and democratization, and the use of federal principles as the basis for a new Iraqi polity.[18] SCIRI, Wifaq, the INC and the two main Kurdish parties took part in the deliberations. Some opposition parties, including Dawa and the IIP, refused to participate on the grounds that the proceedings were designed to satisfy western interests. That said, some of their senior leaders could not resist the temptation to rub shoulders with so many US and UK officials at the same time.

The fact that most of the participants were based outside Iraq had a number of important consequences. First of all, because each party's actual popular support within Iraq (if indeed it had any to speak of) was impossible to gauge, the participants had to find some other mechanism for deciding how much importance to attach to one another. The measure that was adopted was the level of support that each participant enjoyed from foreign powers. This meant that the discussions were principally designed to create a platform for western favourites. Secondly, the ideological discussions that the exiled parties had engaged in prior to 2003 necessarily took place without the participation of the vast majority of the Iraqi population, who were not even aware of what was being discussed (and could not have been meaningfully consulted even if the exiled parties had sought to engage them). The upshot was that consensus was reached within the working group that any future constitution should be based on a federal arrangement, even though the popularity of that idea within Iraq – including among those political forces that did not have any effective representation in the exile community (e.g. the Sadrist movement) – could not be properly gauged.

The working group focused on a number of procedural and substantive questions. Unsurprisingly, the participants rejected any suggestion of a prolonged occupation and recommended an immediate transfer of authority to an interim Iraqi administration, to be composed of leading members of the exiled opposition groups. All the substantive discussions that took place within the working group were just as superficial and self-serving.

When discussing fundamental rights anywhere in the world, the easiest thing to do is to sit down and list the types of rights that should be protected within a national context. Shopping lists are easy to draw up; it is far more difficult to decide how far each right should extend, or what the exceptions to each right should be. For example, although the working group indicated that freedom of expression should be protected, it did not state if that included the right to criticize and level accusations at the president and the government. Freedom of assembly was obviously included on the participants' list, but they did not discuss whether that freedom should include the right to protest against the state, the government or the occupation.

In terms of what system of government was to be adopted after the war, some of the opposition parties (particularly the two Kurdish groups) proposed federalism as a possible model. The idea was controversial within the exile community, as many groups were hostile to the merest suggestion of devolving power from the central government (regarded as weakening the nation in the interests of foreign powers). Other groups adopted a more pragmatic approach, eventually coming to accept what has been described as 'administrative federalism', i.e. federal units are determined by administrative needs, rather than by ethno-sectarian divisions.[19] As expected, the working group only managed to take the conversation so far; after months of deliberations, their agreement merely indicated that Iraq's internal borders should not be determined on an ethno-sectarian basis.[20] They failed to discuss (let alone reach agreement on) any of the rest of the issues, such as what powers the federal units should exercise, where they would get their budgets from, what share of oil revenues they would be given, how they would transition from centralism to federalism, etc.

In a way, the working group's deliberations presaged many of the negotiations that were to take place in post-2003 Baghdad. The talks were chaotic and were attended by all the wrong people, whose real motivations were never discussed openly; the results were limited to a few vague principles that should have been a 'given' before the negotiations even started; and the announcement of the final agreement was followed by a series of self-congratulatory speeches that failed to convince anyone of any real achievement. Even worse was the fact that the participants could not even reach consensus on the few issues that they did manage to discuss.[21] Finally, and perhaps most importantly, the substance of the negotiated agreement was ignored in practice, so the entire exercise was a complete waste of time.

FROM EXILE TO THE HALLS OF POWER

After the invasion and the Baath party's downfall, the former exiles quickly positioned themselves to assume power as soon as they could. Given the near lawlessness that had persisted for years, the question was what these people would finally do with their new positions and with the unfettered access to funds. Would they work for the common good or would they privilege their own interests? Ali Allawi, who served in government from 2003 to 2006 in three different capacities, blamed the eventual breakdown in government on the 'appalling ethical standards of those who were catapulted to power', most of whom 'came from exile'.[22] It turned out that the same qualities that had made it acceptable to work with a baggage-laden foreign military occupation also made it easy to engage in violence and to steal. It was a lesson that Iraqis learned the hard way.

Exile was difficult for many reasons. Those who were cut off from Iraq as it changed and evolved had no way of keeping abreast of developments (apart from a very few who worked in institutions that specialized in the study of Iraq). The country was completely isolated from the international community before 2003: with sparse internet access, almost no uncensored international news coverage and no mobile phones, reliable information on life in Iraq was difficult to get hold of. Exile was so comprehensive during the

Baath era that it often meant not being able to meet or speak to your relatives. For those who did meet, communication would be difficult: there was always the suspicion that someone was working for the Mukhabarat or that the security service might be listening in.

After a long time away, it can be a jarring experience to rediscover one's country and find out again how it operates – not unlike moving to another country altogether. Much changed during the thirty-five years that the Baath party ruled the country: laws, regulations, working practices. In 2003, many returnees noted with disappointment that even cultural values had changed. They knew, of course, that poverty and war had taken their toll on society, but they were nevertheless surprised at how far professional standards had fallen and how pervasive corruption had become. Some former exiles found that the language had also evolved: many of their preferred expressions and idioms were outdated and would often provoke hilarity among those that had remained in the country ('you speak like my grandparents' was a frequent comment); at the same time, so many new foreign terms (mostly English and Farsi) had filtered into the Iraqi dialect that the returnees were often caught off balance and felt uncomfortable.

More importantly, perhaps, the Iraqi state, its institutions and the working methods of its public servants had steadily evolved under Baath party rule, so that whatever knowledge the exiled parties had of the workings of the Iraqi state was decades out of date. This lack of understanding was compounded by the general atmosphere of contempt that the exiles held for anything associated with Baathist rule: whatever the Baathists had done must be undone, regardless of what it was and whether there was any merit in doing so. That attitude created a dynamic of its own that made the former exiles' task even more difficult: many of the bureaucrats, professionals and officials who had remained in Iraq and had continued in their functions for decades (whatever their view of the Baathist regime) were naturally unwilling to accept that everything they had achieved could simply be discarded. After the 2003 war, as the former exiles worked to impose their party cadres on the departments that they controlled, what was left of Iraq's professional class often reacted with barely concealed hostility. This further impaired the workings of the state at a time when efficiency was needed. From 2005 onwards, I witnessed many conversations between experienced officials and former exiles that degenerated into slanging matches, with the former contemptuously accusing the latter of ignorance and of being completely out of touch.

The fact that they no longer identified with, or even understood, the local culture made the exiles' transition into government all the more difficult. The US occupation had brought with it administrators who were often (but not always) highly qualified, but who had next to no knowledge of Iraq's history and its needs. It was thought that the former exiles would be the mirror image of their American counterparts, and that perhaps they would complement each other as they tried to govern the country. In fact, although the former exiles spoke the language, their knowledge of Iraq, its institutions and its culture was either shaky or desperately out of date. The country's rapid decline in the 1990s (a result of the sanctions) had allowed tribalism to re-emerge, corruption to flourish, and the middle class to be seriously undermined. Many of those who expected to occupy senior positions had never worked for the state at all – not even prior to their exile. They would often have to learn everything from scratch, including how the institutions that they were administering functioned, what the operating procedures were, and why officials were behaving in a particular way; and they would be confounded when their decisions reduced efficiency and increased waste.

Moreover, many former exiles did not have any valuable work experience to speak of. Many had been sustained by foreign governments that sought influence in a potential post-Saddam Iraq and that kept exile groups afloat with financial assistance that had very few strings attached and practically no oversight. The result was that many of the former exiles had spent years abroad without work, and with no need to acquire any of the skills that would be needed if they were one day to return home. During their exile, many had been involved in publishing newspapers that were distributed free of charge to a small circle of subscribers (the costs often being picked up by foreign governments). Others had managed party affairs, i.e. keeping up appearances at meetings and conferences, in order to suggest a high level of activity. Yet others had provided assistance to new refugees from Iraq, by helping them to find work of some kind, by assisting them in processing their asylum papers and by helping them navigate their host country's benefits system. Small numbers were involved in direct efforts to topple the regime through sabotage or assassination attempts.

Nouri al-Maliki, who returned to Iraq in 2003 with relatively modest ambitions but who was appointed prime minister in 2006, is a prime example. After a few years at university studying religion and the Arabic language, al-Maliki worked as a lowly clerk in a government office in al-Hilla before being forced into exile in Iran in 1979. There he lived in a military camp near the Iraqi border. After failing to achieve any significant victories against the Baath and having been completely sidelined by the Iranians, in 1991 he settled in Damascus, where he was largely responsible for Dawa's daily affairs. Diplomats who were responsible for maintaining relations with the Iraqi opposition in Syria and who knew al-Maliki have noted that he never seemed to be busy with anything in particular, but also noted his ability to remain calm and composed at all times.[23]

When al-Maliki returned to Iraq in 2003, he had very little in the way of genuine accomplishments: a few years' experience in a minor government office, and twenty-three years of failure and time wasted in exile. Despite his party's initial opposition to the US occupation, its senior membership changed gear early on, once it realized that most of their counterparts in other parties had decided to collaborate. Within a few weeks, al-Maliki had been appointed by the US occupation authorities as an alternate member of the Governing Council, one of the most senior positions in the new state at the time. This was the springboard that enabled him to occupy the position of prime minister in 2006, despite his lack of experience and achievements.

In a different category altogether were the exiles or emigrants who were not necessarily politically active and who had found employment in the private sector. While some had developed successful careers, many had not, and it was largely those people – unproductive and unskilled – who returned to Iraq and who became responsible for directing the state in 2003. One specific individual was born and raised in the US and had worked as a secretary in a real estate firm in California, responsible for keeping the firm's files organized and making sure all files had duplicates. When he decided to return to Iraq in 2003, his family's associations with a specific political party earned him a position as director of research in a key institution of state, where he proceeded to run his department into the ground and prevent any effective research from being carried out for years. Today, never having been held to account for his failures, he lives comfortably in the US, working as a lobbyist for oil companies that have an interest in Iraq.

Those exiles or emigrants who had done well for themselves were never likely to return to Iraq. Having secured a sound education and forged a successful career in banking, law, etc., there was very little incentive for them to put that all aside for an uncertain future in Iraq – particularly since violence and kidnapping had taken root from the start of the occupation. The country would remain a blur for many of these individuals; from London, Dubai or New York, they would shake their heads in disbelief as the levels of violence increased post-2003. They would attend charity events for Iraqi orphans, without ever enquiring whether it would be possible for them to visit the country. The few who did take a chance and returned either left in despair shortly after arriving, were made to leave, or 'were disappeared'.

Ali Allawi is a case in point. Allawi had studied at the Massachusetts Institute of Technology, the London School of Economics and Harvard University, and had worked in a number of leading financial institutions, including the World Bank/IFC Group. He returned to Iraq and in September 2003 became a minister in the Governing Council. He remained in government until May 2006, when Nouri al-Maliki's first administration was formed. By that time, Allawi had joined the many who felt that they no longer had anything to contribute to what appeared to be a failing enterprise. Shortly after departing from Iraq in 2006, he wrote: 'The corroded and corrupt state of Saddam was replaced by the corroded, inefficient, incompetent and corrupt state of the new order.'[24] Mr Allawi has remained out of government since.

The experience of Kurdish politicians and administrators in post-2003 Baghdad is perhaps even more relevant here. When it broke away from the rest of Iraq in 1991, the Kurdistan region was in a bad way. It had suffered not only devastation in war, but also decades of discrimination by central government authorities. Overall, human development indicators were dire, with education and illiteracy rates among the worst in the country. Baath party officials in Baghdad scoffed at the Kurds' attempts to self-organize into an autonomous region, convinced that they would never be able to overcome the challenges that they faced and that they would eventually beg for assistance from central government.

For the next ten years, Kurdish officials worked against the odds and made incredible strides in developing their region; they made improvements in virtually all sectors, so that by 2003 they had transformed their region into the most prosperous in the country. Corruption, bureaucratic inefficiency and poor education were all still problematic, but there was no questioning the progress that had been made. And so, when, in 2005 and 2006, parliamentary elections were held throughout the country, the Kurdish alliance fielded some of the best candidates. Many of these individuals had gained significant experience in raising standards of living, and that much was obvious from their contributions in parliament. In all my time working with that institution, there was a clear consensus that Kurdish MPs and staff were the most competent and most committed to developing parliament's capacity.

When we needed support to develop parliament's oversight capacity, we found it in the Kurdish members, who worked tirelessly to negotiate the agreements that were required to get things going. Conversely, their counterparts from elsewhere in Iraq were generally unmotivated and seriously lacked experience – and it showed.

As the new elites took the reins in 2003, they hid their lack of qualifications behind a screen of deceit, arrogance and supreme self-confidence, which only served to worsen the situation. Iraq, along with many Arab countries, has long had a cultural problem with prestige and titles. Elites have always sought to drive a wedge between the people and to encourage inequality. Former officers' clubs that had been established by the British were taken over by local elites in successive coups d'état. These were at the heart of Baghdad's social life, and the ordinary people were unceremoniously excluded from them. Professors, doctors and engineers demanded status, and that was reflected in their membership of these social clubs, as well as in official policy, which provided special benefits for members of certain professions, such as housing in neighbourhoods that were segregated by class. The Baath party under Saddam Hussein maintained the divisions, even as it undermined them from within: Baath party membership was a new distinguishing factor that enabled the members of any given profession to surpass their peers in privilege, regardless of merit. Loyalty to the image of a strong, chauvinistic Iraq or to the president himself was also rewarded. Chief among the culprits was Saddam Hussein himself, who insisted on wearing a military uniform and on being treated like a war hero during much of his reign – even though he had never served in the army.

Although privilege and deference were a general problem under the Baath, many qualified individuals survived the system (though their numbers had clearly dwindled by 2003). Some even managed never to join the party, despite the prevailing circumstances. But after 2003, whatever remained of Iraq's educated class of professionals disappeared, to be replaced by a caste of former exiles, each of whom demanded to be treated like a monarch. Given their lack of qualifications, they sought to mask their insecurity with even more arrogance than their predecessors. Remarkably, senior officials in the new order almost all claimed to have completed doctorates; some even claimed to have done theirs in English, even though they could not speak a word of the language. Within a short time, anyone who had to address an MP or a senior official would find themselves automatically prefacing their words with the title 'doctor'. In all my years of working with parliament, on only one occasion did I ever hear an MP correct someone who had assumed that he had a privileged background: at lunch during a day-long meeting, a Sadrist MP (not a former exile) who sat at my table noted that he was the father of nine children and was so poor that the whole family lived and slept in the same room; his name had been included on an electoral list without his knowledge, he said, and he became an MP overnight without even having participated in the campaign. Years later, I saw him again. By then he had grown accustomed to the narcissistic atmosphere that the former exiles had created. I noted with disappointment that he had invented a new profile for himself that included having graduated with flying colours from top universities. Those of us who had to work with these people knew that it was all a sham, but we nevertheless felt compelled to acquiesce in the farce that was being played out. In private, those officials who had remained in Iraq and had struggled to survive and serve through the Baath era never wasted an opportunity to express their disdain for the former exiles.

Any attempt to reform institutions that were under the control of the former exiles was difficult: they would pretend to have knowledge of everything, but in fact were ignorant of virtually anything of importance. Correcting a former exile on even a minor point was often virtually impossible. As a result, their ability to learn and to engage in self-criticism was practically nil.

Aside from their undeserved self-confidence and their lack of developmental skills, many of the former exiles were also well schooled in militarism and in the art of distrust and secrecy – so damaging in a multi-party democracy. Throughout Iraq's republican period, but particularly under Saddam Hussein, successive administrations had promoted a chauvinistic military culture. Military officers were granted power, prestige and privilege; propaganda material was prepared to promote their supposed valour and achievements; and military parades were organized to impress (and strike fear into) the rest of the population, as well as Iraq's neighbours. This tendency increased under Hussein, both to mask the fact that he did not have a military background and to cover up his many military defeats.

This culture permeated the country and even extended to opposition parties, many of which developed military wings while in exile, taking advantage of whatever training their members had received while still in Iraq. When these parties returned to Iraq and seized the reins of power, a conscious decision was made to continue to promote the same culture, with only slight modifications. Previously, Iraqis had been forced to endure obscene montages of Saddam Hussein riding a horse ahead of a military parade, his arm outstretched towards the masses of onlookers, or firing a rifle in the air as he savoured his victory over an oppressed population. Although post-2003 propaganda never plumbed quite those depths, the same underlying sentiment could clearly be felt. From 2008 onwards, videos of Nouri al-Maliki silently watching over military parades were broadcast on national television.[25]

Even worse was the impact of the secret police on political culture. All of Iraq's ruling regimes, including the monarchy and all the republican governments, suppressed political opposition by means of violence and intimidation, forcing many underground (see Chapter 1). The Baath, Islamic Dawa and Communist parties (and many others) all relied heavily on secret cells to escape attention, communicate internally, distribute propaganda materials, raise funds, recruit new members, and plot the overthrow of whoever was in power at the time. When it seized power in 1968, but particularly after Saddam Hussein gained full control over the security forces, the Baath party monitored and punished its opponents, even those who were already in exile, by harassing their relatives in Iraq or by engaging in direct assassination attempts. Many perished as a result, making exile not only a lonely but also a terrifying experience.

Fear of the Baathists permeated everything, since just about anyone could be a potential agent. Those engaged in efforts to topple the regime were particularly conscious of this, given the number of assassination attempts on Saddam Hussein that had been infiltrated by spies. Conspirators were invariably found out and executed. If they escaped, they would live out the rest of their days in terror. Many former exiles who returned to Iraq in 2003 had been schooled by the constant conspiracies against them, and by their own plots against the regime. They had learned to trust no one, and would see potential enemies everywhere; they spent years dreaming of power, a power never to be relinquished.

But nothing positive ever came out of the poisonous political atmosphere that the Baath created. And even those exiles that were most conspiratorial in their thinking were not particularly good at what they did. Thousands had been engaged in efforts to topple Saddam Hussein from the moment he acquired the presidency in 1979, yet they all proved incapable of overcoming a single man's determination to remain in power. Untold numbers of coups were botched and many individuals were killed because of poor planning by the exiled parties. It should have been patently clear that these people were not qualified to administer a country. Paul Bremer, the US administrator in Iraq in 2003–04, was to write in his memoirs that the former exiles 'couldn't organize a parade, let alone run the country'.[26]

To make matters worse, many exiles had joined religious or sectarian parties, which meant that they had condemned themselves to seclusion within homogeneous and artificial bubbles that bore little resemblance to Iraqi society. For the most part, living and working in Iraq, particularly in the capital, meant constant interaction with a wide variety of people from different social, religious, ethnic, educational and cultural backgrounds. For exiles in parties such as Dawa, the combination of being in a racially and religiously homogeneous environment and of being in constant fear of the Baath party meant that for decades they had had precious little interaction with Iraqis from different backgrounds. Dawa members would interact with members of other communities only at official gatherings, funerals, conferences, etc. Maintaining close friendships with anyone outside their narrow group of party followers was extremely difficult for a host of reasons, but not least because of the fear and distrust that permeated life in the opposition. That reality contributed to the political environment in Baghdad after the 2003 war. During and after the occupation, the officials who took control of the Iraqi state kept themselves to themselves, hardly interacted with each other, and proceeded with extreme caution and distrust in dealing with anyone from a different party.

When the exiles returned to Baghdad, they took their narrow, isolationist mentality back with them. The one place where all parties could come together was in the new parliament, which first met after the January 2005 elections. The Baathist parliament had been completely dissolved and none of its staff was retained. This meant that an entirely new set of procedural rules had to be established. Unsurprisingly, perhaps, given who was in control, the new parliament became the most sectarian institution in the country. Posts in parliament were distributed on the basis of what was described as 'balance': each of the country's main ethno-sectarian groupings was given adequate representation, based on what their respective demographic weight within the general population was understood to be (though there were no reliable up-to-date statistics available). The speaker's council was responsible for enforcing this rule (which even applied to the parliament's menial labourers), which it did without giving any consideration to qualifications.

Once again, the contrast between the former exiles and those Iraqis who had remained in the country was striking. MPs from the Kurdish alliance, many of whom had graduated from universities in Baghdad, Mosul or Basra and had never lived outside Iraq, were consistently the most willing to break out of the ethno-sectarian formula that had been imposed (except on matters that were of strategic importance to their party leaders). One Kurdish party requested that five of its temporary employees be granted permanent employment contracts; the request was denied when the speaker's council discovered that the employees in question were not Kurdish. Kurds must have other Kurds as their staff members, they were told.[27]

Some institutions managed to insulate themselves against the ethno-sectarian wave: judges boasted that the judicial sector, despite all its flaws, was generally unaffected by sectarianism after 2003. They attributed this to the chief justice.[28] Auditors and other staff from the Board of Supreme Audit (BSA – another decades-old institution) said the same about their institution, and were equally grateful for the cover they had received from their director.[29] Speaking for myself, sectarianism was never an issue in my dealings with these and other professional institutions, but it was a daily problem when dealing with parliamentarians.

The decades that the returnees had spent abroad also flavoured the political negotiations that eventually led to the formation of the new political regime and its institutions. Given the plethora of parties, it was inevitable that the new constitutional arrangement would provide for a multi-party democracy. Given the failures of the past, there was also no question that Iraq would not maintain a presidential system of government. Parliament would therefore play a key role in governing the state, and would be populated by many of the same parties that had made up the exile community. Regrettably, the electoral system that was eventually decided upon was so permissive that there was practically no minimum threshold for entering parliament. This meant that dozens of parties with very little public support would end up with representatives in parliament and would play a key role at many crucial junctures. In order for that type of arrangement to work, it was essential for the parties represented in parliament to develop a solid working relationship with each other, since everything would have to be negotiated. It would be necessary for them to work effectively in parliamentary committees, to appoint professional jurists and economists to develop sound policies, to build effective coalitions, to enter into constructive compromises, etc. And the one key factor that was needed was trust. Without trust, parliamentary life could not work, and any constitutional arrangement that depended on a functioning parliament could not work either.

It should have come as no surprise that right from the start the former exiles were unable to cope with this. Although the pre-invasion negotiation sessions to decide on a unified post-war policy should have been relatively straightforward, they singularly failed to achieve anything. That pattern of failure continued in Baghdad once the war was over. Rather than working to identify common interests and drafting detailed agreements to codify what had been decided upon, officials would spend hours holed up in their offices on their own, trying to decipher each of their rivals' statements to discern the hidden meaning – even if there was none. Rather than getting to the source of the problems that were plaguing the country, former exiles spent their time identifying each other's weaknesses and deciding how they could exploit those weaknesses. The victors in this new dynamic would control the state's security services and its enormous budget; the losers would either be forced out of the country or would disappear. Together, the new political class had re-created the atmosphere and the processes that they were used to, albeit in a different context and with different stakes.

THE OCCUPATION'S EARLY DAYS: A SERIES OF UNFORTUNATE EVENTS

Abandoning security

After the 2003 invasion of Iraq was completed, most Americans were jubilant at what they then perceived as a victory. Iraqis were distraught at having to endure another war, but many expected that, within a few years, Iraq would be free from occupation and relatively peaceful; what they did not know was that post-war planning within the US and the UK governments had broken down, and that orders were not being given to military units on the ground to secure the peace or to prevent any major disturbances. So when widespread looting started immediately after the fall of the Baathist regime, the US military, which was the only organized armed force on the ground and which under international law was responsible for protecting the state's institutions, stood idly by. Some soldiers even assisted the looters by breaking open doors that had been shuttered prior to the war. The US and UK governments made light of the entire affair, claiming that this was just another element of freedom.[30]

Thousands of people suddenly found themselves free to take from the state all those things that (they considered) they had been deprived of. Virtually all public institutions were attacked and stripped of their equipment and fixtures. Entire institutions were destroyed. What could not be taken was torched. Precious archives, legal documents, property deeds, libraries – all were lost. Many officials snapped into action to protect their offices and the state's property: engineers at several water-purification plants not only continued their work in impossible circumstances, but also took up arms to protect their installations from looters; employees at the BSA, which kept detailed audit reports on all the state's accounts, physically transferred all of those files to the auditors' union, where they would be safer.[31]

In the midst of all the chaos, the only institution that remained intact was the ministry of oil, which was protected by US forces. Even the ministry of irrigation, which was next door, was ransacked and torched right under the noses of the US soldiers who had been tasked with protecting the ministry of oil. Two days after the looting began, banners that were attributed to Grand Ayatollah Ali al-Sistani started appearing in many areas of Baghdad. Al-Sistani, the highest authority in Shia Islam (and arguably also the most important religious figure in all Iraq) was at that time a seventy-two-year-old cleric who hardly ever ventured out of his office and home in Najaf, around 150 kilometres south of Baghdad. The banners reminded citizens that theft was forbidden and urged them to return whatever had been taken. Thus the only effort to restore security was made by an elderly cleric who was sitting in a rudimentary office several hours' drive from the capital.[32]

A few weeks after the start of the occupation, the US department of defense announced the establishment of the Coalition Provisional Authority (CPA). This was a civilian authority that had as its mission:

> to restore conditions of security and stability, to create conditions in which the Iraqi people can freely determine their own political future (including by advancing efforts to restore and establish national and local institutions for representative governance) and facilitating economic recovery, sustainable reconstruction and development.[33]

L. Paul Bremer III, a career diplomat who had served for twenty-three years at the US state department, was appointed administrator of the CPA, which made him the highest civilian authority in Iraq.[34] The CPA's staff was largely drawn from the United States and the United Kingdom. It quickly took a number of decisions that were to have a lasting impact on the Iraqi state; these included the creation and dissolution of certain institutions, as well as the launching of the constitutional drafting process.

Entrenching sectarian divisions

Like virtually all countries, Iraq is home to various communities and hosts competing narratives about its past. Although there are clearly no longer any pure races of any kind in the country, and although religion has hardly any impact on the manner in which Iraqis lead their lives, there are other real distinctions that separate Iraqis. Several groups, including the Kurdish and Turkmen communities, speak their own languages as well as Arabic (and increasing numbers do not even speak Arabic at all). Although many countries around the world are host to more than one native language within their borders, language is a long-standing grievance in Iraq because of the manner in which it was politicized in the past.

Conflicting narratives about the country's past have also coexisted in Iraq. Although many countries similarly host various historical accounts that conflict with each other, in Iraq some community narratives have been deliberately constructed in such a way as to demean (and even dehumanize) large sections of the population, all with a view to absolving a particular community or individual of culpability. One of the first individuals to have done this was Iraq's first king, Faisal I (see Chapter 1).

Throughout the twentieth century, various political parties and communities came to challenge the state's legitimacy, as well as the narrative that it was constructing of continuous progress and development. The crackdown on this was violent, particularly in the 1970s and 1980s, as the tools of repression increased. Resistance was led principally by Kurdish political forces (which still suffered from official forms of discrimination and repression) and, particularly after the Iranian revolution of 1979, by Shia Islamist movements. This led to further recrimination and animosity across the communities.

The uprisings that followed the 1991 Gulf War further entrenched divisions, since they occurred in the (Kurdish) north and the (Shia-majority) south. The south in particular felt the effects of the state's repressive measures, on top of having borne the brunt of two conflicts (the war with Iran and the 1991 war). It was the first time that its population had been targeted by such large-scale operations. In the words of Fanar Haddad, one of the leading authorities on sectarianism in Iraq:

> the 1990s and the memory of 1991 served to polarize sectarian relations
> in Iraq perhaps to an unprecedented level in modern Iraqi history . . .
> [The year 1991] and the 1990s in general coloured developments in

sectarian relations from 2003 onwards . . . [T]he fact that the memory
of 1991 was being formulated in conditions of mass poverty, increased
isolation, social breakdown and exile exacerbated the effects of the events
of 1991.[35]

Meanwhile, throughout the 1990s, the Kurdish north was virtually independent from the rest of the country, which contributed to the breakdown in
community relations. By the time the 2003 invasion was complete, Iraq's
community relations had been festering for over twelve years.

US and UK policy makers and their Iraqi allies understood the country's
history and its community relations from a perspective that was informed
by their own prejudices and their own narrow (and often deeply flawed)
understanding of history, according to which the country's communities
had always been antagonistic towards each other. In reality, it was never
the members of Iraq's communities who were guilty of intolerance and
violence, but rather those individuals who had seized power through the
most undemocratic means. A 2009 study by Iraqi and Norwegian academics
found:

[d]uring the long centuries before the excesses of the Baath Party reached
a peak in 1991, large-scale sectarian tension in Iraq was limited to three
episodes – in 1508, 1623 and 1801, all of which were caused by invasions
by outsiders (twice the Persian Safavids; once Wahhabi raiders from
Arabia). In all of these cases, many Iraqis closed ranks against the
outsiders to defend compatriots belonging to the opposite sect.[36]

That fraternal spirit was illustrated in post-2003 Iraq by the fact that, in
February 2004, only 18 per cent of the population supported either the idea
of living in federal regions or outright independence.[37] Thus even Baathist
brutality and prejudice had not left the vast majority of Iraqis with any great
desire to separate from each other. It is worth noting, too, that included in
this figure was the population of the Kurdistan region, which had just
emerged from more than ten years of virtual self-rule and which was famous
for its supposedly unified stance in support of independence. However, even
among people in the Kurdistan region, significant numbers felt part and
parcel of Iraq: in July 2006, only 52 per cent of residents thought that Iraqis
should be segregated on the basis of religion and sect – so by no means all
Kurds.[38] In May 2012, this figure was essentially unchanged: only 53 per cent

of respondents in the Kurdistan region answered that they considered Iraq to be a divided country.[39]

The CPA and its Iraqi allies were thus faced with a choice: either to emphasize unity over division, while nevertheless recognizing and celebrating diversity, or to treat Iraqis as incapable of governing themselves democratically and to reinforce the divisions within the system of government. Sadly, the second option had been selected well before the 2003 invasion.

The CPA and the new ruling elite first made their mark by promoting and exploiting the understanding that, under the surface, sectarianism permeated everything in Iraq. Suddenly, only those who claimed to speak for a specific linguistic or religious group would be invited to play a role in government. And the more extreme their position, the more likely that they would be seated at the front of the table. John Agresto, who served as senior adviser to the ministry of higher education and scientific research in Baghdad from August 2003 to June 2004, described how the CPA promoted the most sectarian elements in society:

> We're more than happy to do exactly the opposite of what [our Constitution tried to do] – we seek out the loudest and most virulent factions and empower them . . . [W]e gather together the representatives of the most antagonistic factions and think that's good democracy. We've done nothing to blur the lines separating people and everything to sharpen them. We will not see moderate and thoughtful people representing the wider interests of Iraq; rather we'll see ideologues chosen for the very reason that they were not mild, moderate, or thoughtful but because they were ideologues . . . Sad to say, in our attempt not to 'impose' our own way of life on the Iraqis, we wound up acting as if the true model of democratic governance was not America but Lebanon.[40]

Disbanding the army, de-Baathifying society and inviting disorder

By 2003, Iraq was short of national symbols and institutions, and was also lacking qualified personnel to participate in what everyone was expecting to be a major reconstruction effort. Many of the ideologies that had been propagated in Iraq's recent past (including Baathism, socialism, communism and Arabism) had either collapsed or no longer attracted the interest of the population. There was no consensus among Iraq's various groups or communities on the record of Iraq's most senior statesmen (including its monarchs, the military leaders of the republican period and even the Baathists). There was also nothing close to an agreement between Iraq's formerly exiled and opposition parties on what direction the state should take, what its ideology should be or what the future should hold. There was a desperate need to rally the country around some positive and unifying image, even if that meant developing or propagating some kind of myth.

As across much of the Arab world, the army was the clear candidate to serve as a unifying symbol for the country and as a 'policing' force to maintain at least a semblance of law and order. The Iraqi military had had a chequered history, particularly in the decades immediately preceding the 2003 invasion. As with virtually all Arab military institutions, it previously enjoyed a reputation among the general public for professionalism and patriotism (despite having few real accomplishments to its name). The army provided a pathway to social mobility for many, and offered a relatively decent salary (until 1991), access to adequate services (including health care) and training in a wide range of fields, not all of them military. Many Iraqis were grateful to the military (as is often the case) for enabling them to escape poverty. Major General Qassem Atta, one of Prime Minister al-Maliki's closest military associates, defended that view well after the army was disbanded and replaced by an altogether new institution. In a 2012 interview with a leading Middle Eastern daily newspaper, he said that 'the former Iraqi army was in large part professional before the former regime distorted it by creating paramilitary forces that were designed to protect the regime itself'.[41]

The US military was in any event unable and unwilling to police the country. To start with, it did not have sufficient numbers: according to its own calculations, it would have needed half a million troops in Iraq to effectively police the country, but the numbers of coalition forces never reached even a third of that figure. Then there was the cultural problem: the military's knowledge of the country, its language, communities and customs was so poor that it prevented any effective peace keeping on its part. Under the circumstances, investigations by US soldiers into any type of criminal activity were essentially pointless. The language barrier by itself was an insurmountable obstacle. A US army captain and West Point graduate who was deployed to Iraq in March 2004 and who was appointed governance officer for al-Dora district, one of Baghdad's most violent areas, was so ignorant of the Middle East that he tested the little Arabic that he had learned from his phrasebook on his kitchen staff, little realizing that they were actually from Sri Lanka and did not speak Arabic.[42] The same individual was later tasked with combating international terrorism in one of the country's most violent areas; his modus operandi was to disburse cash to whoever might pose a security risk. During a visit in 2004, whenever I was pulled over by American patrols, the soldiers meekly pointed to my car's boot and uttered the only Arabic word that they appeared to know (*iftah*, 'open'). That would be the end of our interaction, unless one of them asked if I spoke English. There was no point in requesting anyone's ID, as they would not have been able to read it (let alone tell if it was a forgery). Needless to say, these are problems that trained Iraqi personnel would not have.

Given the lawlessness that had overtaken the streets of the capital, in 2003 the need was to find a way to rehabilitate the military, or at least part of it. Various mechanisms were available. One way would have been to start by identifying a core group of units that could be vetted to weed out war criminals and other offenders. As they resumed their functions, reliable officers could then be entrusted with the task of reaching out to other army units that had not yet resumed their functions. Obviously, in the context, given that the army's principal task would have been to police the country's streets, access to armour and heavy weapons would have had to be limited (not that much was available anyway after the invasion).

It turns out that there was such a plan in the early days of the occupation. For all its flaws, the US's post-war planning at the start of 2003 did involve remobilizing Iraqi military units to carry out low-grade duties such as garbage collection, policing and other services. In his memoirs, Colin Powell, US secretary of state in 2003, confirms that such a plan was approved at the highest level:

> When we went in, we had a plan, which the President approved. We would not break up and disband the Iraqi army. We would use the reconstituted army with purged leadership to help us secure and maintain order throughout the country. We would dissolve the Baath party, the ruling political party, but we would not throw every party member out on the street.[43]

Immediately after they occupied Baghdad, US military commanders were on the ground, collaborating with Iraqi officers to create lists of units that were able to remobilize. By 15 May 2003, the occupation authorities were paying salaries to 30,000 soldiers and there were plans in place to have them back on duty soon.[44] Pursuing such a policy carried its own risks: there would inevitably be violations, some of which could have led to confrontation with the US military. The alternative, however, was to leave the country without an effective policing force altogether – something that was unthinkable. It would also have meant putting hundreds of thousands of young men who were trained in the use of firearms and explosives out of work at a critical juncture in Iraq's transition. To be sure, keeping soldiers on the payroll was a form of bribery – an attempt to encourage them not to turn to illicit means of earning a living.

The issue of what to do with the Baath party was particularly sensitive, given that any mistakes could have a negative impact on the country's prospects far into the future. Some drew comparisons with the South African Truth and Reconciliation Commission – one of the most successful national reconciliation initiatives in modern times (and perhaps in history), which allowed the perpetrators of crimes during the apartheid era to request an amnesty if they admitted to their crimes in open proceedings. Others called for the matter to be dealt with by the courts, and for only those individuals with blood on their hands to be tried and prevented from holding office or working in government. A number of parties and individuals, in particular Ahmed al-Chalabi and his closest associates, insisted that tens of thousands of former Baath party members should be summarily banned from holding public office, and that the process for determining which categories to ban should remain under the full control of the former exiles.

Regrettably, when Paul Bremer arrived in Baghdad, he had already settled on a particular course of action and had a first draft of his initial order as the country's new civilian administrator. Order 1 was issued on 16 May 2003. Under it, the Baath party was 'disestablished' and the four most senior levels of members within the Baath party were 'removed from their positions and banned from future employment in the public sector'. Many of the state's most competent administrators were fired overnight, leaving the bureaucracy in a parlous state. Before any serious public debate could take place on the issue, the CPA formed a de-Baathification commission (eventually renamed the Accountability and Justice Commission (AJC)) which was solely responsible for determining and implementing policy. There was essentially no right of appeal. As with everything else involving the CPA, it did not set detailed rules on how the commission should operate or on how its members should be selected. Al-Chalabi was given free rein to do as he pleased, with no oversight. Thousands of people who had never committed a crime in their lives, including school teachers, engineers and doctors, were fired.

More seriously, however, the commission was used to prevent individuals from contesting national and provincial elections. This was highly inappropriate, since al-Chalabi and his colleagues on the commission were also competing for public office, and were even (for the most part) in the same electoral alliances. A number of blatant absurdities took place: for example, individuals were banned for their supposed links to the Baath party, even though they had spent years in exile for their opposition to the party.[45] Since it was set in motion in 2003, the de-Baathification process has regularly been cited as among the worst transitional justice processes in living memory.[46] The conflict of interest, the opportunities for abuse and the absence of any genuine check on the commission's power have been blatant. In my own experience in Tunisia, Libya and Egypt since the start of the Arab uprisings in December 2010, policy makers have regularly cited Iraq as a model of what *not* to do. Paul Bremer has since acknowledged this mistake, a rare 'mea culpa' for an individual who has remained aloof from Iraqi affairs since leaving the country in 2004.[47]

On 23 May 2003, the CPA issued its Order 2. This was even wider in its impact. Section 1 stated that all entities listed in its annex were dissolved. Many of the institutions on that list were associated with Saddam personally and were deservedly eliminated. But others had been established well before the Baath party and, with the right precautions, could have survived its dissolution. These included the army, the navy, the air defence force, the air force and the ministry of defence, as well as some elements within the presidential diwan, the presidential secretariat and the national assembly (which served as the country's parliament at the time).

The two Orders came as a major surprise to many US officials on the ground. They had assumed that many – if not most – of those institutions would survive and be vetted, rather than eliminated altogether. In fact, they came as a surprise to President Bush, who had been expecting the army to be reconstituted. According to Secretary of State Powell:

The plan the President had approved was not implemented. Instead, Secretary Rumsfeld and Ambassador L. Paul Bremer, our man in charge in Iraq as head of the [CPA], disbanded the Iraqi army and fired Baath party members, right down to teachers. We eliminated the very officials and institutions we should have been building on, and left thousands of the most highly skilled people in the country jobless and angry – prime recruits for insurgency.

These actions surprised the President, National Security Adviser Condi Rice, and me, but once they had been set in motion, the President felt he had to support Secretary Rumsfeld and Ambassador Bremer.[48]

Quite apart from the fact that they had not been approved, the Orders were hugely counterintuitive, given that no alternative existed for any of the institutions being eliminated. Although many were clearly beyond the pale and were rightly dissolved, many others had developed invaluable know-how on vital functions of state, including, for example, on drafting legislation (i.e. drafting skills, as opposed to policy formation). Not only were the institutions disbanded, but none of the technocratic staff were retained. Inevitably, given the new staff's lack of training and experience and given the failure to retain any of the working methods that had been established under the previous regime, the replacement institutions have had huge trouble in standing on their own two feet. This has been the case with the parliament, which was dissolved and replaced with an entirely new structure. Not one single staff member was retained. The institution has been trying to pick up the pieces ever since.

There has been considerable speculation as to what specifically motivated the two Orders. In his memoirs, Bremer justified his decision in purely ethno-sectarian terms. He recalls a conversation on the matter with Walt Slocombe, who was his senior adviser on defence issues. Slocombe suggested that because the previous army had been dominated by Sunni Arabs, Shia soldiers would never willingly follow their orders. Bremer agreed with this assessment.[49]

That conversation and the rationale for decision-making reveal much more about Bremer and his associates' understanding of Iraq than about the country itself. Their vision of Iraq was of a country populated exclusively by people who hated each other because of their religion and in which individual behaviour was irrelevant. The reality was that, in the absence of any data, it was impossible for the CPA to predict how a call to return to duty would have been received. Under the circumstances, it would have been safe to assume that many former soldiers would have welcomed an opportunity to resume service, if only because that would have meant a regular income (particularly at the new rates that would eventually be offered – sometimes hundreds of times higher than pay during the sanction years). Just about any Iraqi could have told Bremer and his associates that blind ethno-sectarian hatred was actually quite rare in Iraq, and that a professional officer was likely to command the respect of his subordinates, regardless of his religion. The CPA's assumption, however, was that Iraqis were so full of sectarian hatred that they would have to be 'dragged out of their homes' to re-enlist. It also assumed that Iraqis were incapable of distinguishing between army units that had been personally loyal to Saddam Hussein (e.g. the Special Republican Guard) and the rest of the army, which was staffed by young men from the general population.

Just as important was the CPA's assumption that Iraq's entire officer class was Sunni and that the lower ranks were exclusively Shia. At the time, there was no evidence to support this view, because (aside from Saddam Hussein's elite units) that level of detail on sectarian affiliation was simply not available: the CPA relied essentially on what it was told by some former exiles. In fact, it has since emerged that this belief was wrong: very many of the top officers in Iraq's new army were officers in the old army, and since there is now greater transparency on issues of sect and race, we know that the majority of those officers are actually Shia. They include Jawad al-Bulani (who was minister of the interior from 2006 to 2010) and Major General Qassem Atta (spokesman for the Baghdad Operation Command under Prime Minister Nouri al-Maliki). Not only was Atta an officer in the old army, but he was also a Baath party member. In his words, 'no one from the former regime was not a Baathist, we were all Baathists and we had to belong to the Baath party'.[50]

Bremer's second argument was that the old army's infrastructure had been destroyed during the war. None of the barracks and units had been left intact. This argument was part of a larger effort by the CPA and the US administration to absolve themselves of blame for the decision to disband the Iraqi military: 'We didn't dissolve the Iraqi army. It dissolved itself.'[51] Events in Baghdad during the first few weeks of the occupation belie that claim, particularly as tens of thousands of soldiers were actually on the CPA's payroll until the army was officially disbanded. The army's infrastructure was indeed badly damaged, but that would apply to any army – whether old or new. In any event, barracks would have to be rebuilt, regardless of which army assumed responsibility for protecting the country.

Reading the accounts of Bremer and others of how Orders 1 and 2 were conceived, it is startling to note how little attention was paid to the implications. Baghdad is the Arab world's second-largest city. Many of its neighbourhoods are little more than slums, with the type of poverty that most Americans would never imagine is still possible in the twenty-first century.

During the sanctions era, criminal gangs had come together to scrape a living by various means, including smuggling. At the end of 2002, Saddam Hussein had ordered a general amnesty, so that by the time the US army arrived in Baghdad in April 2003, thousands of criminals were back on the streets.[52] To make matters worse, very many Iraqis were resentful of the US's history of involvement in their country and were immediately hostile to the presence of US military personnel on the streets. Finally, Iraq was surrounded by nations that were opposed to the Bush administration, particularly Syria and Iran, which were being openly targeted by US officials for future regime change. Even in friendly countries, such as Jordan and Saudi Arabia, people were outraged at the sight of a western occupation of an Arab and Muslim-majority country (while others were indignant at the thought that the country could be led by a Shia political class). The idea that the US army, with all its limitations on the ground and its lack of local knowledge, could control all these forces on its own or prevent trained provocateurs from igniting already smouldering tensions was naïve at best. The CPA apparently never gave any thought to this and created a security vacuum in an area where adequate security forces were desperately lacking.

It is a cliché to say that the Bush administration was ignorant of Iraqi history and culture and that that was one of the reasons for the fiasco that followed the invasion. Not only is this particular cliché true, but the CPA's own decisions prove it.

Virtually every country in the world has a supreme audit institution – a team of auditors that is responsible for overseeing the implementation of the annual state budget law by the government. The information that the auditors gather is then passed on to parliament, which uses it to assess whether the government is adequately implementing the programme that it was elected to implement. Without the auditors, parliaments would be operating in the dark and would be incapable of exercising any effective oversight on government.

Iraq was no exception in that regard. The Board of Supreme Audit was established in 1927. It underwent a number of legal reforms, and by 2003 was legally answerable to the presidential diwan. It was thus inadvertently dissolved by Order 2, along with the Iraqi military. The CPA never considered whether Iraq had a supreme audit institution, and never tried to understand which institutions were attached to the presidential diwan. The BSA's director and its staff, realizing the importance of their mission within the state, continued working for several months without pay and reached out to the CPA in an effort to explain what had been done. It took them four months to make contact with the CPA and to convince it of the error. Order 34, issued on 13 September 2003, reinstated the BSA, which continues to provide parliament with reports on the government's performance.

That was a minor victory. But the army remained disbanded, leaving Baghdad without any effective policing force for years. Criminals acted with impunity, and militias set up shop in the middle of the street, terrorizing the local population in broad daylight. The electrical grid and oil pipelines were constantly targeted by saboteurs. The smuggling of oil in the south was a growth business and funds were used to finance the purchase of arms, further increasing violence on the streets. For years there was no one to challenge criminals and terrorists. It was not until 2007 that some degree of normality began to return to Iraqi streets – partly because the new Iraqi army was finally able to make its presence felt (after a four-year hiatus) and partly because, in many areas, violence had run its course and there was no one left to fight.

Unfortunately, it was from 2003 to 2005, when the violence was daily getting worse, that the state's new framework was negotiated.

CHAPTER THREE

CREATING A NEW POLITICAL ORDER

DEBATING THE TRANSITION TO DEMOCRACY

Two months after its establishment, the CPA was desperate to be seen to be making progress in improving security and transferring sovereignty back to an Iraqi administration – something that would require the drafting of a new constitution and the organizing of elections. At the same time, the US also wanted to exert some control over the process, in order to ensure that its major interests (whatever those were) were protected. Practically speaking, this meant that the US wanted to maintain some control over which Iraqis would administer Iraq when sovereignty was transferred, who would draft its constitution and what the final document would say.

On the other hand, virtually every Iraqi who had a stake in the transition process was concerned that the final constitution should enjoy some form of internal legitimacy. All parties were troubled by the thought of drafting a constitution under foreign occupation (given the amount of influence that the occupying power could have on the final outcome) and agreed that sovereignty should be transferred to national authorities as soon as possible. Several possibilities were put forward. The former exiles insisted that authority should be formally transferred to them – a notion that was rejected by domestic political forces and even by the CPA, which was already becoming disenchanted with the group. The CPA pushed on several occasions for the constitution to be drafted by an appointed body, but the mere suggestion was anathema to many Iraqis: they recalled how the 1925 constitution, which had granted the king sweeping and undemocratic powers, had been drafted by a constituent assembly that was formed by the then-British occupation. They were determined not to repeat that experience.

A third group held the position that the constitution should be drafted by elected representatives and that any other arrangement would be illegitimate. Most prominent in this group was Grand Ayatollah Ali al-Sistani, the most senior cleric in Shia Islam (to which approximately 60 per cent of Iraqis adhere). Although he was an elderly cleric who was rarely seen in public, al-Sistani commanded huge respect. He made his positions known through published remarks or through his representatives. For the CPA, al-Sistani provided the only opposing view worth considering, and so the following few months saw indirect negotiations between the two sides.

There are famously two main camps in Shia Islam – the 'quietist' camp, which rejects any form of intervention in politics, and the 'interventionist' camp, which today dominates the Iranian political system and according to which clerics should be directly involved in governing the state. Ayatollah al-Sistani sits somewhere in between: through his statements and his behaviour since 2003 he has made it clear that he considers that clerics do have a role to play in directing the state's overall direction, particularly in so far as the relationship with religion is concerned. At the same time, however, he has discouraged clerics from actively participating in politics, for fear that they may be corrupted by power. In his view, government should be left to politicians and administrators.[1] Now al-Sistani felt compelled to get involved in the debate on how the constitution should be drafted, in order to prevent the CPA from manipulating the process as its British predecessors had done eighty years previously.

In June 2003, rumours started circulating that the CPA favoured the appointment of a constituent assembly through a caucus system. Although the idea was never finalized, it would have involved the CPA creating caucuses of elders throughout the country; each of those would then have elected or nominated a representative to serve in a larger assembly that would be responsible for drafting the country's new permanent constitution. Many Iraqis noted that the plan mirrored almost exactly the way in which the country's first constitution had been drafted under British auspices. In response, al-Sistani issued a statement on 26 June 2003:[2]

> Those forces have no jurisdiction whatsoever to appoint members of the
> Constitution preparation assembly. Also there is no guarantee either that

this assembly will prepare a constitution that serves the best interests of the Iraqi people or express their national identity whose backbone is sound Islamic religion and noble social values. The said plan is unacceptable from the outset. First of all there must be a general election so that every Iraqi citizen – who is eligible to vote – can choose someone to represent him in a foundational Constitution preparation assembly. Then the drafted Constitution can be put to a referendum. All believers must insist on the accomplishment of this crucial matter and contribute to achieving it in the best way possible.

Given the strength and determination of al-Sistani's position, the CPA felt compelled to allow Iraqis more control over the administration of their country and over the drafting of their new constitution. The first concession came on 13 July 2003, when it established the Governing Council, a body of twenty-five Iraqis who would theoretically be consulted by the CPA when determining future policy, but which in fact was merely designed to give a more Iraqi face to the occupation. The manner in which the CPA chose the Governing Council's membership perfectly reflected Bremer's conception of Iraq as no more than a combination of ethnic and religious groupings. The twenty-five members were apportioned according to a strict ethno-sectarian formula, and each of the council's members had an ethno-sectarian identity foisted upon them, regardless of his or her political beliefs: even Hamid Majid Mousa of the Communist party was counted as a Shia member, despite being obviously non-sectarian.

The CPA stated that it would consult and coordinate with the Governing Council on all matters involving the temporary governance of Iraq. The Governing Council itself appointed a council of ministers and a constitutional preparatory committee, which was responsible for debating how the country's permanent constitution should be drafted. The Governing Council was beset from the outset by internal disagreements and was criticized for being generally ineffectual in its working methods, sectarian in its outlook, unrepresentative in its make-up and detached from Iraqi society because its membership was drawn heavily from the country's exile community. The council also failed to meet most of its responsibilities. Much like the Future of Iraq Project's 'Democratic Principles Work Group' before it, the constitutional preparatory committee was eventually dissolved without reaching agreement on any of the essential elements of the drafting process.

For the next six months, the CPA continued to insist that an appointed body should draft the constitution, and even published a 'final' agreement to that effect. After another series of interventions by al-Sistani, however, the CPA relented and agreed in February 2004 that a constituent assembly would be directly elected in January 2005. It would be responsible for drafting a permanent constitution; that constitution would be put to a referendum and new elections would be scheduled for December 2005. In making this concession, the CPA was effectively acknowledging the weight of al-Sistani's position. At the time this was rightly lauded as a stand for democracy.

The devil, however, was in the detail. The CPA eventually decided that a temporary constitution would be drafted and adopted, above all to establish the rules according to which the state would function over the coming period, but also to create a 'road map' for how the new, permanent constitution would be drafted. It was also decided that a new Iraqi interim administration would be appointed to govern the country during the next step of the transition process. What was not discussed at the time was who should draft the interim constitution, to what extent political forces would be consulted before the document was finalized, and how much importance it would have in the negotiations that would lead to a final constitution. Very few people realized this at the time, and many still do not know the extent to which these details determined how the final constitution was drafted and what it actually said.

In November 2003, work commenced on Iraq's interim constitution, which would later become known as the transitional administrative law (TAL).[3] The document's stated purpose was to establish a system of government for the 'transitional period', and to set out the parameters within which the state's permanent constitution would be drafted. The manner in which the document was negotiated and drafted was supposed to be a one-off – an imperfect process, undertaken under international occupation, the results of which were to be remedied through subsequent elections and a more legitimate constitutional process.

The drafting process that led to the TAL was a classic imperial enterprise. It was so secretive that Iraqis were not even told that an interim constitution was being prepared. To draft it, the CPA appointed a small group of US officials and academics, plus two Iraqi-American jurists, both of whom had been living in exile for decades and who were more fluent in English than Arabic.[4] Needless to say, the text was drafted in English and was only later translated into Arabic, months after the process had started, when it became necessary to share some of the provisions with the Governing Council. The TAL's substantive content was also affected by the drafters' educational and professional backgrounds. Iraqi constitutions have always offered generous social and economic rights (many of which were never delivered, of course), but the TAL's section on fundamental rights was much more in line with US than with Iraqi traditions. Although the TAL maintained some rights, the US drafters were concerned about how constitutional rights could translate into financial obligations that the state could not afford, and so therefore noted that such rights should be granted 'within the limits of [the state's] resources and with due regard to other vital needs'. The drafters also included a provision for the possession of guns, which was unusual not only in the Iraqi constitutional tradition, but also internationally (most world constitutions are completely silent on the issue).

More problematic was the manner in which the constitution's system of governance was conceived. The main bone of contention was the Kurdistan region, which had enjoyed de facto independence throughout the 1990s and which sought to maintain as much of its autonomy as possible. After Saddam Hussein lost control of Iraq's three northern provinces in 1991, the two main Kurdish parties had administered the area as a region with full autonomy from Baghdad (see Chapter 1). A military front separated the two areas, and there was virtually no interaction between the sides. The Kurdish authorities even issued their own currency, which was completely outside the control of Baghdad's central bank. Internationally, Kurdish autonomy was recognized as an acceptable solution to Saddam Hussein's brutality, but outright independence remained a red line throughout the region and beyond.

Given that one of the 2003 war's theoretical goals was to usher in a democratic regime that respected human and community rights, the need to separate Kurdistan from the rest of the country diminished; this meant that the relationship between the two entities would have to be renegotiated, if not redesigned altogether.

There were several options: the Kurdistan region could be dissolved altogether, leaving in its place the original three northern provinces from which it had originally been formed; the region could remain in place, but have more interaction with Baghdad; or it could maintain full autonomy and remain an exception. Given the respective bargaining power of the parties at the time (and noting in particular that the Kurdish parties were by far the best organized negotiators in the country in 2003 and 2004), the most likely outcome seemed to be that the Kurdistan region would maintain almost all its privileges, but Baghdad would regain some of its prerogatives – including perhaps control over currency, airspace and vital economic issues.

It would have been natural to expect this issue of national importance to have been debated by all the country's political forces and social groups in a calm and deliberate manner, over a lengthy period of time, with a view to reaching some form of consensus. Obviously, the Future of Iraq Project had been unsuccessful, as indeed was the Governing Council's own attempt; but both of those initiatives had been dominated by the former exiles, who had a proven track record of incompetence and failure. A dialogue with a more competent and more representative group should have been attempted.

But the CPA's chosen manner of proceeding defied all expectations and common sense: it decided to negotiate directly with the two main Kurdish parties, without the involvement of any other Iraqi groups whatsoever.[5] A series of meetings took place during January 2004, attended by Bremer and the leaders of the two Kurdish parties. These talks were so secretive that even the TAL's drafters were unaware of what was being discussed. The Kurdish parties demanded the maintenance of their autonomy, adopting an inflexible negotiating stance. In the end, the CPA capitulated to almost all the Kurdish demands without any input from the remainder of Iraqi society. It was only well after the agreement was sealed that the US's other allies in the Governing Council were allowed to tweak it slightly.[6]

The point here is not that the agreement reached was not optimal in the circumstances; the point is that it was inherently undemocratic for self-appointed and unaccountable parties to enter into vital talks behind closed doors – negotiations that would have an impact on the state's future. This early on set a very negative precedent – one that would be followed on a number of occasions in coming years, to devastating effect.

The federal arrangement that was ultimately included in the TAL was unique in constitutional tradition and sowed the seeds for future discord in Iraq. The document stated that there should be three tiers of government across the country: central government in Baghdad, regional government, and finally provincial government. Although the Kurdistan regional government (KRG) was the only regional government in existence in Iraq at the time, the TAL allowed up to three provinces (with the exception of Baghdad and Kirkuk) to form new regions of their own. This was a major departure from constitutional tradition: previously there had been only two levels of government in the country (apart from those areas that fell under the authority of the Kurdistan region). In addition, because the Kurdistan region managed to maintain most of its autonomy from Baghdad, any other part of the country that formed a region of its own would benefit from that same level of autonomy. The TAL therefore took what had been the exceptional relationship that had hitherto existed only between the Kurdistan region and Baghdad, and applied it as a general rule throughout the rest of the country.

The TAL's final version set out a list of the powers that were to be exercised exclusively by the Iraqi transitional government (the central authority in Baghdad). It was an incredibly short list. It included only seven powers, some of which were limited to the formulation of policy in certain areas without the ability to actually implement that policy. Central government ended up with power that was far too limited by any standards; real authority rested with the regions and provinces. For example, Baghdad had no control over Iraq's airspace, roads, railways, education, agriculture, health, etc. All of those powers belonged to regions and provinces.

The compromise between the CPA and the Kurdish parties was incorporated into the TAL draft in early February 2004. This left many of the non-Kurdish parties insufficient time to appreciate what was at stake, let alone to suggest any alternative arrangements.[7] In fact, whatever controversy might have existed on federalism was immediately overshadowed by the mechanism for approval of the final constitution. Article 61(c) provided that '[t]he general referendum will be successful and the draft constitution ratified if a majority of the voters in Iraq approve and if two-thirds of the voters in three or more [provinces] do not reject it'. This clause, which was widely interpreted as providing the country's Kurdish population (a large majority of the three northern provinces) with a veto, was considered undemocratic by the majority of Shia negotiators, some of whom were reportedly furious. Significant effort was made at last to negotiate a compromise, but to no avail. At the official signing ceremony, a statement was read out on behalf of almost half of the Governing Council's members that argued against article 61(c) and that promised to seek an amendment as soon as possible (something that never transpired).[8]

With the TAL completed, an Iraqi interim government was to be appointed to administer the country until the election of a transitional national assembly (TNA), which would have as its primary function the drafting of a future constitution. The interim government, which was to be made up of a combination of non-political technocrats and political appointees, was chosen by the United Nations and the CPA, the latter having imposed Ayad

Allawi as interim prime minister. The CPA officially transferred sovereignty to the Iraqi interim government on 28 June 2004, and the CPA and Governing Council were both dissolved.[9] Thus began the second stage of the constitutional process. What was not known at the time was how much had already been decided.

Before it was disbanded, the CPA quickly enacted a large number of rules that would allow for the TNA's election, scheduled for January 2005. Getting the electoral rules right was crucial, given that whoever was elected would theoretically determine how the new state would operate. The rules therefore had to be both equitable and acceptable to the general population. There was, however, strong disagreement between many of the interested parties over how difficult it would be to organize elections, over the type of rules that should govern the elections, and over how long the process should take. The United Nations was eventually asked for its opinion on the matter; it concluded that the entire process should take no less than eight months. That timeframe was eventually accepted, though there was a general desire to hold the first elections as soon as possible. It was assumed at the time that the framework for Iraq's first elections would be adequate, though far from perfect, and that this framework would be improved in the future.

CPA Order 92 established the Independent Electoral Commission of Iraq (IECI) which had the authority to 'promulgate, implement, and enforce regulations, rules and procedures with the full force of law in connection with elections during the Transitional Period'. The most difficult and controversial of the IECI's functions in the period leading up to the polls (particularly given that there was no precedent for such a monumental task in Iraq) would be to '[d]etermine, establish, develop, certify, subdivide, and maintain the voter roll'. The commission's board of commissioners was the sole body competent to 'promulgate, implement and enforce regulations, rules, procedures and decisions . . . to ensure the successful organization, planning, implementation and oversight of nationwide and local elections throughout Iraq'. The board's members were to be nominated by the United Nations, and ultimately appointed by the CPA administrator.

CPA Order 96 determined the legal framework for elections to the TNA that were to take place on or before 31 January 2005. Order 96 established Iraq as a 'single electoral constituency' – a controversial decision that was to affect the election results and the subsequent constitutional process in a number of ways. Most importantly, perhaps, the 'single electoral constituency' meant that if voter participation in a particular area of the country was lower than in the remainder of the country, that area would simply not have any representatives of its own.

Since certain parts of the country had been engulfed in violence, and since some political forces had called for a boycott of the political process, a number of senior policy makers correctly predicted that the residents of Anbar province (for example) would be unable and unwilling to participate in the elections.[10] Sure enough, Anbar was woefully under-represented when the TNA was eventually convened.

Order 96 also established a 'closed list' system, which meant that each party or coalition that was contesting the elections had to submit a single 'list' of its candidates, and voters would have to choose between the lists on offer; they would not be able to vote for individual candidates, even if they wanted to. Given that each electoral list represented large political coalitions, it would be impossible to determine from the electoral results how popular one component of an electoral list was in relation to the others. This would allow certain political parties (namely SCIRI) to dominate constitutional negotiations on the basis not of its actual popularity, but merely on the basis of how popular it was perceived to be by its peers and by US officials.

CPA Order 97 purported to regulate the work of 'political entities' in Iraq. An entity was defined as 'an organization, including a political party, of eligible voters who voluntarily associate on the basis of common ideas, interests or views, for the purpose of articulating interests, obtaining influence and having their representatives elected to public office'. Order 97 established a number of procedural rules that a political entity had to follow if it was to participate in the upcoming elections. These included registering with the IECI. The Order also sought to enforce what it referred to as 'common principles', including that '[n]o political entity may be directly or indirectly financed by any armed force, militia, or residual element' and that '[p]olitical entities must strive, to the extent possible, to achieve full transparency in all financial dealings. In this regard, the Commission may issue regulations with respect to financial disclosure.' The IECI eventually passed a number of regulations that were designed to enforce some of these measures, including Regulation 03/2004 (25 October 2004), according to which political entities that were associated with or financed by an armed force or militia would, in theory, not be allowed to register with the commission, and would therefore not be able to participate in the elections.[11]

Other provisions required all political entities to adhere to the IECI's code of conduct, under which all political entities must '[s]trive to achieve full transparency in political finances and expenditures'. Despite the fact that these principles are officially supported by Iraqi policy makers, they remain unenforceable, since most of the political parties that have enjoyed electoral success refuse to adhere to them. In particular, parties have refused to publish their accounts or even to provide any details about the source of their income. Most Iraqis assume this must originate outside the country or come from some illegitimate source.

DRAFTING THE CONSTITUTION: SOWING THE SEEDS OF DISCORD

Most commentators – and many international and Iraqi officials – maintain that the 2005 constitution was the outcome of a generally democratic process. According to them, the elections that Grand Ayatollah Ali al-Sistani insisted upon led to the formation of a relatively representative constitutional drafting committee and enabled agreement to be reached between Kurdish and Shia negotiators (who together represented 80 per cent of the population). They argue that the Kurdish negotiators acceded to Shia demands for an 'Islamization' of the draft, in exchange for concessions on the vertical distribution of powers, in particular with a view to protecting the Kurdistan regional government's autonomy.[12] They also claim that the Shia political elite as a whole provided a strong endorsement of the constitution's arrangement for federalism, calling for the establishment of a 'Shia region' in the south of the country that would effectively divide the country in two. The contention is that since the elites that crafted the constitution together represented 80 per cent of the population, that was more than adequate to lend the document legitimacy.

But this commonly held view is completely mistaken. In reality, although the constitution was supposed to be written by the people's elected representatives, in the end it was finalized by self-appointed and unrepresentative individuals, through a series of negotiations that took place in secret. Those discussions steered the document away from what the original drafters had decided just days before. As a result, the constitution is the product of an agreement between three small political parties that probably never represented more than 20 per cent of the population. Those three parties in fact de-Islamicized the draft in a way that the people's representatives had not intended and established a federal system of government that is unworkable and lies far outside the mainstream of Iraqi public opinion.

*   *   *

The elections to the transitional national assembly were held on 30 January 2005, a bloody day that saw over thirty civilians killed. The elections were contested by a number of alliances, most prominent of which was the (Shia Islamist) United Iraqi Alliance (UIA). It was formed following pressure from within the Shia community for it to join ranks and make its collective weight count. This came in the context of rising violence and followed Ayad Allawi's unsuccessful attempt to govern the country as a liberal and secular interim prime minister.

Of the 275 seats that were up for grabs, the UIA won 140, the Kurdish alliance 75 and the liberal/secular Iraqiya alliance (headed by Allawi) 40. The electoral boycott meant that the Sunni community was one of the least well represented groups (relative to its generally assumed size). After significant debate as to how the drafting process should be organized, it was decided that a constitutional committee should be formed from among the members of the TNA to negotiate and draft the country's new constitution, although officially only the TNA could finally approve the draft and put it to the people in a referendum.

This committee was eventually formed on 10 May 2005 and consisted of fifty-five members;[13] since its membership reflected the TNA's own composition, an additional fifteen Sunni Arabs were included on 16 June 2005, in recognition of the fact that the community was under-represented in the TNA. Sheikh Humam al-Hamoudi, a leading member of the SCIRI, was nominated as its chairman on 23 May 2005 – the date on which the drafting process was finally deemed ready to commence (the Sunni Arab members joined later).

Even in its expanded form, the constitutional committee was a flawed body. It included only a handful of women, none of whom played a leading role in the discussions, and practically no youth representatives. Deliberations on the state's future, fundamental rights and even gender rights were therefore monopolized by conservative old men who had accumulated a lifetime of prejudices and bad habits that they would never be able to shake off. However, despite its flaws, the constitutional committee was still more democratic than the CPA, the Governing Council or the Interim Iraqi Government. A significant proportion of its members were not drawn from former exiles, and while its deliberations were not broadcast live, at least they did not take place in secret. Media outlets were sometimes given access to the negotiations and to some committee members; and anyone who followed proceedings closely could gain a sense of what was being discussed and where the controversies lay. There were disagreements between committee members, but broad consensus was reached in relation to many important issues.

The main problem that the committee faced, however, was the timeframe that the TAL imposed on it: the draft constitution was supposed to be ready by 15 August 2005. There was then to be a two-month public outreach campaign, ending with a referendum on 15 October 2005. Given that the committee was formed in mid-May, it had three months in which to negotiate and draft the entire constitution (in fact, by the time the expanded committee was formed it had only two months left). It is worth noting that, in post-totalitarian environments, negotiating a constitution is a particularly difficult task. Parties first have to shake off the vestiges of the state's oppressive methods and then bring themselves up to date with recent developments in modern constitutional practice. They need to decide what their own positions are on a wide range of issues, since open and frank discussion on a future constitutional arrangement would not have been possible under the old regime. They must also understand what their counterparts' positions are, negotiate a reasonable compromise, find a proper formulation for it, and then consult with their constituents to ensure that the compromise is acceptable to them.

Aside from the political negotiations, drafting a new constitution nowadays necessarily involves some effort to understand the workings of the country's institutional framework. Even constitutions that are constructed on the ashes of dissolved state institutions cannot hope to start with a completely clean slate. Many existing institutions will be preserved, and their reporting lines, working methods and other traditions will influence the new constitution's workings. As a result, constitutional drafters should try to understand which institutions are the most efficient and which are dysfunctional, so that they can decide how the new constitution can improve on the existing framework. In addition, changes to the country's overall governance structure can affect the way in which specific institutions operate, even if those same institutions are not mentioned in the constitution itself. In the absence of sufficient foresight in relation to these issues, any changes are likely to have unforeseen consequences, which is never a good thing.

If all this is to be carried out successfully, the negotiators need to have ample time. South Africa's 1997 constitution took – from the very beginning to the end – seven years to negotiate and draft. By contrast, despite their poor track record, Iraq's flawed political parties and former exiles were given just three months. It should have come as no surprise that, as 15 August 2005 approached, the committee was still some way off being finished. A decision was required on whether to extend the process by six months (something that was permitted on a one-off basis under the TAL). Sheikh al-Hamoudi, the committee's chairman, was in favour of seeking an extension, and the United Nations recommended the same.[14]

But it was not to be. The US embassy, intent on ensuring that the referendum was held on 15 October, intervened to block the extension.[15] The embassy's position was supported by a large section of the clerical establishment, which, by August 2005, had lost interest in the constitution's content and was pressuring the political class to forge ahead come what may. This position was based on the mistaken assumption that a new constitution would ease tension in the country and lead to an improvement in security.[16] There was also significant dismay among some Iraqi and US actors on the ground over the direction in which the constitutional committee was taking the draft. Its members favoured a strong role for Islam in the state and a strong central government, but this ran counter to the hopes of some parties, most particularly the Kurdish Alliance.

Consequently, the drafting process was not extended. The committee was dissolved at the beginning of August 2005 and the TNA (which the people had elected to draft the constitution) was never given the opportunity to express its views on the process or to debate any of the drafts that had been produced. A few weeks later, some senior members of the TNA asked the United Nations to print and distribute to the general public several million copies of the most recent version of the draft constitution. When the UN insisted that the TNA must approve the draft before it was distributed, Hussein al-Shahristani of the United Iraqi Alliance read the draft to the assembly on 18 September 2005 without giving members an opportunity to vote on it or even to debate it.[17]

The mystery was how the draft constitution could be completed if the drafting process was supposed to be over. In fact, unbeknownst to the general public, many of the draft's most important sections were completely overhauled, behind closed doors, by unrepresentative officials, who often included so many US drafters that even their Iraqi allies were made to feel uncomfortable. The body that took over the drafting process was referred to at the time as the 'leadership council'. This body emerged (and its membership was decided) through a process of self-selection by some and exclusion of others, as well as through the active encouragement of the US embassy. Pro-democracy activists, including some of the 'internationals' who were present at the time, mounted no serious opposition to its takeover; they felt power-less in the face of what was happening and considered that the negative turn taken by the process was somehow inevitable. There was no sense of struc-ture or organization about the manner in which the leadership council held its meetings; indeed, today there is very little agreement even as to which Iraqi parties were actually present. What is certain is that the two Kurdish parties played a major role during that period and that the United States embassy was heavily involved. The rest is murky. A number of inconsistent accounts have been offered, including the following:

- Two former legal advisers at the United States embassy have written that the council discussions featured the two Kurdish parties and secular Arab politicians, while the Shia Islamist parties apparently played a minor role.[18]
- The United States Institute of Peace, also an active participant in the constitutional process, has said that the Kurds' main counterparts in the discussions were actually the party leaders of the SCIRI and the Islamic Dawa Party (both Shia Islamist parties), and that secular politicians were excluded altogether.[19]
- A legal adviser at the United Nations Office of Constitutional Support who participated in many of the leadership council's discussions has described a much more fluid environment, in which the leadership coun-cil's general discussions at first involved more participants than the constitutional committee's seventy members, eventually evolving into a more informal drafting committee that included two Kurdish members, two Shia Islamists and three legal officers from the United States embassy.[20]

The US embassy's role was controversial, given the implications for Iraq's national sovereignty. Although some US officials have offered accounts of how the leadership council's work progressed, neither the US embassy nor the Iraqi authorities have acknowledged the extent to which the process broke down and what impact that had on the draft. After the constitutional committee was dissolved, the embassy imposed itself on the discussions by organizing meetings between various parties, to try to ensure that final agreement would be reached by the referendum date.[21] This was mainly achieved by hosting discussions between political leaders, by participating in drafting negotiations, and by suggesting wording that was designed to reflect whatever agreement had been reached or to assist the parties in concluding their negotiations.

Some of the participants were uncomfortable at the role that US officials were playing in the negotiations, particularly during one of the leadership council's first discussions, held at the embassy itself and involving a 'small army' of US lawyers and assistants. The sense of interference was said to have been so palpable that, after many complaints, the discussions continued in offices that were made available by some of the Iraqi negotiators, including senior Kurdish leaders.[22] This again led to problems, as the council's deliberations would often be so chaotic that several negotiating sessions were held simultaneously and without the knowledge of other parties, so that for several weeks different drafts were in circulation, none of which was more official than the others.[23]

The result of this ad hoc approach was that many of the people's elected representatives could no longer participate in the negotiations, simply because they were no longer aware of where the discussions were taking place and they had not been invited to participate by whichever unofficial authority was hosting them. Not only was this extremely undemocratic, but the way in which the council steered the draft was equally damaging. Its members tossed out a large part of the draft and replaced it with sections from the TAL, the document that had been drafted by a small number of US-appointed officials in an intensely secretive process. In so doing, they steered the draft in a direction that was completely different from the one in which the constitutional committee had been taking it. The upshot was that the council very clearly diluted the provisions relating to Islam and made sure that central government was as weak as possible.

To make matters even worse, the public was deceived into thinking that it could influence the draft. The constitutional committee had formed a 'public outreach committee' that was supposedly responsible for collecting the views of the public. Hundreds of thousands of survey forms were filled in and submitted by members of the public, but the constitutional committee had already been dissolved by the time they were collated and analysed.[24]

The people scarcely even had an opportunity to review the draft: although some copies were leaked to the press in advance, the official draft was circulated to a limited number of people one month before the referendum date.

Very few people ever obtained a copy or had an opportunity to read the text. Even if they had seen it, they would not have known that it was not their elected representatives who had produced the draft. In any case, it would not have mattered, as further changes were made after the distribution date, again behind closed doors. The only significant changes that were made publicly were those announced at a press conference on 12 October 2005. This had been arranged to announce a last-minute initiative designed to encourage Sunni Arabs to vote in favour of the draft. The Iraqi Islamic Party (affiliated to the Muslim Brotherhood) declared that it had brokered the new changes, which included a provision that supposedly guaranteed that the text would be amended within four months of its coming into effect. The declaration was a logical absurdity: the negotiators were asking the public to vote for a constitution that they were promising would be amended within sixteen weeks! If their intention to amend the text was sincere, they should simply have extended the drafting process; the fact that they did not should have been indication enough that they never intended to follow through on their promise.

In the end, the referendum went ahead on 15 October 2005 and the final constitution was approved by close to 80 per cent of the population. The available data indicated that the population voted along ethno-sectarian lines, with the Kurdish and Shia communities almost wholly in favour of the text and the Sunni community almost unanimously against. Some concluded that this reflected the absence of a real sense of nationhood within the country; others noted that the constitutional process itself – carried out at a time of increasing violence – was just another element of growing sectarian conflict. As if to prove the point, the vote was marked by significant violence – dozens were reported to have been killed in attacks on polling stations on 15 October.

Few members of the general public knew what the constitution actually said and what they were voting for. In fact, the process was so opaque that even some members of the original drafting committee were not clear what the final version actually said.

In order to understand how the leadership council shifted the constitution sharply away from the path that the constitutional committee had been setting we need to review the drafts that the two bodies produced.

It is clear from this exercise that the leadership council was far more liberal on religion and far more extreme on federalism than was the constitutional committee. Also, while the committee started out by using the TAL as a template, by the end it had moved well beyond the TAL's provisions on just about every issue. The leadership council, on the other hand, made sure to bring the TAL back to centre stage: wherever possible, TAL provisions were cut and pasted back into the draft constitution, at the expense of whatever progress had been made by the people's elected representatives.

Let us take religion as an example. The drafts show that the constitutional committee Islamicized the draft constitution very early on. The provisions that it introduced were preserved without any major changes until the second week of August, but were then either eradicated or moderated through the use of safeguards by the leadership council as soon as it took over.

Throughout the Arab region, religion has always played a pivotal role in inspiring legislation. Among other things, Iraqis' 'personal status' issues (marriage, divorce, inheritance, etc.) are either entirely derived from, or are heavily inspired by, religious texts. In recent decades, religious scholars and certain components of society have pushed for religion to influence not just personal status, but all areas of legislation. As a result, many constitutions in the region have included what is referred to as a 'repugnancy clause', according to which the legislature should not pass, and the courts should not uphold, any law that contradicts Islamic sharia. In practice, repugnancy clauses often have little or no impact: most legislation (traffic laws, the regulation of the internet, agriculture, industry, etc.) have no relationship with religion, and so legislators often never bother considering what Islam has to say on the issue. There are also very few effective mechanisms in place to ensure that repugnancy clauses are properly enforced.

Iraq had not amended its constitution to reflect this trend, but during the 1990s society retreated into itself and sought solace in religion as it tried to cope with sanctions-induced poverty. As the 2005 constitutional drafting process commenced, society was generally thought to have become more religious, and many of the main political parties (SCIRI, the Sadrist movement and the Iraqi Islamic Party) were primarily motivated by religion. There was little doubt from the outset, therefore, that religion would be given a more important role than in the past; the question was how far the drafters would go.

The role that Islam should play in influencing future legislation followed the pattern outlined above. The TAL's provision on this issue was the product of significant discussion among Governing Council members and the CPA. The final version read:

Islam is the official religion of the State and is to be considered a source of legislation. No law that contradicts the universally agreed tenets of Islam, the principles of democracy, or the rights cited in Chapter Two of this Law may be enacted during the transitional period. This Law respects the Islamic identity of the majority of the Iraqi people and guarantees the full religious rights of all individuals to freedom of religious belief and practice.

The issue re-emerged at the start of the discussions on the permanent constitution. A draft that was circulated on 21 July reflected the dominant voice of the Islamists in the constitutional committee:

Islam is the official State religion, and it is the principal source of legislation. It is forbidden to enact laws that contradict the principles of Islam. This constitution protects the Islamic identity of the majority of the Iraqi people (by Shia and Sunni majority) and respects the rights of all other religions.

Had this been adopted, it would have introduced a stringent form of Islamic law and would have introduced for the first time in Iraqi constitutional history recognition of the confessional divide within Islam between the Shia and the Sunni denominations. Although that recognition was unlikely to have had any practical impact under the 21 July draft, it was nevertheless a development without precedent in Arab constitutional tradition.[25]

The provision proved controversial with some constitutional committee members and certain members of the international community, and over the coming weeks efforts were made to placate them, but without changing the provision's fundamental aspects, on which the constitutional committee would not budge. However, the leadership council toned the provision down as soon as it assumed control over the drafting process in mid-August. A draft produced on 16 August marked a clear departure from the previous version. This would remain essentially unchanged until the referendum. The leadership council's solution was to go back to the TAL and use the exact wording found there, albeit now organized into a small number of sub-paragraphs. The new version therefore provided that:

(1) Islam is the official State religion, and it is a principal source of legislation. It is forbidden to enact laws which contradict:

(a) the principles and tenets of Islam (unanimously);

(b) the principles of democracy;

(c) the rights and freedoms that are provided for in this constitution.

(2) This constitution (protects) and respects the Islamic identity of the majority of the Iraqi people and it guarantees full religious rights to all individuals, freedom of belief and of religious practice.

Not only was the role of religion in preparing future legislation tempered by the fact that it was now just 'a' principal source of legislation (rather than 'the' principal source as in the 21 July draft), but with this wording Islam also had to compete with the vague and undefined 'principles of democracy' and with the constitution's section on fundamental rights, which at that point included detailed provisions on gender, racial and social equality. Although these provisions would remain largely theoretical, in that they would never be applied by parliament or by the courts, they clearly illustrated the difference in opinion between the leadership council and the constitutional committee.

On the relationship between religion and women's rights, a draft provision that was produced by the constitutional committee on 20 July (heavily inspired by Egypt's 1971 constitution) stated that '[t]he state guarantees the fundamental rights of women and their equality with men, in all fields, according to the provisions of Islamic Sharia, and assists them to reconcile duties towards family and work in society'.

The committee, which was dominated by Shia and Sunni Islamists, clearly sought to impose its vision of Iraqi society on the entire country. The draft imposed specific duties on women, without any similar provisions for men; so while women were expected to care for their families and also to work, the drafters were silent on what was expected of men. Women would be encouraged to become mothers, regardless of their own personal choice; to dress in a way that would not bring their male relatives into disrepute; and to care for their children, as well as for elderly and sick relatives, without necessarily being assisted in any of these tasks by their menfolk. This provision attracted the attention of Iraqi civil society organizations and of the international community, which pressured committee members to guarantee equal protection for women. Over the following three weeks, the drafters modified the provision on several occasions in an effort to mollify the critics, but they maintained the essential principle that men and women were not equal and that women had special family obligations.

It was only after the constitutional committee lost control of the drafting process during the third week of August that the provisions on women's rights crystallized into their final form. The draft produced and circulated on 16 August completely changed the course of the drafting process on this issue. All reference to the role of women, to family or society was completely eliminated from the draft, so that the general prohibition on discrimination (article 1, chapter 2), including sexual discrimination, was the only provision that dealt with the rights of women. No further changes were made to the issue of women's rights during the remainder of the drafting process.

The transitional administrative law was heavily skewed in favour of the country's regional and provincial governments, at the expense of Baghdad: it stated that the federal government had only seven powers, and it indicated very clearly that any powers not included on that list belonged to the regions and the provinces.

The powers that were granted to the federal government were so weak and so limited that the state was among the most underpowered in the world. According to a literal interpretation of the TAL, the federal government had the authority to devise but not to implement fiscal policy. Thus under the TAL, the federal government had no authority to raise taxes itself. The same applied to foreign policy – Baghdad could devise it but not implement it. This opened the door for the regions to pursue their own foreign policies. The federal government did not have authority over economic or agricultural policy, so these issues were also left to the regions. The TAL likewise established for the first time in Iraq a mechanism for the formation of new regions, aside from the Kurdistan region.

When negotiations on the country's permanent constitution began in 2005, the constitutional committee's initial drafts mirrored the system established by the TAL, duplicating five of the seven powers that the TAL granted to the federal government. Over the coming weeks, however, a number of important changes were made. The committee's members were in general agreement that the federal government should play a much more important role in the state, and so they set about lengthening the list of powers dramatically. By the time the constitutional committee was dissolved, it had tripled the federal government's powers: it now had authority over the country's airports, international highways, ports and airspace, postal communication policy, monetary and banking policies, foreign economic and commercial policy, the state's development policies and its general planning policy, as well as the general census, public service, salaries and benefits, historical, cultural and archaeological ruins and sites, plus historic buildings and other cultural heritage sites. With all the changes that the committee had made, the state was looking far more viable, although some important detail was still missing.

That trend was completely reversed by the leadership council. It deleted all the changes that had been introduced by the constitutional committee and reintroduced the TAL's original wording, despite all the promises that the TAL would not serve as a basis for discussion and despite the fact that the TAL had been devised through an extremely undemocratic and opaque process. By the time the leadership council was done, the federal government had been stripped of the authority to implement fiscal and foreign policy (it could only formulate these policies, not implement them), to regulate public service, salaries, benefits, railways, airspace, national waters, customs, broadcast frequencies and mail. Under the leadership council's model, these powers were all granted to the regions. There was no mechanism to ensure that regions would cooperate with each other or with the central government. Instead, provinces were encouraged to form themselves into regions, in order to acquire the powers that the constitution was offering. They were even given the unrestricted right to merge to become super-regions: any number of provinces could join together and did not even need to have a contiguous border. Thus, thanks to a shadowy, unaccountable and unelected group of individuals that was shepherded by the US embassy, the Iraqi state was consecrated as one of the weakest states in the world – even as escalating violence threatened to tear it apart.

The area in which the constitutional committee had made least progress was oil and gas. That was perhaps unsurprising, given how complex it was and how much depended on it. The committee members had nevertheless reached agreement on a few issues: first, there was general consensus (or at least a lack of formal debate) on how the oil industry should be managed. Up to 2003 (and particularly prior to 1991), Iraq's ministry of oil and its national oil companies had been powerful entities. They employed some of the country's most respected professionals, and were managing to produce 3.8 million barrels per day in 1979 (as soon as Saddam Hussein took over the presidency that figure dropped sharply and never recovered). National ownership of natural resources was not only a source of pride to many Iraqis, it was also the source of virtually all of the state's revenue. It was a matter of some controversy, therefore, that from the time the 2003 war broke out, no real effort was made to revive Iraq's own capacity in the field. Instead, reliance was placed almost exclusively on foreign oil companies. The US and the UK pressed the state to accept liberalization, and the former exiles acquiesced wholeheartedly. Neither the constitutional committee nor the leadership council debated any alternative arrangements.

Within that context, all that was left to be determined was the level of government that would be responsible for interacting with the international corporations that would flood into the country. The constitutional committee's members had been debating this, but had not reached a consensus by the time they were pushed out of the picture. When the leadership council took over, in keeping with its general principles on federalism it imposed a highly decentralized framework, in which the central government had to cooperate with all of the country's regional and provincial governments in the formation of policy and the management of natural resources. It also used the term 'current fields' for the first time; this was apparently included to distinguish those oil and gas fields that were being exploited at the time of the constitutional negotiations from those that either had not yet been discovered or were not yet in production. Effectively, the use of that term meant that, for example, any existing fields in the Kurdistan region would have to be jointly managed by the federal and regional governments, but any fields that were to come on stream in the future would be solely managed by the Kurdistan regional government. Such a distinction was unheard of internationally, and it has since created enormous problems and tensions between Baghdad and Erbil. It has also emerged that one of the international advisers to the KRG who proposed this wording had a financial stake in one such 'future field' in the Kurdistan region; it has been suggested that this may have earned him up to $100 million.[26]

The drafting process suffered from two other problems: a desire to do the opposite of whatever was done during the Baath era; and too little time to negotiate many of the important details of how the state should function.

Under the Baath, parliament was an irrelevance and power was concentrated in the hands of the Revolutionary Command Council, which itself had been commandeered by Saddam Hussein. The new constitution theoretically rebalanced the relationship between parliament and government (giving the former significant powers). The problem is that, while it provided a detailed guide on how parliament should function internally, it offered no guidance on how government should operate. For example, it did not specify how many ministers had to be present for a government meeting to have a quorum, and nor did it indicate the types of powers that the government was entitled to exercise. In modern democracies, there is a clear distinction between law (which is passed by parliament) and regulation (which emanates from the government, and which can only be in application of a law). In Iraq, that distinction is very unclear. The government has acted on many occasions without making reference to a specific law, citing its own legitimacy as the only source of authority. On occasion, the government has also issued specific decisions even though many ministers were absent.

In this context, Iraq's weak rule of law is particularly relevant. Iraqi officials tend to follow a top-down approach in the exercise of their duties: more often than not, they implement the orders that they receive from their superiors without questioning whether they are in conformity with the law or the constitution. That tradition has a number of causes, most important of which is the culture of fear that has been inherited from Saddam Hussein's regime. In post-2003 Iraq, the tradition lives on.

Let us say that an order is issued by the government. But what if it is not in conformity with the law? What if the law does not permit the government to issue an order in relation to a specific area? The order will most likely be applied anyway. What if the minister of the interior orders security forces to make arrests without a court order (which is in violation of the constitution and of the law)? The arrests will almost certainly be made – as was the case in October 2011, when hundreds of former Baath party members were detained without a court order as a 'precautionary measure' prior to the withdrawal of US troops.[27] In the context of intense and violent political competition between political forces, the absence of a strong rule of law transformed the state into a weapon in the hands of whoever controlled government.

Another important structural chasm is the constitution's provisions on the armed forces. Although the text clearly states that the military should not play a political role, it also states that the prime minister is the 'commander in chief of the armed forces' without making any effort to explain what that term means or what its implications are. Does it give the prime minister exclusive authorization to issue instructions to officers? Could the prime minister issue instructions directly to specific military units or does he have to work within the structure's hierarchy? What is the minister of defence's role in the chain of command, and what is his relationship with the prime minister? Given the constitution's wording, it seemed inevitable that the minister of defence must be subservient to the prime minister. The rub is that, because government is also supposed to be shared between virtually all of Iraq's political parties, and so those two positions will almost certainly be filled by individuals who hail from different parties, there is significant incentive for the prime minister to appropriate the position for himself in whatever way he can (as happened in 2010; see Chapter 5).

Taken together, these factors mean that, under the new constitution, a small group of ministers close to the prime minister could essentially direct the state (barring a few institutions) to carry out their bidding, regardless of whether they have the authority to do so. This partially explains the value of occupying the position of prime minister. Though the drafters did not even realize it, the constitution's lack of clarity turned the keys of the kingdom over to whoever occupied that particular position. It was something that almost all of them would come to regret within a few short years.

A TERRIFYING OUTCOME

Like many of his colleagues in the Shia clergy, Ayatollah Ali al-Sistani considered politics a dirty business. Its methods were unclear and encouraged dishonesty and corruption. Politics, however, is more than merely corrupting; it is also incredibly complex. Political actors have to administer the state and deliver services as effectively as possible, and have to manage what is always a difficult relationship with the public. Just as importantly, they also have to keep at bay their adversaries, who are always seeking to prey on the weaknesses of their enemies. Thus, even when agreements between political rivals are painstakingly negotiated and drafted, they are routinely violated by one of the parties, just when the other side has let its guard down. Even worse, manipulators can exploit the lack of detail in an agreement to bring about the opposite result of what was originally intended, without their adversaries even noticing.

Ayatollah Ali al-Sistani demanded a constitution that was crafted by the elected representatives of the people. The elected representatives that he insisted upon were in favour of a conservative vision of society, and a strong central government. However, despite the weight of his authority, democracy was rudely brushed aside in favour of secretive arrangements and special interests. The final constitution, which was supposed to be the result of a democratic process, was ultimately heavily inspired by the TAL, a deeply flawed document.

Although many were grateful that the leadership council had liberalized the final constitution's provisions on religion and women's rights, it had also created a terrifying system of government in which the country's only central authority (already deprived by the CPA of an effective army or police force) was now deprived of any real constitutional power. This was a system that was designed to be dysfunctional; if ever it were actually implemented, it would tear the country asunder.

Because many Iraqi officials were well aware of the constitution's implications, right from the start they devoted themselves to preventing any provinces from forming a region (as was permitted under the constitution). Despite all the rhetoric of building a state of law, of a new era in which Iraqis would all be equal under the guidance of a constitution drafted by the people, the document could never be applied. This contributed to the state of lawlessness that continues to this day. It also meant that, in the absence of law, governance and development, provinces would seek greater autonomy from the central government by whatever means they had at their disposal. In summary, the constitution set in motion a destructive cycle that has wrought havoc since the day it entered into force.

It is not a question of being wise after the event: the writing was on the wall from the very start. In September 2005, the United Nations prepared an analysis of the draft constitution a month before the referendum date and concluded that 'the provisions for the conversion of [provinces] into a region outside Kurdistan create a model for the territorial division of the State which in our view leaves the central government underpowered and possibly under resourced'.[28]

Professor Yash Ghai, one of the world's leading constitutional scholars, was in Baghdad in 2005, acting as an adviser to Sheikh al-Hamoudi, the constitutional committee's chairman. Professor Ghai also wrote an analysis of the draft before the referendum, in which he said that the draft constitution:

> could sharpen even further the divisions within Iraq and pose a serious threat to the unity and territorial integrity of the country. There are also technical deficiencies in the draft which are to some extent tied to key substantive provisions and will be hard to remedy. We have serious reservations whether the [draft constitution] as it stands can be fully and effectively implemented, *without grave danger to state and society.*[29]

Both views were widely circulated within Iraq at the time, but were completely ignored by those Iraqi and US officials who were controlling the process.

Not only was the constitution's framework for federalism dangerous, it was also far outside the popular mainstream. The vast majority of Iraq's political class, including Dawa, the Sadrist movement, the Iraqiya alliance and the Iraqi Islamic Party, were not given an effective voice in the leadership council. Their views on federalism were not taken into consideration, and that has damaged the constitution's legitimacy. Immediately after it came into force, several of the country's most important leaders rejected its application. In February 2006, Moqtada al-Sadr, arguably the most influential Shia political figure at the time, said: 'I reject this constitution which calls for sectarianism and there is nothing good in this constitution at all.'[30] In October of the same year, Prime Minister Nouri al-Maliki stated:

> [even though] federalism has been legally established by our law, I believe that if we succeed in restoring security, political and economic powers to the central government, the need for federalism will diminish. And if federalism has to be, it should be a political system, not a national, ethnic or sectarian federalism. It should be an administrative federalism based on geographical considerations.[31]

Since then, that same view has been expressed on dozens of occasions by Iraq's most senior politicians, mainly because that is what resonates most strongly with Iraqis.

This leads to an important question: why did a large majority of Iraqis vote for the text? It has been well documented that the Kurdish and Shia communities (which together constitute approximately 80 per cent of the population) overwhelmingly approved the constitution, even though the Shia community was at best divided over the issue of federalism (and was most likely overwhelmingly opposed to it). What can explain that level of support, particularly as most voters did not have the opportunity even to review the draft text before the referendum?

The answer lies in the way in which communities behave during conflict and how inter-communal relations are affected by it. Nicholas Haysom was a legal adviser to Nelson Mandela in the 1990s, but in 2005 he was in charge of the United Nations' efforts to support the constitutional process. He put it thus: 'In conflict, people retreat into fundamentalism. In a conflict, the issues that are dominant are not the same issues that will be dominant in a more peaceful setting.'[32] The constitutional committee that was formed after the January 2005 elections was divided on ideological grounds. Some members were Islamists, others were not. A significant majority of the committee was in favour of re-establishing a stronger central government. Instead of allowing the two sides of the ideological divide to come to a workable compromise, those who sought to maintain a weak central government shut out the majority of parties and kept the draft constitution virtually secret from them and the rest of the population right up until the end.

On the other hand, because Iraqis had not been shown the text, their own general situation dictated how they would vote. The country at the time was suffering from ever increasing levels of violence. In 2005, Shiites were under threat because of the conflict and felt opposed to the Sunni community, which had taken a clear stand against the political process as soon as the US military arrived in Baghdad. In addition, SCIRI came out strongly in favour of the establishment of a super-region in southern Iraq as a way of providing security for Shiites against the unnamed but unmistakable enemy. The referendum was therefore presented as a clear choice between war and peace, security and chaos, and not as one system of government versus another. Although all other Shia political parties clearly objected to the establishment of a weak federal state, they also felt compelled to close ranks with their co-confessionalists and to oppose those parties or communities that they were in conflict with, regardless of whether or not they shared the same views on the constitution. Those politicians who were aware of how flawed the process and the outcome were kept quiet until well after the referendum date.

As for the two Kurdish parties – which obtained more than they could possibly have hoped for in the constitutional negotiations – their support was never in doubt.

Conversely, the Sunni community felt that it had been excluded from the process and that the final constitution did not reflect its interests – though of course it had no inkling what was missing from the text. Virtually the entire community voted against the text – and lost, which contributed to a lack of faith in the entire political process. Rather than shaping a new social contract within the country, the constitutional process thus contributed to a sense of division and distrust.

A second, longer-term problem was also created: the constitution set in motion a political process that was imposed by a radical minority and that was essentially designed to split the country apart. Even after the reduction in violence in 2007, Iraq remained mired in a deep political crisis, mainly because the constitution was so difficult to amend.

As the corrupt politicians play Russian roulette with each other, using rules laid down by a flawed constitution, the general population has been pulled, pushed and downtrodden into a state of sullen submission.

CHAPTER FOUR

A COUNTRY BACK FROM THE DEAD

THE WAR OF ELIMINATION

Large-scale acts of violence flared up across the country as soon as the US military occupied Baghdad. These often took the form of kidnappings, assassinations and sabotage, but worst by far were the bombings of busy markets, which often targeted poor Shia areas.

There were many culprits, including surviving elements of the former regime, newly formed militias and Sunni extremist groups, some of which developed strong links with al-Qaida. Despite all the images of bloody destruction and the calls for revenge, for a time the country's Shia clergy and other community leaders successfully counselled mourners to exercise restraint and not to engage in acts of retaliation. Nevertheless, as the explosions continued to rip through people's lives, several armed groups did start to respond. Best organized were the militias that had moved in from Iran when the 2003 war ended, including the SCIRI-affiliated Badr Corps. The Mahdi Army, which had been formed by the Sadrist movement, was a more informal and amorphous grouping, and some of its elements were totally beyond the control of anybody, including Sadr himself. As time went on, the militias on both sides of the divide stepped up their conflict, unimpeded by the US military or the Iraqi state.

At the same time, there were some notable exceptions to the downward spiral in community relations. These included the uprisings in Fallujah and Najaf in 2004 against the US military, which inspired significant empathy and collaboration between the two sides of the community.

There was a significant escalation in the conflict after the January 2005 parliamentary elections, which brought to power a number of political forces that were affiliated to violent militias. So tense was the atmosphere at the time that many parties did not even conceal the fact that they had armed wings. In particular, SCIRI/the Badr Corps and the Sadrist movement/Mahdi Army became more heavily involved in the conflict.

On the Sunni Islamist side, although the Iraqi Islamic Party denied being associated with any militia (and indeed over the years many of its members seem to have been assassinated by al-Qaida and other terrorist groups), many of its allies were widely suspected (and were often accused) of being linked in some way to extremist groups.

Each of the militias considered the political process to be a sideshow and engaged in a conflict to seize control of the capital and of the country by force. Through their connections in government, they were given access to more equipment and weaponry. They were also able to operate with the acquiescence of the Iraqi police, and sometimes even fought from among its ranks. Baghdad residents started complaining that death squads were roaming the streets. The numbers of dead in a month jumped from the hundreds in May 2003 to the thousands in August 2005, when the new constitution was being finalized.[1]

After the constitutional referendum and the December 2005 elections, the conflict entered a new phase, bloodier than anything the country had witnessed in its modern history. The exact cause of the escalation is difficult to trace. Many have said that the February 2006 bombing of the Imam Al-Askari mosque in Samara (one of Shia Islam's holiest sites) was the trigger. Others have argued that the real upsurge in violence came after the formation of Prime Minister Nouri al-Maliki's first government in May 2006. There is significant evidence to support this latter view: Iraqi and US military deaths remained essentially stable from January to May 2006, but more than doubled from June 2006 onwards.[2]

At the start of 2006, as the pace of killings continued to rise in the capital, part of the Sunni community underwent a change in mindset. It was bitterly disappointed that Nouri al-Maliki, another Shia fundamentalist, had been appointed prime minister after the elections. It also took note of the government's apparent failure to improve security to any measurable degree. In particular, following the destruction of the Imam Al-Askari mosque, Shia militiamen went on the rampage for two days, killing dozens – some say hundreds.[3] The government's failure to react and control the generalized violence was taken as further evidence of its partiality in a widening conflict.[4]

Sunni militias decided that their only possible course of action was to retake control of the country by force. This, it was determined, could only be done by seizing control of Baghdad itself.

At the same time, the country's Shia militias recognized the Iraqi government's inability to protect their co-religionists against random attacks. They, too, concluded that the only solution was physical conquest of the capital. Both sides intuitively understood that what they were calling for was tantamount to ethnic cleansing. Both realized, too, that so long as a sizeable group of civilians from the rival sect remained in the city, there might be militiamen hiding among them. Sunni and Shia militias alike came to the inevitable conclusion that, in order for them to win control of the entire city, all their opponents, whether armed or not, had to be removed. In short, they were both engaged in a war to eliminate each other's presence in Baghdad.

To this end, the guerrillas adopted sophisticated military tactics that were designed to allow them to take over entire quarters of the city at a time. Neighbourhoods were attacked as if they were fortresses: within a matter of hours, they were surrounded, cut off from the rest of the city, besieged, invaded, and eventually emptied of all their inhabitants. This was achieved using a number of methods, including establishing checkpoints at each of the neighbourhood's entry points; mounting incursions from different angles; and using a combination of weapons (including car bombs, mortar shells, rocket-propelled grenades and small arms) in order to cow the neighbourhood's inhabitants into a state of utter helplessness.

One of the first manifestations of this new phase in the fighting came on 18 April 2006, when the Sunni Adhamiyah neighbourhood in Baghdad was surrounded by armed men from the ministry of the interior, which at the time was largely assumed to be dominated by the Shia Badr Corps.[5] Their attempt to enter was repelled. On 9 July 2006, however, the predominantly Sunni Jihad district of Baghdad was surrounded early in the morning by the Mahdi Army and was emptied of all its inhabitants. At least seventy people were killed in the process, and many of the rest ended up in camps just outside their former neighbourhood.

Shortly afterwards, the mostly Shia neighbourhoods of Karrada and Zafraniyah were attacked on 27 July and 14 August, respectively. These attacks, responsibility for which was claimed by a Sunni extremist group, involved a combination of mortars, rockets and car bombs and killed more than a hundred people. Both neighbourhoods were emptied of most of their inhabitants. Militias were sometimes the only forces on the ground.[6] In parts of Baghdad – sometimes just a short distance from the infamous Green Zone – armed groups set up checkpoints in broad daylight and ruled over the local population with total impunity. People would leave home uncertain if they would make it back alive – or if their houses would still be standing if they did return. Driving through the capital's streets could be lethal, and there was virtually nothing Iraqis could do to protect themselves (other than flee, which they did in their hundreds of thousands). So rapid were developments in the violence that ordinary civilians could not even follow which side had the upper hand at any given moment.

Apart from the intensity of the violence, one of the most striking elements of this phase of the Iraq war was the relative impotence of all the forces that had previously been assumed to wield considerable authority in the country. The Iraqi government and the American military were heavily criticized by all sides for failing to have any effect on the violence. They were incapable of defeating the militias, and conceded that the best they could hope for was to keep them apart. They therefore resorted to building walls around the capital's neighbourhoods.[7] Construction of the wall to separate the Adhamiyah neighbourhood from the surrounding (predominantly Shia) areas began on 10 April 2006. There was one point of entry and exit for the entire neighbourhood. All government buildings were surrounded by blast walls that were several metres high.

So disillusioned were people with the ruling authorities that many hoped the government and parliament might be swept away in a military coup d'état.[8] Grand Ayatollah Ali al-Sistani, previously considered the most powerful person in the country, was also powerless to prevent the escalation. His calls for restraint had practically no impact.

The conflict had a devastating effect on society and the state alike. In 2003, ministries and other government departments were already mere shadows of their former selves. After decades of war, brutal dictatorship and sanctions, much of Iraq's professional class had settled in safer havens abroad. Many Iraqis hoped that the 2003 war would create a new environment that would allow ordinary Iraqis to rebuild the state. They were initially dismayed at the sight of unqualified CPA officials and former exiles running ministries. De-Baathification was a disheartening process: the sight of so many highly qualified specialists being excluded from employment purely on the basis of party affiliation was worrying, but it did not necessarily sound the death knell for the state. If the occupation could provide officials with a safe and stable environment in which to work, they could still repair the state's institutions and improve the delivery of services – much as their predecessors had done in similarly difficult circumstances.

But it was not to be. From the start of the occupation in 2003, public officials came under attack from assassins, insurgents and ordinary criminals, and no one was there to protect them. Sabotage was one of the insurgency's major objectives. The state's legitimacy depended on its delivering services to the people; so the less electricity people received, the less legitimate was the state. Thus power lines and engineers came under regular attack.

Corruption was a major cause of the violence. Because of its oil reserves, the state's annual budget was among the highest in the region, and high-ranking officials saw it as there for the taking. All they had to do was make sure that investigators, state auditors, prosecutors and judges (as well as potential competitors) did not get in their way. Intimidation and murder became a way of life, and the ensuing conflict meant there was little or no accountability.

There was general violence (intended to damage the state) and there was targeted violence (including kidnapping to extort financial payments). Dozens of the Board of Supreme Audit's staff lost their lives in the course of their duties (including its head, assassinated in 2004). The agency's headquarters on Haifa Street were often inaccessible, for that area witnessed almost daily gun battles.[9] At one point at the start of 2007, snipers were targeting its staff as they entered their offices. A corpse lay in plain view of the deputy head's window for several days, as the officials were too terrified of being shot to arrange for its burial. At times, the fighting was so violent that the board's staff had to hide behind a moving armed vehicle just to reach the entrance. Staff engaged in sensitive auditing jobs were particularly at risk.[10]

Courts, judges and lawyers were likewise targeted during that period, notably those involved in criminal cases. At least thirty-nine judges were killed between 2003 and 2008.[11] Others lost loved ones (including the chief justice, whose son was assassinated in May 2006) or were kidnapped and held for ransom. Some court houses were attacked in an effort to free detainees.

Parliamentary staff were also targets. After the violence had subsided, I sat with a parliamentary aide who had lived through that difficult period. He described his experience to me:

There were militias all over the streets, and there was a danger of running into any one of them. For us, there was no difference between the Mahdi Army [the armed militia loyal to Shiite cleric Muqtada al-Sadr] or al-Qaida. Either would have killed any one of my colleagues. We would never tell anyone where we worked, not even our friends. When I went to work, I would put my identity card in my sock in case I was searched by a militia. When security got really bad, the office would be practically empty for weeks. I couldn't even have business cards printed in Iraq because that would mean telling the card maker where I worked, which would be a risk.[12]

The repercussions were felt throughout the state. During some periods, work ground to a complete halt, as government staff were unable to reach their offices. Ministries remained empty for weeks, either because entire neighbourhoods were cordoned off from the rest of the city or because security forces and armed groups were engaged in pitched battles. In 2007, when I still worked at the United Nations, a colleague and I arranged to meet the deputy minister of planning. My colleague was in control of a fund from a European country set up to provide the ministry with technical assistance and training, and he was trying to decide where and how to invest that money. He had obtained a diagram showing all the ministry's departments and units, and had some ideas of what could be done. When he met the man, he suggested that the economics department would be a good place to launch the training programme. The deputy minister stared at the diagram for a moment before saying with some exasperation: 'Well, there aren't any economists left in that department. They've all had to leave; our most talented person has just left for Amman. The department is actually currently headed by an architect. He has a PhD though.' The discussion moved on to the IT department: 'There aren't actually any people to train in that department at the moment. All of our staff has left, and we are having trouble recruiting qualified people to replace them.' And on and on. By 2007, much of the Iraqi state had been transformed into an empty shell.

The violence has caused millions of Iraqis (estimated at around 15 per cent of the population) to flee their homes – some to other areas of Iraq, others to neighbouring countries. Up to 4.7 million Iraqis have been displaced – the largest population movement in the world.[13] Many Baghdadis fled to their villages and towns of origin. Iraq's rural areas are still largely tribal, and even Baghdadis who had never recognized the legitimacy of the tribal structure could fall back on it for protection during those difficult days. At one point, it was said that close to 2 million Iraqis had moved to Syria – a 10 per cent increase in that country's inhabitants. Those Iraqis who were not part of a tribe were more likely to flee the country altogether; in particular Christians often had nowhere to go other than across the border, and so a dispropor-tionate number of them appeared in the refugee population.

Since 2003, tens of thousands of skilled professionals have been killed or forced into exile. Academics in particular have been targeted in an organized campaign: hundreds have been assassinated or kidnapped. Not infrequently, criminals are motivated purely by financial gain. Boulos, a professor of law at Baghdad University who was from a Christian family, was kidnapped while on his way home in early 2007. Generally regarded as a gifted lecturer, he knew his subject inside out and could cite entire legal texts from memory, together with the reference. He was blindfolded and taken to a secret loca-tion. There his abductors, who identified themselves as members of the Mahdi Army (but who may just have been a group of local criminals), beat him mercilessly for over a week. Every day, several times a day, they would enter the room he was being kept in and strike him with various utensils. He was an unbeliever, they screamed at him, and unbelievers should not be leading groups of Muslims (an apparent reference to his status as a lecturer at the university). The beatings finally stopped when the group's leader learned that Boulos knew most of the Koran by heart. A few days later, they told Boulos that he would be forgiven if he could raise $10,000 and hand over his car. Upon delivery of both items, he was promptly released. Boulos was left wondering why he had been tortured and abused if all the militiamen wanted was money. When his family saw the state he was in and his injuries, they fled the country immediately. After a few years of languishing in the Middle East as refugees, they finally settled in Australia. Before travelling to Sydney, he was warned by the embassy staff that, unlike many of his compa-triots who would be travelling with him, he was likely to be disappointed. The others were mostly manual labourers and would probably have no trouble in finding equivalent work in Australia. 'Given that you don't speak English,' the embassy told him, 'you can forget working as an academic or as a lawyer.' Today, he works as a labourer in Australia and is often moved to tears when he recalls the life that he left behind in Iraq.[14]

In some cases, the levels of violence were such that all work within a specific government department would be halted. Depending on the nature of the work, though, any suspension of activity could result in massive setbacks and increased challenges for the future. An example of this is the impact that the violence had on Iraq's anti-desertification efforts. The ministry of agriculture had had a programme in place for decades, but as the violence increased, work was effectively halted, so that the desert advanced unimpeded, reversing the progress that had been made. One of the programme's managers told me that between 2005 and 2009 the ministry had paid his salary but he never went to the office: 'It was too dangerous. Al-Qaida militants were all over the area that we worked and lived in. I even removed the licence plate from my ministry-issued vehicle to avoid any attention from militias. We were trying to survive.'[15] The desert, meanwhile, thrived and overwhelmed areas that they had managed to reclaim (see Chapter 8).

The little reliable information that is available on budget execution illustrates the impact that all this had on the state. Since US public money was invested in the country, the US Government Accountability Office (GAO) took it upon itself to produce several reports on the matter.[16] In January 2008, the GAO concluded:

> central ministries had spent only 4.4 percent of their investment budget as of August 2007. The discrepancies between the official and unofficial data highlight uncertainties about the sources and use of Iraq's expenditure data.[17]

In August 2008, it wrote: 'While Iraq's total expenditures increased from 2005 through 2007, Iraq spent a declining share of its budget allocations – 73 to 65 percent from 2005 to 2007'; the investment expenditure ratios of central ministries 'declined from 14 percent in 2005 to 11 percent in 2007'.[18]

So Iraq's budget was annually increasing thanks to greater oil revenues, but the violence was preventing the state from investing most of the money that was available, even as the violence was swelling the numbers of those in need by tens of thousands.

One proposed solution to the plethora of problems was 'governments of national unity' – governments in which all (or almost all) of the political parties represented in parliament were also represented in government. The theory was that, if all parties had a stake in government, they would seek to make it function and would desist from violence.

Iraq's first 'government of national unity' was sworn in in May 2005, following the January parliamentary elections. Although it was clearly decided at the outset that all major political forces should participate, a crisis emerged over who should occupy the prime ministerial post, with both SCIRI and the Sadrist movement claiming it. In the end, a compromise was reached, and Ibrahim al-Jaafari, the Islamic Dawa Party's secretary general, was nominated.

It was widely thought that, as a relatively small party, Dawa would not pose a threat to anyone. Following the December 2005 elections, a second government of national unity was formed in May 2006. Although the same arrangement was maintained, with most of the same parties and individuals, al-Jaafari (who had gained a reputation for profound sectarianism and unprofessionalism during the year that he held office) was replaced by Nouri al-Maliki, one of his colleagues from Dawa.

The governments of national unity were formed on the basis of a strict formula: all that mattered was ethnic or religious affiliation; qualifications were meaningless. The result was a sectarian system of government that rivalled (perhaps even exceeded) the failed constitutional arrangement that was put in place in Lebanon during the first half of the twentieth century (in Lebanon, the president must be Maronite Christian, the prime minister Sunni and the speaker of parliament Shia). In Iraq, not only were all government positions allocated according to sect and race, but each senior official had to work with deputies from other ethno-sectarian groups, in order to counter whatever power he (potentially) wielded. From 2006 to 2010, the Iraqi president was from the Kurdish north and had two deputies, one Sunni and one Shia. The prime minister was Shia, with one Sunni and one Kurdish deputy. The speaker of the parliament was Sunni, with a Shia and a Kurd to back him up. The same pattern was repeated at just about every level: virtually every important minister was forced to work with two deputies who were from different political parties and different ethno-sectarian groups.

The rationale was that everyone should have a veto over any significant decisions, and should be able to prevent minorities (and even majorities) from imposing their will. Various parliamentary committees functioned according to the same principle: all parliamentary bills had to be approved by the legal committee, which was headed by three MPs, each of whom represented a specific ethno-sectarian bloc and could prevent a bill from being debated and voted on in plenary. Given the absence of trust between political blocs, it was inevitable that they would set up roadblocks at every turn to impede progress on virtually every issue.

Under the constitution, parliament is required to pass an oil and gas law and a law governing the federal Supreme Court. But since 2005 the mechanisms described above have prevented those bills even being debated, let alone passed into law. Progress has been blocked on virtually every issue, no matter how important, urgent or vital. This, combined with the government's complete lack of coherence, has meant that it is impossible to establish anything even remotely resembling a government programme. Government does not have a policy worthy of the name, and ministries almost never coordinate their actions because they are headed by political adversaries. Iraqis have therefore been treated to the spectacle of a government that seeks to undermine itself.

It gets worse: since all political forces are essentially allowed to choose their own representatives in government, their performance can never be properly evaluated. No matter how incompetent or corrupt, ministers are almost never fired, since all parties have to be represented in government. Whatever their mistakes, whatever their crimes, ministers almost all remain in post until they themselves decide it is time to bow out. Iraq's governments of national unity have turned Iraq into a frozen republic, where next to nothing gets accomplished.

During the turbulent period from 2006, most officials (including those from international organizations that focused on Iraq) recognized that the government was incoherent, but they nevertheless hoped that it could be made to function through a small number of corrective measures. These included a national reconciliation process and planning exercises that would establish a single programme that the government would be required to adhere to. Consequently, a national reconciliation effort (that had actually been in place since 2003) was reinvigorated as a means of improving government performance and as a peace-building initiative. A parliamentary committee was established for precisely this purpose. Untold amounts were spent by the international community on whisking Iraqis on study tours all over the globe, including to such places as Northern Ireland and South Africa.

Aside from the fact that the parliamentary committee and its government equivalent were grossly underfunded, one of the immediate problems that this initiative encountered was that it was engaging with the wrong people.[19] Many of the internationals who had dealings with the committee were (unsurprisingly) not particularly knowledgeable about Iraq and assumed that committee members were linked in some way to the groups involved in the armed conflict on the ground. Although that was true in some cases, generally it was not. That much should have been obvious, given that mainstream Sunni politicians were often the target of assassination attempts by al-Qaida, an extremist Sunni organization that considered many of its co-religionists to be traitors to their community.

Also, although some parties had representatives on the committee, they were never empowered to make any decisions or to engage in real compromise. Any success in terms of making committee members 'reconcile' would therefore have little or no impact on the ground, given that they had no control over the groups that were engaged in the armed conflict. Committee members were essentially already in agreement about participating in the political process. Withab Shaker al-Jubouri MP, head of the parliamentary reconciliation committee, said in an interview in April 2009 that national reconciliation conferences abroad were tantamount to tourism: 'What is the point of conferences in Helsinki, Tokyo and South Africa for Iraqis who in any event meet every day in the parliament? What we need is to reconcile with the people who are outside the political process.'[20]

Some of those who participated in the reconciliation process satisfied themselves with trying to build trust between the government's various components and improve their working relationships – but even those efforts were unlikely to succeed. Although it was certainly true that senior officials were generally not communicating with each other, their poor performance was mostly due to their lack of experience and interest. National reconciliation was never likely to solve the problem that government was populated by lazy and incompetent politicians, particularly as there was no way of holding any of those individuals accountable.

Nor would reconciliation change the fact that each party in government was bent on expanding its own power and weakening that of its many rivals (who were also its coalition partners). At the same time, they paid scant attention to (or even completely ignored) their main obligation – to improve service delivery to the people. Meanwhile, continued fighting and terrorism on the streets made genuine reconciliation impossible in any event. Each major bombing would be followed by inflammatory speeches from one side or the other that would undermine whatever trust existed between political groups and communities and cause parliamentary sessions and government meetings to be postponed. Those officials who were genuinely working to improve the government's performance were caught up in a dynamic that they could not control.

A number of incidents took place in 2006 and 2007 that illustrated how pointless 'reconciliation' efforts were. The main protagonists in the political process had either succumbed to the sectarian climate or were deliberately propagating it; either way, they had become part of the problem. They consciously ignored violence perpetrated by their own community, yet simultaneously accused others of engaging in near-genocidal acts. Whenever complaints were made about the government's failures, politicians would casually dismiss all critics as terrorists, and level very public accusations against each other without ever presenting a shred of evidence in support of the allegations.

Adnan al-Dulaimi, an MP for the Tawafuq alliance, the largest Sunni parliamentary bloc (which was also affiliated with the Muslim Brotherhood), was one of the worst offenders. Tawafuq and its various components were among the first to join the political process in 2003. They had a representative in the Governing Council and participated in the drafting of the constitution in 2005. They never shied away from being openly sectarian, albeit with what was supposed to be a positive outlook (assuming such a thing was possible): they claimed to represent 'their community's interests' by negotiating in good faith with representatives of Iraq's other ethno-sectarian groups. Not only did the national interest rarely feature in their discourse, but their only real concern was the number of portfolios that Tawafuq would be allocated in government.

Between 2003 and 2005 bombs regularly targeted markets that were frequented by poor Shia civilians, but the prominent Tawafuq members (including al-Dulaimi) rarely voiced any condemnation. Even when al-Qaida became more prominent and its leaders spouted the vilest sectarian hatred ever seen in Iraq, Tawafuq and al-Dulaimi refused to issue the kind of denunciation heard from their rivals in other political groups. Many Sunni leaders, including Tawafuq, privately expressed concern that they would be targeted for assassination if they condemned the attacks too forcefully (and indeed many were killed, along with their family members). Their calculation was fatally flawed, however: by seeking to shield themselves from a handful of extremists (who anyway would never accord them any respect), they alienated themselves from the majority of their countrymen – not just in the Shia community, but even in their own constituency.

In 2005 and 2006, though, violence against Sunnis increased. On 13 December 2006, al-Dulaimi delivered a notorious speech at a conference in Istanbul in which he ranted that Iranian-sponsored Shia militias were engaged in a genocidal campaign against Sunnis. He focused exclusively on the violence that was being directed at his own brethren (as he defined them), never once mentioning the grievances of what he perceived as his enemy:

> By God if you are not careful and if you do not wake up, Iraq will be gone and Baghdad will be gone. It is a sectarian war! It is a sectarian struggle that aims to eradicate the Sunnis . . . Your [Sunni] brothers in Iraq and especially in Baghdad will be destroyed. They will be trampled under the feet of the Shia. They will be exterminated.[21]

Despite his extreme views, al-Dulaimi featured regularly on the Iraqi airwaves and in the international media throughout 2006 and 2007, and he took the opportunity to reiterate his sectarian bias on several occasions. The victims of sectarian violence thus saw and heard an elected official dismissing their suffering and talking as if they were an alien and hostile race, against which he and his ilk needed to be protected.

Tawafuq was not the only offender, of course. Nor was sectarianism always expressed quite so bluntly. On 25 January 2007, a few months after being appointed prime minister, Nouri al-Maliki appeared before parliament to provide information on a new security plan for Baghdad. He pledged that there would be no 'safe haven' for militias, and that they would be pursued, regardless of sectarian beliefs, in the interests of protecting human rights. More importantly, the prime minister's prepared remarks (which were clearly coordinated with US officials in Baghdad) sought to contribute to the reconciliation effort within the country. Recognizing that numerous groups, including Sunnis, were being marginalized in Iraq's post-war political settlement, he begged parliament to do all that was required to provide all Iraqis with equality of opportunity:

> I implore you to authorize the government to start recruiting new staff and to ensure all the components of the Iraqi people will be represented in government, including in all departments, embassies, agencies and all other institutions that will be formed.
>
> I hope once more that you will give the issue of marginalization the utmost attention. The Iraqi people expect us to make progress in these areas and expect the government to be faithful to the promises and commitments that were made in its political programme. This should be done either by creating a positive political climate that will discourage

double standards or by eliminating the monopolization of political power and marginalization. However, this cannot be carried out in isolation of all other areas; it requires the establishment of institutions, and monitoring by the people or by their representatives or by the government itself, and this should accompany the formation process so it comes within a context that confirms political integration because in reality we do not want to give, through our statements, a wrong message to the people or to the world, which is observing the political process, that we have a double standard, we are in the government and we are against it.[22]

Although al-Maliki did not mention any specific groups, from the context it was clear that he was speaking about perceived discrimination against Sunnis in the new political order, and that he was offering to establish a mechanism that would redress certain aspects of that inequality. His statement was the clearest and the most high-profile recognition of the inequity of Iraq's new political framework so far. It was a courageous statement, given the conflict that was raging in the streets and the tension that existed within the chamber itself. Many of al-Maliki's allies would not have been happy at the olive branch that was being extended to the other side, and many of his opponents doubted his good faith. But his initiative had the potential to be a positive step in the political process, and would probably have had some impact – if the sentiments that were expressed were genuine.

But all the good that might have been done was undone just a few minutes later, when the prime minister was interrupted by Sheikh Abdul Nasser al-Janabi MP . . .[23]

It should be remembered that in January 2007, the civil conflict was at its height, with tens of thousands of deaths and countless reports of torture and abuse by Sunni and Shia militias, as well as by the security forces that the prime minister was responsible for. Some Sunnis even complained that the security forces were complicit in the killings taking place in their neighbourhoods, and there was a good deal of anger at central government. In his remarks to the prime minister in parliament that day, al-Janabi raised some of the issues that were most important to his constituents, including the alleged abuse by security forces:

MP Abdul Nasser al-Janabi: I would like to ask the prime minister: why are our cities under siege? The siege that has been imposed on Haifa Street should be lifted. A siege should not be imposed on Haifa Street or on Sadr City or on any other city. Why are civilians being trapped and killed everywhere? The prime minister should be held responsible for the death of any civilian. You should be killing terrorists and not besieging civilians.

- *The release of detainees in the prisons controlled by the Ministries of the Interior and Defence.* We talk about the past prisoners while the worst types of violations of human rights are taking place in the government's prisons . . .
- Information received by the security agencies should be scrutinized by two different sides because some agencies are infiltrated which results in a continuous conflict. Arresting women should be forbidden in all cases. [applause] The security and defence committee should have access to the security plan otherwise the Council of Representatives will not be able to exercise its oversight role.
- The firing of officers and civil servants under the pretext of de-Ba'athification should stop. What kind of national reconciliation are you talking about when you are implementing rules that marginalize Sunnis? The emergency law ended on 3/1/2007. The policy of sentencing innocent people to death should stop because such sentences are politically motivated . . . We cannot trust the prime ministry!

Nouri al-Maliki: The Sheikh will learn to trust the prime ministry after I reveal documents that incriminate him and after I hold him accountable for what he has done. [applause] 150 people have been kidnapped in the Buhayrat area and he hasn't mentioned them! He is responsible for those kidnappings!

Speaker Mahmoud Al-Mashhadani: It is unacceptable for the Prime Minister to make such accusations against a member of the Council of Representatives within the parliament itself! How will the Baghdad security plan work if you are divided in this way? It is equally unacceptable for members to applaud an accusation that is made against a member of the Council of Representatives, when that member has immunity . . . You are dividing the Iraqi people. What will people watching this say? We are fed up of sectarianism.[24]

The session was broadcast live on national television, however coverage was suspended. An edited version was broadcast later that day.[25]

Al-Janabi's comments were designed to undermine the prime minister, no matter what was on offer or whatever the opportunities for reconciliation. At the same time, the prime minister's response to al-Janabi was highly damaging to the national consciousness; with just a few words, he reminded people watching at home of the chauvinism and bigotry that dominated Iraqi politics. All criticism directed against him was met with threats and accusations of terrorism. It was the polar opposite of the inclusiveness that he had been advocating just a few minutes earlier.[26]

A FIELD OF OPPORTUNITY

After around two years of almost total lawlessness, security started to improve at the end of 2007, and by late 2008 the number of security incidents had declined markedly. It was then that government officials realized that they could go back to the office and resume their activities, albeit behind high blast walls and other forms of protection that cut them off from the people they served. Targeted attacks on public servants and state institutions waned, although not to the extent that those individuals could feel completely safe. There were dangerous gaps in the system (including the outrageous handheld bomb detectors mentioned in the introduction), which allowed thousands of civilians and security personnel to be killed every year in terrorist-related crime. The country was still highly dangerous for many officials, especially those seeking to control the flow of state money and to prosecute criminal activity. Public auditors and judges learned to cope: despite a clear legal obligation to do so, the auditors did not publish their reports; meanwhile many judges lived behind blast walls on the premises of the Higher Judicial Council and rarely ventured out to see their families.[27]

There has been some dispute over the reasons for the improvement. The 'surge' of American forces that was ordered in January 2007 and that started arriving in Baghdad later that month is often cited as a primary reason. Others have argued that the war had simply run its course, and that previously mixed areas had been cleansed of one group or the other.

A study of satellite images taken since 2003 showed a marked decrease in the night-time light in Baghdad after the surge commenced. The study's conclusion was that large parts of the city had become depopulated.[28]

Although the debate on this issue will likely continue for some time, if there is one single factor that has contributed to the restoration of (a degree of) normality in Iraq, it is the reconstruction of the Iraqi army. By 2009, it was the only presence on the streets in Baghdad, Najaf, Tikrit, Basra and many other cities. Some irregular armed groups did continue to operate, but they could no longer do so openly.

By 2009, Iraqi institutions, including parliament and the courts, no longer relied on direct US military protection.[29] Responsibility for day-to-day security had been transferred to the Iraqi state, and it was now under the control of an institution that understood the people it was protecting, spoke their language, and had a legitimate interest in keeping the streets safe. In December 2009, I had dinner with two friends in Abu Nawas, Baghdad's most famous nightspot by the side of the Tigris River. At 1 a.m., we drove to the Amariya district, which just a few months previously had been declared capital of the Islamic Emirate of Iraq by al-Qaida, and had been one of the capital's most dangerous areas. The entire outing would have been borderline suicidal in 2006 or 2007, but by 2009 it seemed almost normal. A robbery had just taken place and a group of soldiers that was searching for the culprits spotted our vehicle and hailed us. 'Do you live here?' asked one of the soldiers. The driver responded that he did. More questions followed: 'On what street? How long have you lived here? What is your father's name? Who do you know on your street?' After a few minutes, the soldiers politely waved us through, persuaded that the driver did genuinely live in the neighbourhood and was not criminally inclined. It was the type of conversation that a US soldier could never hope to have in Iraq.

During the civil conflict, driving north from Baghdad to Tikrit could be fatal. What should have been a two-hour drive could often take half a day or longer, as American forces engaged in battles along the way. By 2009, over sixty Iraqi army checkpoints dotted the highway. Drivers had to slow down as they approached, but were waved through nine times out of ten by the soldiers. When a vehicle was stopped, the soldiers would inspect it and the passengers' identity cards within less than a minute.

Most travellers from Baghdad to Najaf would pass through Latifiyah on one of the most dangerous stretches of road in the world. During the conflict, the landscape was frightening, with burnt-out cars and corpses lining the highway. Drivers would recite Koranic prayers as they entered the area, pleading with God to allow them to make it through safely. By 2009, it was entirely peaceful, manned only by the Iraqi army, which allowed Iraqis to make their way to the south without difficulty.

Regional accents are easily identifiable throughout the country, and it was obvious to any Iraqi in 2009 – including those driving to Tikrit – that many of the soldiers manning the checkpoints along the highway were from the (mainly Shia) south of the country. Interaction with travellers was consistently smooth and friendly. Similarly, the highway south from Baghdad to Najaf was lined with over seventy checkpoints, also manned by soldiers from the whole country, and also fair in their treatment of travellers.

The overall improvement in security led to a remarkable transformation in the country. The 2003 invasion had brought ethno-sectarian politics to the fore. By 2008, convinced that sectarian parties had contributed to the country's ruin, most Iraqis were demanding a change in political discourse. The Sunni Iraqi Islamic Party and the Shia Islamic Supreme Council of Iraq (sectarian parties that were at opposite ends of the spectrum) were both being abandoned by their former supporters, who were seeking more moderate middle ground. Iraqis in the capital and in the provinces launched a number of personal initiatives to rebuild community relations.

Gatherings and meetings between various tribes, many of which were of different confessions, took place in accordance with custom: there was a welcome, poems were recited in honour of the visiting guests, flattery was indulged in (as was required by tradition), all held hands and danced together and then retreated to a joint reception. Reconciliation was also encouraged (and engaged in) at a more institutional level. In 2010, the chairman of the Journalists' Union, based in Baghdad, decided to visit each of the country's provinces for meetings with the local chapters. Being Shiite, he was nervous about travelling to the western, Sunni-majority provinces. And so half the local chapter of the western Salah al-Din province travelled to Baghdad to escort him back to Tikrit. When he arrived there, he discovered a banner of welcome outside the conference hall; some of his local colleagues had even brought a cake with them. Many members took to the podium to express both their relief at seeing the chairman in such good health and their sadness that they had not seen him for so long. When I asked why they had gone to so much trouble, they responded simply: 'To make him feel at home.'[30]

During a visit to Najaf in 2010, when Shia tribal leaders learned that I have relatives in Sunni-majority Salah al-Din, one of them stood proudly and placed his hand on top of his head. 'I will carry you on like a crown on my head', he said smiling broadly. 'The people of Tikrit have always respected us and treated us with dignity.' He later told me that he had been stationed in the province for years when he served in the military and had nothing but good memories.

On a pleasantly mild evening a few weeks later, I joined a group of tribal sheikhs in the countryside near Samara for dinner. It was a purely informal gathering and everyone was comfortably speaking their mind. When I asked what their opinion was of Baghdad's political order and of the fact that it was dominated by individuals from a different ethno-sectarian grouping, an elderly sheikh responded: 'It does not matter to me. All I want is for there to be enough food on the table for my family.'[31]

Again in 2010, my wife and I met farmers who had left their lands in Dyala, Tamim and Ninewa provinces because of drought and had resettled in Salah al-Din province. They were all Sunni, but had nothing but sympathy for their Shia countrymen and fellow farmers south of Baghdad. 'Our situation is bad, but theirs is much worse. God help them', a distraught farmer from Tamim province told me. Government officials in Tikrit, the capital of Salah al-Din complained to me of the state of service delivery in their province. I asked if they thought they were being treated unfairly by central government, which is largely dominated by Shia parties. 'The problem isn't discrimination in the system. We have been given our fair share of the annual state budget. The problem is due to our own failure to perform and corruption in our province', they replied.[32]

Public expressions of support for a united Iraqi nation were also far more common after 2008. A number of statements by the prime minister and senior officials bolstered this sense, but even at an individual level Iraqis were once again expressing pride in their country and a willingness to make sacrifices for it – even as regional and international media outlets continued to promote the idea that Iraqis were hopelessly divided. In October 2011, I was in Tikrit when Salah al-Din's provincial council announced the formation of a federal region. Whatever the media outlets claimed about the country falling apart, my discussions in Tikrit at that time revealed a different reality. Some of the people I spoke to were keen to know whether the announcement was legally effective (it was not); but mostly they were determined to convey to me that they opposed the initiative. A young lecturer in law at Tikrit University said candidly: 'I will never accept the formation of a region here because that would mean the end of Iraq. I would never accept that, no matter the consequences.'[33]

One outcome of the new national spirit was that the people forced political discourse away from politics and towards services and corruption. The state had come close to collapse after 2003, a result of sabotage, corruption, mass dismissals, assassinations, violence and intimidation. The demand for change was great and so were the challenges: the official unemployment rate stood at close to 20 per cent; Iraq was close to the bottom of all international comparison tables on corruption; the environment had deteriorated alarmingly since 2003, leading to (among other things) large-scale respiratory problems; the electricity supply was not improving. Finally, even at a very basic level, individual rights were not being respected. Young men and women were being detained without charge, were denied access to legal counsel and to a fair trial, and were often abused and even tortured in prison – sometimes to extract confessions, but other times for no apparent reason. There was much to be done, and the public lent its support to political alliances that claimed to champion a strong, united Iraq, in which the rights of the individual would be respected. Thanks to oil revenues, there would be sufficient funds to finance the recovery. Two rounds of elections were due to take place, and these presented a unique opportunity to redefine government in favour of the people.

In the run-up to the January 2009 elections there was an important realignment. The United Iraqi Alliance, which was established in 2004, had brought together virtually all Shia Islamist parties under one political umbrella and had been the main vehicle by which Shia Islamist parties had governed the country. But towards the end of 2008 the alliance fell apart as the prime minister's Islamic Dawa Party refused to remain a junior partner: regarding himself as one of the country's pre-eminent players, the prime minister planned to see that reflected in the provinces and in parliament. He therefore formed his own political group, the State of Law alliance, which brought his party together with a loose federation of prominent Shia Islamists, known as the Independents. The decision could be interpreted cynically: the prime minister's former allies refused to appoint him head of their alliance, and so he bolted and used the benefit of incumbency to win votes. No doubt personal ambition did play a role, but that is a mainstay of electoral campaigns the world over.

Al-Maliki managed to emerge from his first term in office relatively unscathed by all the scandals, recriminations and serious allegations of corruption and mismanagement that were levelled at his electoral rivals. For the first two years of his term, he was essentially a nonentity. He had very little political clout to speak of, compared to the powerhouses that inhabited government, including the Sadrist movement, SCIRI and the Kurdish alliance. His presence was so underwhelming at first that many analysts barely noticed him.[34] Al-Maliki only registered on people's radar after he launched the Charge of the Knights campaign against the Mahdi Army in Basra in March 2008 and when he took credit for the resulting reduction in violence.[35]

Al-Maliki launched his electoral campaign a few months later, and used his history in government, as well as his few achievements, to construct a powerful picture in the popular imagination. First, he benefited from the fact that he had had such a low profile for two years of his term in office: he often managed to avoid any of the blame for the escalating conflict and the declining services, which allowed him to portray corruption as everyone's fault but his. Secondly, the fact that he had moved against both Sunni and Shia militias meant that he could genuinely claim non-sectarian credentials. Therefore, when State of Law campaigned in favour of national unity, it could attempt to win votes on that basis. He argued that, although he and many of his electoral allies were Shia, they had proved that they were not sectarian in their approach and that they were willing to defend their country against narrow community interests, even if that community was their own. His campaign strategy clearly had some success: in my conversations around that time, Iraqis from all backgrounds (including traditional Sunni circles) were eager to praise al-Maliki, and even expressed a desire to support his political alliance in the elections.

Al-Maliki had charted a course for the unknown, since he could not predict with any degree of certainty what his actual level of popularity was. He was also taking a major risk, given that he was flouting Iran's call for intra-Shia unity. Iran was concerned that divisions within the Shia community could potentially lead to the formation of cross-sectarian political alliances that might leave some of its closest allies out of government; it therefore pushed for al-Maliki to rejoin the ranks of the United Iraqi Alliance. His refusal to do so likewise worked in favour of his nationalist credentials and increased his cross-sectarian appeal.

Al-Maliki's gamble paid off and earned the State of Law alliance 19.1 per cent of the vote in the 2009 provincial elections. The losers included the Fadhila (Virtue) party and SCIRI. They had previously controlled provincial governments across the Shia south, but were practically wiped out.

In the March 2010 parliamentary elections, State of Law obtained 24.2 per cent of the vote and won eighty-nine seats in the new parliament. This time, however, it was joined by the Iraqiya alliance, a secular list that had been formed under the leadership of Ayad Allawi and which drew most of its support from Sunni Arabs around the country. Iraqiya campaigned on a nationalist platform (i.e. in favour of a united Iraqi nation) that was officially anti-sectarian and anti-clerical and that claimed to prioritize the fight against corruption. It gained 24.7 per cent of the popular vote, which translated into ninety-one seats in the new parliament. Its success came at the expense of the (Sunni Islamist) Iraqi Islamic Party, which lost 90 per cent of its support base between 2005 and 2010. Together, the two alliances obtained 180 out of the 325 seats, a clear majority, and represented very large sections of two of the country's main communities. Their ideological similarities were tantalizing, and the prospect of a coalition government excited many Iraqis. The people had done their part. All that was left to secure a national revival was for the politicians to do theirs.

CHAPTER FIVE

DEFECTIVE POLITICS

Despite the clear message that voters delivered to politicians in 2009 and 2010, talks between the country's major political alliances failed before they even began. Politicians the world over are perfectly content to undermine each other; but the tactics that were used in Iraq in 2010 were without parallel.

Notwithstanding the controversy surrounding de-Baathification and the manner in which it was set in motion by the CPA in 2003 (see Chapter 2), Ahmed al-Chalabi and his colleagues remained in charge of the process for years, and often sparked anger with their decisions. In mid-January 2010, two months before the crucial parliamentary election, the de-Baathification commission intervened by banning 511 candidates for alleged (but undisclosed) links to the Baath party. The decision was enormously problematic, since al-Chalabi and many of his colleagues on the commission were themselves candidates in the elections. There was thus a clear conflict of interest, as they were in effect eliminating the competition. Worse still, however, was the fact that the allegations on which their decision had been taken appeared to be suspect.

Many of the 511 banned individuals were candidates on secular lists, and most (if not all) of the better-known political figures targeted were Sunni Arabs. Of the banned candidates, 334 were simply replaced by the political parties; of the remaining 177, only 37 managed to lodge an appeal – and most of those were subsequently rejected by the courts.

The upshot was that some of the country's most prominent politicians were banned from participating at extremely short notice, on the basis of flimsy evidence. Salih al-Mutlaq, leader of the National Dialogue Front, which was a leading member of the Iraqiya alliance, was the most prominent. He was a member of the constitutional drafting committee in 2005 and had been elected to parliament in December 2005, so he had already been vetted twice by the Accountability and Justice Commission. No explanation was given as to why he had been banned on this occasion, but had been allowed to participate in the political process in the past. It was also curious that the many ex-Baathists who surrounded the prime minister (including many of his military staff) were allowed to continue in their duties without any scrutiny.

Although it is tempting to assume that al-Chalabi and his colleagues abused the de-Baathification process to eliminate their electoral rivals, in fact the individuals targeted were not their rivals. The Iraqiya alliance enjoyed significant support among the country's secular middle class and the Sunni community, whereas the AJC was under the control of individuals who were candidates for the National Alliance, which relied on support from Shia Islamists, a completely different constituency. A less obvious and more sinister objective was therefore likely: al-Chalabi and his colleagues were seeking to improve their electoral prospects by reigniting sectarian tension.

If that indeed was the strategy, then it worked: the remaining two months of the campaign featured heated discussion of the Baath party and of its supposed master plan of returning to power in the guise of secular parties. What had been a people-driven debate on corruption and sectarianism was now struggling to compete for attention on the airwaves, all of which were controlled by the parties anyway. The State of Law alliance's campaign, which sought to portray the prime minister as a national candidate who had wrested the country from the brink of disaster, was severely undermined.

Al-Maliki was faced with two choices: either to denounce the de-Baathification process altogether and risk alienating a large section of his Shia base (which could interpret his position as a sign of weakness) or to support it and lose whatever votes he might have picked up from Sunnis in Iraq. In the end, he opted for the less risky of the two strategies and intervened in favour of the de-Baathification process: he endorsed it and put pressure on the courts to complete their review prior to the elections. The moderate middle was therefore successfully undermined by some of the worst elements among the former exiles.

Until this episode, al-Maliki's State of Law alliance had been expecting to win around 120 seats in the March 2010 elections.[1] The tally of eighty-nine seats therefore came as a shock; it was a double blow to learn that it had been beaten into second place by the secular Iraqiya alliance. On 21 March 2010, days before the official results were confirmed, Prime Minister al-Maliki arranged a press conference. Standing on a podium, surrounded by many of his closest allies, he issued a thinly veiled threat:

> Because the elections held on 7 March represented an important step towards promoting Iraq's democratic experience, and because of demands from several political blocs for a manual recount of ballots and to safe-guard the democratic experience and maintain the credibility of the electoral process, I demand, in my capacity as the direct executive authority responsible for the formulation and implementation of state policy and *in my capacity as commander in chief of the armed forces*, that the Independent High Electoral Commission respond immediately to the demands of these blocs to safeguard political stability and prevent security from deteriorating and violence from increasing.[2]

Al-Maliki's suspicions were based on a supposed international conspiracy against his alliance in favour of Iraqiya. There was no doubt that Iraqiya did enjoy significant support from some of Iraq's neighbours. In particular, it was an open secret that Turkey and Qatar had encouraged Iraqiya's various components to group together under Allawi's leadership, and that they had even mediated in some of the negotiation sessions leading up to its establishment. Those two countries were ostensibly motivated by a desire to counter Iran's influence in Iraq, which that country had used to pressure all Shia Islamist parties to unite in a single electoral alliance after 2005. It was also true that the Independent High Electoral Commission for Iraq was the recipient of a significant amount of assistance from the United Nations. But those two facts alone did not constitute a conspiracy. In any event, al-Maliki's reference to the military was highly inappropriate and extremely concerning. The 2005 constitution does state that the prime minister is the commander in chief of the armed forces; but it also unequivocally states that the army 'shall not interfere in political affairs, and shall have no role in the transfer of authority' (article 9). If there were doubts about the election result, there were various legal avenues that could be explored; but neither the constitution nor the law allowed for the army to play a role. In any event, the die was cast and the prime minister was making it clear that he was not willing to transfer authority to Iraqiya, even if that meant relying on the military.

In the end, a recount was organized; despite some anomalies, the preliminary results were confirmed. An overjoyed Iraqiya alliance, stunned by how well it had performed, immediately claimed the right to form a government under its leader, Ayad Allawi. Its position was based on a constitutional provision, by which the nominee of the 'largest bloc' should be tasked by the president of the republic with forming a government. The State of Law alliance objected that this could be interpreted as meaning the largest parliamentary bloc, which would open the door to post-election negotiations to form new alliances. An appeal was lodged with the federal Supreme Court, which eventually found in the prime minister's favour; but the entire exercise was actually a waste of time, given that Allawi never had enough parliamentary support to form a government himself.

He and his Iraqiya alliance did have a different course of action open to them, though: they could immediately have conceded the prime ministerial post to State of Law, in exchange for a commitment to a reformist and conciliatory government programme that would allow the country to get back on its feet. That would have been in keeping with what voters were demanding, and would have allowed for genuine reconciliation and the possibility of establishing a real government programme. Some mid-ranking members of Iraqiya claimed after the event that they had suggested such a course of action to Allawi and the rest of leadership, but there is no evidence that any such plan was seriously considered at the time.[3]

For months, the parties proved unable to form a government. Altogether, the negotiations – surely the most lethargic and directionless in recorded history – lasted for eight months, during which time the parties hardly ever met. Eventually, some momentum did develop and all interested parties assembled in the Kurdistan region in November to hammer out an agreement that allowed the formation of yet another government of national unity on an ethno-sectarian basis.

This agreement (which was kept secret for years) was variously termed the 'Barzani initiative' (on the basis that it was Masoud Barzani, the Kurdistan regional president, who supposedly broke the deadlock) or the 'Erbil agreement'. Either way, it was brokered by US Ambassador James F. Jeffrey.[4] Just about every parliamentary bloc was allocated a specific number of ministries according to a strict formula that was theoretically designed to prevent any single group dominating the political scene. The only exceptions to this were the Gorran Movement (a breakaway from the Patriotic Union of Kurdistan) which had won eight seats and was essentially barred from the talks by the two main Kurdish groups, and the Islamic Supreme Council of Iraq (which had sixteen seats but refused on principle to join yet another government led by al-Maliki). All the other parties that had parliamentary representation (i.e. more than a dozen) were represented.

Although some of the main elements of the Erbil Agreement were made known to the general public, the text of the agreement was not published and the details were kept secret (for reasons that were not immediately obvious). On 11 November 2010, parliament finally reconvened. After the usual self-congratulatory remarks, it elected the Iraqiya alliance's Usama al-Nujaifi speaker.

At this point the illusion of consensus was shattered: Iraqiya's members then demanded that the de-Baathification commission's decisions be officially overturned, claiming that this was what the Erbil Agreement stipulated; meanwhile the rest of the chamber pushed for the president of the republic to be elected first. A large majority of Iraqiya's MPs walked out of the session; al-Nujaifi was visibly perplexed as he sat before the remaining members. He eventually mumbled 'there is no confidence' and walked out as well.

However, the session continued and brought into existence al-Maliki's second government. Two days later, Allawi declared that 'the concept of power sharing is dead now' and said the bulk of Iraqiya would not form part of the government.[5] Yet Iraqiya did not withdraw from government – not even when it realized that the government posts it received (when finally they were allocated) were not in proportion to the size of its parliamentary bloc.

So far as ordinary Iraqis were concerned, the whole issue was of no importance whatsoever. A few more ministers from one group and a couple less from another would not have made any difference, given that the entire crop was rotten.

In the months that followed, the various groups complained about the government's performance and argued that the decisions being taken were in violation of the (still unpublished) Erbil Agreement. Every now and then, a politician would threaten to publish the agreement's full text. In time, these threats became increasingly mysterious and intriguing: what was in the agreement that was so embarrassing to the political class?

Eventually, eighteen months or so later, copies were leaked to the press and circulated online.[6] It made for painful reading and there was no doubt why politicians on all sides had been reluctant to release it: although the parties had supposedly been negotiating for eight months, all it consisted of was an agreement on which individuals should get which positions, and who would be granted amnesty from the de-Baathification process. The vital reforms that Iraq so desperately needed received barely a mention; the text merely listed the types of legal reforms that the parties had supposedly agreed to – all of them required by the constitution in any event. Finally, there was no detail on timetables (at best, specific items were listed as having to be made 'within a few days'), which just went to show how hurriedly the document had been drafted. It all served to illustrate how focused the political class – especially Iraqiya – was on retaining senior positions for itself, and how little it cared about anything else. Perhaps the worst failure of all was the lack of any enforceable arrangement on who should occupy the positions of minister of defence and minister of the interior: the appointments were to be postponed until a later date. This is what allowed al-Maliki to procrastinate for several years, during which time he effectively seized control of both ministries.

AL-MALIKI'S LONG VIEW

For al-Maliki, the entire episode was a life-changing experience. His electoral campaign had been based on the assumption that Iraqis would be attracted by a strong national leader who eschewed sectarianism. He had been counting on the people to give him a solid mandate, but instead he trailed in behind Iraqiya, which was led by a convincing prime ministerial candidate and therefore came within a whisker of taking over. Al-Maliki learned that he could not rely on his own popularity to retain his position and to govern. Instead he decided on a new strategy that would define Iraqi politics for the coming few years.

Rather than build on the electoral message that the people had sent in March 2010, his sole concern became to capture the state and to divide and conquer opponents, in order to remain in power for as long as possible. He set his sights on the key institutions, starting with the parliament, the armed forces and the courts.

Although, under the constitution, parliament had wide powers of discretion and could block any part of his agenda, this was not something that al-Maliki had to bother about during the first few years of his tenure. When his first government of national unity was formed in 2006, it represented 240 out of 275 MPs. Naturally, this large coalition controlled virtually all key positions in the state, including the speaker of parliament, who ensured that

not a single government official was summoned to be questioned by the legislature, despite huge inefficiency and skyrocketing corruption. There were no
rules in place to ensure that the little parliamentary opposition that did exist
could exercise oversight, which meant that government was never held to
account for its many failures. That arrangement frayed momentarily in 2009,
when certain political forces that had previously assumed al-Maliki to be a
weak individual who could never represent any threat panicked following his
encroachments on state institutions and after his success in the provincial
elections. Parliament sought to withdraw confidence and start criminal
proceedings against the ministers who were closest to al-Maliki; but its
success was limited to a single minister, who eventually fled to London
unscathed. Following the March 2010 parliamentary elections, al-Maliki's
second government of national unity represented 301 out of 325 MPs – a
majority that restored parliament's state of passivity.

At the same time as parliament was being subdued, al-Maliki moved to
gain exclusive control of the armed forces. The springboard was the particularly vague constitutional provision by which the prime minister was the
'commander in chief of the armed forces'. There was no indication what that
meant or what level of control the prime minister should personally have
over the military. The lack of detail was particularly alarming, given that the
president of the republic enjoyed only ceremonial powers and had no
authority whatsoever to play any role in the administration of the armed
forces.

The drafters' assumption was presumably that, because the constitution
gave wide discretion to parliament to appoint and dismiss governments,
prime ministers and individual ministers, individual politicians would be
prevented from seizing too much power. The problem, however, was that
Iraq's constitution was drafted and initially applied during a state of complete
lawlessness. In 2005–07, the priority was to re-establish some semblance of
security; good governance, accountability and transparency were not high on
the agenda when the new military's command structure was established.

Al-Maliki exploited the unclear constitutional arrangement by seizing
control of the military. He established the 'office of the commander in chief',
which served as a type of command centre; he obtained the mobile telephone
numbers of commanders all over the country and took to calling them direct in
order to issue instructions, circumventing the chain of command; he established
military units that were personally answerable to him; and finally, he appointed
and dismissed officers at will, changing the make-up of the officer corps.

Between 2006 and 2010 Al-Maliki had to contend with ministers of the interior and of defence who had been selected through consensus between various political forces, and who had been vetted by the US embassy. These two ministers used to disagree sharply with al-Maliki on many issues, leading to a number of tense standoffs. But during the government formation process that followed the March 2010 parliamentary elections, al-Maliki outmanoeuvred all his opponents by persuading them to join a new national unity government without any agreement on who would occupy those two key posts. After 'temporarily' heading both ministries for eight months, al-Maliki nominated Saadoun al-Dulaimi as acting minister of defence in August 2011. By not referring al-Dulaimi's appointment for parliamentary approval, al-Maliki was clearly circumventing the constitution, as well as the logic of the separation of powers, to ensure that he would retain the power to replace the acting minister if he so wished – and could therefore exert significant influence over policy. Al-Maliki thus continued to exercise personal control over the ministry of the interior; he had his personal brigades; and he had control of the ministry of defence through a pliant minister.

Since that time, the al-Maliki government has used the security forces to intimidate anyone opposed to his rule – by oppressing protesters, by carrying out repeated waves of arrests against alleged former Baathists in governorates with a heavy Sunni population where Iraqiya had polled strongest (Salah al-Din, Anbar, Ninewa and Dyala), and by threatening specific high-ranking political rivals.[7] In August 2013, the Baghdad offices of a relatively small Sunni Arab coalition that had previously been allied with al-Maliki were raided by the security forces after it had refused to support some of his candidates for provincial governors.[8]

The judiciary was far easier to capture, but potentially just as important. The 2005 constitution gave the Supreme Court the power to interpret the constitution, which was potentially a powerful political weapon. What better way for a prime minister to impose his will than by arguing that he was merely applying the laws, as determined by the country's most important court? Medhat al-Mahmoud, a prominent judge who commanded significant respect in the Arab world, was appointed chief justice of the federal Supreme Court in 2003 and to date remains in control of the court and of the court system's administration. All that al-Maliki had to do to control the court's considerable authority was to lean on al-Mahmoud and the few people who surrounded him.

For the first few years following the 2003 war, al-Mahmoud was credited with having successfully insulated the judiciary against sectarianism and other forms of discrimination, at a time when most of the country was engulfed in civil strife. For a time he also managed to distance the Supreme Court from all political forces. However, as the security forces became progressively more concentrated in the hands of the prime minister, there was increasing pressure to bow to the government's political will. In 2010, most judges had come of age under Baath rule, and so were accustomed to accommodating political power. They had also suffered terribly during the civil conflict (see Chapter 4). The threat of violence was impossible to ignore.

Since 2010, a series of cases has come before the Supreme Court (usually initiated by the government) to determine how specific constitutional provisions should be interpreted and applied; the court has almost always come down in favour of the government's interpretation. After the decision by the de-Baathification commission to ban 511 electoral candidates, an appeals court ruled that the matter should only be finally resolved after the elections and that the banned candidates should be allowed to contest the elections in the meantime. Al-Mahmoud immediately met al-Maliki and some of his allies and reversed the appeal court ruling, insisting that all de-Baathification cases had to be resolved within a matter of days (see above). Al-Mahmoud came under sustained criticism for allowing such a clear violation of the principle of separation of powers.[9] It was not the court's rationale that was at issue, but the fact that it had reversed a decision reached only days earlier and that it did so after a high-profile political meeting involving the prime minister.[10] There were further disconcerting rulings: in August 2011, when it was decided that one of al-Maliki's most strident opponents in parliament should be removed from his seat;[11] and in May 2012, when parliament was prevented from questioning the minister of higher education (one of al-Maliki's closest allies), despite a clear constitutional mandate to do so.[12]

With the courts firmly under its thumb, the government's inner circle could use legal authority to move against other state institutions. The state's independent agencies were particularly vulnerable, since they were, by design, not protected by any specific political actors. They were also a highly attractive prize, as they allowed whoever controlled them to influence elections (through the electoral commission), prosecutions for corruption (through the integrity commission) and even the economy (through the central bank). In a January 2011 decision,[13] the Supreme Court made independent agencies answerable to the government, despite constitutional provisions that attached them to parliament.[14] The court faced a barrage of criticism from al-Maliki's political opponents and commentators over the weakness of its rationale.[15] Although the court eventually partially back-tracked, its decision remained binding on a number of institutions, most notably the integrity commission.

From that time onwards, the government's inner circle issued instructions to particular agencies to control their actions and policies. When some officials resisted, it was decided that the agencies' senior administration had to be completely captured as well. Judge Rahim al-Ugaili, head of the integrity commission, was forced to resign in September 2011 (see Chapter 7), and criminal charges were brought against the central bank's governor in October 2012 and against the deputy governor in December 2012. The government has also set its sights on one of the last major bastions of independence, the electoral commission, so that it could influence policy in a way that would impact future elections. Although the commission is clearly a flawed institution, it has managed to operate at arm's length from Iraq's major political parties, which has allowed elections a measure of credibility thus far. Given al-Maliki's strategy and his reaction to the March 2010 electoral results, that independence is clearly at risk.

One of the government's most important institutional weaknesses has been that it lacks clear rules of procedure. It is unclear who can issue decisions on the government's behalf, how many ministers are required for a quorum and how the prime minister's personal authority differs from the government's. The constitution requires the government to draft its own rules of procedure; the Erbil Agreement reaffirmed that this should be done as a matter of priority, but it never was. So, for example, although the constitution states that ministers and senior military officials can only be appointed by parliament (a rule that has frequently been violated by al-Maliki anyway), who is mandated to appoint their deputies or their advisers? Is this something that each individual minister is responsible for, or can the government (or even the prime minister) get involved as well? There are no rules on the matter at all (apart from Baathist era custom, which naturally could not be continued). Al-Maliki and his closest allies have deprioritized the drafting of rules of procedure and have exploited the status quo to place their own people everywhere, often with a view to preventing specific ministers from making any progress in implementing policies, or in order to pursue alternative policies of their own (see below). In effect, al-Maliki and his closest allies have set up a parallel government of their own.

Having made major inroads within the state, al-Maliki's other challenges included preventing any significant forms of popular dissent. Throughout his first term, there were hardly any civilian protest movements to speak of: everyone was too busy navigating the sea of militia checkpoints and trying to stay alive. But it did not take long for a new dynamic to emerge after the March 2010 election. By June of that year, parliament had managed to meet for only eighteen minutes on one solitary occasion, and had failed to appoint a government, despite a clear constitutional timetable that required the job to be completed within a few weeks.[16] Despite the fulsome promises made during the campaign, everything remained on hold: no new policies, no decisions and no movement on services. But members of parliament did make sure that their astronomical salaries (which, including benefits, amounted to tens of thousands of dollars per month) were paid.

The prospects of a rapid improvement in the standard of living were melting away as fast as the summer temperatures were rising. This encouraged young activists to take their struggle onto the streets.

At the start of summer 2010, a charity organized a satirical play in the centre of Baghdad in which an MP was seen using ordinary Iraqis as furniture. Then one morning, as commuters set off for work, they were surprised to see on a building that overlooked the Green Zone a huge photograph of an eye, with the words 'We can see you' written below it.

Amidst an unprecedented summer heat wave, thousands gathered spontaneously in over half of Iraq's cities to protest about the inadequate electricity supply. Government buildings were torched and officials were threatened, prompting some (including the minister of electricity) to resign. The government could not (even if it wanted to) deliver any immediate improvement, and so it resorted to intimidation: future protests were banned, and warnings were issued every morning for weeks by police squadrons that drove through the streets of provincial capitals.

The revolutions that spread across the Middle East and North Africa in 2011 gave fresh impetus to the call for better governance. Spontaneous demonstrations broke out in February 2011 in Suleimaniya – partly in solidarity with the Tunisian and Egyptian revolutions, but also to protest about the rule of the two main Kurdish parties in Iraq. A new generation of youth leaders then sought to capitalize on this momentum, launching nationwide demonstrations on 25 February, which they dubbed a 'day of rage'. These activists were motivated by neither religion nor race; they wanted simply to hold the government to account for its actions.

Prior to the demonstrations, the government was concerned enough to make a series of pre-emptive concessions, including an announcement by al-Maliki that he would halve his salary and not seek a new term in office after the next elections, scheduled for 2014. The council of ministers, fearing an increase in inflation, voted to suspend a decision that had been taken a few weeks before to introduce higher customs duties on the import of certain goods (a decision that was intended to protect the agricultural sector against dumping and other non-competitive practices by neighbouring countries – see Chapter 8). Parliament switched almost $1 billion that had been earmarked for the acquisition of military aircraft to social programmes in the 2011 annual state budget.

The security forces were also concerned about the mass protests, and they, too, undertook a number of pre-emptive measures, including beating and intimidating anyone who participated in the warm-up demonstrations in the days leading up to 25 February. Baghdad was declared a 'no-drive zone' on the day of the protests, leaving residents with no means of getting to them (the city is twice the size of Paris). Nevertheless, thousands took to the streets in Baghdad and at least sixteen other cities, torching government offices and forcing the resignation of several public officials, including the governors of Basra and Babel, as well as the head of the Fallujah municipal council. In Baghdad, protesters fought police who were protecting the Green Zone and managed to partially destroy one of the entrances to it. The reprisals were swift: security forces killed close to twenty demonstrators on 25 February and wounded many more. In the weeks that followed, continued government violence and intimidation succeeded in quelling the demonstrations.

Two days after the dust settled, al-Maliki announced that he had imposed a hundred-day deadline on the government to improve service delivery and reduce corruption. When the deadline passed, the government engaged in a campaign to silence its critics, while it continued to shirk its commitments on governance. Weekly demonstrations once again gathered pace, attracting thousands of people. One such demonstration met with a violent response on 10 June, when pro-government thugs armed with sticks and knives attacked protesters. It was alleged that among them had been terrorists who had committed atrocities, and dubious confessions were aired on national television.

Intimidation and violence continued throughout the summer, peaking on 9 September, when Hadi al-Mahdi, a prominent journalist who had previously been arrested for leading protests, was assassinated at home.[17] Although the culprits were never identified, the incident created an unmistakable air of fear among critics of the government, and by the end of 2011 the movement had been crushed.

During the summers of 2012 and 2013, as Basra once again sweltered (for days on end it was well over 50 degrees Celsius), residents organized a series of night-time demonstrations to protest about the lack of electricity. Stones were thrown at the security services, which responded by firing into the air, arresting protest leaders and intimidating demonstrators.

State officials who were brave enough to raise the alarm over government practices were also subjected to organized witch hunts. Judge Rahim al-Ugaili, who resigned in September 2011 as head of the integrity commission, generally kept a low profile after that, but he would offer his opinion on corruption-related issues when asked by the press.[18] Clearly his views were unflattering to the government, but his presence hardly registered in the Iraqi and international press after he stepped down. Nevertheless, the decision was taken that he should be silenced: his replacement at the integrity commission alleged that he had run a secret prison where detainees were tortured, had engaged in massive corruption and had spied for the US.[19] A press conference organized by the integrity commission in August 2013 to officially release its annual report was instead devoted almost entirely to vilifying al-Ugaili.[20]

As increasing numbers of Iraqis complained about the government's performance and its failure to improve services, Iraq's ruling elites once again took refuge in sectarianism, although this time for a completely different reason. Previously, sectarianism had been the principle on which the country's new political order was established, and the mechanism that political parties had used to place their members in senior ministerial positions. But by 2011, sectarianism had acquired two different functions. First, it was used by politicians to deflect attention from their own dire performance. Second, in the absence of genuine progress on the standard of living, government officials and their associates sometimes suggested that at least ethno-sectarian 'interests' were being protected and promoted. Sectarianism had thus become the only line of defence in the face of state failure and the only objective worth pursuing: the achievement that excused all the failures of the past.

Al-Maliki himself was one of the principal culprits in the retreat from national unity and the return to sectarian-style politics. Following his poor showing in the March 2010 parliamentary elections, from the second half of 2010 he came to argue that Iraq's particular ethno-sectarian balance meant that the prime minister would have to be Shia for the foreseeable future, and would have to represent Shia interests. It was the type of opinion that he would never have expressed openly during his earlier days as a national leader. There was no basis in law, or even in tradition, for insisting that a Shia must be prime minister – although there was clearly an argument that, given the crimes of the past, Iraq's various communities would not entrust their security to individuals or groups that they did not feel entirely comfortable with. More cynically, under this proposed ethno-sectarian arrangement, to remain in control of government al-Maliki would only have to ensure that he was his community's candidate, rather than the national candidate that he had once hoped to become. If he could persuade his co-religionists to support him, or if he could impose himself on them, then his chances of staying as prime minister would remain high. Unsurprisingly, although many Iraqis generally understood the sentiment underlying al-Maliki's comments, they were unhappy that it was being expressed publicly and in such sectarian terms. They were also deeply dissatisfied with sectarian statements that were issued by politicians on the other end of the spectrum, including former Vice President Tariq al-Hashimi after he fled Baghdad in 2011.

Over the following two years, the same logic was employed by the ruling elites to divert attention from their every failure. In December 2012, the prime minister ordered security forces to arrest several individuals at the ministry of finance, including security guards who had been assigned to Rafi al-Issawi (a member of the Iraqiya alliance and minister of finance), whom the prime minister and his inner circle had long suspected of being linked in some way to terrorist organizations (although the US military never found any evidence to support the allegation).[21] It was not immediately obvious what prompted the arrests, particularly as real and immediate security threats and violations went unpunished; but in any event the episode was interpreted by Sunnis as motivated by sectarianism and led to demonstrations in al-Issawi's native Anbar province. The true motivation for the arrests was revealed in the reactions and counter-reactions of senior politicians.

Accusations and insults were traded in parliament and on the airwaves, perhaps none so blatantly sectarian as during a televised debate that took place in December 2012 between Saad al-Muttalabi (one of the prime minister's closest allies), Anas al-Tikriti (the son of one of the Muslim Brotherhood's leaders) and Hiwa Osman (an independent journalist from Kurdistan). The question posed by the moderator was whether the government's performance was in any way responsible for the increase in sectarian tension. The discussion lasted for half an hour, which was enough time for al-Muttalabi to insult just about everyone in the entire country, apart from his own ethno-sectarian group.

His first insult was directed at the Kurdish people, whose representatives he blamed for all the government's failures:

> Baghdad is probably one of the worst places to live in and Iraq has failed and that is all thanks to the Kurdish ministers who have miserably failed in their works in Baghdad and are known to be corrupt and a group of thugs and probably worse than that.

Later in the debate, when Anas al-Tikriti compared al-Maliki unfavourably with Saddam Hussein (a clear exaggeration, but one that is regularly made as a form of provocation), al-Muttalabi accused him of supporting the Baathist regime:

> Maybe you do not belong to the Baath party but you belong to the institution that gave Saddam Hussein the authority to rule over Iraq. Do not make the mistake; everybody knows who you are; your organization provided Saddam Hussein with the political authority to rule over Iraq.

Al-Tikriti, who was born in exile because of his father's adherence to the Muslim Brotherhood, was clearly startled and furious at the suggestion. It was the worst form of guilt by association possible, and marked a clear decline in political discourse among the country's more senior leaders.

Popular disillusionment with the ruling class was so palpable as a result of this type of behaviour that, in the run-up to the 2013 provincial elections, Iraqis were encouraging each other to stay away from the polls. Across the country, including in the Shia-majority south, there was a common refrain: 'What have we obtained? Nothing has changed.'[22] The growing sense of apathy was terrifying for the ruling elite, as it could lead to volatile and unpredictable election results. An effort was made to get people to vote, although this time it was through the explicit use of sectarianism in public spaces. The clergy were encouraged to drum up xenophobia – and many were all too eager to deliver. On this occasion, however, sectarianism was also used to exonerate the ruling elites of any wrongdoing; the message was that the only thing that mattered was defending 'the sect's interests'.

Throughout 2012 and 2013, Sheikh Salah al-Tufayli, a relatively young Shia preacher who was a favourite of a few party-owned satellite channels, delivered himself of a series of fiery sermons designed to get the vote out. The following is an extract from what was perhaps the most incendiary, delivered in December 2012:[23]

> There will be elections coming up soon. There is confusion in the street. What have people in our community been saying? 'Do not vote. Do not go to the polls. What have we got from this person? What have we been able to arrange from that person? Do not vote at all.' That is not the way things work . . . Who should power go to in that case? To Ezzat al-Douri [the then leader of the outlawed Baath party] who will force Umayyid rule on us? Let the person who governs us come from among us. Choose someone honourable, someone decent. Use your mind, use your vote to change the odds. Iraq is a state of institutions, and we live in a democracy. Use your vote to change the odds but do not say that you will not go to the polls and that you do not want to vote because this is a war between us and them. We are being broadcast live [so I cannot be too explicit], but you know who 'us' and 'them' are. Go to the polls in support of our community. Vote for anyone, even if the government is corrupt, even if it has daily problems and even if we curse them on a daily basis. Despite that, they have done what was required of them. At least they recognize that Ali is God's divine appointee. Even if they are dishonest and they do not mean it, it does not matter. Even if all they do is talk and they do not satisfy their promises, set that aside. At least they recognize that Ali is the Wali of God.
>
> . . . If you ask me about the general situation, I can tell you that it is very bad. But we rely on God and Ahl al Beit [the descendants of the Prophet]. Hopefully, hopefully, a government official who steals once, twice, three times, may one day get tired of stealing and will send us a mouthful from the leftovers. Yes, maybe God will guide them to the right path. What can we do?

Corruption, incompetence, failure after failure – Iraqis were blatantly being told that none of it mattered so long as their leaders pretended that they were sectarian. It was apparently even too much to expect politicians to exhibit genuine expressions of solidarity to their co-religionists, so Iraqis were instead being told that they should satisfy themselves that their leaders were at least making the effort to lie to them. In the end, the politicians and their allies managed to drum up significant controversy and forced Iraqis out to vote. The campaign was framed in entirely sectarian terms; all that mattered suddenly was who was best suited to represent 'Sunni' and 'Shia' interests. Some voters agreed with the sentiment, but many voted in the hope that they could identify the least of several evils.

Tension ran high in the weeks preceding election day, as al-Maliki was considered to be encroaching on Sunni provinces by offering support to some of the more pliant candidates. After a series of incidents during the campaign, it was during the week of 21 April 2013, as the votes were being counted, that the explosion occurred.

According to various accounts, on 23 April an army checkpoint in Kirkuk province was attacked. Security forces pursued the attackers and claimed that they had sought refuge at a sit-in in al-Hawija, a tribal area that borders Salah al-Din province. Officers demanded that the demonstrators give up the men. The protest leaders refused to allow the security forces access to their camp. A confrontation ensued and ended in bloodshed. Reports indicated that around fifty protesters were killed, mostly with shots to the head and chest.[24] It was the first time since the sectarian violence had abated in 2008 that security forces had been used so blatantly and in broad daylight against apparently unarmed civilians.

Because of the role that it had played in reducing the violence, for several years the army had been regarded with a certain degree of respect throughout the country. But as al-Maliki acquired full control of the institution, that reputation gradually faded. The events of 23 April were yet another nail in its coffin. Throughout the rest of that day, the airwaves were filled with highly provocative statements. Sunni politicians demanded an inquiry; tribal leaders dismissed the idea and issued ultimatums against the government and the army, which they referred to in blatantly sectarian terms ('Iranian', 'Persian', etc.).

For years, a core group of Iraqis argued that the politicians who were seeking to divide the nation would not succeed. On the day of the massacre, I contacted a friend who had adamantly defended that perspective to ask for his view of what had happened, and to hear what I expected would be his reassuring confidence in the face of this new outrage. His voice was both determined and dejected: 'Iraqis have been divided into two groups, Sunni and Shia. There is no longer any mistaking the matter.'[25]

Over the years, the proportion of people favouring some form of separation has ebbed and flowed in line with security concerns: from 18 per cent of
the population in 2004, the proportion reached 42 per cent in 2007, as the
violence peaked.[26] When security improved in 2008, Iraqis very clearly shifted
their focus of concern to services, unemployment and corruption. It is worth
noting, however, that regional and separatist sentiments have never returned
to their 2004 levels, hovering around 30 per cent from 2008 to 2013. After ten
years of occupation and ethno-sectarian rule, Iraqis have become more – not
less – willing to separate from each other. It is the clearest condemnation
possible of the entire post-2003 political order.

When it became clear in late 2011 that popular protest had failed to
achieve even a modicum of success, Iraqis sought out other avenues by which
to improve their situation. The 2005 constitution theoretically established a
quasi-confederal model of governance, granting significant powers to the
provinces and the regions, and very little authority to the central government. But outside the Kurdistan region, and in violation of the constitution,
that system was deliberately not applied by al-Maliki and his colleagues in
the central government. Among other things, parliament passed a decentralization law in 2008 that gave the provinces virtually no powers, in direct violation of the constitution. Almost all state employees at the provincial level
continued to receive their instructions from (and were paid their salaries by)
central ministries. Provincial governments' annual budgets were in fact not
for them to spend; they merely reflected the money that central ministries
were granted by the central ministry of finance to continue operating in the
provinces. Baghdad was completely in charge.

During the early days of the occupation, and until the civil conflict that
peaked in 2007–08, most Iraqis eschewed any suggestion of regionalism as a
dangerous fantasy that could easily cause the entire country to break up.
This was despite the fact that, as violence spiralled out of control, the state
practically collapsed, leaving schools and hospitals to decay and most of the
country with almost no electricity. It was also despite the relatively positive
example that had been established by the Kurdistan region, which enjoyed
good security and better service delivery than the rest of Iraq after 2003.

But as the years passed with no progress on the ground, some provinces
pinned their hopes on invoking the constitutional provisions that allowed
them to organize a referendum within their own borders on the formation of
a federal region. And by 2011, with state services continuing to underper-
form and amidst unending security threats, a number of provincial officials

acted against their own patriotic instincts and initiated the process to form new federal regions.

The move was a risky one. The local populations in each of the provinces involved were demanding action. The federal government was not delivering on its promises, public expressions of discontent were being crushed, and elections were unlikely to produce any significant change. Activating the constitution's provisions was seen as a last resort. Some felt that it could lead to partition of the country, but others retorted that under the circumstances they had no choice.

Basra province was the first to debate the possibility. For decades its population had suffered terribly from war (Basra being on the front line during most of Iraq's wars), international sanctions, bombings by the US and the UK during the 1990s, invasions, militia-led violence after the 2003 war, government repression and lack of investment.

Because of its network of canals, Basra was once upon a time referred to as the Venice of the East; but by 2011, the canals were full of garbage and were highly polluted. Most of the local population did not have access to a reliable source of drinking water, often as a result of the toxic munitions that were left to rot in the city's outskirts.[27] Hospital officials reported huge increases in birth deformities, attributing the phenomenon to the use by international forces of depleted uranium and other such materials.[28] Its educated class of engineers and professionals was well aware that the largest share of Iraq's oilfields was located within its provincial borders, and this caused increasing resentment.

An initiative in 2008 to transform the province into a federal region had failed to garner sufficient interest among the local population, which was then still willing to give central government a chance, particularly as security had only just recently improved. By 2010, though violence remained relatively low in the city, corruption and incompetence had continued to prevent any real progress on service delivery. Basra's provincial council called for a referendum and went on to repeat the call on several occasions.

Soon a number of other southern provinces became interested in the idea, having failed to reap any of the rewards that many assumed would come their way from having their co-religionists in power in Baghdad. Even people in al-Maliki's home town could not believe how little development had occurred in the area.[29]

In late October 2011, Salah al-Din and Anbar provinces threw their hats into the ring. This came in reaction to a wave of arrests and dismissals from

Tikrit University for alleged links to the banned Baath party. Salah al-Din's reaction was particularly indignant and sustained. In fact, provincial council members were so excited about the prospect of a referendum that they neglected to check the legal requirements that had to be met before a region could be formed and thereby skipped a number of formalities: Salah al-Din's provincial council announced the formation of the region on 27 October 2011 without consulting the people. After realizing its mistake, it called for a referendum in the province.

Prior to 2011, the government's response to any calls for the formation of a federal region was either to ignore them altogether, or else to cajole the local population with promises of extra employment (which usually took the form of useless jobs in the already bloated security sector) or with the petrodollar scheme (through which provinces are given a fixed dollar amount for each barrel of oil produced). From October 2011, however, the government stated that it would block any attempt to form federal regions, despite the fact that it did not have the authority to do so. Under the constitution, if a province expresses the desire to form a region, there is a process involving the provincial authorities and the electoral commission; central government has no formal or official authority to influence the process whatsoever.

When Salah al-Din province pushed for a referendum within its borders, the Independent High Electoral Commission, which was theoretically responsible for organizing any referendum, bowed to pressure from the prime minister's office and simply did not respond. The provincial authorities threatened to print their own ballot papers, but abandoned that idea when they realized that they simply did not have the capacity to organize a referendum of any type.

Several weeks later, on 15 December 2011, in response to similar circumstances, the provincial council of Dyala, a governorate with a mixed population[30] but dominated politically by Iraqiya since the January 2009 provincial elections, also voted in favour of forming a federal region.[31] The next day, armed protesters (some say members of the Sadrist militia, the Mahdi Army) occupied parts of Baquba, the provincial capital, and several highways leading into and out of the province. They ransacked the council building, forcing members to hold an emergency session in Khanaqin, a Kurdish-controlled district in a far corner of the province. It was a provincial coup d'état, and the council's elected members remained in exile for months, while the security forces that were under al-Maliki's control did absolutely nothing to restore order or constitutional authority to the province. This was a power war, where the only interests that mattered belonged to political mafias; the people's needs and concerns were not even part of the equation.

Despite these very clear breaches of the constitution, the international community, most notably the United States, supported al-Maliki in his efforts. The story is a familiar one: western powers are largely indifferent to governmental practices in Middle Eastern countries, so long as nothing is done to threaten a number of vital interests, including natural resources. As a result, diplomatic and material support will be offered to ideological opponents of the most illiberal kind – just so long as oil and gas flows unimpeded. Even as the Iraqi government's practices deteriorated (albeit with a relative improvement in security), the US and others heaped public praise on al-Maliki for the successes he had supposedly engineered. On 12 December 2011, at a joint press conference in the White House's South Court Auditorium, President Obama was effusive:

Today, I'm proud to welcome Prime Minister Maliki – the elected leader of a sovereign, self-reliant and democratic Iraq . . . Iraq faces great challenges, but today reflects the impressive progress that Iraqis have made. Millions have cast their ballots – some risking or giving their lives – to vote in free elections. The Prime Minister leads Iraq's most inclusive government yet. Iraqis are working to build institutions that are efficient and independent and transparent. Economically, Iraqis continue to invest in their infrastructure and development. And I think it's worth considering some remarkable statistics. In the coming years, it's estimated that Iraq's economy will grow even faster than China's or India's. With oil production rising, Iraq is on track to once again be one of the region's leading oil producers. With respect to security, Iraqi forces have been in the lead for the better part of three years – patrolling the streets, dismantling militias, conducting counterterrorism operations. Today, despite continued attacks by those who seek to derail Iraq's progress, violence remains at record lows. *And, Mr. Prime Minister, that's a tribute to your leadership and to the skill and the sacrifices of Iraqi forces.* Across the region, Iraq is forging new ties of trade and commerce with its neighbors, and Iraq is assuming its rightful place among the community of nations.[32]

No mention of the capture of democratic institutions, the corruption, the lack of progress on infrastructure and economic issues, the simmering discontent, the human rights violations, the crushing by security forces of

public protests just a few months earlier. . . Even the economic growth that
Obama referred to was almost entirely fuelled by growth in the oil and gas
sector and depended on factors over which Iraq's government had no control
(see Chapter 6). The US president was aware, of course, that the rest of the
economy was stagnating, but that was not worth mentioning. Obama's
support contributed to the cloak of international legitimacy and respecta-
bility that the Iraqi government has used for years to pursue its selfish and
inept policies.

The only trouble that al-Maliki has ever had from the international
community has been from Turkey and Qatar, which sponsored the formation
of Iraqiya and which were particularly unhappy when the alliance was
marginalized after the elections, when the government was being formed.
They expressed their displeasure in a variety of ways, including through
statements to the press and by hosting some of Iraqiya's leaders as they fled
Iraq. But al-Maliki brushed off their opposition, which he sometimes even
used to feed the divide-and-rule policies that he adopted in 2010.

AN INSURGENT PARLIAMENT AND THE CONSTITUTIONAL IMPASSE

Governments of national unity are designed to prevent any particular
party or individual from dominating others. If any such attempt is made,
the system intervenes, and the mechanism that it employs is parliament. If
a particular faction in government seeks to impose its will, it inevitably
has to prepare legislation to support its agenda; at this point, its allies in
government become parliamentary opponents, ready to vote down the
proposed bill.[33]

Al-Maliki's first government of national unity worked in tandem with
parliament for three years, until the results of the 2009 local elections brought
that arrangement to an end. Although the relationship was formally reconstituted after the new parliament was elected in March 2010, it could not last
long, as al-Maliki pursued his strategy of dominating the state at the expense
of his allies. Within a few weeks, therefore, a majority of parliamentarians
rebelled against al-Maliki. But they did so for the wrong reasons and using
the wrong mechanisms. Although the 2005 constitution granted parliament
the power to withdraw confidence from government and the prime minister
without having to call fresh elections, al-Maliki's opponents could not agree
on who should replace him. And so they left him in place, preferring instead
to block key components of his legislative agenda. MPs from al-Maliki's own

State of Law alliance remained loyal to him and to his agenda, but they often found themselves entirely isolated within parliament on a number of key issues.

As soon as al-Maliki's government allies understood that the Erbil Agreement was never going to be applied and that the prime minister was intent on pursuing his 'long view' throughout his second term, parliament approved a series of laws, each of which was designed to counter the government's policies.

In July 2011, a new law on the integrity commission was passed, according to which the head of the body should be appointed by parliament with no government involvement (in the end, the government just ignored the procedure and appointed a new acting director when the existing head stepped down under pressure; see Chapter 7). Parliament also moved to block al-Maliki's efforts to capture the electoral commission. In September 2012, he introduced a bill that would have expanded the number of commissioners from nine to fifteen. This would have given smaller parties (some of which were allied to al-Maliki) more representation and would have caused al-Maliki's opponents to lose some of their own influence. The proposal was rejected by parliament, which voted to keep the existing nine commissioners, of whom State of Law could not control more than two or three.[34] There were complaints that parliament did not have a quorum and there was the threat of an appeal to the Supreme Court; but any repeat vote would almost certainly have produced the same result.[35] Shortly thereafter, a new group of commissioners was selected by parliament and State of Law was left with a minority.

Then in December 2012 a new law on the Higher Judicial Council was passed, which reduced the council's powers significantly and prevented one of al-Maliki's closest allies from presiding over it. State of Law MPs once again immediately threatened to appeal against the new law's application.[36] In February 2013, parliament refused to vote on an 'information crimes' bill that had been drafted by the government and that would have imposed harsh penalties for unspecified crimes involving the internet. It was stated that the law would clearly have infringed basic freedoms and was unjustified.[37]

Most importantly, perhaps, following the failed 2011 attempts by Salah al-Din, Basra and Dyala to create federal regions, parliament passed a new provincial powers law in June 2013, which amended the original 2008 law. The amendments were in complete opposition to al-Maliki's own policy on decentralization, and granted the provinces wide-ranging powers, including exclusive authority over education, health, agriculture, finance, sports and youth. The new law also required the security forces to obtain the governor's approval in the event of any security-related mission, and gave governors the authority to communicate directly with the security services should their work be unsatisfactory. Finally, the law vastly increased provincial budgets, at central government's expense. The legislation was a clear slap in the face for al-Maliki, giving as it did each province a veto over security and unprecedented authority over significant areas that central government had previously monopolized.[38]

As the theory and practice of the separation of powers have evolved around the world, it has become standard for the various branches of government not only to check each other's power, but also to seek to undermine each other's constitutional authority. Governments in particular always seek to sideline parliaments, and often gain the upper hand for a number of reasons. It is tempting to conclude that al-Maliki's attempts to consolidate his authority and parliament's concomitant insurgency were simply manifestations of this phenomenon.

In Iraq, however, the problem is not simply that the means that political forces use to undermine each other have involved violence, intimidation and other practices that would be deemed inappropriate in most other countries. It is also that we have actually reached an impasse: without an overhaul of our constitutional and legal system, our defective politics will prevent any significant improvement in the quality of governance, service delivery or standard of living, which will spell disaster for the state's survival in the mid to long term.

The 2005 constitution granted government and parliament very specific, interdependent roles, and it is on the exercise of those roles that the success or failure of the parliamentary system of government depends. The Iraqi government is responsible for establishing general and specific policies, and for implementing those policies. Parliament is responsible for ratifying all the government's policies, whether by approving its programme and the annual state budget law, or by approving individual bills. Where the government deviates from its programme or fails to meet the expectations of parliament or the public, parliament is mandated to impose sanctions through a number of mechanisms, including by withdrawing its confidence in government.

The parliamentary insurrection that started in 2009 and that intensified in 2011 pushed constitutional practice in a different direction. Faced with a number of choices (including the possibility of withdrawing confidence from the prime minister), parliament followed the government in bastardizing constitutional conventions by formulating its own policies through legislation without the government's involvement, and did so not in the country's interests but in its own.

The sight of state institutions acting contrary to their given functions in a parliamentary system is cause for significant concern, particularly in Iraq. Any policy that is established by parliament will necessarily – almost by definition – quickly encounter a number of limitations, some of which may actually cause a worsening of governance. Government, which is the only body mandated and able to implement policy, will necessarily resist applying any law that it does not agree with. Court cases will be commenced to challenge the law's constitutionality, which will lead to significant delay and confusion; meetings on implementation will be boycotted and delayed; regulations designed to specify how a policy should be implemented will not be forthcoming, etc.

This does not merely bring us back to square one; it leads to an impasse and to a weakening of the rule of law. State officials and citizens no longer know what the law is and are led to believe that it can be resisted and is of little value without the support of a narrow group of politicians.

Even more serious, perhaps, is that any policy designed by parliament – particularly the Iraqi parliament, which is renowned for its lack of capacity and administrative incoherence – will have been conceived without any real understanding of whether the state is capable of absorbing the changes that are called for, or of how it is likely to react. Under ideal circumstances, policies are developed after long and detailed discussion involving experts, ministers, senior officials, economists, etc. When a policy is designed to bring about fundamental change, the process can – indeed should – take years and should involve significant public debate, in order to allow proper consideration of what the implications might be.

A decade after the end of the 2003 war, there is no question that government has been incapable of organizing any such effort. But parliament is even less likely to succeed in doing so. In fact, it may not even be aware of how complicated the whole procedure is, since it does not have the tools to gauge whether its policies are being implemented.

Let us take the decentralization law of 2013 as an example. The manner of its adoption by parliament guarantees that a number of difficulties lie in wait around the corner – difficulties that are likely to worsen governance in the short to medium term. First of all, the law makes no provision for how provinces will manage their greatly increased budgets and portfolios. In some cases, particularly in Basra province, the increases are likely to be astronomical. This raises a serious question, for the residents of the southern provinces have for years been complaining that their local governments have been unable to fully disburse the limited budgets that they have at their disposal. The problem is that there is a dearth of effective project managers at all levels of state. Even Baghdad, where the country's best managers are concentrated, has had significant difficulty in fully disbursing its budget. If the new law were to be applied, the first few years would almost certainly witness large amounts of money unspent at the end of each fiscal year, which is likely to lead to significant frustration among the local populace.

Secondly, the law does not even mention the measures that should be taken to prevent or reduce opportunities for corruption. Even if provinces were able to disburse their budgets, it is very unlikely that the local populations would obtain value for their money. In particular, provinces do not have sufficient capacity to oversee the implementation of large-scale projects, have close to no capacity to examine environmental impact, and do not have adequate auditing experience to root out waste, inefficiency and corruption. Although Baghdad is home to many of the country's most competent administrators, since 2003 it has been incapable of answering many of these questions satisfactorily. Given also that government will resist preparing a genuine transition plan for decentralization, there is little doubt that the issues will not be addressed at the provincial (or regional) level for some time. By the time a solid legal framework is established and competent institutions are created to oversee its implementation, waste and corruption will have swamped the newly formed region. This will erode the new authorities' legitimacy and their ability to serve the interests of the people.

The 2013 law stipulates that a new commission should be set up to supervise the law's application and the transfer of ministerial departments to the provincial governments. The key to the law's implementation lies in how that commission will operate in practice. Transferring the authority of departments from one level of government to another is no simple matter; merely ensuring that staff salaries are paid without interruption can be challenging enough. So far as the 2013 law is concerned, the difficulty is that the commission is to be headed by the prime minister and requires his close cooperation to ensure that its work is done properly. The prime minister's opposition to the entire enterprise is clear, so he is likely to resist putting in place the measures and regulations needed to ensure the law's success. It is also very likely that much of the remainder of the state, particularly the central ministries in Baghdad, will resist the law's application, since it runs counter to almost a hundred years of centralization. Of course, bureaucracies everywhere resist change; where that is the case, government normally steps in to enforce matters. But once again, here the opposite is more likely: government will almost certainly work to prevent the law from ever coming into force.

In so far as motives are concerned, parliament's activism was not a response to a government that had failed to deliver; rather, it was an attempt to save itself from al-Maliki's attempts to capture the key institutions of state. Since 2011, all the legislation that it has adopted in the face of government opposition specifically relates to the balance of power within the state – and is designed to curb the prime minister's power.

Similarly, parliament's actions have not been concerned with the people's welfare or with improving governance: it has not undertaken to resolve disputes over oil and gas that the government allowed to fester since 2005, and nor has it drafted a law on political parties. Both matters are of vital importance to the population, but parliament has not seen fit to prioritize them – not least because they do not affect its survival.

In summary, since the 2005 constitution came into force, neither government nor parliament has focused on developing a functioning democratic system. Government has been preoccupied with undermining itself from within, while both government and parliament have been busy undermining each other. The only reason why parliament has resisted government policies has been to protect those political parties that are not allied to al-Maliki from being emasculated.

PERSONAL FAILINGS

Even if al-Maliki and his rivals were to resolve their political differences, there is one thing above all else that will continue to prevent any further consolidation of their authority in the country: their personal failings as administrators. This – a result of their poor educational and professional backgrounds and the negative instincts that they developed while in exile – will forever constitute a barrier to improving the state's performance, and therefore to achieving genuine popular legitimacy in the country. More particularly, the former exiles' insistence on micromanaging every aspect of policy formation and implementation, including on issues that they do not understand, is particularly damaging.

The drafting of the annual state budget law is a case in point. Every year, senior officials at the ministry of finance and in all government ministries communicate over a period of months, feeding one another information about the funding needed over the coming year. The process is complex and painstaking, as every department has to predict what ongoing and future projects will cost. Every country should theoretically undertake the same process every year, but not all of them succeed (where a budgetary process fails, one option is to carry over the previous year's budget law, which means that the government's finances are not adjusted in line with the country's needs or with policy).

Despite all its problems, Iraq has managed to get the job done on every occasion, thanks to the dedication of its mid-level bureaucrats. Every year, however, when the draft is in its final stages, it must be approved by the government before it can be sent to parliament for a final reading and approval. It is at this stage that Iraq's former exiles reveal their worst traits, as they misunderstand everything that is done and said and accuse one another of misleading each other. One year, the government's inner circle tried to increase the amount of deficit spending by 30 per cent, bringing the total budget to around 130 trillion Iraqi dinars (at the time about $100 billion). The suggestion came at the last minute, with no thought given as to whether Iraq could raise the necessary funds, what the consequences would be if it failed to do so, or what a deficit of that magnitude would do to Iraq's credibility internationally. The initiative led to a shouting match that lasted for days, with ministers accusing each other of obfuscation or ignorance. In the end, the additional amount was removed from the budget when a number of Iraqi and international officials intervened to explain that the proposal was essentially unworkable.[39]

It is rare that this type of breakdown occurs openly, but that is what happened in July 2012, when the then minister of telecommunications resigned. Mohamed Allawi was a senior member of the secular, Sunni-backed Iraqiya alliance. Allawi, who is related to Ayad Allawi and is from a well-known Shia family, is known as a devout and honest technocrat who has long tried to eschew politics when carrying out his work. He joined al-Maliki's second government in November 2010 and, although his political alliance was involved in a dangerous contest with al-Maliki, Allawi kept his head down, refused to speak to the media and focused on improving the delivery of services. Less than two years later, he abruptly resigned.

He had been working to secure the construction of a fibre-optic line that would link Iraq to Turkey and the rest of the world, but the project was cancelled by al-Maliki, who had been advised that Turkey would be able to intercept sensitive communications. Allawi responded that all fibre-optic cables are protected by sophisticated password and encryption systems, and that all countries used fibre optics because it is the most secure technology available. The prime minister refused to budge, however, and opted to maintain Iraq's current system, which relies on satellites (and is far less secure).

This was enough to cause Allawi to resign and to go public with his misgivings about how the government is run. He published a letter that he had written to the prime minister in July 2012, in which he highlighted examples of mismanagement and imposed an ultimatum. The prime minister, he wrote, had appointed Hiyam al-Yasiri, previously of the ministry of higher education, as an adviser to the ministry of telecommunications and had given her the power to overrule the minister. If Ms al-Yasiri was not dismissed from the ministry, he wrote, he would be compelled to resign:[40]

I have tried to the best of my ability to deal with you in a professional way. I have refrained from making political statements during my tenure as minister, and instead focused on carrying out my work. Unfortunately I was confronted with a malicious, deliberate and negative campaign against me. These include the following:

- There was an attempt to undermine the ministry by marginalising its staff and by transferring them to other ministries. It is unacceptable that staff should be appointed to and fired from a specific ministry without the relevant minister even being consulted. A number of senior professionals and honest officials were fired and replaced by unprofessional individuals who have already been accused of financial and administrative corruption.
- Another attempt was made to undermine the ministry by cancelling important and useful projects for the communications sector and for the country in general. You personally granted some individuals in the ministry, in particular the adviser to the cellphone department Dr Hiyam al-Yasiri who is just an adviser to the minister, a mandate to cancel projects. These individuals used the fact that they were associated with you personally to force the cancellation of projects.

The ministry's staff and the relevant companies did not dare confront them, as a result of which a number of projects were either delayed or cancelled.

. . . You are aware that the adviser in question has made many false accusations against the ministry and, instead of holding her accountable, she was appointed to the Integrity Commission to lead investigations against innocent staff.

She fought any project that was for the benefit of the country and that develops the communications sector. To be as accurate as possible, there is a group of people inside and outside the ministry who have fought all the projects that I tried to launch.

I ask that the adviser Dr Hiyam al-Yasiri be transferred back to the ministry of higher education or to any other position outside the ministry of telecommunications. I would consider such a measure to be sufficient. Otherwise, I will present my resignation because I am incapable of working in such an infested environment.

The prime minister refused to transfer the adviser in question and accepted Mr Allawi's resignation.

Mismanagement is so pervasive that it has even affected the oil sector and the decision as to whether or not specific foreign workers and consultants should be granted visas to assist with large-scale projects that have been approved by the government. The representatives of companies that have been awarded large contracts by the state might have to wait months (if not longer) for a visa – and sometimes do not receive one at all.[41]

Another example: in November 2012 the government sought to replace what was left of the food rationing system of the 1990s with a cash-based system. The day after the announcement, religious authorities in Najaf bitterly condemned the decision as running counter to the people's interests. In particular, Ayatollah al-Nujaifi complained that the decision would lead to significant inflation in market prices, would reduce purchasing power and increase food insecurity.[42] Protests erupted all over the country, and two days later the government backtracked, announcing that it would not be cancelling the ration system after all.[43]

Corruption and mismanagement have been a constant theme of al-Maliki's time in office; although he has sought to portray himself as entirely clean, many of his closest allies have had serious accusations levelled against them and have had their names dragged through the mud. As a result, al-Maliki's own reputation has been well and truly sullied.

Al-Maliki and his allies are so disorganized that even calling meetings and conferences has proved a challenge for them. In 2010, the Arab League announced that it would hold its twenty-third annual summit in Baghdad on 29 March 2011 – a major leap of faith, given how poor security and services were in the capital. The government was elated and announced major new construction projects to beautify the capital. The airport road (previously the most dangerous road in the world) would be replanted with thousands of palm trees and decorated with water features; big hotels would be constructed to host the event and Turkish contractors were retained for that purpose. However, as March 2011 approached, almost no work had been completed. The only improvement to the airport road that I could discern was that a small stretch had been relaid.

The Arab League postponed the event for two months and then for a year. The summit finally took place in March 2012, and those dignitaries who showed up (most did not) were quickly ferried from the airport to the conference centre and then back. A public holiday was announced and curfews were imposed by the security forces to prevent any car bombers from getting near. Mobile phone lines were blocked for days. While the government boasted that the event had been a major achievement, ordinary Iraqis cursed the Arab League – and the government for agreeing to host the summit.

Worst of all is how security policy has been affected by the involvement of unqualified politicians, including al-Maliki and his appointees. We have already looked at the scandal involving the patently fraudulent equipment used throughout the country as 'bomb detectors', but throughout al-Maliki's second term his political appointees have bungled security. In particular, al-Maliki was ridiculed by Iraqis across the country in October 2013, when he spoke on national television about his twenty-six-year-old son's role in security operations in Baghdad. Apparently an unnamed individual had managed to amass a small, undeclared army inside the Green Zone (which by all accounts should be the most protected part of the country) and the security forces had seemingly been unable to bring the gunmen under control, even though arrest warrants had been issued. Al-Maliki bragged that his son (who is said to be employed by the prime minister's office) then took control of a special police unit and successfully arrested the gunmen, because 'he is harsh in upholding the law'.[44] By 2013 militias had rearmed in many parts of the country, coordinated bombings were once again taking place on a regular basis, and spectacular prison breaks were being organized with relative ease, even though the government had advance warning.[45] In one 2012 incident, prisoners dug a kilometre-long tunnel, pouring much of the earth they excavated down the prison toilets. Although plumbers were called several times to clear the blocked soil pipes, the security system at the prison was so poor that no one ever linked the plumbing problems with a possible escape attempt.

The agony of the situation is that, as bad as al-Maliki and his colleagues have been, the rest of the political elite are unlikely to have been able to do any better. When Allawi, al-Mutlaq, Tariq al-Hashimi, Usama al-Nujaifi and others joined together to contest the March 2010 elections as the Iraqiya alliance, a moderate and non-sectarian bloc, it provided a formidable opportunity to change Iraq's political dynamic and to have a positive impact on discourse. Instead, their repeated blunders turned them into just another part of the political elite.

For many years, Ayad Allawi was regarded by many as the only credible alternative to al-Maliki. Although his supporters claimed that he had what it took to improve security and restore services, during his time as interim prime minister (2004–05), he presided over a general deterioration in security, including the sieges of both Fallujah and Najaf. The state's inability to deliver on such basic services as electricity continued throughout 2004, and although there have been no meaningful accusations of corruption levelled at him personally, several members of his government (including his ministers of defence and electricity) are widely believed to have embezzled billions of dollars.

Since 2005, Allawi has been in parliamentary opposition, where he has been particularly ineffectual. He has been parliament's worst truant, preferring to indulge in photo opportunities with foreign heads of state in western and Arab capitals, and leaving his party practically leaderless in the process. His failure to engage in the drafting of the constitution in 2005 (when he let the process be dominated by a group of parties that today represent less than 20 per cent of the population and whose views are far outside the mainstream) was particularly damaging and illustrative of his lack of interest in anything other than the exercise of power.

Although the formation of his expanded coalition in late 2009 gave him a new lease of life, the manner in which he shuttled between foreign capitals during the campaign and avoided contact with the people he claimed to represent strongly suggested that he remained as aloof and detached as ever.

When his alliance narrowly defeated the State of Law alliance in the March 2010 parliamentary elections, Allawi miscalculated badly. He completely misjudged his opponents' obstinacy, and in the process attracted vitriol from both them and the security services. Allawi's major failure was that he never understood the opportunity opened up by al-Maliki's decision to form a separate electoral list from the rest of the Shia Islamists. Had he realized, he would have been the statesman that so many expected him to be.

Salih al-Mutlaq, another of Iraq's prominent politicians from the Iraqiya alliance, earned a reputation in 2005 for being a secular-minded and sharp negotiator who insisted on Iraq maintaining a strong central government. In 2010, during the negotiations over al-Maliki's second government, he single-mindedly insisted that the charges brought against him personally by the de-Baathification commission be dropped, completely ignoring his broader constituency's interests and needs. His fortunes declined even further in 2012: after referring in a televised interview to al-Maliki as a dictator who was 'worse than Saddam Hussein', he was declared persona non grata and prevented from attending government meetings until he apologized. Although no further public statements were made on the issue, al-Mutlaq was suddenly allowed to attend government meetings again a few months later, strongly suggesting that a backroom deal had been struck. The public's bitterness showed when, in December 2012, demonstrations broke out in Anbar province against the government's supposed anti-Sunni discriminatory practices. When al-Mutlaq tried to address the demonstrators, he was met with a volley of shoes and was chased to his car to make his escape.[46]

Iraqiya's leaders likewise found it impossible to keep on message in relation to the centralism/federalism debate. The cracks within the alliance's ranks were first exposed in June 2011, when the parliamentary speaker, Usama al-Nujaifi, stirred up controversy by claiming that the growing sense of disenfranchisement and persecution among Sunni Arabs would increase their desire for self-rule. In response, a number of Iraqiya's leaders held a press conference in July 2011 to reassert the alliance's support for centralism. Ayad Allawi commented that he nevertheless supported greater decentralization (as opposed to federalism), which provoked a walk-out by Deputy Prime Minister Salih al-Mutlaq, who supported a strongly centralized system of government. By December 2011, al-Nujaifi was openly calling for regionalization as the best way to solve the problem of failing services and government repression.

The Kurdish alliance and the Sadrist movement, two of Iraq's other important political forces, are far more cohesive in terms both of their

members and their ideology; but both represent relatively narrow constituen-
cies that cannot hope to attract enough support to play a leading role in
government. Although the Sadrists claim to represent all Shias, they in fact
command the support of the *mahroumin* ('the disenfranchised'), or about
8 per cent of the general population. In Iraq, no one genuinely speaks for the
poor masses, and the Sadrists have carved out their own niche constituency
in that regard. But their influence is unlikely to extend beyond the poor of
one particular ethno-sectarian group, given that the movement is clearly led
by Shia clerics, and also that Sunnis (and others) are unlikely to forget any
time soon its role in the bloody civil conflict. Finally, the Sadrists have never
really managed to distance themselves from the rest of the political pack:
their representatives and senior officials have been guilty of the same kind of
mismanagement, corruption and opportunism as their counterparts from
other alliances. The Kurdish alliance, meanwhile, makes no pretence of
representing anyone other than its own constituency, within which it does
not enjoy a monopoly of support.

BREAKING OUT OF THE IMPASSE

By 2013, the occupation, the constitution that it produced, and Iraq's defective politics had led to an impasse. What solutions existed to break out and
refocus politics on improving the standard of living and rebuilding a common
identity in the country?

Iraq is ostensibly a democracy, and elections supposedly offer a means of
replacing underperforming politicians on a regular basis. However, although
Iraq tried a number of different electoral systems between 2005 and 2013 –
including closed and open list systems, the 'largest remainder' method and
the Sainte-Laguë method – the results have varied only slightly from one election to another. For the most part, and with very few exceptions, the same
parties and the same individuals that were part of the US's original governance framework have been returned to parliament and to government on
each occasion.

The fact is that, although elections have taken place regularly and have
been fairly transparent, they have been neither free nor fair – mainly because
government and parliament have refused to pass a law on political parties,
but also because of the misuse of government funds to buy votes. In the
absence of a law on political parties, there are no rules on how parties can
raise funds, where and in what form those funds may be kept, how the funds

can be spent or how much can be spent. There is also no obligation to submit or publish accounts, to declare income or expenditure.

The absence of rules is so extreme that during the 2010 parliamentary elections, although complaints were made against the State of Law alliance for having offered golden revolvers as gifts to tribal leaders in the south (all at government expense), no investigation or remedial action was undertaken. The only rules that are in place were established by the Independent Electoral Commission (which was established by the CPA and which is the predecessor of the Independent High Electoral Commission). In 2005, it issued a code of conduct according to which political parties cannot 'have or be associated with an armed force, militia or residual element', cannot 'be directly or indirectly financed by any armed force, militia or residual element' and 'must strive to achieve full transparency in political finances and expenditures'.[47] The code's provisions were widely violated, and there is no evidence that the commission ever imposed any penalties.[48] The code was updated for the 2010 elections, but it still contained no mention of how parties should be funded.

The result was the Wild West of political finance. The absence of rules meant that funds could be raised anywhere – from within Iraq, in Arab countries, Europe, the US, China; from foreign states, the private sector, individual donors or groups. Funds could be obtained illicitly (through corruption, oil smuggling, or simply by raiding ministry coffers), deposited in offshore accounts or in countries that have strong banking secrecy regulations (such as Lebanon) and then channelled back to Iraq during election campaigns. Unrestricted amounts of cash and gifts can be doled out to powerful elements in the country, including tribal leaders and the heads of armed groups, to buy their support. Funds have also been used to establish television channels, of which there are dozens, most of them broadcasting live every day and streaming online. Not only did this give established political parties unparalleled access to the population, but it also succeeded in dividing Iraqis by funnelling to each household a particular version of the truth (or indeed untruth) that conformed to the interests of the party that was financing the channel in question.

Because Iraq's new ruling elite integrated itself into the state as early as 2003, and because of the lack of rules and the easy access to public funds through illicit activities, political parties have become extremely well-funded operations. Their financial interests are thoroughly entrenched: they own large tracts of land, businesses and media empires, and employ thousands of people. Each has become a little state in its own right. The system (or rather the absence of rules) effectively insulates the entire ruling elite from the possibility of a genuinely democratic movement arising in the country. Viewed from without, the current elites are all equal (although whoever occupies the prime ministerial post clearly has an edge over the others, given the unparalleled access to power and funds that the position affords). Any outsider who seeks to do away with this 'system' will inevitably have a mountain to climb: without access to cash or weapons, he or she will never be able to compete. Any group of individuals hoping to challenge the status quo by establishing a new political party and contesting elections would have to raise funds of their own and establish some means of communicating with the public. That would mean yielding either to illicit, foreign or narrow financial interests. There is little point in replacing one set of corrupt politicians with another.

As a result, under the current constitutional and legal system, elections will not produce any real alternatives to Iraq's ruling elite. The fortunes of some parties may rise, while others may see their popularity wane somewhat; but the chances of anything emerging outside the current crop of incompetent and corrupt politicians are vanishingly small. The 2010 parliamentary election results were evidence of that: despite deep dissatisfaction with the ruling elite, there was no choice on offer other than the same parties and the same individuals that had ruined the country in preceding years, albeit repackaged in new coalitions and campaigning under different slogans. It was the same in the 2013 provincial elections. Voters in southern provinces were clearly disillusioned with Nouri al-Maliki's administration, but their options were very limited; the only real alternatives were to vote for the Sadrist movement, SCIRI (now, of course, the Islamic Supreme Council of Iraq – ISCI) or one of the many smaller parties that have been part of the political equation since 2003. The results removed some of al-Maliki's strength in the provinces, but the winners were those self-same groups that had been in control from 2003 to 2009, prior to the rise of al-Maliki. Subsequent elections are unlikely to be any different. In all likelihood, Iraqis will choose to stay away from the polls in increasing numbers, leaving the politicians to play an aggrandized version of musical chairs while everyone else just watches.

CHAPTER SIX

A COUNTRY LEFT TO LANGUISH

The failed constitutional order and the country's defective politics were not merely abstract concerns. As politicians obsessed over their incessant and violent power struggle, they deprioritized virtually everything else, including a number of long-standing problems that were literally threatening the state's existence. These included rocketing unemployment, the decrepit public services (electricity, water, education), a failing framework to protect human rights that was exacerbating security risks, corruption and environmental disaster. Solutions were desperately needed – additional investment, new legislation and regulations, as well as mechanisms to invigorate the private sector. It was all achievable, because Iraq had sufficient funds for any investment needed, had the support and attention of the international community, and could count on a number of dedicated Iraqis who were motivated enough to resolve these issues.

Without real and speedy progress, there was a genuine danger that the country could be engulfed in perpetual crisis, even if the security issues were resolved or reduced. By 2008, even though the worst of the civil conflict was over, Iraq found that it was still regressing. Every year that the government failed to take action, the challenges facing the country grew more complicated and difficult to resolve. The negative impacts spread through the country like a disease, further damaging the already bad relations between the governed and the governing. The question was how much government and parliament valued the system that they themselves were perpetuating and what they were willing to do to ensure its survival. Would they offer a solution to Iraq's predicament, even if only a partial one? Would they rely on force and repression to maintain their position? Or would they just allow everything to burn to the ground?

AN OIL POLICY IN DISARRAY

Natural resources are both the cause of all Iraq's problems and the only solution to the crisis brought on by the ruling elites. With approximately 145 billion barrels, Iraq has the fifth-largest proven oil reserves in the world (after Venezuela, Saudi Arabia, Canada and Iran). Its resources are also among the least costly to extract, since they lie just below the earth's surface. The difficulty is, however, that the ready availability of these resources and the absence of any effective system of taxation in the country mean that successive governments have enjoyed relatively easy access to significant income with next to no involvement from the population.

Close to 97 per cent of the Iraqi government's revenue derives from oil resources. By way of comparison, Venezuela gets 45 per cent of its income from oil, Saudi Arabia 90 per cent and Iran 50 per cent – even though they have more resources to exploit. Just 3 per cent of Iraq's income comes from everything else: customs, duties and income tax.[1] The taxation 'bargain' that exists in other countries, by which populations hold their political representatives to account on the basis that they, the people, provide all (or most) of the state's revenues by paying their taxes, has never existed in Iraq. Instead, the country offers one of the best illustrations of the resource curse: the ruling elites feel no incentive to improve performance, since state revenues depend on international oil prices, rather than on the outcome of specific policies. Iraq's economic model can be summed up as follows: the state sells oil on the international markets and uses the proceeds to fund salaries (for staff who are mostly paid to do nothing) and pensions; comparatively little goes on investment.

For that model to survive, particularly given the impending population boom (see below), the state has an interest in increasing and maximizing production so as to boost government revenue. In 2004, Iraq's annual state budget was just under $20 billion, and without additional funds the entire ship was likely to sink. Very early on, the government set itself the objective of dramatically increasing exports, in order to swell government coffers. Plans were drawn up and discussed, and wild predictions were made of soaring production within just a few years. Early in the US occupation, officials were boasting that the record production rates of the 1970s would quickly be surpassed. In 2009, the Iraqi government predicted that there would be an increase from around 2.5 million to 4 million barrels per day by 2013, and eventually 12 million barrels in 2017. In 2012, those figures were revised by the ministry of oil, which announced plans to raise production to 6 million barrels by 2015.[2] The unrealistic targets might have been missed, but the incentive for action is high: clearly exports have only to increase marginally for government to start reaping the rewards.

There was a further advantage to reinvigorating the oil industry: a successful strategy would create a national 'champion' that could inspire the country's workers and the general population. Ever since the 1950s, Iraqi engineers have instilled confidence and pride that the country's workers can stand shoulder to shoulder with the best in the world. At the peak in 1979, they were extracting 3.8 million barrels a day.

These engineers and the nationalized companies they worked for were motivated partly by values that promoted the national ownership of resources, partly by the idea that locals could outperform their international counterparts, and partly by a determination to prove that they could manage on their own.

The imperative to create a national symbol of success was perhaps even greater after 2003 than it had been before the war, given the increasingly gloomy mood at the time – a result of sectarian tension and violence. The people had unifying symbols from their history that they could turn to, but there was a desperate need for a new symbol in the present. Although the breakdown in national education would have made such a strategy difficult under any circumstances, there was still sufficient expertise in the country itself to develop the skill set, and there was certainly enough support among the general population and the trade unions to rebuild the industry.

But Iraq's long-term strategy was different. During their long period of exile, the country's opposition parties had reached a consensus that the previous centralized model should be dropped and international corporations allowed free rein to manage the country's most important oilfields. This view was further reinforced during the 1990s, when Iraqi industry collapsed. The calculation was that it would take too long to rebuild local capacity and, following the removal of the Baath party, the state's need for cash could only be met if international corporations were allowed in. All of Iraq's administrations since 2003 have maintained that position, arguing that the oil sector should be opened up to international corporations that would exploit the country's fields in return for paying royalties.

When the constitutional negotiations commenced in 2005, one of the great surprises (and disappointments) was how little debate there was on this issue. There was hardly anyone among the constitutional committee's members – and certainly no one within the leadership council's shadowy ranks – who argued in favour of rebuilding a national industry. Instead there was some unspoken agreement during all the discussions. At expert meetings that I attended and that involved constitutional committee members, the representatives of major international organizations put their cards on the table: all wanted the greatest possible liberalization of the industry. No one was given any choice in the matter. In any case, de-Baathification forced out many of Iraq's leading oil experts, and many of those that remained made their way to the United Arab Emirates or Jordan when violence spiralled out of control in 2006 and 2007. It was as if the state was doing its utmost to destroy whatever know-how it still possessed.

After the constitution came into force, the core of Baghdad's policy was to negotiate favourable terms with international corporations and to ensure that it remained the only interface for any providers that were interested in doing business in the country. By maintaining overall control of the industry, it could easily negotiate advantageous terms with international corporations that would allow production and revenues to soar.

But Baghdad already had a rival inside the country's borders: since 2004, the Kurdistan regional government had signed exploration agreements of its own with a number of small and mid-size oil corporations. Senior officials in Baghdad were aghast; their nationalist tendencies made it impossible for them to accept that a sub-entity within the state should be entering into international agreements without even consulting the central government. They were also concerned that if there were several levels of government responsible for contracting, their bargaining positions would be weakened – perhaps even leading to a race to the bottom. A solution needed to be found to deal with the contracts that had been signed – perhaps by treating them as an exception, concluded during a period of legal ambiguity.

An additional complication was that the constitution spoke of allowing the Kurdistan region, as well as individual provinces, the right to exploit fields that were not already in production when the constitution entered into force in 2005 (see Chapter 3). Although the distinction between 'current fields' and 'future fields' was unprecedented in comparative practice, and did not appear to have any logical basis other than trickery by one of the foreign advisers who was in the room when the provisions were drafted, the fact remained that the term was in the constitution and was therefore one of the challenges that Baghdad would have to overcome. Predictably, however, Baghdad made a mess of the whole thing. Rather than encouraging progress, it increased political tension in the country and discouraged many corporations from investing.

The Kurdistan region's position was perfectly rational and predictable. It was motivated by a desire to secure its own revenues in the long term, and it also sought whatever guarantees it could obtain from Baghdad that it would no longer be subject to the practices of the past. The 2005 constitution itself was very reassuring for the region, as its representatives had essentially drafted the provisions on oil and gas (see Chapter 3); but it kept a close eye on al-Maliki's administration to see whether it had a partner that it could genuinely trust (particularly as al-Maliki had not played a major role in drafting the constitution's oil and gas provisions and appeared to be opposed to them).

Soon after the occupation, Baghdad had developed the practice of transferring 17 per cent of the national budget to the Kurdistan region (roughly in proportion to the region's population). This money had been the cornerstone on which the Kurdistan region built its internal economy after 2003, but it was based solely on a gentlemen's agreement between the country's main political forces. What the region truly sought was a legally binding arrangement by which it would have an important role to play in the formation and execution of oil policy and would be guaranteed a fair and equitable distribution of revenue. One way of achieving that would be through a new hydrocarbons law. A draft of such a law was prepared as early as 2007 and provided for an oil and gas council, with representatives from central government, the Kurdistan region and provincial governments. That arrangement reflected the political reality that all major political parties would want a say in forming oil policy.

There were many contentious issues that needed to be resolved – not least the fact that the draft law threatened to politicize what should have been a purely technical issue. If the goal was to maximize production and revenue through the most appropriate economic and industrial models, then the decision to give political parties influence over the formation of policy was potentially highly damaging.

But the parties could not reach agreement: some argued that central government was given too much influence on the oil and gas council; others complained that it had too little influence, compared to the Kurdistan region and the provinces. Several solutions were tabled, including depoliticizing the draft altogether, while still offering the type of guarantees that all sides were seeking, or even offering incentives to particular parties to create enough support in parliament to allow the law to be passed.[3] However, rather than negotiate a grand bargain with the Kurdistan region that would provide the necessary guarantees, Baghdad stalled on finalizing the law. It then threatened to blacklist any corporation that entered the Kurdish market, gambling that the lure of Iraq's southern oilfields would be too great for anyone to risk being boycotted.

What Baghdad did not realize was that geology alone was an insufficient incentive for international markets: legal frameworks, infrastructure and corruption were all vitally important as well, and Iraq scored poorly on all fronts. In November 2011, an official at an oil company complained that 'they can't get equipment through customs, they can't get visas for their experts, and they can't deploy the capital they've carved out on their balance sheets for these projects'.[4] Visas, in particular, are an especially difficult issue: obtaining one is difficult enough, but renewing it once in country presents a bureaucratic nightmare. It often involves blood tests, getting the results certified by the ministry of health, presenting the certificate to the residency department at the local police station, providing fingerprints, signing dozens of forms – and then having the entire file reviewed by the police station's chief officer. Even that does not guarantee that non-Iraqis will be able to leave, as airport officials often take it upon themselves to decide that particular procedures have not been followed and send their victims back to Baghdad or to the relevant provincial capital to renew a particular stamp or obtain an additional signature. These are only some of the reasons why Exxon, which signed a contract for exploration in Kurdistan in November 2011, sought to sell its stake in the giant West Qurna field in southern Iraq – and why production rates across the country have barely increased since 2007.

In July 2012, Chevron and Total purchased rights in two oil exploration ventures in the Kurdistan region, and did not seem particularly bothered by Baghdad's announcement that they would be barred from entering the southern oil market as a result.[5] Others also expressed an interest in investing in Kurdistan, and there was even news of several wildcat corporations entering into agreements with provinces south of Kurdistan (including Salah al-Din, Anbar and Wasat provinces) – something that was certain to provoke

Baghdad's ire. Finally, just when everyone thought things could not get any worse after another disagreement between Baghdad and Erbil, the KRG announced that it was building a pipeline to the Turkish border to link up with a line that was being planned by the Turks.[6] In January 2013, while the controversy surrounding the pipeline was still fresh, it was announced that oil extracted from the Kurdistan region was officially and openly being exported to Turkey for the first time, with the KRG's consent, by Genel Energy plc.[7] Baghdad's reaction was merely to threaten Genel with law suits and to demand that Turkey respect its sovereignty (as if it had any leverage over either). Baghdad's own oil policy, which was theoretically designed to increase production, was instead contributing to the country's break-up.

What impact did all of these surprising and unnecessary developments have on production? In 2009, as sectarian violence receded from its peak in 2007, the government finally set out to implement its strategy to increase production rates. By 2013, the annual state budget had indeed increased by 600 per cent in eight years, to reach $118 billion. The government used that additional income to expand an already bloated public sector and to fund some investment. The difficulty, however, was that revenue was increasing not because the state had managed to meet its objectives, but merely because of an increase in global prices. The data showed that production rates had barely risen between 2001 (when Iraq produced an average of 2.58 million barrels a day) and 2013 (when it produced an average of 2.9 million barrels a day).[8] But the price of oil had jumped from $28 a barrel in 2001 to over $100 in mid-2013. Iraq had therefore benefited from market forces. But it had also become very vulnerable to factors that were completely beyond its control. Any combination of factors that caused international prices to fall, even if only slightly, could precipitate a fiscal crisis, particularly if the prices stayed low for a few years.

By way of example, international prices declined from $124 a barrel in mid-2008 to $35 in 2009 as a consequence of the banking crisis that spread from the United States to many parts of the world.[9] Although prices recovered the following year, this drop forced Iraq to fall back on its reserves and to seek a loan from the International Monetary Fund. If a similar decrease were to take place in the coming few years (which is certainly possible, given the technological advances that are enabling shale gas to be extracted in many parts of the world), and were to last for several years, the government would be forced to enact severe austerity measures, which would be certain to lead to civil unrest.

THE LOOMING JOBS CRISIS

A major crisis has been brewing for at least a decade – one that should, by all rights, be keeping senior officials awake at night endeavouring to find a solution. Iraq's population has been soaring for over half a century. In 1960, it stood at around 8 million; by the time of the 2005 parliamentary elections it was estimated to have reached 27 million; by 2010, it had climbed to around 32 million and looks set to continue to rise.

The 2011 fertility rate was far above the regional average, at 4.64 children per woman. In contrast, the rate was 2.87 in Syria, 2.74 in Saudi Arabia, 2.06 in Turkey and 1.64 in Iran (the latter two being below the accepted replacement rate, meaning that if current trends hold, their populations are projected to decline in the foreseeable future). The trend has a number of causes, but can mainly be traced to an absence of government policy on the issue and to the breakdown in the education sector. The youth bubble that had been on the cards for some time had unquestionably arrived by the time al-Maliki embarked on his second term as prime minister: 64 per cent of the population was under twenty-four years old and the median age was twenty. In other words, between 2007 and 2011, approximately 250,000 young Iraqis joined the workforce each year, increasing to 290,000 annually from 2012.[10]

In the past, Iraqis would favour the public sector for employment. Historically (and particularly given its socialist past), Iraq's ministries and state-owned enterprises have employed the largest share of workers in the country and have offered generous benefit packages, including privileged access to credit from state lenders. Although the state was never as effective as it led people to believe at the time, it did employ many hundreds of thousands in an effort to develop a manufacturing and engineering sector. The war with Iran led to a surge in the armed forces and actually created a labour shortage; millions of workers were brought in from abroad to make up the shortfall. The 1991 war changed that dynamic once again, this time by destroying Iraq's infrastructure and ruining what was left of its fiscal position. Following all the wars and sanctions, the collapse of ideology and the rise of corruption, the state stopped trying to produce anything and contented itself with trying to ensure that the population had enough food so as not to starve and enough money to keep a roof over their heads. Industry could not survive and ground to a halt.

The 2003 war did little to change that dynamic, except that it eventually saw an end to the sanctions and therefore restored Iraq's ability to engage in international trade. The new elites arrived just in time to have to deal with a ticking demographic time bomb. Hundreds of thousands of young Iraqis were entering the workforce and the state needed to direct them towards some form of employment if it wanted to avoid increased unrest. The public sector was already bloated and extremely ineffective, and so the obvious thing would have been to encourage growth in the private sector. Private enterprise represented a tiny proportion of overall economic activity in Iraq: the oil sector on its own represented over 60 per cent of GDP, and much of the rest was public sector activity, too.

A number of factors would have to be addressed for that trend to be reversed, and the first was education. In the 1970s, Iraqi schools and universities produced some of the best-qualified professionals and scientists in the region and attracted students from countries as far afield as Morocco and Lebanon, which had a developed education sector of its own. Three decades later, education had collapsed. All the most qualified staff had long since left and the teaching curricula were woefully out of date. There was general agreement that this situation had to be reversed, but the renewed violence of 2005–07 exacerbated the problem. By 2013, more than six years after the violence had abated, there had been hardly any reform – other than to expunge Baathist ideology from textbooks. Academics and trainers who were supposed to be teaching English to Iraq's newer generations could not understand a word of the language themselves.

Even if the new generation had received the education and training they needed, they were still reliant on the state to create employment. Given that the public sector was already oversubscribed, this should have meant creating an environment in which the private sector could thrive. In 2003, Iraq suffered from a decrepit legal framework that was in desperate need of reform. In particular, the rules governing the availability of credit, starting a business, engaging in cross-border trade and enforcing contracts and court judgments were archaic. Every Iraqi who thought of opening a business and of engaging with the state knew what was required: either you could slowly shuffle through innumerable decrepit government departments to obtain the necessary permits or you could pay someone handsomely to do the job for you. In 2012, five years after the reduction in violence, the World Bank found that Iraq's legal procedures for doing business were among the most cumbersome in the world: it ranked the country at 177 out of 185 countries for ease of doing business. By 2013, only a little progress had been made: it was ranked 164 out of 183 countries.[11] For years, key legislation that the business sector desperately needed had languished in draft form, and there was no light at the end of the tunnel. One sector that was most in need of assistance was agriculture, which has traditionally provided the largest share of private sector jobs. Because of the incoherent and unfair legal framework that had been established by the CPA, Iraqi farmers were subject to unfair competition from regional producers, and could not attract the kind of capital that they needed to rebuild capacity. Ten years after the CPA was disbanded, precious little attention had been paid to these issues by the state, so that underemployment and urbanization had increased.

To add insult to injury, foreign workers took a significant number of the few private sector jobs that were created. Also, when the ministry of health noted that hospitals were suffering from a shortage of trained nurses, it retained the services of international hiring agencies to recruit non-Iraqis. In late 2012, the message was sent out internationally that the ministry was specifically looking to recruit 2,000 nurses from the Philippines, even though the country discouraged its citizens from travelling to Iraq following a number of kidnappings in earlier years.[12] The oil sector was likewise importing much of its expertise and was using as little Iraqi labour as possible. Even restaurants in Abu Nawas, one of the traditional focal points for night life in Baghdad, were importing staff from Bangladesh, since they had better training than their Iraqi counterparts.

Having failed to improve both education and the business environment, the state pursued the only course open to it at the time. This was both the easiest and the worst option: it doubled the number of public employees by creating positions wherever it could, even if there was no need. By 2013, the state employed approximately 4 million individuals, equivalent to 60 per cent of full-time workers (the proportion is said to be even higher in the Kurdistan region),[13] and 12.5 per cent of the population.[14] By way of comparison, in 2011 some 32.3 per cent of Sweden's workforce consisted of public employees, while the figures were 16.42 per cent in the US and 6.35 per cent in Singapore.[15] The security sector alone was said to employ close to a million people.[16]

What, if anything, would all these new staff be doing, given that the state was already extremely unproductive? By 2010, two years after the reduction in violence, state employees had returned to work, but were finding that they were essentially being sent home for long periods of time. Official holidays were proclaimed almost every other day – to commemorate religious pilgrimages, because of high temperatures, or just to keep the roads empty when high-level meetings were organized in the capital. A staggering one hundred public holidays were declared in 2011.[17]

One can obtain extended paid leave for all sorts of reasons: two years of maternity leave, study leave, etc. Under normal circumstances, generous benefits of that kind, which encourage a healthy family environment or allow doctoral studies to be carried out at the state's expense, would be ideal. However, circumstances in Iraq are not normal: there is a desperate need to have these people working and delivering services; instead the state is encouraging everyone to stay at home for as long as possible.

Equally surprising, even when they are supposed to be working, employees have nothing to do. In my experience of various institutions, very few can actually be described as busy. For the most part, when they have work, employees waste their time following outdated or ineffective practices or endlessly reporting to each other; but more seriously, most never seem to have anything to do. Foreign diplomats who communicate regularly with the ministry of oil, which should by rights be a hive of activity, are always surprised at how quiet and empty the building seems.[18] A recent study has calculated that state employees work for seventeen minutes during an average day. There is some doubt about the study's methodology, but the fact that the figure was picked up and remained essentially unchallenged in the capital is in itself revealing.[19]

ELECTRICITY, WATER AND WEAPONS

One of the main things hampering the oil industry is the same problem that has plagued the population for decades, but particularly since 2003: service delivery, particularly education, health, transport and electricity. These are a source of considerable anxiety in Iraq, and have been for some time.

In the late 1980s, the national grid was capable of producing 9,295 megawatts per day (MW/d), at a time when demand peaked at around 5,100 MW/d; 87 per cent of the population had access to electricity twenty-four hours a day.[20] Iraqis had come to rely heavily on their infrastructure by the time the 1991 war swept their country back to the stone age. Production fell to 2,325 MW/d, but the Baathist regime, always conscious of appearances and determined to create the illusion of defiance and progress, invested all the human capital it had at its disposal in restoring electricity in the capital. Immediately prior to the 2003 war, production had recovered to 4,400 MW/d and Baghdad enjoyed round-the-clock supply, though that came at the expense of the provinces, which received far less power than the capital.[21]

Following the 2003 war, services collapsed once again, but this time expectations were quite different from 1991. Sanctions had been lifted, oil prices were rising, there were promises of significant financial assistance from donor countries, and the US military, with all its expertise as the most powerful army in world history, was on the ground and supposedly playing a leading role in the reconstruction effort. In the early days after the war, it seemed certain that electricity at least would be fully restored within a few years. Education and health were more problematic, as they required tens of thousands of staff to be trained, but they, too, would surely follow on the path to recovery.

Iraq suffers from severe weather conditions that can range from over 50 degrees Celsius in summer to freezing in winter. This makes heating and air conditioning imperatives. Although I have travelled extensively in most of the Arab region, Iraq is the only place where the heat has caused me serious difficulties. Like anyone who has spent significant time in the country outside the Green Zone, I have spent weeks on end without a regular power supply at home. This includes the hours of darkness: each night, I have desperately shifted from one place to another to try to cool down; I have tried sleeping in bed, on the floor, on the roof, in a doorway, in the bathroom. But all to no avail: it is hard to get more than a few winks of sleep at a time.

During the day, it is difficult to achieve anything much after a sleepless night and in the blazing sun. On one occasion, I thought I would faint as I left a friend's car just to cross the street on my way to a building opposite. The wind was so thick with heat that I could feel it cutting through my skin. As we drove back home, I was left speechless at the sight of manual labourers working in the midday sun with nothing but Arab headscarves to protect their heads.

One morning, I sat in our kitchen as my uncle struggled to describe how hot he felt: 'Today, the temperature is . . . It could be as hot as . . . It's at least, at least . . .' His son interrupted to complete the sentence: 'Today, the temperature weighs a ton!'

During summer, I was always very happy to head for the airport and put it all behind me for a while; but millions of others have had to endure the same misery for years and decades, with no hope of even a temporary respite. On one occasion, shortly after I arrived in Beirut, I received a call from a friend in Baghdad. 'Where are you?' he asked. 'Sitting indoors with the air conditioning on. How about you?' Although his response was meant as a joke, I knew it contained a lot of truth: 'I'm in hell.'

One of the most painful aspects of summer is the sight of Iraqis scrambling to access electricity when one source after another fails them. On a blistering summer's day, a relative spent four hours in his Baghdad shop without enough electricity even to power a fan, and then laboured for close to eight hours in the blazing sun trying to replace the private generator that had powered his home but that had succumbed to the heat earlier that day. It was a race against time as he searched for cables, wire cutters, ladders, extensions and a generator that had enough capacity for his home. His young children and elderly mother heaved a sigh of relief as he finally secured an alternative source of energy late that afternoon. His face red with anguish, his jaw still tense, he sat before me, stared into the distance and muttered: 'Life in Iraq is a constant struggle.'

The high temperatures regularly cause severe health problems among the elderly and other vulnerable groups, including heat stroke and dehydration. Travelling around the country by car during summer without air conditioning is torture and could lead to a trip to hospital for some. The temperature is sometimes so high that car windows crack and electricity generators explode. A cousin who took his car to a garage to replace the windscreen ended up having to pay double, as the back window cracked while he waited.

The humanitarian and practical need to overhaul the grid must have been obvious to anyone in Baghdad immediately after the 2003 war; and indeed many CPA officials did recognize the importance of this for the country's stability and future.[22] But US and Iraqi officials were also very well aware right from the start just how difficult a task it was going to be. Aside from the grid's generally dilapidated state, there were a number of other factors that were bound to complicate matters. There were the usual problems of security, regular acts of sabotage and the brain drain; but also the demand for electricity increased dramatically in the years immediately after the war and was bound to rise over time, given how fast the population was growing. Household appliances (particularly air-conditioning units and refrigerators) poured across the unregulated borders, leading demand to more than double – from around 5,100 MW/d prior to the 1991 war to 12,000 MW/d in 2010.[23]

In response to these challenges, the US invested close to $5 billion between 2003 and 2008, and the Iraqi government stumped up $23.3 billion from 2006 to 2012.[24] Various promises and projections were made, although these kept shifting and slipping every time a target was not met. In 2008, the government's national development plan estimated that the grid would reach twenty-four hours of power a day nationwide by 2015, and would exceed demand by 10 per cent soon after.[25] By June 2013, that projection was clearly not going to be met; but still the deputy prime minister for energy affairs, Hussein al-Shahristani claimed that by the end of the year, Baghdad residents would enjoy eighteen hours of power a day, and even said that Iraq would be exporting energy to neighbouring countries soon thereafter.[26] Despite the impressive sums of money (far more than had ever been invested in the electricity sector before) and the endless promises, electricity production has seen hardly any improvement.

In 2007, a household socio-economic survey published by the Iraqi Central Organization for Statistics and Information Technology described what this meant for the average household:

> The public electrical grid . . . provides on average of only 7.9 hours of power per day. The lowest rate is in Baghdad, with only 5.0 hours of power supply per day. Only 22.4% of persons are able to rely solely on the public network for electricity to their housing unit. 75% of individuals supplement the public network with one or two other power sources. On average, community generators provide 6.4 hours and private generators provide 4.0 hours of additional power per day.[27]

Another survey, this time from 2009, found that during a six-day period, the daily supply of electricity from the grid met only 52 per cent of demand and that Baghdad residents were receiving 7.8 hours of electricity supply a day.[28] By 2011, the figure had increased only very slightly, to 56 per cent.[29] By 2012 the national grid was still barely capable of producing more than 6,000 MW/d. Though that represented a 33 per cent increase over 2003, it was still around 30 per cent below what the grid had been capable of producing on the eve of the 1991 war.[30] Iraqis were forced to endure debilitating power cuts that could last hours (and sometimes longer, depending on the location). By the summer of 2013, supply had hardly improved. Even journalists writing from Baghdad complained that they were not receiving more than six hours of power a day, and that the supply actually seemed to be deteriorating.[31]

Iraqis generally do not care what the reasons for all these failures are. Responsibility clearly rests with successive administrations, and in particular with the two governments led by al-Maliki from 2006. The actual details of what has gone wrong are enough to make one weep: they involve a series of mistakes that can be attributed to the government's incoherence and to incompetent senior officials.

First, for any strategy to improve the grid, those individuals responsible for building, upgrading and maintaining power plants throughout the country need to coordinate closely with those officials who are responsible for allocating and distributing fuel. The difficulty from the outset has been that, for long periods, the ministry of oil was under the control of ministers who were (and still are) personally close to al-Maliki and his political alliance, whereas the ministry of electricity was under the control of individuals who had different allegiances. As a result, there was a general lack of coordination at the two ministries: the wrong fuel was often sent to power plants, which increased maintenance costs and the frequency of power cuts. There was frequently no fuel at all to power the turbines.

A separate problem was the general lack of capacity in the ministry of electricity to carry out professional planning exercises and to oversee large-scale projects. During al-Maliki's first government, major pieces of equipment were commissioned, built and delivered long before they were needed. They then had to be stored for years in warehouses. All of this soaked up funds that could have been better used elsewhere.

There was also the usual problem of political interference in the ministry's operation, leading to abrupt transfers of key staff from one position to another and the appointment of unqualified party cronies to oversee major projects. Predictably, positions were effectively left vacant for months at a stretch, just when the sector was in desperate need of direction.

In 2008–09, I was contacted on several occasions by clients I had worked for in my law practice. Worryingly (but unsurprisingly), they asked me informally how they should interpret the fact that their counterparts at the ministry of electricity had stopped responding to correspondence and answering phone calls, for no apparent reason and despite the fact that significant down-payments had already been made. Some even queried what procedure they should follow to cancel their contracts, since they could not operate without a client to give them directions. In 2008, Iraqi and international economists and engineers were lamenting the lack of progress and calling for the government to carry out a serious planning exercise to set out what needed to be done and in what order. Although that exercise was ready by the time al-Maliki's second government was formed in late 2010, the same problems kept recurring.

The worst and perhaps most embarrassing episode came in July 2013, when al-Maliki admitted, during a televised debate with a small group of academics and journalists, that the officials responsible for improving production rates were guilty of 'failures and stupidity'. They had arranged for major contracts to be negotiated with General Electric and Siemens to construct large-scale generation plants that would be powered by natural gas, even though Iraq did not actually have any gas to fuel them! The turbines should have been designed to use diesel. He insisted that he could not be blamed for the blunders, even though he had signed the contracts, because he 'did not specialize in electricity'. Al-Maliki also rebuked his deputy prime minister for energy affairs, Hussein al-Shahristani (also one of his closest allies), for making false promises on the future rates of supply (see above). He said an investigatory committee had been tasked with determining who was at fault for all these failures.[32]

Not only did the government's poor performance affect the standard of living throughout the country; it also infuriated Iraqis. For years, demonstrations broke out every summer in the southern provinces, where the heat was most oppressive. Demonstrators would make their way through the streets at night, carrying symbolic coffins in which they had laid electricity's corpse to rest. On occasion, the protests would degenerate into riots, with arson attacks on government buildings and violence by the security services. In the summer of 2013, the demonstrations were persistent, taking place every day for weeks in several cities[33] and attracting the ire of senior government officials, who referred to the protesters as 'barbarians'.[34] In early August 2013, in an effort to calm things down, the minister of electricity paid a visit to Nasiriya, one of the cities that had witnessed sustained demonstrations. When he left, protest leaders made a point of noting that the power supply had actually been worse than usual during his visit.[35]

Despite all the failures, the closest anyone came to being held responsible was in June 2010, when Karim Wahid, the minister of electricity, resigned after a series of violent protests in the southern provinces. But even that smallest of victories was incomplete: Wahid had merely resigned from what was a caretaker government, and was unlikely to return as minister in the new government (eventually formed a few months later), given that he had lost the support of the political forces that had initially brought him into government in 2006. In any event, Wahid's resignation speech showed his bitterness: he complained that the government's performance was not to blame, but rather Iraqis 'are not sufficiently patient'.[36]

In August 2011, Minister of Electricity Raad Shalal was fired for signing contracts worth $1.7 billion with two fictitious companies, one German and one Canadian. Despite years of planning exercises, and the constant flow of complaints about corruption and mismanagement, the minister had not bothered to follow a proper procurement procedure for these, some of the most important contracts he would ever sign, and had somehow managed to select companies that were clearly not qualified to fulfil an order for light bulbs, let alone to build major power plants. He later complained that the contracts had been countersigned by the prime minister, but by then he had already been shown the door.[37]

The only solution for the general population is to find alternative sources of power, no matter how inadequate, just to keep the lights on at night. For years, local businessmen have invested in mid-size generators that are capable of providing significant wattage to dozens of homes at a time. If they are lucky enough to live close to a neighbourhood generator, Iraqis can buy a few hours of electricity a day (although prices are often exorbitant in Baghdad, and generator owners always provide power for less than the agreed time). Those who can afford it keep a small generator just outside their homes (in the garden, on a balcony or beside the front door), simply to keep the lights on in case both the national grid and the neighbourhood generator fail.

Even households that can meet all these costs present a depressing sight: people have constantly to switch from one source to another, often leaving the house in darkness for long periods as they do so. In addition, each household has to have a system in place to ensure that high-consumption appliances are not plugged in when the lower-capacity generators kick in. Some organize automatic systems, but others scrabble around the house several times a day, shutting down air-conditioning units every time the state supply is cut off. The surrounding environment is also heavily impacted: a canopy of power cables blots out the sky in most residential areas, and the din from all the generators running at any one time is indescribable. Then there is the damage caused to air quality and to residents' health, as pollutants are constantly spewed forth in close proximity to living quarters. Rather than prioritizing electricity production, the state has essentially admitted defeat by buying into this ad hoc and inadequate system: it now provides fuel practically free of charge to neighbourhood generators, in order to keep them running as long as possible.

After al-Maliki's second government was formed in 2010, and when the power supply failed to improve, some provinces decided to take matters into their own hands. Prior to 2011, Kirkuk province, home to some of the country's most important power plants, together generating 500 megawatts, received just four hours of electricity a day. Although the province was notoriously divided along ethnic and religious lines, after a string of promises from Baghdad of improvements that never materialized, the provincial officials were able to set their differences aside and face up to the government. In January 2011, with local police officers at their side, they cut off the supply of electricity to the rest of the country. Governor Abdel Rahman Mustafa organized a press conference, attended by virtually all of the province's dignitaries, at which he declared that he would not budge until the ministry of electricity addressed the province's needs.[38] Provincial council member Hassan Torhan, a leader of Kirkuk's Turkoman bloc, defended the decision: 'Electricity is not distributed equitably in Iraq. We are receiving four hours a day while other provinces receive ten hours.'[39] It was a brave decision that exemplified just how far Iraqis' expectations had fallen. Eventually, in another major affront to Baghdad, Kirkuk resolved its difficulties by purchasing electricity from a private supplier based in the Kurdistan region.[40] Following that example, other provinces also purchased electricity from private providers who had set up their own power plants in the Kurdistan region (where the regional government has managed to increase production so that supply is available for close to twenty-four hours a day).

Electricity has been the most obvious and pressing problem; but all other public services have suffered similarly. At some of the country's most prestigious medical institutions, patients have died for lack of oxygen, even though hospitals are supposed to be equipped with oxygen generators. Doctors have had to operate on patients without adequate anaesthetics, which have had to be rationed. Accordingly, Iraqis have been travelling to Jordan, Lebanon, Syria and even India to have basic medical procedures carried out. In summer 2012, doctors at the American University of Beirut told me that 20 per cent of their patients were Iraqi.[41]

Even those parts of Iraq's infrastructure that were buried deep underground suffered from the same neglect. On Christmas Day 2012, 6.75 centimetres of rain fell on the capital – around double the monthly average for December. As the day progressed, it became apparent that the drainage and sewerage systems could not cope with the pressure; streets were flooded, buildings collapsed and several people died. An official in Baghdad's municipality indicated that the cause of the flooding was 'the outdated sewer pipes, the fact that some are broken as well as the fact that we have not received the necessary funding to undertake the projects that are needed to save the capital and upgrade them in the area of services and infrastructure, particularly water drainage'.[42]

For weeks, television screens and the web carried humiliating pictures of furniture floating inside people's homes and of children diving from concrete blocks into filthy water that was stagnating in the streets and in underpasses. A month later, the rain continued to pour all over the country, revealing that the problem existed virtually nationwide: floods were reported in Ninewa, Kirkuk, Baghdad, Anbar and Karbala, as well as in the Kurdistan region. Some of the main roads in Karbala were completely flooded; schools and businesses were shuttered up in some places for weeks; islands of garbage formed in the middle of stagnant water, while residents complained that they were left to their own devices by the state, which did not send any assistance whatsoever. When the water levels finally receded, local officials termed the operation a success.[43] Tempers boiled at the irony of Iraq's situation: every time the country's budget increased, the position of its population seemed to deteriorate.

An image widely circulated on Facebook summarized the popular mood. The upper half of the image showed the skyscrapers of Dubai, with a caption indicating that the state budget was $12 billion. Below it was a photograph of Baghdad during the floods, with battered cars and a horse-drawn cart navigating a flooded street, which noted that the state budget has now exceeded $100 billion.

Faced with complaints about the condition of public services, senior officials always lamented that the state did not have the financial wherewithal to provide the type of relief that Iraqis so desperately needed. But the government's own numbers tell a very different story. Iraq's 2012 annual state budget was $100.6 billion – the highest it had ever been (the 2013 annual budget was even higher, at $118.6 billion).

The way in which this money is allocated reveals the state's skewed sense of priorities. Taking the 2012 budget, $14.7 billion were allocated to defence; $5.6 billion to the electricity sector; $9.9 billion to education; and $4.9 billion to health and the environment. Altogether, from 2006 to 2012, the government's military budget was $71.7 billion – 16.07 per cent of the total. Electricity came in at just over 5.1 per cent; education at just under 8 per cent; and health and the environment at 5.05 per cent.

Some comparison is useful here. In 2011, Iraq's gross domestic product was around $115.39 billion, which means that its military budget stood at 10.5 per cent of GDP that year. By contrast, the US's military budget was 4.7 per cent of GDP; Russia's was 3.9 per cent; the UK's was 2.6 per cent; and South Korea's was 2.7 per cent. Even Saudi Arabia, well known for its extravagantly wasteful defence contracts, spent 'only' 10.1 per cent of GDP.

Not only has the government prioritized military expenditure over essential public services and efforts to improve the standard of living, but the money spent on defence has been largely wasted. Although operating costs (salaries, pensions, etc.) represented a large proportion of the funds, much of the investment budget has been literally squandered on the purchase of items that have absolutely no application to the security risks faced by Iraq. After the US's own disastrous experience, there was little prospect of any other country invading or of Iraq's own military engaging in a conflict outside its borders; so the purchase of fighter jets and tanks is extremely difficult to justify, particularly in a country where children often go to bed hungry.

Since 2003, Iraq's principal security risk by far has been terrorism and insurgency, but the type of military aircraft that Iraq was investing in clearly had no relevance or application to this threat. The beauty of military spending, of course, is that it is almost never subject to oversight in Iraq, the Arab region or even beyond: national security, we are always told, requires that the details remain secret and therefore away from the scrutiny of auditors, the press and the public. Iraq, however, is a country of surprises, where government officials can be so inept that their most precious secrets find their way into the public domain, simply because the corruption and waste are too obvious to hide (see Chapter 7).

The sad reality is that, even if such huge military expenditure was essential and was unavoidable, the annual state budget could easily have been boosted sufficiently to safeguard the investment required by the electricity and other sectors. If only those individuals in charge of government had been capable of organizing their work as they promised, they could have met the projections for oil extraction and exports, which would have meant a substantial increase in the state's revenues and its budget. With sufficient vision, capacity and compassion, all these things and more could easily have been achieved.

FAILING HUMAN RIGHTS

Under the circumstances, the least the government can do is restore some sense of security to the country. After all, it has thrown astronomical amounts of money at the security forces, and has encouraged the perception that it has been effective in the war against terrorism and the militias. Despite the reduction in violence in 2007–08, the government has made a mess of security policy: first by deploying faulty equipment to protect its citizens (e.g. the magic wands described in the Introduction), and secondly by creating unnecessary security risks through its own terrible practices.

Human rights abuses have long been a problem in Iraq. They should have been among the most urgent priorities after the 2003 war, and certainly should have been prioritized after the reduction in violence in 2008. The failure to protect human rights, particularly among detainees, has always increased the security risk: people who are picked up and tortured by the security forces are more likely to engage in criminal activity than if their constitutional rights are maintained and the rule of law is respected. Under the previous regime, the constitution guaranteed detainees certain rights, and torture was prohibited in all cases. Those provisions were widely violated either in an effort to extract confessions through the use of threats and physical violence, or just as a matter of routine. It emerged shortly after the 2003 war that many of these practices had not changed; as the civil conflict worsened, so did the number of reported cases of abuse. Torture in detention and the use of confessions as evidence in court proceedings were widespread. Irregular militias and state security services were both said to have been to blame. The civil conflict resulted in the death of tens of thousands, sometimes at the hands of the security services.

When the reduction in violence came in 2008, there was some expectation that a corresponding improvement in human rights protection would follow. The new constitution contains a number of provisions that theoretically prohibit all forms of physical and mental abuse in detention. In addition, dozens of international and local organizations have arranged training sessions for security officials, to teach them about human rights. Tens of millions of dollars have been spent on trainers and on studies for this purpose. For a time, there was hope that all this would help turn a new page and that there would be a reduction in human rights abuses. But the hope has been in vain.

A 2008 report by the ministry of human rights indicated that it had received hundreds of complaints of torture in detention centres run by the ministry of the interior and the ministry of defence, as well as by the Kurdistan regional government; in relation to these claims there was 'supporting evidence, including physical signs of torture on victim's bodies'. The report also noted that there was a 'worrying' number of detainees who had never been charged with a crime and of detainees who had not been freed after having been found innocent of all crimes.[44]

In December 2008, Human Rights Watch supported the ministry's findings. It reported that '[a]buse in detention, typically with the aim of extracting confessions, appears common' in the new Iraq.[45] In 2009, the US state department reported that it had found 'credible reports of torture, some resulting in death' in the Iraqi penal system.[46] In 2011, in a report entitled *Broken Bodies, Tortured Minds: Abuse and neglect of detainees in Iraq*, Amnesty International reported that the rights of criminal defendants were regularly being violated throughout the trial process.[47] Indeed, large numbers of detainees were kept in detention without charge, there was an over-reliance on confessions in the court system, with a corresponding lack of reliance on physical evidence (which led to a large number of miscarriages of justice, including the execution of young men who were wrongly accused of crimes), and the court system failed to provide adequate protection for juveniles and women. Despite unending conferences, seminars and training sessions, virtually no progress has been made on any of these issues, and all the practices described above continue unabated.[48] Even more worrying is the practice of maintaining 'secret prisons', a number of which have been uncovered since 2003, where holding conditions are deplorable.[49] Although the Iraqi authorities deny their existence, so many people have been held there that no one takes the denial seriously.

There is an important distinction between individuals who are accused under Iraq's vague anti-terrorism law and those who are accused of having committed ordinary crimes (see below).

The 2005 anti-terrorism law contains eight articles and has been used to accuse and condemn thousands of people of vague offences. Some are arrested because they visit their local mosque too often; others because they have been traced visiting opposition websites. Once the security forces get hold of them, they often disappear for weeks, if not months. Some are never given access to a lawyer and never appear before a judge. They are never officially charged, but are told straight away that they should confess to their crimes. Methods of coercion include being forced to stand in a cell overnight; if the detainee tries to rest, he receives a hail of blows. Then there are the beatings to the head and neck and the electrocutions. Any attempt by a detainee to protect himself will usually encounter more violence. Once in detention, it is often extremely difficult to get out; it usually depends either on being well connected or on paying a bribe (typically tens of thousands of dollars).

Why are human rights still regularly violated under the new regime, despite the new constitutional framework and all the efforts to improve the system? The answer is simple: because human rights are never protected merely by being enshrined in a constitution. There needs to be a monitoring system that constantly investigates and reports on security services, detention centres and the judicial process. And there needs to be an enforcement mechanism to ensure that human rights violations are punished. But Iraq's judicial system depends on one single institution – public prosecutors – to fulfil both functions. The system is inquisitorial, which means that judges question witnesses directly to seek out the information that the court requires to make a decision. In that sense, judges are considered to represent the interests of the state and of society. Public prosecutors need to be present throughout the process (from the time of arrest, through the collection of evidence, to the trial) in order to ensure that all procedural rules and the defendant's rights are upheld. Public prosecutors are therefore supposed to oversee not only the police, but also judges themselves in the exercise of their duties. The law governing public prosecutors has been on the books since 1979.[50]

In practice, prosecutors have been described as worse than useless in so far as defendants' rights are concerned. In order for them to be effective, prosecutors would have to be completely independent of the courts, the police, etc. But that type of independence is never respected: prosecutors mingle with judges, sipping tea and discussing cases in a way that is completely inappropriate.

Part of the problem stems from the manner in which judicial training is organized in Iraq. Law graduates seeking to become judges pass an entrance exam to be admitted to the judicial training institute. Once they are admitted, their careers will depend on their grades. The top students become judges; less successful students become less well-paid prosecutors. As a result, for decades, prosecutors have felt a deep sense of inferiority towards their former classmates, and have learned to submit themselves completely to their authority. Just as importantly, the Higher Judicial Council, which is responsible for managing the entire judiciary, is also responsible for managing prosecutors. Its leadership is almost entirely composed of judges, who do not look kindly on intrepid prosecutors accusing their colleagues of wrongdoing. This lack of institutional independence has essentially paralysed prosecutors, and the impact is plain to see. Prosecutors never raise any objections, even in the face of overwhelming evidence of abuse. An official at the ministry of justice who was responsible for working with serious offenders told me:

'I have never seen a public prosecutor do anything. They just stand idly by and never take any action, which has forced many lawyers and officials at the ministry to act on their own initiative to help some of the accused through the trial process.'[51]

The problems facing prisoners accused of ordinary crimes are rather different. Criminal defendants are often destitute and are not provided with adequate representation by the state. Usually only lawyers without any paid work agree to be appointed by the court. Some will take on dozens of cases at a time, so that they have only a few minutes to devote to any given brief. They can often be spotted shuffling through their papers during a trial, trying to make sense of the facts and the charge before the judge makes up his mind. As a consequence, many detainees are left without any real representation and get completely lost in the system.

None of this is a secret; it has been known to judges, legal advisers, court workers and policy makers for years. There are also many potential and recognized solutions to the problem. Possible small-scale reforms would include creating a separate training institute for prosecutors, redressing the salary imbalance, publishing statistics on their performance, etc. Further-reaching reforms would include abolishing public prosecutors altogether and imposing on investigatory judges an obligation to ensure that abuse does not take place. Another possibility would be to completely separate the institution of public prosecutor from the judiciary and to establish a new oversight body that would hold prosecutors accountable for any failures.

The reality, however, is that very little reform is likely to take place in the foreseeable future, because Iraq's current ruling elite will almost certainly not take any action. They are too concerned with engaging in political disputes that have little or no impact on ordinary people's lives; and anyway, they do not feel sufficient compassion for the accused and their families to act on their behalf.

Even those individuals who are most vulnerable are not immune from violence and apparently do not merit the state's protection. Iraq's Christian community in particular has been targeted for years, precisely because it is vulnerable and has had nowhere to turn.

Iraqi Christians have a proud history. Theirs is a story of brotherly integration with all their neighbours, though obviously this has not been unproblematic. As a community, Iraqi Christians are immensely proud of their contribution to Iraq's heritage; as individuals they are proud of their own achievements.

Christianity was introduced to Mesopotamia in the first century after Christ.[52] Christian poets contributed to the regional enlightenment, whether in the desert or in urban settings. Both during and after the Islamic expansion, Christians were generally protected, and came to occupy senior positions in the state bureaucracy. Several cities were planned by Christian architects under Muslim rule, including Kufa, just south of Baghdad. Christians also lived throughout the capital and were not relegated to particular neighbourhoods. Indeed it was quite common for Muslims to celebrate religious festivals together with their Christian neighbours.[53] In the modern state of Iraq, Christians were part and parcel of the intelligentsia and worked closely with their compatriots as journalists, senior public officials, men of religion, etc. During the British occupation, prominent Christians discouraged any discussion of an independent state for their community in the north and contributed hugely to the development of the state of Iraq as it is known today.[54] The community was estimated to have numbered half a million in 1975 and perhaps around 1.5 million in 2003.[55]

Like the rest of Iraq's population, Christians encountered violence and terrorism after 2003, but they suffered disproportionately. First, religion was often used by ordinary criminals as a pretext to target Christians, even when they were only interested in their cash and possessions. Secondly, as a small minority (around 3 per cent of the population) Christians were unable to defend themselves as the state broke down completely and the US occupation forces were unable (or unwilling) to protect anyone.

During the height of the violence in Baghdad and Mosul, as individual families no longer felt secure in their neighbourhoods, many fled to the countryside and their tribal territories. Even those families that had never spent any considerable time with their tribal brethren could still count on them for protection, if necessary. Thus, in 2006–08 many neighbourhoods in the capital were emptied; meanwhile many of the provinces that took in the internally displaced peoples witnessed a housing boom as a result. As mentioned above (Chapter 4), because Christians do not have tribal connections to rely on, they were far more vulnerable to attack. Their response was to flee the country in disproportionate numbers: an estimated 1 million Christians left the country in the years following the 2003 war, which means that they accounted for about a quarter of all refugees.

Baghdad's Christian community was targeted from the start of the war. Dora district, where Christians have always lived peacefully, was the scene of immense violence during the sectarian conflict, and the community was essentially eradicated. Churches were attacked, homes were destroyed, prominent members of the community were kidnapped and killed.

In 2008, it was Ninewa's turn. This province is home to some of Iraq's oldest Christian communities. Its churches are heritage sites, and are often visited by Muslim families seeking good fortune. Although they suffered from the very earliest days of the occupation, their situation deteriorated markedly in September 2008. For about ten days after 28 September, there was a series of murders and threats against Christian civilians; their homes were rigged with explosives and blown up. This resulted in the displacement of close to 2,000 families in just a few weeks. Most made their way to various villages on the Ninewa plain, including Tal Asquf. Under intense pressure from Iraqi and international groups to respond to the crisis, on 13 October the prime minister formed a committee of high-ranking officers, headed by Lieutenant General Ali Ghidan Majid, commander of Iraq's ground forces, to investigate the attacks and displacement of Christians from Mosul specifically, and from Ninewa generally, and to determine whether any security leaders had failed in their duties.

The committee completed its work on 20 October 2008, which is when the prime minister's office received the final report. The document, which was never published, confirmed that Iraqi security officials had failed to protect Christians and had ignored a number of warnings of imminent security threats. It also confirmed that, despite these failures, the same military unit had been responsible for protecting the area for over four years without any rotation.[56] Specific officers were identified as having failed to do their duty, but they were never held accountable. Worse still, the committee found that Ninewa's operations command did not have clear procedures to deal with the security crisis and that its officers did not seem to have any sound idea of what was happening in the area that was supposedly under their control. The committee also found that the province's security forces did not coordinate their activities with the governor, which resulted in more crime and an increasing number of displaced Christians. The committee recommended that the military unit responsible for the area be replaced as a matter of urgency, and that special investigators be commissioned to locate the criminals who had been intimidating members of the Christian community.

The findings of the report made no difference and the community was left to fend for itself. Attacks against Christians continued throughout 2008, 2009 and 2010 – well after violence in the rest of the country had abated – precisely because criminals were aware that no one was prepared to defend their interests. The violence peaked on 31 October 2010, when a brutal attack targeted the Our Lady of Salvation Church in the Karrada district of Baghdad. Several gunmen (the exact number is unknown, but it seems there were no more than twelve) entered the building during mass. They held the hundred or so worshippers hostage until Iraqi special forces raided the building. In the ensuing bloodbath, over forty Christians were killed. This massacre led to another exodus of relatives and friends of the deceased and wounded.

Some days later, I was at a conference in Amman which was attended by several senior Iraqi government officials. Asked to evaluate the state's performance generally, they showered themselves with praise, describing success after success, but making no mention of how the vulnerable were continuing to suffer and to flee the country in their thousands.

✻   ✻   ✻

Given the context, it should have come as no surprise that after ten years of attacks and abuse, the rates of violence rose generally in 2013, reaching their worst levels since 2008.[57] Although certain regional factors – including the conflict raging in neighbouring Syria – did have an effect, the principal reason for the increase was the never-ending series of policy failures by the state. The cycle of violence was reinvigorated by a sense of helplessness, of marginalization and of injustice at the state's brutal practices. A terrorist or a militiaman is never excused for his atrocities; the state, too, ought to shoulder responsibility for having fanned the flames of extremism at home.

CHAPTER SEVEN

THE RAVAGES OF CORRUPTION: THE SECOND INSURGENCY

Since 2003, Iraq has witnessed an alarming rise in corruption. The international watchdog organization Transparency International has ranked the country near the bottom of its global corruption perceptions index for three years running – in 2012, it came in at 169 out of 174. Billions of dollars have been embezzled and public investment projects have either been ignored or have floundered while the population has suffered.

Graft was so out of control in 2006 that Stuart Bowen, the US special inspector general for Iraq reconstruction, referred to it as the 'second insurgency'.[1] Corruption in today's Iraq, albeit more dramatic than in the past, continues a long tradition of exploitation of the people by political elites, and of grotesque economic disparities between the ruled and the ruling.

A number of factors have encouraged the phenomenon: the juxtaposition of the previous regime's selfishness with a decade of harsh deprivation caused by the sanctions; the sheer mass of capital that suddenly flowed into the country after the 2003 war; a breakdown in security and the criminal justice system that has allowed officials to operate in an environment of impunity; targeted assassinations of state officials and random violence, both of which have seriously hindered oversight agencies in their work; and gaps in the legal and institutional framework that was supposed to provide a check on government. Meanwhile, both government and parliament have been unwilling and unable to engage in the type of reform that would help to bring corruption under control, and have even sought to manipulate the phenomenon for political ends.

The impact on the average Iraqi has been enormous. The state has not just stagnated; it has regressed by leaps and bounds – at a time when much of the rest of the world has moved forward. Government funds have been diverted from those areas that are in urgent need of reform and improvement, including the sectors of education, health and agriculture. Corruption is so widespread that it even impacts on citizen security, to the extent that security forces are obliged to use a useless piece of plastic to protect themselves and the country from car bombs (see Introduction).

The government has become skilled at exploiting constitutional, legal and institutional gaps to avoid any form of accountability. Also, senior officials have grown accustomed to manipulating whatever investigative bodies exist, in order to threaten their political rivals. Given that Iraq's annual state budget continues to grow year by year (the 2013 budget was the largest in the entire Middle East, second only to Saudi Arabia), this negative trend bodes ill for the future.

CORRUPTION AND WASTE PRIOR TO 2003

Iraq was certainly no stranger to corruption before 2003. There were many dimensions to the phenomenon, most important of which was that unlimited funds were available to Saddam Hussein, his family and his closest associates to indulge in whatever earthly pleasures they desired. Presidential orders made state funds, properties and palaces available to a privileged few for their personal use and enjoyment. By way of example, in the 1980s several large properties were developed on a tract of land that ran alongside the Tigris river south of Tikrit, supposedly to accommodate Arab heads of state and officials who were due to travel to Iraq for a summit meeting (each of the properties was built in accordance with a specific Arab country's architectural traditions). The summit never took place and the guests never came; instead the properties were made available to the president, his relatives and a select band of officials. (Following the 2003 war and after Salah al-Din's first elected provincial council suffered some security breaches, the council's members moved into the properties and used millions of dollars of state money to refurbish them.)

State funds were also used to prosecute the president's narrow and petty rivalries throughout the region (given that archives have been destroyed and many of the main players are either dead or dying, it is almost impossible to know how much of Iraq's wealth was wasted in this manner). A case in point was Iraq's provision of military support to Lebanese militias during the 1975–91 civil war, purely because they were engaged in a conflict with Iraq's Syrian rivals. Not only was this not a legitimate use of state funds, but it was done carelessly. The Iraqis would ask the Lebanese militiamen what type of equipment they required, but not the quantities needed. They would then send over large amounts without ever investigating whether their sizeable donations were actually required.[2] The same militias were also in receipt of material support from Israel, but the Israelis required specific details of the exact quantities of each type of unit requested.

Setting aside high-level corruption, Baathist rule did combat corruption by state officials, for two main reasons. First, like many unelected governments in the Arab region and the developing world, the party had to ground its rule on some form of legitimacy. Although it pretended to enjoy the people's support, that claim was always frivolous: it had seized power through a coup d'état in 1968 and only allowed parliamentary elections after 1980, when the Communist party had been forced underground. Legitimacy therefore had to be derived from other sources. As with many countries in the region, Iraq relied on international and internal sources of legitimacy.

On the one hand, internationally it claimed to be working to address a number of genuine concerns (while simultaneously it strove to ensure that those concerns would always remain unsatisfied). It was supposedly committed to both Arab unity and the Palestinian cause: in its rhetoric it promoted both of those goals (though in fact it pursued a number of policies that militated against them, engaging in vitriolic and infantile disputes with its neighbours and promoting individuals who worked against unity at every turn).

On the other hand, as was the case in many socialist republics at the time, Iraq invested heavily in economic and social development. The state had to be seen to be engaging in major construction and infrastructure projects at all times, in order to justify its existence; the projects would provide employment and improve standards of living. They also cost a lot of money, but that ceased to be a problem for the Baathist government once the oil industry was nationalized and the price of oil rocketed in 1973 (see Chapter 1). The thinking was that the population would be willing to sacrifice their freedoms if they were given good employment opportunities and if their country was seen to be a major player in the region.

In the context, then, it was dangerous for civil servants (and even most ministers) to engage in corruption prior to 1991. First of all, stealing state funds was tantamount to stealing from the head of state, given that the treasury operated at his personal discretion. Secondly, to engage in corruption meant reducing the funds that were available for development, which would damage the state and the Baath party's internal legitimacy. To work against development was to work against the Baath party, which in turn was to work against the president. Unsurprisingly, therefore, the state cracked down ruthlessly on graft by anyone outside a small inner circle and put in place a number of mechanisms to curb corruption. Given that all Iraqi citizens were expected to report any illicit behaviour to the Mukhabarat, the scope for corruption within the country was often limited. The best opportunities presented themselves during foreign trips, particularly to a contractor's facilities. As a result, a Baath party cadre would always accompany every mission abroad. He (or she) would always attempt to disguise himself as someone with technical knowledge – someone who was legitimately part of the mission – but it was always clear who was there merely for reporting purposes: usually that person would not participate in the substance of the discussions and would keep very quiet.[3]

More importantly, however, there were harsh penalties imposed on anyone who was even suspected of being involved in corruption, waste or mismanagement. Depending on the situation, acts of corruption could lead to the death penalty: a significant number of officials who were convicted of corruption-related crimes were executed.[4] In one such case, an official was found to have taken bribes from a UK company that manufactured buses and was publicly hanged. There were other officials who were executed for gross negligence, including senior officials in the ministry of health who were found to have allowed the import of medicines that were unfit for human consumption, and agricultural officials who imported spoilt foodstuffs.

The upshot was that officials were afraid to take bribes; on the downside, though, few would take even a minor decision without referring the matter to the relevant minister. Thus, although Iraq was relatively clean at the time, bureaucratic procedures had ground to a halt. In the words of one Lebanese businessman who had significant commercial interests in Iraq:

> I would ask for my Iraqi counterpart, who was a state official, to grant me a change order because of changed circumstances. He would review the request and would tell me orally that he had no reason to object and that he agreed that the change was necessary, but he would refuse to sign it, because he was simply too afraid of making a mistake. He would send it

to his director general, who would in turn send it to the minister. Every small matter would take ages, because they were all too afraid to take a decision and to make mistakes.[5]

Just as importantly, Iraqis themselves, as a people, were generally opposed to the notion of corruption, theft and waste. Despite regular political upheavals and the virtual absence of any form of democracy, the country benefited from heavy investment in education, agriculture and infrastructure (all financed by oil revenues) that led to significant economic growth. Iraqis were generally conscious and proud of their place as a developing nation and rejected practices such as sectarianism and theft as regressive and unworthy of a nation such as Iraq. Although citizens by and large eschewed religion at the time, corruption was often referred to using the religious term *haram* ('forbidden'). The country's generally improved economic situation was obviously an important factor in encouraging that moral stance. Although Iraq was still a very unequal country, the growing middle class was increasingly self-confident, and this determined society's values.

Everything changed following the Gulf War of 1991. GDP and the annual state budget plummeted. State employees' salaries were cut to just a few dollars a month, while unemployment soared. Although its engineers and scientists managed to rebuild part of the infrastructure within a few months of the end of the war, the country was but a shadow of its former self. Iraq's foreign policy was in complete tatters; its army was severely diminished; and its regional and international standing had completely collapsed. The regime had lost all its sources of legitimacy. Those who had continued to 'believe' in the regime prior to the war were now devastated. Millions were suddenly thrust below the poverty line and were reduced to living on handouts from the state and from the fortunate few who could make ends meet.

The change was reflected even within the regime's inner circle: with collapsing revenues and international sanctions, senior officials actively sought out new sources of income. After the Oil for Food Programme was instituted by the United Nations, senior Iraqi officials demanded (in violation of the sanctions programme) that all companies either purchasing oil or selling goods to Iraq must pay an undeclared commission into Iraqi-controlled accounts in Jordan and elsewhere. Iraq received $1.8 billion in illicit income during this period, much of it used to finance the grotesque lifestyle that Saddam Hussein's family had grown accustomed to.[6] Inequality in Iraq was probably at its worst during this period: while the average state employee was paid a mere $2 a month, luxury goods were still being imported to satisfy the cravings of a greedy few. With the population suffering oppression from within and without, by March 2003 any sense of obligation to the state felt by the ordinary citizen had clearly dissipated.

A POLITICAL SYSTEM THAT ENCOURAGES GRAFT

By 2003, the scene was set for a monumental upheaval in Iraq's social fabric. After more than a decade of grinding poverty and inequality, the country was transformed by the US and its Iraqi allies into the world's most recent incarnation of the Wild West, in which corruption and incompetence reigned supreme. The US had successfully organized massive aid programmes in the past – most notably the Marshall Plan, through which it sought to prevent the spread of communism in Europe. Although it is impossible to completely prevent corruption, this plan was relatively free of fraud because of the deep ideological and security-related concerns that underlined the entire effort. Many of the individuals involved considered that freedom itself was under threat from the Soviet juggernaut, and viewed corruption as tantamount to treason.

In Iraq, there was no such ideology or threat. Very few of those who were involved in the war and reconstruction effort understood why the US had invaded the country in the first place; and after a few years of occupation, almost everyone was certain that the whole venture had been at best a distraction from the real security challenges elsewhere, and at worst (to borrow the words of novelist Ben Fountain) 'a bullshit war'.[7] Even to those US officials who still mistakenly clung to the belief that Iraq had been involved in 9/11, the likelihood of the country overrunning American cities was preposterous. That, combined with decades (at least) of prejudice against Iraq, Arabs and Muslims (plus the fact that no one was really checking to see what was happening), made the prospect of stealing funds seem somewhat innocuous.

After the CPA was established, it was given possession of incredible sums of money, which it was empowered to spend in more or less any way it saw fit. United Nations Security Council Resolution 1483, issued just weeks after the occupation started, established the Development Fund for Iraq (DFI), to be financed through unspent funds from the Oil for Food Programme, and indicated that this money would have to be audited, which it was. However, there was no indication of whether or how corruption, incompetence, waste and mismanagement would be punished, so essentially any amount of audits would make no difference.

After more than thirteen years of international sanctions, billions of dollars were suddenly flowing into the country unimpeded, most of it in cash (wads of which were distributed all over the country by incredulous American officials to placate potential enemies). To make matters worse, neither Iraqi, nor American nor British procurement rules were followed by the US and UK occupation authorities. Massive contracts were granted without competitive tender, without proper instructions or planning, and were paid for in cash. Iraqis could not help but notice the absurdity of what was happening: the supply of electricity did not improve, sewage and garbage continued to line the streets, and schools that were scheduled to be rebuilt were simply given a fresh lick of paint. Even after the world's journalists wrote scathing articles about the CPA's lax methods, those same practices continued – well after the CPA was dissolved.

In 2004, after Iraq regained sovereignty, control over the DFI was transferred to the Iraqi government, which in turn authorized the US government to administer the DFI funds. The US department of defense received $9.19 billion from the DFI from 2004 to 2010. An audit by the special inspector general for Iraq reconstruction, carried out in July 2010, discovered that $8.7 billion (around 96 per cent) of that amount was not properly accounted for. The audit found that the department of defense had followed neither the US treasury's rules, nor its own. It concluded that the 'breakdown in controls left the funds vulnerable to inappropriate uses and undetected loses'.[8] In other words, the US government cannot say with any degree of certainty what happened to $8.7 billion of Iraq's money.

The consequences were appalling: schools that were supposedly rebuilt were left in ruins; projects that were supposed to create employment were in fact staffed by ghost employees, with the salaries being pocketed by a handful of individuals; factories that were built at great expense lay idle and were eventually stripped for spare parts because a regular electricity supply had not been provided. And the failures continued for years.[9] A project to develop Fallujah's sewerage system that commenced in 2004 and was originally budgeted at $33 million was found in late 2011 to have cost more than $101 million, even though it served only a third of the homes originally intended.[10] As late as August 2010, more than seven years after the alarm was first raised about the CPA's poor accounting, a slaughterhouse that had been funded by the US on behalf of the DFI to the tune of $5.6 million was found to be a shambles. An audit concluded that the instructions were 'poorly written and confusing', and that the contractor had been overpaid. It also found that, nineteen months after the contract had been signed, the project was still lacking a reliable power source, potable water and sewerage.[11]

THE FAILURE TO ENACT REFORM

When the CPA was disbanded and replaced by Ayad Allawi's nominally sovereign interim Iraqi administration in June 2004, corruption-related problems continued to accumulate. The flow of capital into Iraq was accelerating and was now officially under local control, even if everyone knew that US officials still had enormous influence at all levels. In May 2005, Prime Minister Ibrahim al-Jaafari's government formally took on the role of forming and implementing policy on all issues, including anti-corruption. Although US advisers still had an important role to play, a line had clearly been drawn in the sand: outside security-related matters, the US could no longer impose any specific decisions or outcomes on the Iraqis. It had been shown over the previous year that many of the Iraqis who had been placed in control of the state were just as incompetent as their CPA colleagues, and that many had taken advantage of the lax oversight standards to siphon off billions in state funds. From then on, there was a clear onus on al-Jaafari's administration (and al-Maliki's after him) to shake off the legacy of the CPA and the first Iraqi government and to crack down on corruption through legal reform and stringent enforcement mechanisms. It was not rocket science: if the will was there, the country's leaders could achieve this objective without significant difficulty.

It turns out, however, that there was no appetite for reform of any kind, and that the gaps in the legal framework that the Iraqis had inherited from the CPA were to remain in place for another ten years at least. Although the CPA's much-reported penchant for allowing ideology and political nepotism to drive policy is now almost universally considered to have contributed to its mismanagement,[12] the failure of successive Iraqi administrations to redress the administrative framework they inherited is more difficult to understand and explain. The lack of action on corruption is at best a powerful illustration of how inept the constitutional framework is – and at worst proof that the ruling elite has a vested interest in keeping a corrupt system in place.

Before the 2003 war, Iraq's legal system included a number of institutions, including criminal investigators and a supreme audit organization. The CPA instituted reforms which created a number of loopholes. The first of these came in January 2004, when it created Iraq's first anti-corruption agency, the integrity commission, as an umbrella institution to coordinate all anti-corruption efforts. This commission was responsible for enforcing basic integrity measures (according to which, for example, all senior government officials must publicly disclose their annual income and assets), anti-corruption laws and public service standards,[13] and for investigating corruption cases and presenting these to an investigative judge.[14] As with many other new institutions, the commission was established at a time when the state was disintegrating and public officials were being targeted by insurgents and criminals. In addition, the commission, which was modelled on elements of the US system and had no precedent in Iraqi administrative culture, had a poorly defined mandate that created confusion.[15] As a result, it remained ineffective for its first four years and came to mirror the state it was seeking to cleanse of corruption.[16] Its staff and administration developed undesirable practices in order to survive, including the hiring of individuals who had falsified their resumes and had questionable backgrounds.[17]

There was some improvement after the reduction in violence in 2008, but a number of fundamental difficulties remained. Most seriously, its inability to access specific government departments meant that it was forced to rely on the inspectors general in individual ministries to carry out investigations on its behalf,[18] while its own role was limited to desk reviews.[19] Thus the results of any investigation and the quality of information depended on external factors, such as the reliability and independence of the inspectors general – both the subject of repeated criticism.

As with many other institutions, the commission was also vulnerable to political interference, in particular by the prime minister. In common with all other senior state positions, whenever a new director was appointed to the commission, parliament was required to confirm the appointment; in order to guarantee a certain amount of independence from the government, parliament was also the only institution that was mandated to remove a director from office. By 2013, the commission had had four directors, none of whom had been confirmed by parliament and the first three of whom had all been forced from their positions by the government.

In September 2007, Judge Radhi Hamza al-Radhi, the then director, had accused the security forces of complicity in large-scale corruption and of attacking his home.[20] The judge fled to Washington, DC, where he testified before several congressional committees (and many news outlets). The government then appointed Mousa Faraj to be the commission's acting chief. He was dismissed (by the government) a few weeks later, when he began repeating many of his predecessor's allegations,[21] in the process receiving significant support from US anti-corruption officials.[22] His successor in January 2008, Judge Rahim al-Ugaili, was likewise forced from office following immense government pressure (see Chapter 7).

Another body, the Board of Supreme Audit, was already in existence at the time of the 2003 war. Established in 1927, it had been responsible for auditing and inspecting the state's accounts, evaluating its performance in operating expenditure and implementing projects, and detecting 'corruption, fraud, waste, abuse and inefficiency'.[23] To this end, it had the power to access classified state documents relating to public expenditure and to carry out on-site inspections of government offices. Importantly, this board had the authority to refer any suspected criminal activity directly to the courts. Although reliable data is lacking on how it performed before 2003, there is substantial agreement that it did so professionally and relatively effectively in difficult circumstances.[24]

In April 2004, the CPA issued a new order that required the board, for the first time, to refer allegations or evidence of criminal activity to the relevant ministry's inspector general or to the integrity commission, rather than to the courts.[25] The order also stipulated that the board should refer specific requests for information to the inspectors general, instead of obtaining the information directly from the ministries.[26]

Even at the best of times, the CPA reforms would have significantly increased the number of bureaucratic hurdles to be cleared to secure a conviction for a corruption-related crime. However, the CPA forced the board to work through newly created bodies at a time when they had hardly any staff, when violence against public officials was rising, and when public expenditure was increasing rapidly. Given its reduced mandate and the climate of violence, the board made little effort to adapt to the changed environment and the emergence of organized crime in the state apparatus. It continued to audit state institutions diligently, but rarely carried out specific investigations into the impact the criminal elements had on the state's finances.[27]

The last of the CPA's innovations was to establish the inspectors general in 2004, modelling these on the US's own anti-corruption framework.[28] Each ministry now has an inspector general's office, which carries out investigations and audits of the ministry.[29] In theory, the inspectors general support both the integrity commission and the BSA by carrying out specific audits and investigations on their behalf.[30] However a number of structural flaws have impaired the whole system. For instance, the reform failed to provide for coordination between individual inspectors, which partly contributed to important differences in the way they carry out their work.[31] As a result, the inspectors lack any standard operating procedures, so that individual auditors and investigators have no instructions about how specific tasks should be carried out and what each task's objective should be. Lacking capacity, inspectors general remain largely passive, acting only on specific allegations, despite their presence in each ministry.[32]

The law also fails to clarify the exact process by which individual inspectors are recruited and dismissed.[33] This, combined with the obvious interest of individual ministers in controlling the process, has led to the appointment of unqualified personnel, selected solely on the basis of their relationship with the minister in question.[34] There was a highly publicized incident in late 2008, when the first al-Maliki government dismissed several inspectors who had been appointed prior to its formation in 2006, sparking accusations of political interference and further undermining the institution's credibility and effectiveness.[35] Efforts were made to reform recruitment, including by placing it in the hands of a special committee headed by the integrity commission. The problem was that the new process was non-binding, so that some inspectors continued to be recruited through non-competitive processes.[36] Ministers also had significant leeway in dismissing inspectors, which served as a powerful disincentive for the inspectors to take an aggressive stance on corruption.[37]

These difficulties were identified by Iraqi and international experts at the outset. After the reforms, officials at the BSA complained that their hands were tied and they were not provided with support. Experts noted that the CPA's reforms forced the state's oversight agencies to report to each other interminably before a matter could be referred to the courts. A bureaucratic nightmare had been created just when violence and corruption were on the rise and when there was a desperate need for legal clarity to allow existing institutions to function effectively. As early as 2007, a number of expert organizations suggested solutions, many of which were fairly straightforward (e.g. allowing the BSA to refer matters directly to the courts). But all their initiatives were met with faint smiles and stony silence from parliament, which had no interest in enacting any meaningful reform. The cracks in the system may have been obvious to anyone, but parliament did not feel compelled to act.

The clearest illustration of this failure is the fact that it took the government eight years to repeal article 136(b) of the criminal procedure code. That article stated that an investigative judge could not prosecute a state official without the relevant minister's prior permission,[38] which meant that ministers could unilaterally grant their staff immunity.[39] Article 136(b) was actually introduced by the Baath party prior to 2003 so that ministers could ensure that strategic departments were not left understaffed (since anyone accused of corruption would immediately be suspended); the provision was in fact almost never used to block investigations or prosecutions, and was merely taken to mean that a minister had to provide his signature before proceedings could begin. After the 2003 war, the provision took on a new meaning and was universally regarded as an invitation to steal. Although ministers used it hundreds of times – it is impossible to say precisely how often – between 2003 and 2011 to protect political appointees who had stolen vast sums against prosecution,[40] and despite enormous internal and international pressure after 2004 to repeal the provision, successive governments refused to do so. Parliament finally acted on 18 April 2011. Despite continued government objections, the amendment came into force in July of that year. The fact that government had resisted this straightforward but vital reform for so long is a clear indication of its priorities.

Leaving aside this notable (though purely symbolic) instance of progress, no further effort to curb corruption is likely to achieve even a modicum of success until the many other existing legal loopholes are closed. For example, as has already been mentioned, there is no law to compel political parties to publish their accounts or to disclose the sources of their income. Many parties have extensive property portfolios and operate costly satellite television channels, yet they need not provide reliable information on how they have financed these holdings. No one even knows where the parties hold their cash, if they have bank accounts or in what countries those accounts might exist. This has created a general perception that they are largely funded through corruption. For years, civil society organizations, jurists and senior officials have been calling for a law on political parties that would oblige all parties to open their accounts to public scrutiny. But government and parliament have largely ignored those calls. Until an effective law on political parties is passed, anti-corruption efforts are a waste of time.

Draft legislation to reform other, less controversial and more technical aspects of the anti-corruption framework has been in parliament since 2007, but has been progressing at snail's pace due to the ruling elite's lack of interest. In fact, instead of seeking to change or repeal laws that nurture corruption, the government and parliament have striven to repeal a series of draconian Baath-era legal provisions that impose harsh penalties on any public official convicted of (or even under investigation for) corruption. Thus, despite soaring corruption, many of the substantive legal amendments since 2003 have been designed to soften the penalties rather than close the loopholes.

A PARLIAMENT PARALYSED

So parliament has been unwilling to engage in reform. Between 2005 and 2009, it was also precluded from exercising its constitutional obligation to exercise oversight, since it was essentially indistinguishable from government. The process of negotiating the first governments of al-Jaafari and al-Maliki was challenging and time consuming, and there was no appetite for allowing parliamentarians (who, within Iraq's rigid and deeply hierarchical party structures, are looked down upon by ministers) to disturb the delicate balance that had been struck. In any event, even if MPs had wanted to engage in some form of oversight in those early years, they would have had considerable difficulty, given how little experience they had in parliamentary affairs and their lack of understanding of how the state functioned. In particular, most parliamentarians were unaware of the BSA's work and did not realize that they were supposed to be reviewing the many reports it was issuing to them, in order to assess whether government was performing properly. The BSA was designed in part to act as parliament's eyes and ears, and it was essential that whatever information is gathered by the former should be transmitted seamlessly to the latter. Without the BSA, MPs would have to rely on rumour and media spin, particularly as Baghdad was too dangerous to have many face-to-face meetings with senior officials.

In fairness, if the MPs were unaware of what was happening around them, this was also because the BSA viewed parliament as an upstart institution with no sense or understanding of what oversight meant. It therefore paid scant attention to its relationship with individual MPs, legislative and oversight committees or the institution as a whole. In practice, this meant that the BSA did not bother to draw the attention of MPs to any of the reports it was producing. It simply couriered the reports to parliament with a compliments slip, and never called to make sure that they had been received – let alone read and understood. At a meeting that I attended in 2008, the leaders of the finance and economics committees admitted to the BSA's head that (more than half way into their terms in office) they had not read a single one of his agency's reports. They started by complaining that the reports were too long, to which the BSA's head responded (only half jokingly) that he was prepared to make audio recordings if they preferred. They could not even agree on how many reports the BSA had sent parliament that year. Without the knowledge contained in those reports, there was no way MPs could understand what the government was doing – assuming any of them were interested.

As noted earlier (Chapter 5), the only time the delicate balance between parliament and government was disturbed was following the 2009 local elections, when a number of parties were fearful of being eradicated by al-Maliki's new State of Law alliance. They took control of parliament and activated its oversight capacity, hoping to withdraw confidence from al-Maliki's closest allies and to commence criminal proceedings against them; if a sufficient number could have been publicly humiliated, that might have reinvigorated al-Maliki's opponents' chances in the coming parliamentary elections.

Mahmoud al-Mashhadani, a leading figure in the Tawafuq alliance, had been appointed speaker of parliament in 2006 and had prevented the legislature from exercising any oversight of government for almost three years. He was ousted in December 2008 for a combination of reasons, not least of which was that most MPs had become exasperated with his incompetent administration and eccentric outbursts. The post remained vacant for months, as various parties vied to control parliament. However, when the January 2009 election results were announced, a number of forces within parliament converged to make sure that an opponent of al-Maliki's became the new speaker.

Ayad al-Samarai, of the Iraqi Islamic Party, was the main candidate, thanks to his reputation for professionalism and efficiency. Al-Maliki saw in him a potentially dangerous opponent, and did what he could to prevent his appointment; however he only managed to delay it. Al-Samarai was elected in April 2009, and the floodgates opened for parliament to be used as a political weapon by the losers in the local elections against the winners.

The first person they set their sights on was Faleh al-Sudani, minister of trade and one of al-Maliki's closest allies. Prior to the 2003 war, the ministry had been responsible for making food rations available to citizens by purchasing staple goods on international markets and making them available to all Iraqis without restriction. This service was undermined after 2003 – partly as a result of a restructuring of the national economy and partly as a result of graft. The ministry started by cutting back on the quantities of rice that were distributed to the population. After a number of other items were cut, it was discovered that some of the goods still being distributed were actually contaminated. Iraq's millions of disenfranchised poor were the hardest hit, as many had no alternative but to eat what they were given by the state. Rumours circulated throughout the country that international traders were offloading their expired goods on Iraq with the knowledge of the ministry, which had called off its health inspectors in exchange for significant kickbacks. Al-Sudani had operated with impunity for years. When one of his inspectors general questioned specific practices, he was promptly reassigned to the Iraqi embassy in China as a commercial attaché in November 2006.[41] For years there was no accountability and no transparency, until the web of silence that protected the minister was suddenly rent asunder.

As the violence receded and it became possible again to travel around the capital, a number of investigators and auditors decided that they could no longer keep quiet about the ministry. They carried out aggressive on-site investigations, insisting on being given access to incriminating documents that revealed significant irregularities. During one such investigation, someone must have realized that the new attitude meant trouble: as the auditor left the building and climbed into her car, a live grenade found its way in as well. The auditor survived the explosion, but her body was peppered with shrapnel.[42] Importantly, however, her sacrifice was not in vain: she and her colleagues at the integrity commission managed to accumulate significant evidence against the ministry's senior staff.[43] Arrest warrants were issued against several senior officials, including two of the minister's brothers. Security forces visited the ministry on 29 April 2009 to make the arrests, but the suspects put up a fight and there was an exchange of gunfire.[44] Most of the suspects managed to escape, but the security forces arrested Sabah al-Sudani, Faleh al-Sudani's brother, on 9 May 2009.[45]

It was in this context that parliament called Faleh al-Sudani before a plenary session to answer a string of questions relating to allegations of corruption. He was accused of embezzling funds that were supposed to finance the state's ration system. In particular, he was accused of stealing millions of dollars that should have been used to purchase and distribute cooking oil; of importing sugar and grain that was unfit for human consumption; of neglecting to take action against corrupt officials in his ministry; and of ignoring the fact that many trucks transporting foodstuffs across the country had disappeared. His accusers also claimed that, as a result, for years several provinces had not received any foodstuffs from the ministry.[46]

Al-Sudani appeared before parliament on 16 and 17 May 2009. Sheikh Sabah al-Saadi MP, a well-known anti-corruption campaigner from the al-Fadhila party, led an aggressive interrogation session at which all these matters (and many others) were raised. The minister appeared not to take the process seriously and refused to answer most of the questions on the grounds that they were too detailed. But he had clearly misread the tea leaves: his assumption was that the arrangement that had been in place for the past three years remained in place, and that the government would come to his defence. It had not dawned on him that a majority of parliamentarians were fighting for their political survival and that they were using the one institution that they controlled to eliminate their rivals.

Eventually he did realize, however: he resigned on 25 May and booked himself on two flights – one to Amman in the morning and the other to the Emirates in the afternoon.[47] He boarded the second plane, hoping that anyone seeking to arrest him would be looking for him on the first flight. His plane took off, but the pilot was ordered to turn around. Al-Sudani was forced to disembark and was arrested for financial and administrative corruption.[48] It was the first time in years that a minister had been held to account for his actions.

Parliamentarians were energized. Here was an opportunity to lock up all their enemies and to increase their own chances of being returned to parliament in the coming elections. They now indicated that the ministers of foreign affairs, natural resources, finance, transport and the interior would all be called to answer charges of mismanagement of public funds and/or substandard performance.

The government baulked at what it maintained was intolerable interference in its work and politicization of the oversight process. Khaled Attiyah, the deputy speaker and al-Maliki's most senior ally in parliament at the time, bluntly accused the 'losers' in the local elections of seeking to punish the 'winners'. The preparations for the next round of hearings were well under way when, on 12 June 2009, Harith al-Ubaidi, one of al-Samarai's closest associates, became the first Iraqi MP in years to be assassinated. He was killed just after Friday prayers by a lone gunman, who blew himself up as he was about to be apprehended by al-Ubaidi's bodyguards.

No evidence has ever been presented to indicate who might have been responsible for the killing. However, it is undoubtedly the case that the assassination put the dampers on parliamentary activity. As soon as news of the killing spread, the entire enterprise ground to a halt and no further ministers were called before parliament. Meanwhile, al-Sudani was replaced by another of al-Maliki's close allies.

The entire episode is symptomatic of what is wrong with Iraq's politics. Under the new constitution, the country's system of oversight is broadly based on the Westminster model, but in the latter ministers are never called to give evidence before any of the House of Commons committees (not even the powerful public accounts committee) – precisely in order to avoid any politicization (or even the appearance of politicization) of the process. It is taken for granted that the government would leap to the defence of any of its members, which would cause the entire system to collapse. Instead, public servants, who remain in their posts regardless of who is in power, are called to provide evidence – mostly to discuss the efficiency of their ministry's work and whether the taxpayer has obtained value for money.

In 2009, oversight in Iraq took on a completely different dimension. Since corruption is the result of both an institutional and a legislative breach, it is pointless for parliament to deal with corruption's outward manifestation without first tackling the underlying cause. It should have been obvious that, in the context, a vacant ministerial position would merely be filled by someone from the same crop of corrupt politicians. A more effective approach, which would also have helped parliament avoid accusations of electoral posturing, would have been for it to reduce the scope for corruption by requiring all political parties, politicians and officials to declare their financial interests; to set out in detail the procedures to be followed by anti-corruption bodies; and to defend their independence from the bodies that they are overseeing. Instead, the parliamentary majority sought to force its main opponents from office and into prison. What many saw as a victory for parliamentary oversight and for government accountability was actually nothing more than a political vendetta, which had no impact on public wellbeing.

In any event, following the March 2010 elections, another government of national unity was formed, which renewed the arrangement by which parliament would not hold individual ministers responsible for their actions. Parliament would not engage in reform, and would not exercise any oversight. It would only move to protect its own existence, which was why, in summer 2012, a near majority of parliamentarians threatened to withdraw their confidence in al-Maliki, in response to his increasingly autocratic tendencies and his refusal to name ministers of defence and the interior. When the MPs failed to muster enough votes, even the idea of forcing al-Maliki to appear before parliament merely to answer questions was dropped. Once again, the initiative was never about improving government's performance; it was all about politicians trying to save their own skins in a volatile environment.

Coincidentally, at just the same time, a court of appeal sentenced al-Sudani (who had fled to the United Kingdom) to seven years in prison for corruption-related crimes. He subsequently scoffed at the court's decision, saying it was not worth the paper it was written on as he was a UK passport holder and could not be extradited to Iraq.

Naturally, none of these events inspired the government or parliament to enact any major reform of the country's anti-corruption framework, which suffers from all the same problems that the CPA left behind when it was dissolved in 2004.

GOVERNMENT MANIPULATION

Not only was parliament emasculated, but the government itself created opportunities for corruption, preventing specific investigations from proceeding and using corruption and other forms of mismanagement as a political weapon against its opponents.

In most cases, even when some agency or other amassed information on corrupt practices, government intimidation ensured that the relevant files were allowed to gather dust. Senior government officials and politicians would occasionally publicly embrace the prosecution of a particular act of corruption in order to convey the impression that they were being tough on graft; but they allowed more egregious violations to go unpunished, either because it was politically expedient to do so, or because it served their personal interests.

Ahmed al-Chalabi was one of Iraq's most ambitious and least popular politicians. By 2010, many of his fellow elites had decided that he was more trouble than he was worth. In particular, his continued control over, and manipulation of, the de-Baathification process was a major nuisance that poisoned the country's political atmosphere. It was just a matter of time before senior elites moved against him.

The move came in May 2011, when the government gained control of the Trade Bank of Iraq. This bank, established in 2003 as an independent government agency, is a vital artery for international transactions and lines of credit, and al-Chalabi (notwithstanding his questionable earlier experience in international banking) had played a major role in setting it up and managing it. He had Hussein al-Uzri, his great-nephew and close associate, appointed as its director.[49] In May 2011, the government accused al-Uzri of irregular practices and corruption, and took the bank under its control. The government's accusations were based on investigations begun in 2007 and that had been going on ever since.[50]

At almost the same time, on 26 May 2011, one of al-Chalabi's closest allies, Ali Faisal al-Lami, (nominally) the director of the de-Baathification commission, was assassinated in Palestine Street in downtown Baghdad.

Many officials interpreted these two events as somehow linked, constituting a multi-front campaign to marginalize al-Chalabi.[51] Similarly, throughout 2011, the State of Law alliance raised allegations that had been made against the Independent High Electoral Commission's senior officials in an effort to have them impeached in parliament and replaced. While many MPs from other blocs agreed with the allegations, they opposed the initiative, fearing that it would enable al-Maliki's allies to dominate the commission's future composition.

More serious, perhaps, was the manner in which the government seized control of the integrity commission. In January 2008, after his only two predecessors had been forced from their jobs, Judge Rahim al-Ugaili was appointed the commission's acting head. Although (as mentioned above) the law requires any individual appointed to the position to be confirmed by parliament, so as to afford him or her immunity against political interference, al-Ugaili's appointment was never referred to the legislature, so for the next few years he was obliged to operate under constant threat of dismissal by al-Maliki. During his time in post, al-Ugaili was applauded by Iraqi and international officials alike, who praised his efforts to cleanse the commission of corruption, sectarianism and the political influence. They also expressed admiration for the commission's increasing professionalism in investigating graft and in reporting its findings on its website and in the press.

Privately, al-Ugaili would voice exasperation at his position and the lack of success in dealing with high-level corruption. Senior politicians were untouchable and were preventing any real progress on graft. Whenever his staff was about to finger a specific individual, senior officials would threaten to have him replaced, citing his supposed incompetence. Things came to a head in 2011, when investigators at the integrity commission and the Board of Supreme Audit discovered that various ministries had entered into contracts with hundreds of shell companies that were registered abroad, and that those companies were all linked with political parties and senior officials.

Procurement laws required all government tenders to be carried out openly and according to relatively strict and transparent regulations. However, the commission discovered that ministries were circumventing these rules by entering into 'cooperation agreements' with the shell companies, without any competition or oversight.[52] For the most part, the companies had no staff to speak of and no capacity to fulfil the contracts. Consequently, not only were the political parties profiting directly from these contracting procedures, but most of the contracts were never actually fulfilled, despite the fact that the contract value was always paid by the ministries. When the commission sought to commence prosecutions in the courts, officials again suggested having al-Ugaili replaced on the grounds of corruption and incompetence. The courts also refused to hear the cases, almost certainly because they feared the repercussions. Under the circumstances, al-Ugaili resigned on 9 September 2011 in protest against the political pressure brought to bear. Thus to date, three commission chiefs have either resigned or been fired – all during al-Maliki's time in office.

In fact, al-Ugaili's resignation worsened an already desperate situation. A few days after he made his announcement, on 24 September 2011, parliament snapped into action and passed a new integrity commission law. A draft had been on the table for years, and Iraqi organizations, departments and analysts (as well as international bodies) had been begging for it to be passed, but all to no avail. Suddenly, the matter became urgent, as parliament realized that al-Maliki could appoint any successor to al-Ugaili that he pleased. The new mechanism stipulated that the head of the commission could only appointed by parliament; the prime minister and the government would have no say in the matter.[53]

MPs were jubilant at what they perceived to be a victory over al-Maliki. And yet, just a few days later, al-Maliki ignored the new law and appointed Judge Alaa Jawad Hamid, a docile and pliant official. In the period following his appointment, the commission's investigators and officials complained that all matters, including training sessions abroad, were being referred by the new head to the prime minister's office for approval.[54] In 2013, two years after his appointment, a western diplomat based in Baghdad said of Judge

Hamid that 'he has blocked all of the commission's work'.[55] The commission was weakened and, in case anyone needed any reminding, parliament's irrelevance was highlighted once again.

UNCARING (OR INCAPABLE) INTERNATIONAL ASSISTANCE

Corruption and incompetence do not necessarily go hand in hand, but in Iraq they are firm companions. Iraqi failures have been well documented, but less well known is the damage caused by the international 'assistance' that Iraq has been receiving since 2003.

Any major international crisis in the world is invariably followed by a swarm of organizations that descend on the relevant country to implement projects that are ostensibly designed to improve the situation on the ground. Much of that aid is provided through short or medium-term projects, which is convenient for the individuals involved, as they tend to move from one crisis to another. Thus many of these people come across one another regularly in places that have been hit by a catastrophe of some sort. The greater the crisis, the more irresistible it becomes for these people, since salaries spike according to how much international attention is focused on the stricken country. Although many (if not most) of the individuals who are part of this effort are well intentioned, the Iraqi experience clearly brought out the worst in many of their organizations.

The sheer incompetence of the CPA effectively lowered the bar when it came to assessing the 'success' of project implementation in Iraq. The CPA was eventually replaced by the US embassy (and its provincial reconstruction teams) and all sorts of international organizations, including various United Nations agencies. But the golden rule of intervention has never changed: whatever happens, whoever is funding and implementing the project, the average Iraqi should not benefit.

The first problem was that very few US and international staff spoke Arabic – and equally few cared whether Iraqis would benefit from the 'reconstruction'. Almost no one made any effort to learn the language or anything about the country. Officials who were responsible for major reconstruction projects often had to rely on the *New York Times* or the BBC for news about Iraq, even though they were based in Baghdad. Indeed, articles had to be on the relevant website's homepage for anyone to notice them. If someone did spot a story, it would be forwarded hundreds of times that day by internationals who were amazed to learn something new about Iraq. Yet many of these clueless individuals were responsible for multi-million-dollar projects, and were funnelling much of the money to phoney civil society organizations. Some of this was corruption, with internationals cutting deals with suppliers and Iraqi organizations to split the profits; but much of it was sheer incompetence.

It was actually very difficult to get to know Iraq, as the security risk meant that there were severe restrictions on people's movements. From 2003 onwards, it was strictly forbidden for any internationals to move around Iraq without a security presence. They were limited to working either from Amman or from the Green Zone (which was perhaps even more isolated from Iraq than was Amman). It was thus hard to meet Iraqis – any Iraqis. Some internationals went for weeks without speaking to any of the people that they were supposedly helping. Others never went to Iraq at all – not even to the Green Zone. This raises some important questions about what so many highly paid international officials were doing with their time in Jordan. And it was all compounded by their uncaring attitude. Decisions were made by internationals after 2003 that allowed corrupt senior officials in Iraq to wrap themselves in the mantle of international legitimacy or that wasted vital funds on useless programmes in the face of basic human needs.

In 2007, a meeting was arranged in Amman between a leading international organization and the Iraqi integrity commission to discuss how a generous grant from a wealthy European nation could be used to develop the commission's capacity to tackle corruption. The internationals had informed their Iraqi counterparts that they would present a detailed plan that would be up for discussion. It is no exaggeration to say that, apart from purchasing plane tickets, reserving a conference room and hiring an interpreter, absolutely nothing had been done to prepare for the meeting: there was no plan available for discussion.

Moreover, a number of people from Western Europe who had nothing to do with Iraq had been invited to attend the meeting. One friendly individual I spoke to was an academic who specialized in the Farsi language and had no knowledge of either Iraq or of corruption, but who was thrilled to be visiting Jordan for the first time.

The half-day meeting got off to a bad start, as the interpreter struggled with what was being said in English and was not particularly familiar with the Iraqi dialect either. The discussion was equally disorganized: the first two hours involved a free-flowing, surreal monologue by the chairman on the values of international aid and the hopes that it inspires, while the rest of the time was taken up with an update by the commission's head on security in Baghdad. The few exchanges that did take place were borderline comical, given the quality of the interpreting.

Four gruelling hours later, and five minutes before the meeting was due to close, it suddenly dawned on some of the internationals that the assistance programme had not yet been discussed and that they had nothing to present anyway. A last-minute recess was called, during which one of the meeting's organizers got one of her colleagues to jot down some suggestions of what the programme could involve. Initially reluctant, he finally grabbed the first piece of paper to hand (which was torn along the edges) and recorded some generic ideas ('capacity building', 'satisfying infrastructure needs', etc.). When the meeting reconvened, these were read out to the commission's head with great ceremony, as if they were the result of an intense fact-finding mission. To my dismay, he responded by nodding in approval and saying that he was greatly satisfied with what had been proposed. At the time, I thought he might not have realized what had just happened; later on, it occurred to me that he may not have had any choice but to react in the way he did.

Despite the CPA's terrible record on corruption, for years the US authorities barely addressed the issue, restricting themselves to issuing strongly worded statements and publishing reports by their own anti-graft agencies. The Bush administration hardly used the tools it had at its disposal to encourage the type of legal reform that was needed, and was content to limit its involvement to security-related issues and what it termed 'reconciliation'.

By late 2007, that position was no longer tenable and a special department was established at the US embassy in Baghdad in response to the growing realization that corruption was getting worse and that the US had to share responsibility for having provided so much support to the elites that were now at the helm of state. The department was staffed by US law enforcement officials, and a special anti-corruption ambassador was appointed. They battled with the baleful legacy of the CPA and the Bush administration and with the obstacles erected by their Iraqi counterparts.

Someone at the embassy eventually took matters into his or her own hands and leaked a secret report to the press. It was untitled but was marked 'sensitive but unclassified', and it contained a number of damning conclusions, as well as some detailed information on specific acts of interference by senior government officials. It noted that 'Iraq is not capable of even rudimentary enforcement of anticorruption laws' and '[i]n addition to the lack of capacity within the anticorruption agencies, politicization and fear of accountability are serious impediments to the enforcement of anticorruption laws'.[56] The report also noted that the prime minister's office had expressed 'open hostility' to the principle of institutional independence. This manifested itself in the alleged withholding of material support from the integrity commission and the issuance of 'secret orders' by the prime minister's office, which tried to prevent the commission from referring cases involving high-ranking officials to the courts. Finally, the report stated that individuals in both al-Maliki's office and that of Vice President Adel Abed al-Mahdi had prevented cases from coming to court, and maintained that al-Maliki's staff had ordered the replacement of certain of the commission's personnel.[57]

While the individual who leaked the report was rightly commended, the Iraqi government's reaction was less inspiring. Although it denied the report's contents, it realized that the matter was a public relations disaster and sought some way of restoring its reputation. The first available avenue was provided by the United Nations, which was struggling to remain relevant in Iraq and was grateful for any attention it could get from senior government officials. It was suggested that there could be a joint initiative with the Iraqi government to declare 2008 'the year of anti-corruption'. The UN was encouraged in this undertaking by a number of western governments, including the Bush administration. No thought was given as to whether the government's intentions were genuine or whether the press conference that was planned to launch the initiative would afford corrupt officials some international legitimacy, even though their internal credibility was crumbling. The conference was finally arranged in Baghdad, photo opportunities were seized, speeches were made – and, predictably, nothing positive came of it. Between 2008 and 2011, millions of dollars were invested by the UN and the US to train and reform the oversight agencies, even as the Iraqi government refused to improve the legal framework governing the agencies and continued to encroach on their independence.

At the end of 2008, I participated in a senior-level meeting at the United Nations, where project implementation over the previous twelve months was reviewed. Several projects, worth tens of millions of dollars, were discussed and evaluations were offered on the basis of what percentage of the available funding was actually spent. Out of more than a dozen major projects, one was singled out as being 'outstanding', since 100 per cent of the available funds had been disbursed. As the discussion neared its conclusion, and as attendees started to pick up their notepads, ready to leave the conference room, one Iraqi (not me) said: 'Wait, we haven't discussed whether any of this has had any impact.' The official who had been leading the discussion looked exasperated: 'We don't have the luxury to consider impact.' That was the end of the discussion.

The following year, I attended a major governance planning meeting for all UN agencies. I travelled to Amman from Baghdad, where I had been visiting relatives. I was happy to leave, as I had just lived through one of the worst dust storms on record. I had choked on the red dust that was blotting out the sky. I had been unable to see more than a few metres ahead of me. And I had been overcome with emotion when I heard cries from the local mosque (completely obscured by the dust) begging God for rain to clean the air (see Chapter 8).

I landed at Queen Alia airport and took a taxi straight to the meeting. The discussion quickly focused on what could be done to get ordinary Iraqis to take a greater interest in the political process. Several of the officials in attendance, some of whom had been working on Iraq for more than five years, suggested that the constitution should be translated into more minority languages, such as Chaldean. I could scarcely believe my ears! Although many Iraqi Christians *speak* Chaldean, only a few people – priests and specialists – can read it. Most Christians can only read Arabic. Five years was apparently not long enough for the internationals to learn some of the basics of the society that they were supposed to be helping, or to come up with a single project that could be of use to the country.

The discussion moved on to what could be done to improve the Iraqi health sector. Much attention was paid to an ongoing HIV/Aids programme. I immediately protested that, although HIV/Aids was a problem that should be addressed in all countries, there was very little information on how many people actually suffered from it in Iraq, and in fact the figure was probably relatively low. I reminded everyone that Iraq's environment was deteriorating rapidly and that dozens of people were dying during each of the increasingly frequent dust storms. I showed some of those present photos that I had taken just a few days before (not very good photos, as the camera could not cope with the thick red dust).

Iraqis were choking to death and were desperately in need of assistance, but one participant responded that the meeting's focus was on governance, and that I should raise environmental issues at the proper 'cluster meeting'. Another retorted that climate change had been classified as a 'cross-cutting issue' and so was a relevant concern at all meetings relating to Iraq. I found myself still choking – but now it was bureaucratic jargon that was clogging my throat. In the end, I was bluntly told that the United Nations did not have a budget for the environment and that in any event the HIV/Aids programme would continue. The ignorance and lack of genuine compassion were difficult to fathom, but were all too real.

THE IMPACT

Corruption is not an abstract concern. It translates into reduced financial resources and human capacity to improve public services. More importantly, it also means that whoever is in control of the government and its policies does not have the interests of the public at heart, and that the formation of the kind of policy that could address basic needs is not prioritized.

In Iraq, the result of this has been that the state's capacity to deliver basic services has declined over the years, while reforms that can and should be passed quite easily never see the light of day. This has caused significant distress to all Iraqi citizens, and has contributed to the state's lack of legitimacy.

There are no precise figures for the amount of public funds stolen or wasted as a result of corrupt practices; but it is safe to say that it must amount to billions of US dollars annually.[58] This order of magnitude is supported by information that comes to light in the wake of the relatively few convictions achieved for corruption-related crimes. In 2005–07, 111 electricity ministry officials were convicted of various corruption-related offences involving sums totalling $250 million. Some 319 defence ministry officials were also convicted of crimes involving more than $1 billion.[59] In 2010, the number of convictions reached an all-time high, although few were high profile. Ministries with security-related portfolios are the worst offenders, but corruption has also spread to the judicial sector, provincial governments and the Kurdistan regional government.[60]

Corruption affects the country at a number of levels and is one of the main factors preventing improved public services. It manifests itself in the following ways:

• Nepotism is a regular feature: unqualified staff are hired at all levels of government on the basis of family, friendship or party affiliation. Every Iraqi has come across examples of this, but perhaps the worst instances are to be found in parliament, where almost every MP has taken on relatives as staff members (virtually impossible to remove). This has affected just about every part of the institution. Parliament may have a generous budget, but it took years for it to secure a regular internet connection and a reliable intranet, because the relevant official (who is a nice enough person but lacks nous) was foisted on parliament by one of its most senior members, who also happens to be his father.

- Bribery has become indispensable to obtain services or favours: in particular qualified graduates often complain that, unless they pay substantial bribes, they cannot hope to secure stable employment. Another outrageous manifestation of this is that defendants who have been found not guilty and criminals who have served their time often have to paid bribes to prison guards and judicial officials merely to be released.

- Throughout government, the public procurement process is riddled with corruption: public funds are embezzled, placing an additional strain on public finances.[61]

The US state department in June 2008 summarized the impact that all this was having on Iraq, in rather diplomatic terms: 'widespread corruption undermines efforts to develop the government's capacity by robbing it of needed resources; by eroding popular faith in democratic institutions, perceived as run by corrupt political elites; and by spurring capital flight and reducing economic growth'.[62] There was agreement among a large number of anti-corruption officials that despite the relative increase in the number of corruption-related convictions (97 in 2008; 296 in 2009; and 481 in the first nine months of 2010),[63] court action had barely made a dent in the problem.

In 2012, the government launched a military spending spree, purchasing equipment from all over the world. The ministry of defence was still populated by officials who held dangerously militaristic and chauvinistic tendencies. The military, in their view, should rearm as quickly as possible with heavy armour – not to protect the people, but to intimidate the neighbours. The government, naturally, was in favour for a number of reasons, including that such weapons could be used internally in the event of a massive deterioration in security. Concern was voiced in many quarters over the size of the purchases and their nature: the government appeared most interested in acquiring offensive material, such as fighter aircraft and tanks. Such weapons are usually employed in conventional warfare, and did not appear to have any application to Iraq's real and ongoing security challenges. What good, after all, would a fighter aircraft be against a handful of individuals planning a car bomb attack in secret?

Discussions with Russia on the purchase of arms are said to have started as early as April 2012. Acting Defence Minister Saadoun al-Dulaimi visited Moscow and ended up staying for several weeks to discuss the details of a possible agreement and strategic military cooperation.[64] In October 2012, a high-level delegation headed by al-Maliki travelled to Moscow to sign the final agreement. The delegation also included al-Dulaimi, the head of the counter-terrorism unit, the commander of Iraq's air defence forces, the director general of armament and equipment, members of the directorate general of budget and programmes, and members of the army aviation command. The deal was interpreted as an attempt by Iraq to diversify away from American suppliers (also a way of obtaining greater leverage with Washington in future arms negotiations).[65] It involved the purchase of surface-to-air missile systems, anti-aircraft artillery, MiG-29M/M2 aircraft, thirty Mi-28 attack helicopters and other heavy weaponry.[66] The Iraqis, as usual, claimed to have obtained a big discount from the Russians, ostensibly to impress the general populace that its money was not being wasted.

Even before the Iraqi delegation returned from Russia, however, rumours began circulating that the entire deal was rotten. The spectacle of Iraqi officials drooling over a multi-billion-dollar arms deal with a country that had corruption problems of its own was enough for many people; but it was the fact that officials were inconsistent about the size of the discount that raised most questions. Iraqis immediately speculated that part of the discount was in fact being redirected to offshore accounts. Russian arms experts have since speculated that kickbacks as high as $500 million might have been paid.[67]

The public was treated to the spectacle of an open feud between two senior officials. On 10 November, government spokesman Ali al-Dabbagh, who had been accused of receiving commission, asked for an investigation to clear his name. Ali al-Moussawi, the prime minister's media adviser, saw an opportunity to eject his rival al-Dabbagh from government, and announced that 'when al-Maliki returned from his trip to Russia, he had some suspicions of corruption, so he decided to review the whole deal'.[68]

This was denied by Acting Defence Minister al-Dulaimi, who claimed that the deal was still on, that no payments had been made, and that he would shoulder any responsibility for impropriety. He accused various media outlets and senior officials of seeking to 'blackmail' his ministry and bizarrely invited his enemies to 'drink sea water'.[69]

Ali al-Dabbagh responded that the deal had indeed been cancelled and that it would be renegotiated with the Russians.[70] On 21 November 2012, he claimed that there was a conspiracy against him that was being led by (once again) media outlets.[71] But the pressure was too great, and al-Dabbagh finally resigned on 26 November. In a letter to the prime minister, he accused al-Moussawi of orchestrating 'an unfair media campaign aimed at distorting my name and my reputation and I find it difficult to continue to perform my work in this hostile environment'; he left it up to al-Maliki to decide on his position in government.[72] Although al-Maliki accepted the resignation, al-Dabbagh's contract of employment was extended to the end of 2014.[73]

A few days earlier, parliament had voted to form a special committee to investigate the deal. When it approached al-Dabbagh, he claimed that he had been the first to notify the prime minister of possible corruption, and that he did so forty days before the delegation actually made its way to Russia. In response, al-Maliki denied that al-Dabbagh had shared his suspicions and stressed that the two had never even discussed the matter. Talal Zawbai MP, a member of the committee of enquiry, said on 25 December 2012 that the Russians had given a 30 per cent discount on the equipment, but that only 9 per cent had been officially reported by the Iraqis, strongly suggesting that the rest had been pocketed.

The committee also found that Iraqi procurement laws had been blatantly violated: according to rules that had been in force for quite some time, the minister of defence was only authorized to sign contracts worth up to $100 million. Anything above that value had to be signed by the prime minister, but that rule had not been followed in this case.[74]

The committee's final report was submitted for discussion at a plenary session of parliament on 9 January. MPs voted to refer al-Dulaimi, al-Dabbagh, Abdul Aziz al-Badri (an adviser to the presidency who had also been involved in the negotiations), Majid al-Qaisi (an Iraqi businessman), two Lebanese businessmen and a director of a Russian oil company to the integrity commission and the public prosecutor.[75]

Six months later, the deal appeared to be back on track. There had been no prosecutions, no resignations, no apologies and no action.

CHAPTER EIGHT

THE THIRD INSURGENCY: ENVIRONMENTAL DISASTER

SURROUNDED BY DESERT AND DUST

If corruption is Iraq's second insurgency, then the collapse of its environment since 2003 is its third.

From 2005 onwards, it became increasingly frequent for meetings with friends or colleagues outside Iraq to be delayed for several days at a time. At first the reason given tended to be security related, but more and more often a new explanation crept in: '*ajaj*, the Iraqi term for a dust storm. When they did arrive, friends would apologize profusely, but it was clear that they were relieved to have left the dust behind.

Over the years, security became less of an impediment to travel or work plans; but the storms started to become a regular obstacle. Until 2009, I had somehow managed to avoid the worst of them, but they were described to me in stark terms: red skies, thick air, an entire city at a standstill. It sounded incredible – exaggerated even. But in 2009 I saw it for myself.

As I approached central Iraq that summer, I became aware of a gradual process: from blue, the sky slowly turned grey and blotted out the sun; grey transformed into bright red, which then darkened considerably. I started worrying about breathing. Finally, I realized that I could not see more than a few metres ahead of me. Police officers and soldiers manning checkpoints wrapped whatever they could around their mouths to lessen the effects of their constant exposure to the dust. The skin around their eyes was all that was exposed to the elements, and it was deeply cracked. As we passed each checkpoint, the soldiers would strain to peer at us and would wearily and wretchedly raise an open hand, wave to us and wait for a response of some kind – as if merely to confirm to themselves that they could still be seen through the dust and that they had not been completely swallowed up by the storm. A thick layer covered everything: parked cars, garbage on the street, trees, bushes. . . Everything was the same red colour. Children played football just a few metres ahead of me, but I could barely make them out. Indoors, rooms that would otherwise be bathed in sunshine were dark in the middle of the day. And there was dust everywhere: on tables, inside closets, in bathrooms, on clothes, toothbrushes, on keyboards. Nothing was spared. Words cannot describe the phenomenon; it evokes utter despair.

Dust storms are distinct from sandstorms. The latter are a naturally occurring phenomenon that the Middle East has witnessed throughout recorded history. As strong winds blow across the Sahara, they carry with them particles of sand and dust in incredible rushes that engulf entire cities. Often referred to as *khamaseen* (from the Arabic word for 'fifty'), they typically occur during the spring and blow sporadically over a fifty-day period.

Dust storms are different. Winds have always blown across Iraq, but now, as they skim the surface of the land, they pick up parched and cracked biological material where once there were rich agricultural fields, lakes and marshes. Once upon a time they were a rare occurrence. Iraqis who lived through the 1990s recall as remarkable an event from 1994: a dust storm changed the sky's colour to red and reduced visibility to a bare minimum, forcing everyone to stay at home. A family friend had bought a red BMW earlier that year, and now his children and neighbours marvelled at how the colour of the air rendered the car almost invisible, even just a few metres away. This was a landmark event, but it was also a portent. These days the storms can blow up several times a week during summer.

During the storm that I experienced in summer 2009 (and which I reported at the Amman conference – see Chapter 7), all afternoon I could only see a few metres ahead of me when the dust cleared a little; for the rest of the time, the world was a red-tinged haze. At the time, NASA reported that particular storm as 'the worst in living memory'.[1] Since then, the storms have increased further in both frequency and intensity. The Iraqi environment ministry has estimated that the country could witness more than 300 days of dust storms a year for the next ten years (in 2008, the estimate was 238 days). Clear blue skies are set to become the exception rather than the rule.[2]

There are a number of factors that have coalesced over the past ten years to contribute to this new state of affairs. Some are outside Iraq's control, but others have been of its own making. Climate change has reduced the little seasonal rainfall that the country used to have, and this has lowered the level of its two great rivers, the Euphrates and the Tigris. The construction of upstream dams and the diversion of rivers in Turkey, Iran and Syria have compounded the problem, leaving some of Iraq's tributaries and lesser rivers completely dry. The increased use of fertilizers and pesticides upstream has raised the levels of pollution in what waters remain, and agriculture has declined markedly as a result.

Decades of mismanagement of water resources by the Iraqi state, including the absence of effective waste management and the use by farmers of outdated irrigation practices, have not helped.[3] The general population also displays wastefulness and an alarming lack of awareness.

Saddam Hussein's military campaigns made matters far worse, first of all by diverting essential labour to the front (the resulting huge reduction in farming led to the land turning to dust) and secondly by destroying fields (and the topsoil) that were in the way of military supply lines. The incessant bombing of southern and northern Iraq also littered the landscape with toxic munitions that have contaminated the water supply. The US contributed to this problem through its bombing campaign of 1991 (when depleted uranium was used against Iraqi armour) and in the aftermath of the 2003 invasion, when similarly questionable munitions were used in many parts of the country.

Vast tracts of land that were previously rich in life have been transformed into a desert wasteland. The process began with Saddam Hussein (who drained the southern marshlands to curb insurgent activities against his rule) and continued with the US occupation, which eradicated significant areas of forest to prevent militants from using it as cover from which to launch attacks and which also destroyed much of the topsoil by using military vehicles on what had been agricultural land. The Iraqi state did the rest: it reduced state subsidies on oil products, which increased production and transport costs for farmers. They can no longer compete with their counterparts in neighbouring countries (many of whom benefit from generous subsidies) and large numbers have gone out of business. Finally, as the state collapsed completely (first as a result of the sanctions during the 1990s and then because of the occupation), law enforcement disappeared along with the electricity: ordinary citizens had no choice but to fell trees for heating or cooking – and little fear of being punished for doing so. The people have also completely ignored zoning laws that previously prevented construction in agricultural areas; many of these areas have now been completely urbanized, further reducing Iraq's green cover.

All of this has contributed to speeding up desertification. Iraq's western deserts have been moving eastwards for some time now. However, as lack of state support means that more and more land is abandoned to the elements, soil that was previously cultivable becomes parched and then crumbles to dust. Winds carry what remains into the atmosphere, forcing even more people to leave their land. Natural defences against the desert are rapidly being eroded and trees (whose roots used to bind the soil together) have been cut down. According to Iraq's ministry of agriculture, 80 per cent of Iraq's landmass is affected by desertification.[4]

DAMS AND DISAPPEARING MARSHES

Some of the factors that have had an impact on Iraq's quickly changing environment are indeed beyond its control. For example, the United Nations estimates that Iraq emits 0.34 per cent of the world's carbon dioxide; so on its own this has little impact on global climate change. Nevertheless, Iraq has been made to suffer the consequences of climate change, and these are likely to worsen over time.

In particular, reduced rainfall has proved a major challenge. In the past, parts of Kurdistan in northern Iraq and Ninewa province had sufficient rainfall to produce cereals and vegetables without relying on the two great rivers. But severe drought has affected the region over the past few years, and that has hit crop yields. The rest of the country is almost entirely dependent on the Tigris and Euphrates, as no significant rain falls outside the northern mountains. Both rivers rise in Turkey's east and are fed by rain and meltwater, so both are highly sensitive to climate change. Reduced rainfall immediately translates into less water for irrigation in the rest of the country. Yields have been consistently low in recent years and are likely to decline still further. The first (and so far only) projection for rainfall in the Fertile Crescent was carried out in 2008. It presents a number of stark conclusions:

> The current climate model projects decreasing precipitation in the Fertile
> Crescent region. Changes in streamflow become more severe, which may
> result in substantial damage to rain-fed agriculture in the Mesopotamia

area. Ancient rain-fed agriculture enabled the civilizations to thrive in the Fertile Crescent region, but this blessing is soon to disappear due to human induced climate change. The fate of people in this politically vulnerable region depends on global management of the limited available water. Countermeasures have been planned for a long time, and global climate models that sufficiently represent the Fertile Crescent and project its future change can now be utilized for such purposes.[5]

The construction of upstream dams by three of Iraq's neighbours has contributed to the problem. Both the Euphrates and the Tigris rise in Turkey, and both run through Syria. Many of the Tigris's tributaries (including the Wand and the Karun rivers) flow from Iran. As drought affects the entire region, each of these countries has constructed reservoirs to support irrigation. Turkey's south-eastern region borders both Iraq and Iran. To manage the drought that this area has been subject to for several decades, the Turkish government has the Greater Anatolia Project, which, it is estimated, will cost $32 billion and will eventually involve the construction of twenty-two dams and nineteen hydro power plants. Although the project has been on the books since the 1970s, funding and security concerns have meant that planning and construction work has been rather spasmodic. However, construction restarted in earnest in 2009 and the project is now set for completion in 2017.[6] It will divert even more water from Iraq's two rivers to feed irrigation in Turkey and to fill reservoirs.

Dams also reduce water flow over the long term, as they lead to significant evaporation. In 1990, when the Atatürk Dam (one of the largest in the world) was completed, water flow into Iraq was reduced by 75 per cent for a month. At the time, the Iraqi government threatened to bomb the dam, significantly raising tension between the two countries.[7] (Attention was diverted from the issue by the invasion of Kuwait that same year.)

Iraq also has to compete with Syria for whatever waters flow from Turkey. During an acute drought in 2009, Turkey agreed to release additional water into the Euphrates to feed Iraq's fields. However, there was no obvious improvement, which led Iraq to accuse Syria of hoarding the water to fill its own reservoirs.[8]

Iran has also been busy diverting water from Iraq to irrigate its own land. The Karun is Iran's only navigable river. It eventually joins the Shatt al-Arab, which is formed by the confluence of the Euphrates and the Tigris. Several dams already lock in a significant volume of its waters, and several more are under construction. On many occasions since 2003, the flow from the Karun has been reduced to a trickle, causing an environmental catastrophe in Basra province.[9] The Wand River is one of the most important tributaries of the Tigris and it also feeds the traditional agricultural areas of Iraq's eastern Dyala province, which is famous for its orange groves. Since 2003, its flow has also been completely cut off several times by Iran.[10] The Dyala River, which rises in Iran and flows into the Iraqi province of the same name, has also been at risk for years, with greatly reduced levels.[11]

Successive Iraqi administrations have mismanaged their water resources. Iraq has built a number of dams of its own, and the sheer number of them has impaired water resources downstream.[12] In addition, the country's infrastructure is in desperate need of repair: surface water is often contaminated by sewage and other waste; the water distribution network is in a parlous state; and poor agricultural practices have reduced groundwater levels and led to increased salinization.[13] Finally, at the individual level, there is a general lack of awareness of water issues: garden hoses are left on for hours for no reason, and when pipes burst entire streets are flooded for days before anyone repairs the damage. Illegal wells are dug and run dry by families; in Kurdistan, centuries-old subterranean aqueducts (known as *karez*) have been damaged through overuse, after water pumps were installed and deeper wells were dug.[14] The weak legal framework means that pollutants (including drained batteries, used refrigerators and other household appliances) are dumped in rivers with no repercussions: the financial penalty for environmental crimes is ridiculously low and is practically never applied.

The country faces a number of serious difficulties. First of all, reduced water levels mean that Iraq's hydroelectric dams cannot generate as much electricity as they otherwise would. Then there have been several impacts on irrigation: one very obvious consequence of lower water levels is that many irrigation pipes, built when water levels were far higher, now hover more than a metre above the river level. Irrigation pipes and canals – previously a lifeline for many fields – lie idle and silted up. Not only do upstream dams abroad reduce the amount of water that is available, but they also have an impact on the quality of water: the reservoirs are used to irrigate farms, from where pesticides and other chemicals find their way into the river as it flows down into Iraq. Even if treated, the quality of the water is greatly reduced and this contributes to lower yields and the spread of disease. As the flow of fresh water recedes, so salt water from the Persian Gulf finds its way into the Shatt al-Arab. Officials have noted that salinity has increased markedly, which has had an impact on local inhabitants and their fields.[15] Drinking water is now salty, and the soil has lost much of its quality, causing palm groves and other fruit trees to wither. When many of Basra's districts were declared a disaster zone in 2009, Iranian officials patted themselves on the back for offering to deliver fresh water by ship.[16]

Most serious of all is the way in which environmental degradation has had an impact on Iraq's marshlands. Traditionally, as the winter snows melted in northern Iraq, Turkey and Iran, Iraq's rivers overflowed and fed the stagnant marshes of southern Iraq. These once occupied an area of 20,000 square kilometres. The marshes were an incredible sight, a place of legends. The local inhabitants, whose way of life had changed little in 5,000 years, lived in reed huts that floated on tiny artificial islands that were grouped together as villages. They dwelt side by side with water buffalo, which provided milk, yoghurt and butter and were a rich source of manure. The low-lying waters were also ideal for growing rice.

In terms of biodiversity, the marshes were of regional and global importance. In particular, they were a stopover point for birds migrating from Siberia to parts of Africa. Much has been written about the area, including a seminal work by Wilfred Thesiger, who lived in the marshes during the 1950s.[17] Unfortunately, the area's inhabitants have regularly suffered discrimination in Iraq's urban centres and by the state.

Plans to manipulate Iraq's southern waters for various purposes were drawn up as early as the 1950s (some experts say that plans even existed in the pre-Islamic era).[18] One objective was to deal with soil salinity by developing an effective drainage system; another was to reclaim part of the marshes for agriculture. A far more ambitious plan was developed in the 1970s to channel the Shatt al-Arab's flow into a complex system of irrigation canals, all of which would eventually run into the Gulf. Before the work could commence, however, Saddam Hussein ordered the invasion of Iran, which diverted attention from the project altogether.

The conflict with Iran saw a front of activity emerge near Iraq's southern border. In order to allow the flow of machinery and armour, the area was dredged and parts of the marshes drained. The eastern marshes actually cross into Iran and were themselves part of the front. Later, after the 1991 war, an uprising in the south prompted the Baathist regime to drain the marshes completely in order to prevent potential enemies from using them as cover. Enormous irrigation canals were constructed around the marshes to divert water directly into the sea.[19] As soon as the canals were completed and

were connected to the Tigris and Euphrates, the marshes virtually disappeared, leaving only a few patches here and there. Hundreds of thousands of
Iraqis were displaced, and many of them fled to Iran. Dozens of species of
wildlife were also wiped out.

Moreover, in typical Baathist fashion, the original plan to replace the
marshes with a system of irrigation canals was abandoned in favour of a
much quicker plan, which was simply to drain the marshes and allow the
water just to flow into the sea. The land formerly covered by the marshes was
transformed into parched, salt-encrusted earth, and the winds that had
previously been broken by the reeds in the water were left to blow
unimpeded.

Maysan province lies just to the north of Basra. Previously two-thirds of
it was covered by marshes that largely supported the local population. After
the devastation, 50 per cent of the province was left desert, and only a small
proportion remains arable.[20] This was not just a humanitarian or an ecological crisis; it was a recipe for disaster. Before the current epidemic of dust
storms started, a detailed report, completed in 2001 by the United Nations
Environmental Programme, predicted many of the environmental changes
that were about to take place:

> Rapid desiccation of over 9,000 km² of wetlands and lakes is bound to
> have significant ramifications on the regional micro-climate. As the
> moderating role of the wetlands is eliminated, evapotranspiration and
> humidity rates will sharply decrease. Rainfall patterns will be modified.
> Temperatures will invariably rise, particularly during the hot and long
> summers. Strong and dry winds reaching temperatures of over 40 °C,
> previously broken by the reed beds, will blow unhindered. *With salt crusts
> and dry marshland soils exposed, windblown dust laced with various
> impurities will considerably increase, affecting thousands of square kilo-
> metres well beyond Iraq's borders.* Ecosystem degradation at such a grand
> scale may have serious drawbacks on human health, ranging from the
> effects of water scarcity and pollution to increased exposure to thermal
> extremes and potentially toxic dust storms blowing off saltpans and dried
> marsh bed. Furthermore, the fragile arable lands surrounding the former
> marshlands are likely to suffer from land degradation and desertification,
> caused by wind erosion and sand encroachment from the dried marsh bed
> and surrounding deserts.[21]

It was prophetic. Within a few years of the report's publication, as water levels continued to recede, dust storms started engulfing the entire country for days on end, and with increasing frequency.

Fortuitously, the marshlands have great appeal both in Iraq and internationally, and this has translated into significant efforts to have them restored. A group of activists and Marsh Arabs broke down some of the dykes that had been constructed in 1991 and 1992, which led to parts of the marshes re-flooding. Over the coming years, government institutions and international organizations embarked on a number of projects, which by 2006 had restored water to 50 per cent of the marshes' 1973 area. This was hailed as a major victory and was promoted by the US military and its allies. A CBS report that was aired in November 2009 (and which had relied on US military units for protection during filming) claimed to show the extent to which the marshes had been restored.[22]

The reality on the ground is rather less inspiring, however. In 2009, during a period of drought that coincided with an effort by Iran to divert waters from Iraq, the area of the marshes receded to the 2003 level. The water-covered area continues to fluctuate, but in recent years it has not exceeded 50 per cent of the area previously covered.[23] Much of the rest remains a desert that will continue to feed dust storms far into the future. In addition, in 2009 Iran completed construction of a six-metre-high dyke along its border, dividing what had always been a united marsh into two independent entities. The Iranians argued that the dyke was necessary to crack down on the drug trade; but its impact was entirely in keeping with Iran's other water policies – essentially to prevent as much water as possible from crossing into Iraq. As the Iraqis were in the process of reviving the marshes, they asked for the dyke to be destroyed, but this met with a flat refusal.[24]

Life has not returned to the marshes in the way that many hoped or imagined it would. Very few of the displaced inhabitants have come back, and the plant and animal life remains a shadow of its former self. Once again, reduced water flow has meant that the marshes are now far saltier than they once were. This alters the area's biodiversity completely and prevents its former inhabitants from growing traditional crops, such as rice. The rapidly changing climate means that even if all of Iraq's waters were allowed to flow freely, the marshes would almost certainly never return to their former glory. But even if only a partial solution is sought, the Iraqi state will have to reach agreement with its neighbours, particularly Turkey and Iran, to ensure a more equitable sharing of the region's precious water supplies.

POLITICS BEFORE BREAD (AND CLEAN AIR)

Rivers that cross several countries are not subject to any binding international rules. The United Nations adopted a convention on the non-navigational uses of international waters in 1997, but as yet it has not come into force, since not enough states have signed up to it. Turkey, Iran and Iraq have not signed any international or regional treaties on the matter, and so there are no regulations whatever governing the flow of the Tigris, the Euphrates or the other rivers. The only way in which Iraq can prevail upon its neighbours to share water more equitably is through diplomacy: if Iraq asks nicely and offers something in exchange, it might obtain concessions. Otherwise there is nothing it can do to enforce any type of arrangement – short of declaring war.

So what has the Iraqi government done in the face of environmental disaster? Instead of trying to negotiate a solution, it has actively contributed to a marked deterioration in relations with Turkey, and has done almost nothing to encourage Iran to act. Until recently, economic relations with Turkey were almost exemplary: in 2010, Turkish corporations dominated foreign commercial activity in Iraq, with the announcement of twenty-two major deals involving Turkish firms (total value of just under $15 billion), including a real estate project in Baghdad's Sadr City, the construction of five hospitals in several provinces and power plants in Karbala and Ninewa provinces. The Turkish Petroleum International Company was also awarded a contract to drill forty-five wells in Rumaila oilfield (Basra province). And smaller Turkish businesses were in evidence all over Iraq: furniture stores in Baghdad, clothes shops in Basra, restaurants in Erbil. Shoppers equated Turkish goods with European standards: in Iraq, 'made in Turkey' meant high quality.

By 2011 everything had changed. Turkish goods were still flooding the market, but its big corporations were no longer being favoured for the largest projects, and some tenders that it had been won were taken away. The final straw came when the Turkish Petroleum International Company was unceremoniously booted out of the Rumaila oilfield in favour of a consortium of Kuwaiti and Emirati firms.[25] Abdul Mehdi al-Amidi, head of the oil ministry's contracting and licensing department, attributed the decision to 'non-technical issues that were outside the responsibility of my office and me personally . . . The decision is from the cabinet.' The Turkish authorities described the decision as 'childish'.[26] In 2010, Turkish companies together topped the rankings of foreign investors in Iraq; by the end of 2011, they had fallen to fifth place, behind the South Koreans and Dutch.[27]

Between 2009 and 2011, just as Iraq's water shortages were worsening, Ankara and Baghdad engaged in a series of tit-for-tat rhetoric, straining relations to breaking point. The initial spark was Ankara's support in 2009 and 2010 for the Iraqiya alliance, which was led by Ayad Allawi and which enjoyed the support of the vast majority of Sunni Muslims. Members of al-Maliki's entourage privately seethed that Iraqiya – which, as we have seen, outperformed the State of Law alliance in the 2010 parliamentary elections – had been formed at the instigation of the Turkish government.[28] Over time, that resentment festered and gave rise to a campaign against many of Turkey's main allies in Baghdad: an arrest warrant issued against former Vice President Tariq al-Hashimi in December 2011; and the temporary banishment of Deputy Prime Minister Salih al-Mutlaq around the same time.

The Turks meanwhile thumbed their collective nose at al-Maliki by giving refuge to al-Hashimi, and improved their ties with the autonomous Kurdistan region (just when its relations with Baghdad were deteriorating). Finally, as Baghdad and Erbil engaged in a tense military face-off in Kirkuk in November 2012, Turkish Prime Minister Recep Erdogan accused al-Maliki of pushing Iraq towards civil war.[29]

A few weeks later, on 6 December 2012, al-Maliki lamented the current state of relations between the two countries and called for a 'new chapter' to be written. In an interview with the Turkish press, he said: 'Despite our differences, we would like to have a good dialogue with Turkey. I am extending an olive branch, we would like to cooperate in all areas with Turkey. But Turkey must not interfere in Iraqi internal affairs.'[30] This call was followed by further action against a politician who was close to Turkey – Finance Minister Rafi al-Issawi, who was accused of terrorism and forced to resign from his position.

Turkey's influence in Iraq was rapidly becoming a polarizing issue: demonstrations were organized in Basra to demand the boycott of Turkish goods,[31] and members of al-Maliki's parliamentary coalition accused Erdogan of sectarianism and demanded the expulsion of the Turkish ambassador.[32]

To cut a long story short, Baghdad remains some way away from resolving the country's water crisis through its negotiations with Turkey. Al-Maliki and his allies have promoted narrow political interests over the country's wellbeing. It is not that the environmental crisis should trump all other issues; rather the problem is that water is not even part of the calculus. Instead, the airwaves are dominated by old-fashioned political conflicts that revolve around the monopolization of power. Meanwhile farmers continue to toil using the precious resources that they need to survive, while the soil continues to crack and turn to dust beneath their feet.

Turkey's water policies have certainly had an impact on the Euphrates and the Tigris, but it is hard for the average citizen to gauge the extent of this impact, given that both rivers continue to flow (albeit at much reduced levels). On the other hand, the impact of Iran's policies is much easier to trace: they have caused a number of the Tigris's tributaries to go completely dry.

In the absence of any solutions from their political representatives, farming communities that have depended on these rivers for centuries have decided to take matters into their own hands. On several occasions, ordinary farmers and citizens have prevented Iranian pilgrims from entering Iraq, in protest at Iran's water policies,[33] and have even closed down a number of border posts.[34] Maysan province, which is on the border with Iran and has been among the worst affected by Baathist, American, Turkish and Iranian policies and by the new Iraqi government's neglect, even banned the sale of Iranian goods in its markets.[35] These modest actions, desperate and well intentioned, have singularly failed to provoke any reaction or to give rise to a new set of policies in either country.

ABANDONING AGRICULTURE

Prior to the discovery of oil, agriculture was Iraq's primary economic activity. It traditionally employed millions of people, and contributed a significant proportion of the country's GDP (8 per cent in 1976). Even today, agriculture provides employment for 30 per cent of the population.

As mentioned before, parts of northern Iraq enjoy sufficient rainfall to produce cereals without the need to rely on irrigation. Rainfall in the rest of the country is minimal, and so farmers depend on irrigation. While the agricultural sector has accommodated other major crops, including barley and wheat, and a wide variety of fruits and vegetables, date palms are intimately bound up with the country's mythology. Iraqis used to be fond of saying that there were three palm trees for every inhabitant of the country. And the myth was not far off the reality: in 1970, for a population of around 9 million there were 21 million date palms.

There are hundreds of varieties of dates. Many are considered great delicacies and are a source of huge pride. Any Iraqi who can afford it will plant palms either on his farm or in his garden. Iraqi exports once upon a time represented around 50 per cent of the world's date consumption.[36] From a distance, palm groves are a majestic sight: forests of date trees standing in serried ranks, so densely packed together that you can barely see past the first few. To stand in a grove is to be transported into another universe.

Since 1958, Iraq has come to rely increasingly on food imports. In the 1970s, increased investment in the agricultural sector was supposed to reverse that trend, but mismanagement and a rapidly increasing population prevented the goal from being realized. And then the war with Iran put paid to any ideas of a recovery: the much-needed labour was diverted to the war effort and significant areas of agricultural land near the border were badly damaged. Things got even worse after 1991, when the US-led coalition destroyed much of the country's industry and then imposed sanctions which made the import of any equipment extremely difficult. By way of illustration, the number of date palms has declined by around two-thirds as a result of these conflicts and lack of care by the authorities.

In 2003, the Coalition Provisional Authority set the country on a new disaster course, and since then successive administrations have been unable or unwilling to change direction. One of the CPA's first decisions was to slash customs and duty on all imports to 5 per cent.[37] The order, which was dubbed a 'trade liberalization policy', was unprecedented – both in Iraq and internationally. There is hardly a country in the world that does not seek to protect its domestic industry and agriculture to some extent, and the United States is certainly no exception in that regard.

This new measure also subjected the Iraqi market to the vagaries of world trade at a time when it was totally unprepared for competition with even unsophisticated traders. The country had just emerged from thirteen years of the most comprehensive international sanctions regime ever devised. Furthermore, these had been imposed just when much of the rest of the world (including many neighbouring countries) was taking a great leap forward, with unparalleled technological advances. Local businesses and farming interests were completely cut off from those changes by both the sanctions and the Baathist regime.

Thus, at the worst time imaginable, the borders were flung wide open to anyone who wanted to export anything to Iraq. The Iraqis were forced to pay the price for the same type of neo-conservative shock therapy that had brought misery to Eastern Europe after the fall of the Soviet Union.

By 2004, Iraq was also negotiating the cancellation of its debt with its international creditors and loan agreements with the IMF. As part of the package, the government agreed to drastically reduce its subsidies on a number of goods, including oil and its derivatives. Prior to 2003, oil was all but free in Iraq (it cost around 20 dinars a litre, when the exchange rate hovered around 1,500 dinars to the dollar). This subsidy cost the state billions of dollars a year. It gave manufacturing and agriculture a massive boost (though it was one that they could never fully capitalize on in the international markets on account of the Baath party's disastrous foreign policy and its military adventures). But the subsidy also encouraged a degree of complacency: in Iraq's heavily regulated economy, local producers never had to compete with international producers, and so did not really seek to cut their production costs.

The government's decision to reduce subsidies now revolutionized Iraq's economy. It reduced the incentive to engage in a number of negative practices, including smuggling, and freed up a significant portion of the annual state budget. State employees saw their salaries increase exponentially, and their improved purchasing power reflected positively on the consumer market. At the same time, however, transport and production costs soared with the increase in the price of oil. The state made almost no effort to mitigate the impact of its policy on manufacturers and farmers, who now had no cushion to protect themselves against international corporations that had spent the previous decades lowering production costs by consolidating and mechanizing and by investing in new technology (which was in any case unavailable in Iraq).

Suddenly the Iraqi market was flooded with fruit, vegetables and meats from Syria, Iran and Saudi Arabia, where farmers had made significant technological advances and benefited from generous government subsidies. The local market could not compete. It was overwhelmed by foreign markets that had, in the past, imported foodstuffs from Iraq. Suddenly, everything on sale in Iraqi stores was foreign: watermelons from Syria, apples from the United Kingdom, bananas from Central America, canned foods from Turkey.

On the highway between Baghdad and Tikrit, farmers put their freshly grown potatoes in cardboard boxes and offer them at reasonable rates to passers-by. Less than an hour away, Baghdad's markets have only Saudi potatoes (which are much cheaper than the local produce, because of the Saudi state subsidies). During summer 2010, I asked some Baghdad store managers if they would consider selling Iraqi produce. The response was uniform: 'too expensive'.

Even dates – traditionally Iraq's largest agricultural export and part of the country's national heritage – are nowadays imported from Saudi Arabia. Many of the date palms that have survived the ravages of drought and economic hardship are no longer cultivated, their fruit hanging disconsolately – a sad reminder of what used to be. Iraqi farmers are simply unable to compete.

On top of everything else, the occupation and the war ensured that any farmers who had access to enough capital to ride out the government's measures would not have been able to invest the funds effectively. As noted in Chapter 6, the electricity supply throughout the country was extremely unreliable after 2003, as was the distribution and accessibility of fuel. Thus, farmers could not rely on state-provided electricity to pump water from the river or the irrigation canals, and often could not even buy fuel to power any generators they might have purchased.

Over time, as more and more farms were abandoned to the elements, they turned dry, contributing to desertification and to the ever-present dust storms. Rural unemployment increased, so that more Iraqis went to the capital and other major cities in search of work. This led to even more unplanned urbanization. It took the government almost seven years to realize that some of its policies needed either to be reversed or at least modified.

A new law was finally passed in 2010 to increase customs and duty to between 10 per cent and 20 per cent (depending on the goods being imported). Although the law was designed principally to boost the state's revenue, farmers heaved a sigh of relief, as foreign producers would at last be faced with increased costs, which would go some way towards balancing the benefits they received from their home governments.

Public debate on the issue, however, was markedly negative: the focus was entirely on the impact that the new law might have on the capital's consumer market and on inflation. News reporters asked shopkeepers for their views, while farmers and environmental experts were ignored.[38]

Then, typically, as the revolutions in Tunisia and Egypt brought down those countries' leaders, the Iraqi government drew the wrong conclusions. It postponed the new customs law in an attempt to appease an urban population that was up in arms not about inflation, but about corruption and incompetence.[39] For the next two years, the government maintained its moratorium on the law's application, despite the fact that it did not have the authority to do so in law or under the constitution. Finally, in December 2012, it called for the new law to be suspended indefinitely, on the grounds that there were not enough trained technical staff to monitor implementation.[40] This was a clear capitulation to the government's own ineptitude: it had sponsored a law in 2010, only to admit in 2012 that it did not have the capacity to implement it. The government had squandered the previous two years (which it had bought itself by unilaterally and illegitimately not applying the law) by failing to carry out any of the training that it claimed was so essential. At the earliest, then, the law can be applied only in 2015 – twelve years after the 5 per cent flat rate was first applied. By then the agricultural sector will have shrunk even further.

The government has implemented a number of strategies to mitigate climate change, but these have so far proved inadequate. Up until 2012, Iraq did not really have a national strategy to combat desertification. There were isolated programmes in various parts of the country, but they were essentially powerless to stop the advancing sands. A unit was established in the 1970s in the border area between Kirkuk and Salah al-Din provinces. Its handful of staff were obliged to suspend their work on several occasions because of violence, most recently between 2005 and 2008, when the surrounding towns were under the control of militias that would gladly have kidnapped or assassinated any government employee they could get their hands on. When they were finally able to resume their activities, they found that the desert had advanced significantly. The unit maintains a small nursery, which cultivates a bush known in Iraq as *shawkasham*. It grows to a good height and its roots push deep into the soil within two years, even in the desert. The staff worked on their own (apart from a few dozen casual labourers) in extreme conditions and against all the elements. Until recently, theirs was one of only a handful of small-scale projects to combat desertification.

In 2012, though, Iraq established an anti-desertification office, which launched a major effort in Karbala province to plant around 20,000 palm trees, as well as thousands of olive trees. It remains to be seen whether the project's size (tiny in relation to what has been lost in the past few decades) and its implementation (requiring as it does vital water resources) will be sufficient to halt the desert's advance.

The lack of action is palpable. The prime minister and his closest associates involve themselves in negotiating huge defence contracts with foreign providers, but discussion of how to tackle Iraq's environmental catastrophe seems to be very low down the government's agenda. Its argument is that security issues must take priority; all other matters, including the need to increase electricity production, to halt desertification and to tackle rural migration, are of secondary importance.

AS THE REGION SUFFERS, THE IRAQI STATE IS PARALYSED

Many commentators have charged that Iraq has become completely subservient to Iranian interests since 2003; but it seems that even Iran cannot force its western neighbour get its act together. Dust storms are highly mobile and do not respect national borders; they have been finding their way into Iran, including Khuzestan, Sistan and Baluchistan provinces. The storms have affected people in the same way as in Iraq, impacting on their breathing, their work and their quality of life.

In July 2009, an unprecedented dust storm enveloped more than half of Iran. It affected the provinces of Qazvin, Kermanshah, Hamedan, Qom, Isfahan, Fars, Markazi, Khuzestan and Tehran. Offices, businesses, schools and universities closed for two full days because of the high levels of dust. State television said air pollution in the capital, Tehran, had reached levels not seen for thirty years. Visibility was close to zero, forcing the cancellation of domestic flights. Iranian researchers found higher instances of silicon dioxide, calcium, potassium and carbon in the air. Unsurprisingly, respiratory disease increased in the country: the elderly, children and people with heart and respiratory problems were told to stay indoors.[41] Experts at the time complained that the dust storms had descended on Iran from deserts and former marshlands in Iraq and Saudi Arabia.[42]

The issue was raised officially in November 2009, when Iranian Majlis Speaker Ali Larijani held a meeting with his Iraqi counterpart Ayad al-Samarai in Baghdad. The Iranian speaker urged Iraqi officials to take the necessary steps to prevent severe dust storms like the ones that had spread to Iran over the previous year: 'The issue of dust storms is a regional problem, and the neighboring countries should cooperate.'[43] The two sides signed an agreement, under which mulch was to be poured on abandoned farms in Iraq to prevent the topsoil from breaking up. A biological mulch would be tried first; if that failed to do the trick, petroleum-based mulch would be used. This was the first of many agreements that Iraq would sign with Iran to combat climate change, and particularly dust storms. In September 2010,

Iran, Iraq, Syria, Qatar and Turkey reached an accord in Tehran to establish a network of meteorological stations and to regenerate vegetation in order to stabilize the soil, specifically with a view to curbing the incidence of dust storms. The agreement was important enough for Iranian President Mahmoud Ahmadinejad to encourage other countries in the region to sign as well.

Just over a year later, on 3 October 2011, Iran and Iraq set out a more detailed version of their original agreement. It indicated the measure of investment that would be required from both sides ($1.2 billion in total) and set out a five-year timetable for completion. It also confirmed that the two sides would attempt a natural solution to the dust storms, but if that failed, then oil derivatives would be used.[44] Yet another agreement was signed on 1 November 2012, this time to establish a joint fund on environmental matters financed by the two countries.

However, despite all the talks and agreements, Iran's environment continues to deteriorate. In mid-April 2011, severe dust storms hit twenty of Iran's thirty-one provinces, including Lorestan, Kordestan, Kermanshah and Khuzestan. Schools and government offices were closed, and flights to and from some western Iranian cities were cancelled because of dust storms that were said to have originated in Iraq. The storms even reached Tehran, where experts were alarmed at the level of pollution, which aggravated respiratory problems. In Lorestan province, the quantity of airborne dust particles was nine times the permitted level. Members of the Iranian parliament criticized the government for failing to take appropriate measures to mitigate the environmental issue, and called on the foreign ministry to resolve the issue with the neighbouring countries, citing Iraq in particular.[45] In April 2012, yet another dust storm hit the western and south-western provinces of Iran and reached Tehran.

The deterioration, the Iranians said, was a result of Iraq's lack of action. Despite the many agreements that had been signed, Iraq was doing almost nothing to implement them. Criticism started in May 2012, when Mohammad Javad Mohammadi Zadeh, head of Iran's environmental protection organization, accused the Iraqi government of failing to meet its commitments. He also said that Iran's foreign minister, Ali Akbar Salehi, had urged al-Maliki at a meeting in Tehran to step up the government's actions. The Iranian side likewise raised the matter with the executive secretary of the United Nations Convention to Combat Desertification and asked him to personally exert pressure on Iraq.[46] Over the coming months, many Iranian officials and politicians criticized their Iraqi counterparts in the strongest terms, describing them as 'showing no interest' in implementing the agreements that had been entered into,[47] and threatening to raise the matter at international and diplomatic forums. Several Iranian delegations travelled to Baghdad to push for the existing agreements to be implemented, only to find that the little progress that was being made in tree planting was taking far too long.[48]

Iran's accusations of Iraqi inaction are partly self-serving: they mask the fact that Tehran itself has failed to act to curb desertification on its own territory, including in the south-west region of Khuzestan.[49] But Iraq is an easy scapegoat, given the lack of progress by Baghdad. Indeed it has failed to respond coherently to the accusations: the government is too busy with other, far less important issues. In a February 2013 joint assessment by all development agencies present in Iraq, the United Nations sought to give the government's inaction on environmental issues a positive twist by focusing on the development of a risk-management strategy. However, the UN's assessment could not conceal the lack of government interest: 'One of the main impediments to combating [sand and dust storms] today is the nascent understanding about the urgency for concerted action, limited regional cooperation, as well as a significant funding gap.'[50]

A DYING LANDSCAPE, A FLOUNDERING ECONOMY

The impact of drought, desertification and dust storms on the local population is immeasurable. When the sky is red and the air is filled with dust, it becomes too dangerous to travel, and so schools, universities, businesses and other institutions remain closed. Education is hit badly, economic activity is affected, and the business of governing the country grinds to a halt.

The health of Iraqis has deteriorated markedly. The dust enters people's lungs and impairs their breathing, particularly if they are asthmatic. Doctors in affected areas report a jump in respiratory problems and sometimes mortality during dust storms, especially among the elderly and the young. During a particularly bad episode on 16 April 2011, thirteen people died of respiratory difficulties in Najaf province alone.[51] Dust storms also cause bronchitis, headaches, sinusitis and pharyngitis.[52]

To add to the problem, power cuts in summer leave houses without air conditioning. The sweltering heat inside forces people to leave their doors and windows open – and so they are exposed even more to the dust. During dust storms, emergency hospital admissions for respiratory problems can jump from less than 5 per cent of all admissions to about 80 per cent. Even those lucky enough to reach hospital are not guaranteed treatment: mismanagement and corruption have led to a shortage of oxygen and inhalers.[53]

The lack of water and the poor quality of what water remains (a result of the pesticides, fertilizers and untreated sewage dumped in the rivers) have similarly contributed to the health crisis, particularly in children. Low aquifer levels mean that wells that have supplied farmers for decades cannot now be replenished and have dried up. And so the rural population is obliged to buy water from tankers that transport untreated water direct from the Tigris. Many people have contracted gastroenteritis, with children being particularly at risk. Every summer, more than fifty children are admitted to Tikrit Teaching Hospital alone with gastroenteritis; in recent years this disease has accounted for a quarter of child deaths in the area.[54]

More cases of cholera were reported in 2007 than at any time since 1966, which led one Tikrit hospital to be quarantined. A physician based in Salah al-Din's countryside told me he had treated over ten cases of cholera in a single year.[55] The dust gets into the water supply as well, leading to a marked increase in kidney stones and urinary tract infections.[56]

Meanwhile, city dwellers have long since given up trying to seal their windows; nothing can stop the encroaching dust from coating the inside of their homes. Within just a few hours, a house can look as though it has been abandoned for decades. Women (who traditionally are expected to keep the house neat) complain of having to clean their homes several times a day. The battle with the dust has resulted in an increased prevalence of back pain, rheumatism and arthritis among women, all of which has led to increased rates of depression. Doctors are finding it ever harder to keep their patients off valium. In the larger context of Iraq today, mental health is hardly a priority, and so the problem is more often than not just swept under the carpet.

Not only is the dust ruining people's health; it is also forcing them from their homes. The dust storms feed into desertification, and are fed by the same phenomenon. As the desert encroaches on cultivated fields, farmers either have to shake the dust off the plants constantly or surrender to the elements and abandon their land in search of areas that are less affected (or seek work in a different sector altogether). If they choose the latter course of action, they worsen an already desperate problem: their fields quickly turn to dust, which is then carried by the winds and follows them to wherever they seek to escape.

Even when farms are still able to produce, the storms make the entire business of farming far harder: roads, railways, irrigation and drainage canals are covered in dust. Consequently, farmers and villagers are forced to abandon their land all across the country. There is a new class of internally displaced persons: entire populations are being forced off their land and reduced to living nomadically, tilling whatever fields are still cultivable in an attempt to survive in the expanding margins of society. By 2009, drought had displaced 300,000 people across the country. In Salah al-Din, during a particularly bad spell in 2007 and 2008, three villages were colonized by the desert, while a further ten were abandoned when their farms failed to produce any crops.[57] Former residents joined other displaced persons in a small township of clay houses that sprang up on the outskirts of the provincial capital. Typically, they are denied fair treatment by the authorities, which view them with suspicion and trepidation.

In summer 2010, I visited farmland near Beiji, on the border between Salah al-Din and Kirkuk provinces. There I found farmers who had been displaced because of the changes to the country's climate. One, from the Ninewa plains, described what had made him leave his province:

> Our village was buried under sand eight months ago. We came here, hoping to make a living. The land here is acceptable, but we're too far away from the Tigris to obtain any water from there. We've dug a well, but the water is salty. We're not sure it will be enough.

The farmer and his family of eight were living in a two-room mud hut; the nearest house, tree or road was a kilometre away. There were others who had arrived from Dyala and Kirkuk provinces, all in search of land that could still be cultivated. Their only source of potable water was a tank that was refilled once a week by a local company – but it was merely providing them with untreated water straight from the Tigris. As I peered inside the tank, I spotted the worms they had told me about.

Iraqis often have trouble expressing how exasperated they have become with the storms. Government officials have described the situation that they 'inherited' as 'disastrous'. But citizens are quick to blame the government for its inactivity. In a radio interview during a particularly bad spell of storms, one Abdel Karim al-Rifa'i, who identified himself as a 'government employee', did not mince his words: 'They are too preoccupied with their political disagreements, financial and administrative corruption and looting.'[58]

The changes to Iraq's environment have had some very far-reaching implications. Since 2002, the quantity of wheat, the area that is available to grow
wheat and the productivity of wheat farming have all declined. Although the
area that is available to cultivate barley has actually increased since 2002,
productivity has declined. Meanwhile, other crops, particularly those produced
in the irrigated south of the country, have fared very badly. Iraq has had to
make up for the shortfall by buying abroad: by 2012 imports accounted for
80 per cent of all the food consumed.[59]

This exposes Iraq to a significant risk of serious food insecurity. If the
price of oil dropped slightly, or if international commodity prices rose,
the country could be overtaken by a food crisis. This would obviously hit the
poor and most vulnerable sections of society worst, particularly as the state's
assistance programmes have essentially been cancelled. One of the ironies of
the post-war period is that while the United States has provided only meagre
assistance to Iraq's agricultural sector, it has promoted its own exports,
encouraging Iraqis to purchase the wheat, rice and barley that they require
on the international markets.

The decline in agriculture has contributed to the rise in unemployment.
Although GDP has been climbing rapidly, growth is concentrated almost
entirely in the oil sector, which generates very little employment. And in
Iraq's case, it generates even less than it normally would, as very many of the
oil workers are imported.

In 2010, the government claimed that unemployment stood at 15.3 per
cent, a figure that was widely discredited. The United Nations estimates that
the real figure for people aged below thirty is closer to 30 per cent.[60] As
mentioned above, the agricultural sector still employs around 30 per cent of
the workforce, but that figure is declining as arable land is lost to desertification. As unemployment increases, so does food insecurity and poverty for
large sections of the population. The government currently has no credible
solution to offer those individuals who are already unemployed or those who
will be swelling their ranks in years to come. There are 250,000 new entrants
to the labour force annually, and the public and private sectors are currently
capable of absorbing only a tiny fraction of that number (see Chapter 6).
Without a comprehensive and credible economic plan that involves regenera-
tion of the agricultural sector, the problem will continue to grow.

The only option that the government provides is for these individuals to
join the security sector. Although a police officer or a soldier is paid far more
than the average farm worker can hope to earn, there are only so many jobs

to go around. Also, as anyone who has been to Iraq has seen, most security personnel are paid literally to sit around and do nothing. Thus, instead of subsidizing the agricultural sector or launching a national effort to regenerate farming as a whole, the state now pays for ex-farmers to provide targets for terrorists and other armed groups. Those who are not killed or maimed then have the privilege of dusting off their hair, face and clothes and spending their salaries on imported dates and rice from the local market, instead of eating the local produce that they themselves used to grow with such pride.

The sense of frustration can be felt everywhere and at all times. In summer 2011, I stood by the side of the road in west Baghdad, waiting for friends to pick me up and drive me to the airport, where I was to catch a plane to Beirut. A soldier who saw me from a distance came over and questioned me briefly. I asked where he was from. 'Nasariya', he said, a southern province that used to be predominantly agricultural, but that now offers up its young men to the security services. He asked what life was like in Beirut, and I told him it would be easy for him to visit and see for himself. 'And what would I do there?' he wondered. 'You could relax, enjoy yourself by the sea or in the mountains.' He smiled ruefully. As he turned and walked away, he muttered: 'There is no enjoyment in this life.'

CHAPTER NINE

WHAT IS TO BE DONE?

Given all the failures, the disappointments and the crimes committed, there is an important question that must be resolved: was Iraq's downward spiral after 2003 inevitable?

Some western and Iraqi analysts argue that it was, and that Iraq's ethno-sectarian divisions lie at the heart of all the country's difficulties. In their view, at the end of the First World War the British forced three communities (the Sunnis, Shias and Kurds) to live together in the same country, even though they had nothing in common – bar a long history of antagonism and hatred.[1] According to them, the violence that rumbled on throughout the twentieth century and the 2006–07 civil conflict were a result not of the state's having been captured by anti-democratic and chauvinistic elites, but of the fact that Iraq is an artificial country whose people cannot and do not want to live together.

This narrative suffers from two main problems. The first is that the facts do not support it. Almost every serious academic study that has been carried out on the question shows that, well before Iraq was established as a single nation state, most of the communities that resided on its territory were fully aware of belonging to a single cultural and political entity (see Chapter 1). There were also, contrary to popular perception in the West, very few recorded instances of sectarian conflict in Iraq. Of course, even if the narrative were true, the mere fact that the nation is an artificial construct is not reason enough for a hundred years of antagonism and violence: many stable nations were created around the same time as Iraq and under similar circumstances. Again, in many cases, the decision was taken by a foreign power or a national elite with no knowledge of, or interest in, the local population; and yet many such nations continue to function today without fear of break-up. Clearly, the reasons for Iraq's difficulties lie elsewhere.

The second problem with the argument is that it distracts from Iraq's real problems and focuses attention on a false debate about ancient history. A hundred years after the Iraqi state was established, the only two questions that matter are, first, whether Iraq's existing borders are viable; and, second, what the likely consequences of changing them might be if they are not. The manner in which the state was established is certainly relevant, but only in so far as it affects Iraqis' current sense of belonging. If Iraq has historical antecedents, so much the better for rebuilding a common sense of history; if it does not, there is still nothing to prevent the inhabitants of the country from living together peacefully. In the end, the determining factor in whether Iraq has a future is how Iraqis see themselves today and how they see their future.

Compared to other countries, Iraq's divisions are not especially marked. There are countries whose cleavages are far more pronounced, but that have nevertheless overcome them in favour of peace and development. Though divided by language, skin colour, religion, a history of imperialism, colonization and even slavery, many countries of Africa and Latin America have emerged in recent years as modern democracies. These countries not only had the benefit of good leadership, but also established clear rules by which they were to be governed. Compared to a country like South Africa, with its clear racial, linguistic, religious and cultural differences, Iraq is put to shame. It had every chance to progress after 2003 (indeed proponents of the 2003 war in the US and UK governments often made that point to justify the invasion), but every opportunity has been squandered.

Simply blaming Iraq's suffering on the way in which the state was established is facile (particularly as the narrative is wrong): any serious analysis needs to examine how the country has been governed over the past century, and particularly over the past ten years, and to try to understand the dynamics that underpinned the decisions taken during that time. I have tried to demonstrate throughout this book how greed, incompetence, personal ambition, foreign interference and many other factors have impaired Iraq's development since 2003. Sectarian divisions have not in themselves been an impediment to progress; rather they have been deliberately politicized by the country's most important actors, who sought to divert attention from their own performance in government.

Much damage has been done, but solutions are still available. To quote Fanar Haddad again:

> The oft-cited failure of Iraqi regimes to provide a narrative of state that effectively encompasses Sunnis and Shias is, I would argue, a failure rooted in the state's narrative rather than in the basics of sectarian relations. In other words, there is nothing inherent in Iraqi sectarian dynamics, in and of themselves, that prevents state nationalism from incorporating both sectarian nationalisms.[2]

In that context, the challenge will be to build a new narrative for the Iraqi state. What better place to start than by replacing the corrupt and sectarian rule of the former exiles with a genuine democracy based on real equality and on a desire to respond to the people's needs and aspirations?

Any attempt to define democracy and its various components will inevitably be incomplete, particularly in countries that do not have significant experience of free expression and elections. However, there has been sufficient debate on the issue since 2003 to identify some of the principal elements. Obviously, the people have been almost constantly on edge as a result of never-ending violence and political tension, and have had little opportunity to engage in substantive discussions; but those debates that have taken place reveal that a core group of the country's population shares a common vision for their country and their state, and that that vision cuts across ethno-sectarian lines. Most fundamentally, perhaps, despite having endured ten years of corrupt politicians and unremitting violence, a large majority of Iraqis consistently pronounces itself in favour of democracy, equality, the peaceful transfer of power, government accountability, equity, etc. This is by no means an obvious outcome: in many regions of the world, where an ostensibly democratic system of government fails to improve standards of living, support for democracy can quickly fall to shocking levels, particularly if the region has recently emerged from an autocratic system of government.[3]

Over the past ten years, consistent majorities of Iraqis have favoured a secular form of government, rather than the ethno-sectarian framework that has been in place since 2003. In a poll published in February 2011, the majority stated that they would prefer politics to be separate from religion (contrary to popular belief, the vast majority of Iraqis either never or only very rarely go to a mosque or a church).

Full equality is consistently cited by Iraqis as one of the essential elements of society.[4] The data confirm what I have experienced time and again with family, friends and colleagues. In 2007, at a meeting of parliamentarians and experts, Salim, an Iraqi Christian lawyer who is also passively nationalist, expressed disappointment with the direction the country was taking: 'The state doesn't represent me.' One of the other participants who was ideologically close to an Islamist party responded: 'Why? You are represented by Yonadam Kana' (a prominent Christian politician who had been involved in government and parliament since the 2003 war). Salim grew exasperated: 'Yonadam doesn't represent me! I want a state that won't discriminate against people, and I don't need a Christian in government for that to happen.'

Even the most sectarian politicians have to shape their discourse carefully, so as to avoid offending popular sentiment. Nouri al-Maliki, who has often been accused of intolerance towards individuals from other ethno-sectarian groups, is subject to the same pressure. Shortly after sectarian violence was brought under control, al-Maliki found himself campaigning in the 2009 and 2010 elections. He was hoping to attract nationalist, non-sectarian voters and delivered speech after speech that promoted his non-sectarian credentials. In one example, in January 2009, he said:

> We have the right to be proud that we stood against the fire of strife. Through rationality and brotherhood, and through a reaction characterized by an Islamic and patriotic humanitarian spirit, we pulled all components of Iraqi society together. All components [of the country] met on one single principle, that of Iraq, and the fact that this strife does not benefit anyone.[5]

Going further, al-Maliki sought to portray himself as above not only sectarianism but also political partisanship. This was music to the ears of most Iraqis. The January 2009 local elections confirmed that his nationalist, non-sectarian rhetoric did resonate with the population. Later, in June of that year, he said:

> When a person reaches a certain position, he has to forget his political partisanship and look after his citizens, as they are Iraqis who are equal in rights and obligation. [We have to open up to] all political forces and

deal with everyone with respect, as the first step towards treason is discrimination among Iraqis.[6]

For a while after the violence abated in 2008, it was very common for private businesses, government departments (particularly at the municipal level) and street signs to be festooned with Shia religious banners. Although these were often merely individual expressions of faith, commemorating historical and religious figures that most Muslims (and indeed even many non-Muslims) regard as role models, the context in which they were displayed provoked some discomfort among people from other confessions, and indeed among many Shia, too.[7] The phenomenon continues, and Sheikh Hussein al-Yassin, one of Grand Ayatollah Ali al-Sistani's representatives, has addressed the issue in a number of sermons. In November 2012, he said:

> Why do people organize official condolences in their government department? A state division belongs to all Iraqis, its function is to be a government department. It is not correct for you to hang banners and flags in your government department. It exists for all Iraqis of all religions and denominations. This is everybody's: government departments, schools, universities, all belong to everybody. It is not that of Shiites, Sunnites, Christians, or a particular political party. For that reason, it is not acceptable for any of the various political parties to campaign at a university or a school. These institutions are for education only. Schools are only for education. Finance divisions are for finance. Military units are only for the army.[8]

Iraqis were very quick to adapt to the idea of a peaceful transfer of power, active political participation and the free expression of ideas. The following extract from a sermon delivered in April 2013 by Sayyed Ahmed al-Safi, one of Grand Ayatollah Ali al-Sistani's closest associates, provides a clear statement of one such element:

> Some areas did not participate in the elections, especially in Baghdad even though Baghdad is suffering in relation to terrorist problems, bombings, road blocking, economic problems, and other similar problems. Then why did they not participate? Government officials have a responsibility to spread awareness on the peaceful transfer of power. If a citizen feels that his vote will not make a difference, he will not participate in the

elections. Our position is not that the citizen is right in so doing. What we are saying is that his decision not to participate is wrong but that it is up to government officials not to allow for citizens to reach that point. Because, without a transfer of power, dictatorship will be consecrated. There will be a return to the rule of the individual and the catastrophes that we witnessed. There is a need for real participation. Change does not come through wishing, or by sitting at home, but through participation. Rights are taken and not given. Your right as a citizen, as a person who wants change, you have to work towards it. You have to make an effort.[9]

Scholars, preachers and pundits have consistently challenged the political elites on a number of occasions, particularly when their practices were blatantly detrimental to the common good. By way of example, the decision in 2010 to move from a closed electoral list system to an open list (allowing Iraqis actually to see who they were voting for, and to choose individual candidates) was forced upon the political class by civil society and the religious class. When, in 2013, several politicians suggested moving back to the closed list system, the initiative was denounced as self-serving by civil society and a host of clerics.[10] Those same forces consistently call for a law that would regulate the financing of political parties, which is one of the measures that the parties themselves have most resisted.[11]

In terms of political preference and values, virtually all the polling data collected since 2003 has shown the same thing (with the exception of data collected during the civil conflict). The message could not be clearer: service delivery and basic economic issues are the top priorities for most of the population; religion and other divisive matters hardly feature. In 2009 and 2010 – the only two election campaigns that have been more about government accountability than sectarianism – the major parties and alliances were forced to discuss the issues that concerned Iraqis; in the process they revealed how remarkably similar they are to one another.

Having reviewed hundreds of pages of campaign materials, dozens of speeches and interviews, and the websites of all the major players, I have compiled a list of core issues that virtually all the candidates prioritized in their campaigns:

(i)   Improving the delivery of public services (in particular the water supply, electricity, health care, education, transport, housing and social care) and supporting displaced families

(ii)   Reducing unemployment
(iii) Fighting financial and administrative corruption
(iv)   Ending the ethno-sectarian system of government and basing recruit-
       ment to government positions exclusively on experience and
       competence
(v)   Fighting terrorism
(vi)   Developing independent and non-sectarian security forces.

Although the issues that were of importance to Iraqis were clearly identifiable, the quality of the debate was wholly unsatisfactory. By and large, the
candidates had no specific proposals; they merely said they would deal with
each of the issues with determination and integrity. But then the political
parties they belonged to had selected the candidates not on the basis of
merit, but through nepotism (so even if they were elected, they would never
work to resolve the issues). Given the right context, the right people and
enough time, a vibrant debate would surely follow.

Iraq's social values are plain to see. Although large swathes of the country
have been urbanized, people maintain a strong link to their traditional
customs – many of them tribal – which form the backbone of Iraqi culture.

In addition, educational programmes that started under the monarchy
and that continued for decades under successive republican regimes (until
they were totally corrupted by the Baathists in the 1980s) instilled a sense of
nationalism in most parts of the country that is still identifiable today.
Although some of those nationalist tendencies are negative (including a
distinct militaristic trend), they do nevertheless contribute to the country's
sense of itself and to a desire for unity.

There is a strong sense in Iraq of solidarity, generosity, kindness, hospitality, honesty and a desire to help others, including people from other countries. In the 1970s and 1980s, millions of foreigners lived, studied and worked
in Iraq; though they left after the invasion of Kuwait in 1990, they spread
tales of Iraqi generosity and customs far and wide throughout the Arab
region. More than two decades later, in my daily interactions with people
across the Arab region, I am invariably asked about life in Baghdad. On one
occasion, a young Egyptian labourer who had never been to Baghdad told me
how much he loved our capital city and its people. When I asked how this
could be, since he had never been to Iraq, he answered: 'Because no one who
has ever been to Iraq ever comes back disappointed. Iraqis are the best of all
peoples.'[12] Similarly, a large number of Arab academics studied at Iraqi

universities in the 1970s; now middle-aged, they still speak of the vibrancy, the sense of solidarity and the hospitality they experienced at the time.[13]

The way in which this plays out in practice may come as a surprise to observers whose only source of information is the western press. For example, in 2003, after twelve years of complete separation from the rest of the country, officials in the Kurdistan region began relaxing entry requirements for Iraqis who lived south of the de facto border. In the first few years, Iraqis from Baghdad were required to have a guarantor in the region if they wanted to visit. At a time of increasing violence in all parts of the country south of Kurdistan, this measure was generally considered to be justifiable, even if people did complain about it.

Later, as the violence receded, the restrictions were replaced by a requirement that the driver of any vehicle entering the region should leave his or her driving licence at a check point. Though unpopular with Iraqis outside the region, the new procedure at least allowed millions to visit the north, either for a holiday or for work.

Academics from Baghdad and elsewhere took up teaching positions in Kurdish universities; some acquired permanent residence in Erbil, while others visited once a week. Doctors opened clinics in Erbil; others joined public hospitals. Many people purchased retirement homes or travelled to the mountains to see snow for the first time in their lives. Meanwhile, resorts and water parks opened throughout the region specifically to welcome Arab tourists from the rest of the country.

Despite the analysts' gloomy predictions, not a single violent incident involving Kurds and Arabs has been reported anywhere (apart from on the militarized so-called 'trigger line' that runs across the disputed territories, which continues to be manipulated for political purposes).[14] Kurdish students are unfazed at being taught by Arab lecturers, and Arab patients are only too happy to seek treatment in Kurdish hospitals. Iraqis from the rest of the country have been made to feel completely at home in Kurdistan. Relations are warm and easy and offer a firm basis for peaceful coexistence.

Finally, Iraqis are imbued with a sense of responsibility and duty. This is most evident in the thousands of mid- to senior-level state officials who work tirelessly to ensure that whatever is left of the state continues to function. Some were trained prior to 2003; others joined after the invasion with the best of intentions. These are the individuals who, between 2003 and 2008, fought off looters to protect factories and government offices, and who worked to ensure that water was still being purified and delivered to people's homes. They work today with whatever means are at their disposal to treat the sick and to provide electricity to as many people as possible. When their bureaucracies stopped functioning entirely, they stepped up to the plate and, at considerable personal risk, did what they could to keep the wheels in motion. Despite (or perhaps because of) their achievements, these individuals are quick to curse the politicians and the racket they are now running. They are caught between hope (that their country can pick itself up again) and despair (which could impel them to emulate the thousands who have emigrated for good).

These people represent the country's best hope of a peaceful future, in which the needs of Iraq's destitute millions are prioritized.

A PLAN OF ACTION

In the final analysis, the question is whether there is any way of translating a desire for democracy and good faith into a plan of action. The answer is that there must be. Other countries with similar (if not worse) problems have successfully strengthened their democracies and have made inroads in the fight against corruption, and there is no reason why Iraq cannot do likewise. While there are many challenges, the ingredients for a successful transition are all present. What is lacking is a road map for the transition. What follows is a modest proposal for the next few years in Iraq.

If Iraq is to achieve a more convincing measure of democracy, the first thing required is a new constitution. The work to draft a new text (or at least heavily amend the 2005 constitution) will draw a line in the sand between the post-2003 period, with all its mistakes, and the future. The original text is highly problematic: it is tainted – partly because of the way it was written, and partly because its actual content is divisive. A new or revised constitution should resolve a number of outstanding issues:

(i) **The armed forces.** The 2005 constitution provides almost no detail on the armed forces and how they should be controlled. This has allowed the prime minister to capture the institution for what is perceived as his own narrow political interests. A new constitutional arrangement should introduce a number of mechanisms, designed so as to prevent any future abuse. First, the chain of command should be clearly set out. Secondly, military policy should not be left in the hands of a single individual: a national defence council (whose members should include military and civilian officials) should be clearly enshrined in the constitution and should be the sole body responsible for determining policy and making senior appointments. Thirdly, the military's role should be clearly spelt out, in considerable detail. Other countries' constitutions (including those of Germany, South Africa, etc.) clearly indicate the circumstances in which the army is required to intervene internally, including natural disasters, and specify what the army should be doing in such circumstances. The army should no longer be allowed to police the country.

(ii) **Political parties.** Any new constitutional arrangement should prioritize the regulation of political parties. The 2005 constitution makes no mention of the rules and standards by which political parties should operate, and this has encouraged a surge of corruption throughout the country. A new or revised constitution should clearly specify that parties cannot register unless they have declared bank accounts within the country and unless they comply with the highest standards of transparency. Foreign funding and donations over a certain threshold should be expressly prohibited. A clear mechanism should also be established to allocate public funding to parties, in order to reduce the incentives to solicit foreign or illicit funds. Finally, the new text should provide specific sanctions for engaging in hate speech.

(iii) **Corruption.** The country's anti-corruption framework should be completely overhauled. Both the country's audit institution and the integrity commission should be able to refer criminal cases directly to the courts. Both should be completely independent of the executive branch of government, and should be responsible for determining their budgets, albeit within limits. The same applies to the courts: under a new arrangement, the courts should be completely free to administer their own affairs; judges should be specifically protected against arbitrary or unfair dismissal, as well as against any sanctions that are designed to apply pressure on judges. All these matters should be specifically stated in the constitution, as is the case in many of the world's most modern constitutions.

(iv) **Natural resources.** The new constitution should redesign the existing framework on oil and gas. The vast majority of Iraqis do not have any views on whether the industry should be centralized or be under the control of regional and provincial governments. They do, however, consider that whatever revenues are generated should be used to finance pro-poor policies and to rehabilitate government services. Given that the politicians have singularly failed to resolve their differences in this area, the matter should be depoliticized in its entirety and left in the hands of an independent expert committee. That committee, which should be composed of economists, oil and gas engineers and jurists, should be tasked with determining the framework that is most likely to maximize profits and establish firm mechanisms in relation to transparency throughout the industry, including in the disbursement of profits.

(v) **Decentralization.** A genuine system of decentralization for the provinces outside the Kurdistan region should finally be established. The current system has given democracy a bad name: provincial elections take place every four years, but the councils have no authority to serve the people. All decisions remain firmly within the control of central government. Thus the current constitution makes provincial officials accountable for matters over which they have no control. Under a new constitutional arrangement, real power should be allocated to the provinces, including the construction and maintenance of schools and hospitals, hygiene and garbage collection in public places, the maintenance of roads and means of transport in the province, the protection of the environment, etc. Naturally, also, provincial authorities should be allocated sufficient funds for these activities, calculated on a per capita basis. At the same time, additional funds should be allocated to those provinces that are still recovering from the effects of war and neglect.

In addition to legal reform, a concerted and deliberate effort should be made to reduce sectarian tension throughout the country. To this end, substantial changes in discourse are needed, as are certain legal and regulatory reforms. Politicians, particularly those in the upper echelons of government, should commit themselves to promoting harmony throughout the country and to condemning any form of prejudice. Specifically, accusations that equate Shias with Iranian agents are clearly mistaken, and there needs to be a commitment to avoid such references in future. Similarly, the tendency to equate all Sunnis with the Baath party and with anti-Shia oppression must stop. Clearly, the current crop of political elites is incapable of reaching any such agreement, let alone of implementing it; but in the meantime changes can be introduced that will at least place a check on intemperate speech in the short to medium term. These changes would include: (i) reform of defamation and other criminal laws, to ensure that hate speech is properly sanctioned; (ii) regulatory reform to ensure that a media commission is empowered to ban hate speech in all quarters; (iii) legal reform to bring an end to the de-Baathification process and to place transitional justice issues completely in the hands of the courts; any individual found guilty of a crime should be punished, and collective or arbitrary punishment should be avoided.

These ideas could serve as stepping stones to a future free of conflict, discrimination and widespread corruption. But what are the dynamics that would allow such a thing?

Clearly, one possibility would be the collapse of the existing political order. As was explained in Chapter 6, unemployment is set to rise steeply in the next few years. Hundreds of thousands of young Iraqis will join the workforce, and the vast majority will have no prospect of finding meaningful employment. The government has no solution to this problem, but is essentially hoping that the projected increases in oil production will generate enough revenue to buy the population's acquiescence and passivity. Under that rationale, financial support will be provided to needy families through the few individuals who are lucky enough to have government jobs. As the rest languish at home with nothing to do, the government will continue to build up its security forces, in case the poor take to the streets and riot (as they have done on many occasions since 2003).

But this fragile construct could fall apart for many reasons: even a modest drop in the price of oil on the international markets could cause a budget crisis of colossal proportions. If oil prices remained low even for just a few years, the pressure would probably lead to the collapse of the government. That could force a complete change in direction for the state.

Even without a fall in oil prices, the gap between the social and economic classes is set to widen, as the number of the unemployed poor rises while the ruling elite amasses greater wealth. The smallest spark could cause the simmering anger to explode.

That said, simply waiting for economic realities to wreak havoc is not a strategy for change. Therefore another possibility would be a concerted and organized grassroots campaign over a period of years to force change. There is significant evidence that a national campaign for reform could be successful, given the right conditions. Since 2003, civil society and the clerical establishment have mobilized on several occasions to curb the political elite's undemocratic tendencies. In particular, they have arranged nationwide campaigns against corruption and have even forced parliament to amend the electoral law from a closed to an open list system. In August 2013, demonstrations were organized simultaneously in twelve provinces to protest against the high pay, privileges and retirement packages that the politicians have offered themselves. The good will, organizational ability and influence that these institutions wield can and should be directed towards creating momentum for significant constitutional reform. That initiative will be difficult and will take years; but it is achievable and is one of the only avenues leading to genuine democratic reform from within.

The ultimate threshold or target for any campaign for reform should be the parliamentary elections due to take place in 2018 (2014 is already a lost cause). The objective should be to obtain a sufficient number of representatives in parliament to impose a reform programme on the government. This is easier said than done, of course, considering that the ruling elite has access to virtually unlimited funds and considering the number of candidates who have been killed in previous electoral campaigns.

However, all the opinion polls carried out in recent years show that voters are looking for credible alternatives to the parties currently in charge. In May 2012, 68 per cent of the population (76 per cent in the south, and 80 per cent in the west) said that they would prefer to vote for someone other than the current ruling elite. The stage is set; all that is needed is a united front, a clear political platform, and enough credibility to attract voters in sufficient numbers.

To this end, the 2017 provincial elections should be regarded as a stepping stone. The past ten years have shown that local protest movements can attract significant support during provincial elections. In 2009, a single candidate ran as an independent in Karbala province, where he outperformed all the major electoral alliances. Though he had almost no funds and could not mount a serious campaign, his reputation as an honest individual who cared about the welfare of his province gained this one man 37,846 votes; put together, all the candidates on the Sadrist list (a major national alliance) polled 26,967 votes. In 2013, a local alliance in Najaf also clearly outperformed all the heavyweights.

Thus there are precedents. A core group of civil society activists and organizations, combined with the clerical establishment, could initiate the campaign by preparing a new programme for reform. Local independents and movements with a reputation for integrity, compassion and professionalism should be invited to debate the programme, to become accustomed to it – and ultimately to campaign for it. The campaign's success will depend on whether sufficient momentum can be generated and whether it can be maintained until the national elections.

If Iraq's problems today are caused by political parties that are devoid of any ideology other than personal gain, then the best solution for the country is to develop a programme for reform that does not rely on specific parties. After all, the Arab Spring's initial successes in January and February 2011 were the result of campaigns that had been launched by civil society years earlier.

By 2017, Saddam Hussein will have been out of power for fourteen years. The new ruling elites should finally be made to take responsibility for their failures. Their inability to empathize with the people's suffering will provide enough fuel for a credible and organized national campaign to get rid of them.

ENDNOTES

INTRODUCTION

1. ATSC Limited previously maintained a website on which it provided background information on the Advanced Detection Equipment ADE 651. That website (www.atscltd.com/advanced-detection-equipment-ade651.html) now appears to be defunct. Background information is available: http://en.wikipedia.org/wiki/ADE_651
2. Radwan Mortada, 'Lebanon: The great explosives detector hoax', Al-Akhbar.com, 12 September 2013, at: http://english.al-akhbar.com/node/17005
3. Henceforth all reference to dollars should be assumed to be US dollars.
4. Ministry of justice official, interview with the author, Baghdad, January 2011.
5. 'Export ban for useless "bomb detector" ', BBC *Newsnight* website, 22 January 2010, at: http://news.bbc.co.uk/2/hi/programmes/newsnight/8471187.stm
6. 'Investigation revealed that Jabiri recommended that Iraq sign five contracts to supply security forces with the detectors for between 23,548.37 pounds and 34,702.86 pounds each even though the real cost of the devices is no more than 61.97 pounds, the senior official said.' http://uk.reuters.com/article/2011/02/17/uk-iraq-britain-explosives-idUKTRE71G3H120110217
7. 'Six charged with fraud offences relating to substance detection devices', Crown Prosecution Service, 12 July 2012.
8. *R v. James McCormick*, Sentencing remarks of his honour Judge Hone QC, 2 May 2013, at: www.judiciary.gov.uk/media/judgments/2013/r-v-mccormack
9. Prime Minister Nouri al-Maliki's speech dated 20 March 2013 can be viewed in full at: www.youtube.com/watch?v=CdlC45ucM2Q#t=8m00s (my emphasis). Here and throughout, unless otherwise stated, all translations are my own.
10. 'Thi Qar's police switches from handheld devices to police dogs', Iraqiyoun.com, 15 March 2013, http://iraqiuon.com/index.php/permalink/4492.html

CHAPTER 1: A LEGACY OF OPPRESSION AND VIOLENCE

1. Jim al-Khalili, *Pathfinders: The golden age of Arabic science*, Penguin, London, 2010.
2. Abbas Kadhim, *Reclaiming Iraq: The 1920 revolution and the founding of the modern state*, University of Texas Press, Austin, 2012, Kindle edition locations 171–84.

3. Reidar Visser, 'Historical myths of a divided Iraq', *Survival*, 50:2 (April–May 2008), pp. 95–106.
4. Quoted in Kadhim, *Reclaiming Iraq*, Kindle edition locations 197–210.
5. ibid., location 2782.
6. An annex to the Treaty of Sèvres provided that Iraq's only national oil company would remain 'under permanent British control' and that 'native interests' would be permitted to hold no more than 20 per cent of that company's stock. See 'Anglo-French oil agreement is out', *New York Times*, 24 July 1920, at: http://query.nytimes.com/gst/abstract.html?res=FA0716FA3B5910738DDDAD0A94DF405B808EF1D3 See also more generally, Daniel Yergin, *The Prize*, Free Press, New York, 1991, pp. 184–206.
7. Majid Khadduri, *Independent Iraq*, Oxford University Press, London, 1951, pp. 14–15.
8. ibid., p. 16.
9. Hanna Batatu, *The Old Social Classes and the Revolutionary Movements of Iraq: A study of Iraq's old landed and commercial classes and of its communists, Ba'thists and Free Officers*, Saqi Books, London, 2012, p. 25.
10. Kadhim, *Reclaiming Iraq*, location 3018.
11. David McDowall, *A Modern History of the Kurds*, I.B. Tauris, New York, 2005, p. 180.
12. Kadhim, *Reclaiming Iraq*, location 3029.
13. Philip Williard Ireland, *Iraq: A study in political development*, Russell and Russell, New York, 1937, p. 372; Ernest Main, *Iraq from Mandate to Independence*, G. Allen & Unwin Ltd, London, 1935, p. 166.
14. Batatu, *Old Social Classes*, p. 471.
15. World Bank, *The Economic Development of Iraq: Report of a mission organized by the International Bank for Reconstruction and Development at the request of the government of Iraq*, Johns Hopkins Press, Baltimore, 1952, p. 1.
16. Batatu, *Old Social Classes*, p. 475.
17. ibid., pp. 730–9.
18. See, for example, Mohamed Baqir al-Sadr al-Sayed, *Our Economics*, 1962, available at: http://lfile.ir/feqhi-library/book469.pdf
19. My father, Salah Omar Al-Ali, was a member of the RCC and was purged in 1970 when he protested over a number of the government's policies.
20. Tareq Ismael, *The Rise and Fall of the Communist Party of Iraq*, Cambridge University Press, 2007.
21. Joseph Sassoon, *Saddam Hussein's Ba'th Party: Inside an authoritarian regime*, Cambridge University Press, 2012, pp. 102–3.
22. Imad Khadduri, *Iraq's Nuclear Mirage: Memoirs and delusions*, Springhead Publishers, Ontario, 2003, p. 147.
23. When Nouri al-Maliki returned to Iraq in 2003 after a long period of exile, he discovered that his younger relatives had never even heard of his existence. Ned Parker and Raheem Salman, 'Notes from the underground: The rise of Nouri al-Maliki', World Policy Institute, 2013, at: www.worldpolicy.org/journal/spring2013/maliki. My father and I were in a similar position: he was completely ostracized by the regime after he decided to actively campaign for Hussein's downfall and his relatives never spoke of him again. Upon our return to the country after the 2003 war, we discovered that many of my generation of relatives had never heard of us.
24. Interview with the author, January 2011.
25. Conference entitled, 'Iraq 2013: Achievements and Challenges', Chatham House, 20 March 2013, at: www.youtube.com/watch?v=xse9AB_iQhg
26. Denis J. Halliday, 'The deadly and illegal consequences of economic sanctions on the people of Iraq', *Brown Journal of World Affairs*, 7:1 (Winter/Spring 2000), p. 229.
27. Interview with the author, October 2013.

CHAPTER 2: ON THE ORIGINS OF IRAQ'S NEW POLITICAL ELITES

1. In 2007, SCIRI changed its name to the Islamic Supreme Council of Iraq (ISCI). For the sake of clarity, I shall refer to SCIRI throughout.

2. 'President Bush meets with His Eminence Abdul-Aziz Al-Hakim, Leader of the Supreme Council for the Islamic Revolution in Iraq', White House website, 4 December 2006, http://georgewbush-whitehouse.archives.gov/news/releases/2006/12/20061204-7.html

3. A number of the Kurdish alliance's advisers have subsequently written their own accounts of the alliance's starting positions, many of which do not coincide with the draft constitution that was agreed upon in 2002. See, for example, Brendan O'Leary, *How to Get Out of Iraq with Integrity*, University of Pennsylvania Press, Philadelphia, 2009, ix–x.

4. United States Department of State and the Broadcasting Board of Governors, Office of Inspector General, 'Review of awards to Iraqi National Congress Support Foundation', Report Number 01-FMA-R-092, September 2011.

5. A small number of the US and the UK's preferred collaborators were so unpopular that they were never able to attract any public support to speak of, including Ahmed al-Chalabi and Adnan al-Pachachi.

6. Shane Harris and Matthew M. Aid, 'Exclusive: CIA files prove America helped Saddam as he gassed Iran', *Foreign Policy*, 26 August 2013, at: www.foreignpolicy. com/articles/2013/08/25/secret_cia_files_prove_america_helped_saddam_as_he_ gassed_iran?print=yes&hidecomments=yes&page=full

7. *Iraq's Weapons of Mass Destruction: The assessment of the British government*, at http://news.bbc.co.uk/nol/shared/spl/hi/middle_east/02/uk_dossier_on_iraq/pdf/ iraqdossier.pdf

8. 'Bush, Blair: Saddam has to go', CBS News, 7 September 2002, at: www.cbsnews.com/ stories/2002/09/08/attack/main521177.shtml

9. Joseph Curl, 'Agency disavows report on Iraq arms', *Washington Times*, 27 September 2002, at: http://www.washingtontimes.com/news/2002/sep/27/20020927-091051-4501r/ ?page=all; Richard Norton-Taylor, 'Doubt cast on PM's "nuclear threat" claim', *Guardian*, 9 September 2002, at: www.guardian.co.uk/international/story/0,3604, 788336,00.html

10. '[W]e know from Khidhir Hamza, the head of the Nuclear Program for Saddam . . . that there were and are hundreds of sites where weapons of mass destruction are worked on in Iraq. Many of them are buried. Many of them are quite small. Saddam . . . is using centrifuges and other facilities that can be relatively small. His biological weapons laboratories can be quite small . . . We know through Khidhir Hamza, who headed the program and came out of Iraq in 1994, how well developed the program was in terms of design, in terms of expertise, in terms of the components of the weapon other than the fissionable material' ('US policy toward Iraq', Hearing before the Committee on International Relations House of Representatives, One Hundred Seventh Congress, Second Session, 19 September 2002, Serial No. 107–115, at: http:// commdocs.house.gov/committees/intlrel/hfa81813.000/hfa81813_0.htm).

11. Khadduri, *Iraq's Nuclear Mirage*, pp. 91–2; 'Nuclear weapons expert warns of Hamza evidence', *Lateline*, transcript on ABC website, 25 September 2002, at: www.abc.net. au/lateline/stories/s686055.htm

12. This statement is not made with the benefit of hindsight. At the time, I spent considerable time investigating the matter on my own, using sources that were publicly available, and concluded that all the allegations that were made in the UK's case for war were incorrect. I put all of my conclusions in a letter to my MP in the UK parliament, in which I urged him not to support the conflict. I then circulated the letter as widely as possible and published it online in an effort to influence public debate at the time (unsuccessfully, obviously). The letter, dated 23 January 2013, is available at: www. casi.org.uk/discuss/2003/msg00242.html

13. On 29 May 2003, President George W. Bush said: 'We found the weapons of mass destruction. We found biological laboratories. You remember when Colin Powell stood up in front of the world, and he said, Iraq has got laboratories, mobile labs to build biological weapons. They're illegal. They're against the United Nations resolutions, and we've so far discovered two. And we'll find more weapons as time goes on. But for those who say we haven't found the banned manufacturing devices or banned weapons, they're wrong, we found them' ('Interview of the President by TVP, Poland', George W. Bush White House Archives website, 29 May 2003, at: http://georgewbush-whitehouse.archives.gov/g8/interview5.html). A few years later, President Bush reluctantly admitted the failure to locate any weapons, which he attributed to an 'intelligence failure' and described as the 'biggest regret of the presidency' (Alex Spillius, 'George W. Bush says Iraq intelligence failure is his biggest regret', *Daily Telegraph*, 1 December 2008, at: www.telegraph.co.uk/news/worldnews/northamerica/usa/3540733/George-W-Bush-says-Iraq-intelligence-failure-is-his-biggest-regret.html).

14. Greg Muttitt, *Fuel on the Fire: Oil and politics in occupied Iraq*, Vintage, London, 2012, Chapter 4.

15. Constitution Project, 'The report on the Constitution Project's Task Force on Detainee Treatment', Washington, DC, 2013, at: http://detaineetaskforce.org/read/

16. Daniel Somers, a veteran of Iraqi Freedom, took his own life in June 2013. In a letter that he left for his family, and which they have since decided to make public, he wrote: 'During my first deployment, I was made to participate in things, the enormity of which is hard to describe. War crimes, crimes against humanity. Though I did not participate willingly, and made what I thought was my best effort to stop these events, there are some things that a person simply cannot come back from. I take some pride in that, actually, as to move on in life after being part of such a thing would be the mark of a sociopath in my mind. These things go far beyond what most are even aware of. To force me to do these things and then participate in the ensuing cover up is more than any government has the right to demand.' The full letter is available at: http://gawker.com/i-am-sorry-that-it-has-come-to-this-a-soldiers-last-534538357

17. Although collaboration did allow some actors to enjoy an important popular profile at a crucial time in Iraq's transition, that advantage was still not enough for others to achieve any level of popularity, either because they were too far outside the popular mainstream and were too lacking in personal charisma (as in the case of Adnan al-Pachachi), or because they were simply too disliked in the country or too closely associated with foreign interests (as in the case of Ahmed al-Chalabi).

18. David L. Phillips, *Losing Iraq: Inside the postwar reconstruction fiasco*, Westview Press, New York, 2005, p. 36.

19. For more on Shia opinions on federalism, see Reidar Visser, 'Shi'a perspectives on a federal Iraq: Territory, community and ideology in conceptions of a new polity' in Daniel Heradstveit and Helge Hveem (eds), *Oil in the Gulf: Obstacles to democracy and development*, Ashgate, Aldershot, 2004. A United Nations official who was intimately involved in the 2005 constitutional negotiations agrees with this account: 'There were two basic strands within the Shia negotiators. One strand involved some form of regionalization in the south of the country, although there was much disagreement between them as to which provinces should be the focus of attention. There were some that were concerned with Najaf province and its surrounding provinces. Others were concerned with Basra becoming its own province, while still others were hoping to convert the entire south of the country into one region. The second strand had the opposite view, and were arguing in favour of a majoritarian democracy' (interview with the author, July 2010).

20. Democratic Principles Work Group, *Final Report on the Transition to Democracy in Iraq*, 2002, at www.iraqfoundation.org/studies/2002/dec/study.pdf

21. The INC's Ahmed al-Chalabi angrily rejected the transition plan that had been discussed, arguing in favour of a government-in-exile that would have him as its head. See Phillips, *Losing Iraq*, p. 87.

22. Ali Allawi, *The Occupation of Iraq: Winning the war, losing the peace*, Yale University Press, New Haven and London, 2007, p. 351.
23. Interview with the author, 2006.
24. Allawi, *The Occupation of Iraq*, p. 460.
25. One such promotional video was posted on YouTube but has since been removed.
26. L. Paul Bremer, *My Year in Iraq: The struggle to build a future of hope*, Simon & Schuster, New York, 2006, p. 171.
27. Interview with the author, January 2011.
28. Interview with the author, June 2011.
29. Interview with the author, January 2011.
30. Muttitt, *Fuel on the Fire*.
31. Interview with the author, July 2010.
32. 'Oil ministry an untouched building in ravaged Baghdad', AFP report, 16 April 2003, at: www.smh.com.au/articles/2003/04/16/1050172643895.html
33. L. Elaine Halchin, 'The Coalition Provisional Authority (CPA): Origin, characteristics and institutional authorities', CRS Report for Congress, Congressional Research Service, 6 June 2005, at: www.fas.org/sgp/crs/mideast/RL32370.pdf
34. ibid., p. 6.
35. Fanar Haddad, *Sectarianism in Iraq*, Columbia University Press, New York, 2011, p. 13.
36. Norwegian Institute of International Affairs (NUPI), *More than 'Shiites' and 'Sunnis': How a post-sectarian strategy can change the logic and facilitate sustainable political reform in Iraq*, Oslo, 2009, p. 18–19.
37. 'Poll finds broad optimism in Iraq, but also deep divisions among groups', ABC News Poll: Iraq – Where things stand, 12 December 2005, p. 21, at: http://abcnews.go.com/images/Politics/1000a1IraqWhereThingsStand.pdf
38. 'Survey of Iraqi public opinion', International Republican Institute, 14–24 June 2006, p. 41, at: http://www.iri.org/sites/default/files/2006%20July%2019%20Survey%20of%20Iraqi%20Public%20Opinion,%20June%2014-24,%202006.pdf
39. 'A major shift in the political landscape: Results from the April 2012 National Survey', Greenberg Quinlan Rosner Research on behalf of the National Democratic Institute, May 2012, p. 30, at: http://abunoass.net/uploads/pdf/greenbergen.pdf
40. John Agresto, *Mugged by Reality: The liberation of Iraq and the failure of good intentions*, Encounter Books, New York, 2007, Kindle edition, locations 1410 to 1462.
41. Hamza Mustapha, 'Baghdad operations' official spokesman: The majority of terrorist attacks are carried out by officials' security guards, and through the use of official cards and IDs', *Asharq Alawsat*, 2 February 2012, www.aawsat.com/details.asp?section=4&issueno=12119&article=661740&feature
42. Jason Whiteley, *Father of Money: Buying peace in Baghdad*, Potomac Books, Washington, DC, 2011, pp. 31–2.
43. Colin Powell, *It Worked for Me: In life and leadership*, Harper, New York, 2012, Kindle edition, location 2820.
44. Thomas E. Ricks, *Fiasco: The American military adventure in Iraq*, Penguin, New York, 2007, p. 162.
45. Interview with the author, February 2013.
46. See, for example, Miranda Sissons and Abdulrazzaq al-Saiedi, 'A bitter legacy: Lessons of de-Baathification in Iraq', International Center for Transitional Justice, March 2013, at: http://ictj.org/sites/default/files/ICTJ-Report-Iraq-De-Baathification-2013-ENG.pdf
47. Paul Martin, 'Paul Bremer on Iraq, ten years on: "We made major strategic mistakes. But I still think Iraqis are better off" ', *Independent*, 18 March 2013, at: www.independent.co.uk/news/world/middle-east/paul-bremer-on-iraq-ten-years-on-we-made-major-strategic-mistakes-but-i-still-think-iraqis-are-far-better-off-8539767.html

48. Powell, *It Worked for Me*, location 2827. There is some dispute among US historians and those officials involved in these decisions as to who would have authorized Bremer to overrule the plan that the president had already approved, and it has been suggested that his instructions might have emanated from the vice president's office. That is a matter that is beyond the scope of this volume.

49. Bremer, *My Year in Iraq*, p. 55. Bremer repeated this view in a July 2012 interview with Rudaw, a popular English-language Kurdish website: 'Practically, it would've meant sending American forces into the villages, farms and towns to force the conscripts, the enlisted men, back into the army they hated, under Sunni Arab officers they hated' ('Paul Bremer shows little regret about role in Iraq', Rudaw, 26 July 2012, web page no longer available).

50. Hamza Mustapha, 'Baghdad operations' spokesman: The majority of terrorist attacks are carried out by government officials and with government vehicles and IDs', *Asharq Alawsat*, 2 February 2012, at: www.aawsat.com/details.asp?section=4& issueno=12119&article=661740&feature

51. Mark Fineman, Warren Vieth and Robin Wright, 'Dissolving Iraqi army seen by many as a costly move', *Los Angeles Times*, 24 August 2003.

52. David Blair, 'Saddam empties Iraq's jails', *Daily Telegraph*, 21 October 2002, www. telegraph.co.uk/news/worldnews/middleeast/iraq/1410858/Saddam-empties-Iraqs-jails.html

CHAPTER 3: CREATING A NEW POLITICAL ORDER

1. Allawi, *Occupation of Iraq*, p. 210.

2. ibid., p. 204.

3. The Law of Administration for the State of Iraq for the Transitional Period, usually referred to as the transitional administrative law or the TAL, is available at: www. iraqcoalition.org/government/TAL.html

4. Allawi, *Occupation of Iraq*, pp. 220–1.

5. ibid., pp. 221–2.

6. Bremer, *My Year in Iraq*, p. 288; Larry Diamond, *Squandered Victory: The American occupation and the bungled effort to bring democracy to Iraq*, Times Books, New York, 2005, p. 163; Phillips, *Losing Iraq*, p. 188.

7. Allawi, *Occupation of Iraq*, p. 222.

8. Diamond, *Squandered Victory*, p. 177.

9. Article 29 provides in full that: 'Upon the assumption of full authority by the Iraqi Interim Government in accordance with article 2(B)(1), above, the Coalition Provisional Authority shall be dissolved and the work of the Governing Council shall come to an end.'

10. Adnan Pachachi, 'Delay the elections', *Washington Post*, 2 January 2005, at: http:// www.washingtonpost.com/wp-dyn/articles/A40055-2004Dec31.html

11. The regulations, codes of conduct and other rules issued by the Independent Electoral Commission of Iraq are available in both English and Arabic at: www.ihec.iq/en/

12. Nicholas Haysom, 'The Iraqi constitution-making process – critical evaluation', Office of Constitutional Support, United Nations Assistance Mission for Iraq, Unpublished, December 2005 ('In the end, the Sunni negotiators were presented with a draft text based on agreements made between the UIA and the Kurdish alliance. This was justified on the basis of inadequate Sunni response and engagement on the textual issues whenever approached'); Noah Feldman and Roman Martinez, 'Constitutional politics and text in the new Iraq: An experiment in Islamic democracy', *Fordham Law Review*, 75:2 (November 2006) ('These provisions embody compromises between Shi'i Islamists seeking to maximize the document's Islamic and majoritarian aspects on the one hand, and, on the other, a loose coalition of Kurds, secular nationalists, and the United States urging greater protection of individual

liberties and minority rights. Ultimately, all sides made concessions, but the final constitution reflects the dominant political strength of the Shi'i Islamists'); Jonathan Morrow, 'Iraq's constitutional process II: An opportunity lost', United States Institute of Peace, November 2005, at: http://www.usip.org/publications/iraqs-constitutional-process-ii-opportunity-lost-arabic-edition ('The model of federalism the Kurdish and Shia "kitchen" finally offered to Sunni Arab negotiators would not only consolidate a large degree of autonomy to the Kurdistan region, but would also allow for other future federal regions, including a southern, predominantly Shia, federal unit').

13. Mona Iman, 'Draft constitution gained, but an important opportunity was lost', United States Institute of Peace website, October 2005, at: http://www.usip.org/publications/draft-constitution-gained-important-opportunity-was-lost

14. Interview with the author, July 2010.

15. Interview with the author, July 2010.

16. Interview with the author, February 2013.

17. Sameer N. Yacoub, 'Iraqi lawmakers OK amended constitution', Associated Press, 18 September 2005.

18. Ashley S. Deeks and Matthew D. Burton, 'Iraq's constitution: A drafting history', *Cornell International Law Journal*, 40:1 (2007), p. 4 ('The Kurdish Alliance and secular Sunnis and Shia, such as Hajim al Hassani, Ghazi al Yawer, and Ayad Allawi, were frequently present. However, for large parts of the summit negotiations, not all of the relevant principals attended the meetings. The Shia Alliance, represented chiefly by Abdul-Aziz al-Hakim, Ahmed Chalabi, and Humam Hamoudi (the Chairman of the Constitutional Committee), also were present for some sessions, but not to the extent necessary to make the gathering a true leadership summit' [footnotes omitted]).

19. Morrow, 'Iraq's constitutional process II', p. 9 ('In its basic form, the Leadership Council consisted of SCIRI leader Abdul Aziz al-Hakim, Shia Dawa party leader Prime Minister Jaafari, Kurdish PUK party leader President Jalal Talabani, and Kurdish KDP party leader Masoud Barzani . . . These were meetings at which the Sunni Committee members had no right of attendance, to which they frequently requested attendance, but were not often invited'). An American adviser to the two Kurdish parties, who played a major role in the negotiations, agrees that the leadership council was essentially a series of discussions between senior Kurdish and Shia leaders; see Peter W. Galbraith, *The End of Iraq*, Simon & Schuster, London, 2006, p. 192 ('Days after taking up his post in early August, [US Ambassador Zalmay] Khalilzad had summoned Iraq's top leaders to the capital's Green Zone, initiating three weeks of non-stop talks that produced the Kurdish-Shiite deal that is the basis of the Iraqi Constitution').

20. Interview with the author, November 2005.

21. Although there is broad agreement between all parties that the US embassy played a major role in the leadership council phase, opinions vary slightly as to the precise nature of that involvement. According to one participant, the embassy essentially acted as a secretariat to the leadership council by 'record[ing] agreements, incorporat[ing] them into the text, and prepar[ing] drafts'; see Galbraith, *End of Iraq*, p. 193. Another participant noted that the first of the leadership council's meetings took place at the US embassy itself, during which a 'small army of US drafters, lawyers and assistants of every kind and specialty' was present, which caused many Iraqi negotiators some discomfort and forced US embassy officials to play a more low-key role. According to the same participant, the US embassy continued to play an important role at all stages of the negotiations, with at least two officials present at all times (interview with the author, April 2010).

22. Interview with the author, May 2010.

23. Morrow 'Iraq's constitutional process II', p. 3.

24. United Nations Assistance Mission for Iraq, 'History of the Iraqi constitution-making process', December 2005, Unpublished, paras. 104–7.

25. Note, however, that article 12 of the 1979 Iranian Constitution is far more divisive in that regard, choosing to recognize not only Shia Islam as the official religion of the state, but even specifying the Twelver Ja'fari school, one of the many schools of thought in Shia Islam, as the dominant trend. It provides that: 'The official religion of Iran is Islam and the Twelver Ja'fari school, and this principle will remain eternally immutable. Other Islamic schools are to be accorded full respect, and their followers are free to act in accordance with their own jurisprudence in performing their religious rites. These schools enjoy official status in matters pertaining to religious education, affairs of personal status (marriage, divorce, inheritance, and wills) and related litigation in courts of law. In regions of the country where Muslims following any one of these schools constitute the majority, local regulations, within the bounds of the jurisdiction of local councils, are to be in accordance with the respective school, without infringing upon the rights of the followers of other schools.'
26. Ruth Wedgwood, 'Peter Galbraith's $100m oil patch', Forbes, 19 November 2009, at: www.forbes.com/2009/11/18/peter-galbraith-diplomats-politics-world-opinions-contributors-ruth-wedgwood.html
27. 'Baathists arrested in Iraq, accused of conspiring to seize power', Reuters, 26 October 2011, at: www.almasryalyoum.com/node/508760
28. Nicholas Haysom, 'The United Nations' Office of Constitutional Support, summary and critical review of the draft constitution presented to the TNA on 28 August 2005', 15 September 2005, Unpublished; a leaked copy of this paper was quoted in Scott Johnson, Babak Dehghanpisheh and Michael Hastings, 'Iraq: Loose federation or violent disintegration?', Newsweek, 10 October 2005.
29. Yash Ghai and Jill Cottrell, 'A review of the draft constitution of Iraq', 3 October 2005, at: www.law.wisc.edu/gls/arotcoi.pdf (my emphasis).
30. Michael Howard, 'Moqtada Sadr throws Iraqi unity talks into disarray', Guardian, 20 February 2006, at: www.guardian.co.uk/Iraq/Story/0,,1713411,00.html
31. 'Interview with Iraqi Prime Minister al-Maliki', USA Today, 15 October 2006, at: www.usatoday.com/news/world/iraq/2006-10-15-al-maliki-full-length_x.htm
32. Interview with the author, July 2010.

CHAPTER 4: A COUNTRY BACK FROM THE DEAD

1. There is some dispute over death rates in Iraq. Various studies have been carried out, some finding that (as of 2013) close to a million Iraqis have perished as a result of the conflict, while others have found that just over 100,000 were killed. The most recent study, published in October 2013, found that at least 500,000 deaths were attributable to the 2003 war and the occupation. See Salman Rawaf, 'The 2003 Iraq war and avoidable death toll', PLOS Medicine, 10:10 (2013), at: http://www.plosmedicine.org/article/info%3Adoi%2F10.1371%2Fjournal.pmed.1001532. I do not take a position on which estimate is correct.
2. US Department of Defense, 'Measuring stability and security in Iraq', March 2009, p. 23.
3. Patrick Cockburn, 'Diary', London Review of Books, 6 April 2006, at: http://lrb.co.uk/v28/n07/cock01_.html
4. '[Former Prime Minister] Jaafari was not only ineffective but also sectarian. He refused to impose a curfew to stop the retaliatory killing after the Shia mosque in Samara was bombed in February; he said the Shia needed to "let off steam" ' (Linda Robinson, Tell Me How This Ends: General David Petraeus and the search for a way out of Iraq, PublicAffairs, New York, 2009).
5. Nelson Hernandez and Bassam Sebti, 'Mystery hangs over Baghdad battle', Washington Post, 19 April 2006, at: www.washingtonpost.com/wp-dyn/content/article/2006/04/18/AR2006041801630.html
6. International Crisis Group, 'After Baker-Hamilton: What to do in Iraq', Middle East Report Number 60, 19 December 2006.

7. See four-part film entitled 'Baghdad: City of Walls', *Guardian* website, 16 April 2009, at: www.guardian.co.uk/world/series/baghdad

8. Joshua Partlow and Saad Sarhan, 'Iraq official warns against coup attempt', *Washington Post*, 29 July 2006, at: www.washingtonpost.com/wp-dyn/content/article/2006/07/28/AR2006072801746_pf.html

9. Interview with the author, July 2009.

10. Interview with the author, August 2009.

11. The Higher Judicial Council, which oversees and administers all of the judiciary's affairs, maintains a list of assassinated judges and court workers on its website at: www.iraqja.iq

12. Interview with the author, February 2011.

13. Joseph Sassoon, *The Iraqi Refugees: The new crisis in the Middle East*, I.B. Tauris, New York, 2011, p. 1.

14. Interviews with the author, August 2009.

15. Interview with the author, July 2010.

16. The GAO is the US's supreme audit institution. Since US public funds have been invested in Iraq since 2003, the GAO has a mandate to ensure that such funds are being properly utilized. This is achieved partly by ensuring that the Iraqi state is not wasting its own funds, and this has prompted the GAO to carry out a number of investigations in Iraq in relation to the state of budget execution and corruption.

17. GAO, 'Iraq reconstruction – better data needed to assess Iraq's budget execution', January 2008, GAO-08-153, at: www.gao.gov/new.items/d08153.pdf

18. GAO, 'Stabilizing and rebuilding Iraq – Iraqi revenues, expenditures and surplus', August 2008, GAO-08-1031, at: www.gao.gov/new.items/d081031.pdf

19. Michael Eisenstadt and Ahmed Ali, 'How this ends: Iraq's uncertain path towards national reconciliation', Washington Institute Policywatch 1553, 17 June 2009, at: http://www.washingtoninstitute.org/policy-analysis/view/how-this-ends-iraqs-uncertain-path-toward-national-reconciliation

20. Adi Hatem, 'Withab Shaker al-Jubouri to al-Hayat: National reconciliation conferences are just touristic trips abroad, and they don't include the opposition', *Al-Hayat*, 28 April 2009.

21. Al-Dulaimi's conference speech is available at: http://www.youtube.com/watch?v=j7ESihwrULM

22. An official transcript of the exchange is available at: www.parliament.iq and a video extract is available at: www.youtube.com/watch?v=BvnwUCC70X4

23. Al-Janabi is a Salafi cleric who, at the time, was a member of Tawafuq and of the parliamentary defence and security committee. He was one of the fifteen Sunni members who joined the constitutional drafting committee late, in June 2005. Although he supported the process at the time, he was dismayed at the way in which the leadership council seized control of the process in August 2005, and he called on Iraqis to vote against the text in the October referendum.

24. The full exchange is available at: http://www.metacafe.com/watch/714027/?code=AQBbSm8YKrNz-8e3-BrnNUSAX3KLbXA3ZRJXDBR6InTOuB90xFq2iwwV5Hsh tqGEz1XuRMcNnOUMUaZeFvOOJEc0VIKXM6c1SrOROp0A5Z-kDtVU188gs71 QfDIp87px2L9NBw0hVPFk_JNoe_4jPyqiFai-DfshiTPSmN82Y9zkZTEqUzevUrd WQvQLenfC7FU#_

25. Marc Santora, 'Iraq leader and Sunni officials in clash on security', *New York Times*, 26 January 2007, at: www.nytimes.com/2007/01/26/world/middleeast/26iraq.html?_r=1

26. Following the session, the Higher Judicial Council announced that it was commencing legal proceedings against al-Janabi based on the prime minister's accusations, and requested that the Council of Representatives lift al-Janabi's parliamentary immunity. Although no charges were ever brought, and although no convincing evidence was ever presented against al-Janabi, in July 2007 he announced that he was 'joining the armed resistance'. He was later expelled from the Iraqi Accord Front. In 2012, there

was still little sign of any genuine evidence against al-Janabi, who was by then living in Amman.
27. Interview with the author, February 2011.
28. See J. Agnew, T.W. Gillespie, J. Gonzalez and B. Min, 'Baghdad nights: Evaluating the US military "surge" using nighttime light signatures', *Environment and Planning A* 40:10 (2008), pp. 2285–95.
29. Interview with the author, June 2009.
30. Interview with the author, June 2011.
31. Interview with the author, August 2010.
32. Interview with the author, July 2010.
33. Interview with the author, October 2010.
34. In a thirty-four-page report on Shia politics in Iraq, published in November 2007 by the International Crisis Group (widely considered to be among the informed sources on Iraq at the time), al-Maliki was mentioned only four times, and only in passing (International Crisis Group, 'Shiite politics in Iraq: The role of the Supreme Council', Middle East Report Number 70, 15 November 2007, at: www.crisisgroup.org/en/regions/middle-east-north-africa/iraq-iran-gulf/iraq/070-shiite-politics-in-iraq-the-role-of-the-supreme-council.aspx).
35. Marisa Cochrane, 'The battle for Basra', Institute for the Study of War, at: http://www.understandingwar.org/sites/default/files/reports/Iraq%20Report%209.pdf

CHAPTER 5: DEFECTIVE POLITICS

1. Interview with the author, February 2010.
2. Naseer al-Ali and Qasem al-Qaabi, 'Maliki demands a recount, and warns against a return to violence', *Asharq Alawsat*, 22 March 2010, at: www.aawsat.com/details.asp?issueno=11700&article=561983#.UfjwCG2CDLM (my emphasis).
3. Interview with the author, January 2011.
4. Although the Erbil Agreement's exact terms were kept secret for some time, several versions which generally agreed with each other were published in the Iraqi press in December 2012. One version was published by *al-Mada* and can be found (in Arabic) at: http://almadapaper.net/ar/printnews.aspx?NewsID=4241
5. Arwa Damon, 'Allawi: "Power sharing is dead now" ', CNN website, 12 November 2010, at: http://edition.cnn.com/2010/WORLD/meast/11/12/iraq.allawi/index.html
6. 'Exclusive: Al-Mada publishes the Erbil Agreement', 2 May 2012, Voice of Iraq website, at: www.sotaliraq.com/mobile-news.php?id=54370#axzz2bqOBUa3W
7. International Crisis Group, 'Iraq's secular opposition: The rise and decline of al-Iraqiya', Middle East Report Number 127, 31 July 2012, at: www.crisisgroup.org/~/media/Files/Middle%20East%20North%20Africa/Iraq%20Syria%20Lebanon/Iraq/127-iraqs-secular-opposition-the-rise-and-decline-of-al-iraqiya.pdf
8. 'Attab al-Douri: The raid on al-Hal's offices by the security forces was reprehensible and unjustified', Al-Forat News website, 9 August 2013, at: www.alforatnews.com/index.php?option=com_content&view=article&id=47432:2013-08-09-08-03-32&catid=36:2013-03-27-10-35-00&Itemid=53
9. Steven Lee Myers, 'Candidates to stay off ballot in Iraq', *New York Times*, 13 February 2010.
10. International Crisis Group, 'Iraq's uncertain future: Elections and beyond', Middle East Report Number 94, 25 February 2010, at: http://www.crisisgroup.org/en/regions/middle-east-north-africa/iraq-iran-gulf/iraq/094-iraqs-uncertain-future-elections-and-beyond.aspx
11. In August 2011, the federal Supreme Court issued a decision that removed former Interior Minister Jawad al-Bolani from his parliamentary seat. Bolani stood for election in March 2010 in Baghdad governorate but failed to obtain enough votes to secure a seat. He subsequently entered parliament after a member of his Unity of Iraq

list, who had stood in Salah al-Din province, was given a ministerial portfolio and released his seat to Bolani. The court held that Bolani could not replace a candidate who had stood in another province and so unseated him. Although the court's decision was well reasoned, it is unclear why that same reasoning did not serve to unseat Salim Abdullah al-Jubouri, an Iraqi Islamic Party member who had not obtained enough votes to represent Dyala province, but entered parliament when he replaced a party colleague who had been elected in Salah al-Din province and had resigned for health reasons.

12. Decision 35 (2012), dated 2 May 2012, at: http://iraqja.iq/viewd.975/
13. Decision 88 (2010), dated 18 January 2011, at: www.iraqja.iq/view.729/. Critics were concerned in particular about the fate of the Independent High Electoral Commission, given the potential for government manipulation in future elections. See, for example, 'Heavy criticism of the decision to attach independent agencies to the prime minister', *Al-Hayat*, 23 January 2011 (in Arabic).
14. Section Three, Chapter Four of the Constitution is devoted to the powers, responsibilities and reporting lines of independent agencies, including the Board of Supreme Audit, the integrity commission and the Martyrs' Foundation.
15. To reach the conclusion that all independent agencies should be attached to the council of ministers and not to parliament, the federal Supreme Court had to set aside specific constitutional language, such as article 103(2), which provides that the Board of Supreme Audit and the communication and media commission are 'attached to the Council of Representatives'. The court's reasoning that this wording is redundant (given that all administrative officials are in any event answerable to parliament) stands against the widely established legal principle that specific wording should be given meaning and not set aside in favour of general principles. Moreover, the court held that where the constitution provides that specific agencies are attached to parliament, this meant that the latter should be responsible for 'establishing [the agency's] general policy, without interfering in its decisions, procedures, and professional affairs, because these commissions were given administrative and financial independence to guarantee the neutrality and independence of their decisions and procedures, within the context of their jurisdiction' (unofficial translation). Nevertheless, the court found that the government should 'supervise' those same agencies, without providing any indication as to how it should exercise that supervision and whether it would have authority to overrule an agency's decisions.
16. Leila Fadel, 'Iraq's new parliament convenes but defers on appointing leaders', *Washington Post*, 15 June 2010, at: www.washingtonpost.com/wp-dyn/content/article/2010/06/14/AR2010061401780.html
17. 'Who killed the journalist Hadi al-Mahdi?', Buratha News Agency, 2 September 2011, at: http://www.burathanews.com/news_article_135672.html
18. See, for example, a televised interview on al-Baghdadiya News which aired in March 2013 and is available at: www.youtube.com/watch?v=XEF2ycavTPw
19. 'Judge Rahim al-Ugaili: The anti-corruption commission has now become the anti-Ugaili commission', Ain News, 28 August 2013, at: www.ahewar.org/news/s.news.asp?nid=1323555
20. 'Rahim al-Ugaili in the balance of justice', Integrity Commission, 28 August 2013.
21. Letter sent from US Military Commander Raymond T. Odierno to Prime Minister Nuri al-Maliki, Inside Iraqi Politics website, 18 January 2013, at: http://www.insidei-raqipolitics.com/Files/IIPOdiernoLetter.pdf
22. Interviews with the author, March 2013.
23. Available at: http://www.youtube.com/watch?v=fl9DNtEUkZ8
24. A parliamentary commission was charged with investigating the killings. Its findings were published in a report that was completed on 29 April 2013. The full report is available at: www.wijhatnadhar.com/2013/05/blog-post_7804.html. An English-language summary is also available ('Hawija investigation results revealed', Shafaq

News, 30 April 2013, at: www.shafaaq.com/en/archive/5953-hawija-investigation-results-revealed-.html).

25. Interview with the author, April 2013.

26. 'Iraqis' own surge assessment: Few see security gains', ABC News/BBC/NHK Poll: Iraq – Where things stand, 10 September 2007, p. 21, at: http://abcnews.go.com/images/US/1043a1IraqWhereThingsStand.pdf

27. See the Iraq Living Conditions Survey 2004, a joint study by the Iraqi ministry of planning and development cooperation and the United Nations Development Programme, and which was first published in 2005. The full study is available at: http://reliefweb.int/report/iraq/iraq-living-conditions-survey-2004

28. See, for example, 'Doctors in Basra report rise in birth defects', BBC News, 21 March 2013, at: www.bbc.co.uk/news/world-middle-east-21873892. See also M. Al-Sabbak, S. Sadik, O. Savabi, G. Savabi, S. Dastgiri and M. Savabieasfahani, 'Metal contamination and the epidemic of congenital birth defects in Iraqi cities', *Bulletin of Environmental Contamination and Toxicology* 89 (2012), pp. 937–44.

29. Mohammad Hamid al-Sawaf, 'Visiting Iraqi PM's hometown: "even the street next to his house is still full of holes" ', Niqash, 12 July 2012, at: www.niqash.org/articles/?id=3088

30. Dyala is home to a sizeable Shiite population – around 20 per cent – and experienced extreme violence during the 2005–08 sectarian war.

31. Security forces arrested provincial officials in Dyala throughout 2011. Most were Iraqiya members; some were high-level officials, including the deputy governor, who was arrested on 20 January 2012.

32. 'President Obama's press conference with Prime Minister Maliki', White House website, 12 December 2011, at: www.whitehouse.gov/photos-and-video/video/2011/12/12/president-obama-s-press-conference-prime-minister-maliki#transcript (my emphasis).

33. The only way to overcome that reality would have been to organize an explicit coup d'état against the constitution, something that would essentially have been impossible given the political context.

34. 'The parliament approves the electoral commission by a majority of its members', Al-Hurra, 17 September 2012, www.alhurra.com/content/iraqi-parliament-vote-election-commission-members/211857.html

35. Hamza Mustafa, 'The Iraqi parliament resolves the controversy surrounding the electoral commission, and the State of Law alliance objects', *Asharq Alawsat*, 14 September 2012, at: www.aawsat.com/details.asp?section=4&article=695249&issueno=12344#.UQy6IGdqOSo

36. 'State of Law: We will appeal against the application of the judicial council law', 19 December 2012, Iraqi Media Net, at: http://imn.iq/news/view.17444/

37. Ali Abed al-Sada, 'Public pressure forces the parliament to halt legislation that would curb freedoms', Al-Monitor Iraq Pulse, 10 July 2013, at: www.al-monitor.com/pulse/ar/contents/articles/opinion/2013/07/iraq-parliament-media-law-halted.html

38. The full text of the law is available at: www.parliament.iq

39. Interview with the author, May 2012.

40. 'The text of Telecom Minister Mohamed Tawfiq Allawi's resignation letter, which was presented to the prime minister', Khabaar News, 28 August 2012, at: http://khabaar.net/index.php/permalink/7915.html

41. Omar al-Shaher, 'Iraq to simplify visa procedures for foreign oil workers', Al-Monitor Iraq Pulse, 23 May 2013, at: www.al-monitor.com/pulse/originals/2013/05/iraq-eases-oil-worker-visa-procedures.html

42. 'Urgent: The clergy in Najaf express surprise at the reasons offered by the government to cancel the ration card system', Al-Forat News website, 7 November 2012, at: www.alforatnews.com/index.php?option=com_content&view=article&id=25340&Itemid=53

43. Najah Mohamed Ali, 'Iraq suspends the decision to cancel the ration card system', Al-Arabiya, 11 November 2012, at: www.alarabiya.net/articles/2012/11/11/248917. html

44. An excerpt from the interview, conducted by Sumaria News on 10 October 2013, is available at: www.youtube.com/watch?v=5QVBTxbw9NM&feature=youtu.be. For an example of the reaction that the interview provoked, see Bushri al-Mudhfer, 'Ahmed al-Maliki is the Green Zone's "policeman" ', *Al-Hayat*, 13 October 2013, at: http://alhayat.com/Details/561372

45. Kareem Raheem and Ziad al-Sinjary, 'Al Qaeda militants flee Iraq jail in violent mass break-out', Reuters, 22 July 2013.

46. 'Two hurt as protesters attack Iraq deputy PM', Agence France Presse, 30 December 2012, at: www.arabnews.com/two-hurt-protesters-attack-iraq-deputy-pm

47. 'Code of conduct for political entities', at: www.elections.ca/imie/pdf/Political_Entity_Code_of_Conduct.pdf

48. International Mission for Iraqi Elections (IMIE), *Final Report: Assessment of the January 30, 2005, Election Process.*

CHAPTER 6: A COUNTRY LEFT TO LANGUISH

1. Iraq country profile, Revenue Watch Institute, 2013, at: www.revenuewatch.org/countries/middle-east-and-north-africa/iraq/overview

2. Sinan Salaheddin, 'Iraq officially retreats from ambitious oil plans', Associated Press, 10 October 2012, at: http://bigstory.ap.org/article/iraq-says-oil-production-can-be-doubled-2015

3. See for example International Crisis Group, 'Oil for soil: Toward a grand bargain on Iraq and the Kurds', Middle East Report Number 80, 28 October 2008, at: www.crisisgroup.org/en/regions/middle-east-north-africa/iraq-iran-gulf/iraq/080-oil-for-soil-toward-a-grand-bargain-on-iraq-and-the-kurds.aspx

4. Guy Chazan, 'Exxon looks to quit Iraq oilfield', *Financial Times*, 7 November 2012, at: www.ft.com/intl/cms/s/0/aba9f240-2906-11e2-86d7-00144feabdc0.html#axzz2I QkrIXOX

5. Ahmed Rasheed, 'Iraq blacklists Chevron for Kurdish oil deals', Reuters, 24 July 2012, at: www.reuters.com/article/2012/07/24/us-iraq-chevron-idUSBRE86N12A20120724; Brian Swint, 'Total follows Exxon, Chevron into Kurdistan region of Iraq', Bloomberg, 31 July 2012, at: www.bloomberg.com/news/2012-07-31/total-follows-exxon-chevron-into-kurdistan-region-of-iraq.html

6. David Obyrne and Kate Dourian, 'Iraqi Kurdistan planning 1 million b/d pipeline to Turkey', Platts, 4 October 2012, at: www.platts.com/RSSFeedDetailedNews/RSSFeed/Oil/8788014

7. 'Oil firm to boost exports from Kurdish area despite Iraqi threats', Associated Press, 18 January 2013, at: www.cbc.ca/news/world/story/2013/01/18/oil-iraq-genel.html

8. Ahmed Rasheed, 'Iraq oil exports stagnate, deep cuts ahead due to port work', Reuters, 7 August 2013, at: www.reuters.com/article/2013/08/07/iraq-oil-production-idUSL6N0G81L520130807. Historical data on production and export rates is available at: www.eia.gov/countries/country-data.cfm?fips=IZ#pet

9. Ziad Daoud, 'The IMF programme in Iraq', Awraq website, 20 May 2013, at: http://ziaddaoud.blogspot.co.uk/2013/05/the-imf-programme-in-iraq.html

10. USAID/Tijara, *USAID–Tijara Provincial Economic Growth Program: Assessment of current and anticipated economic priorities in Iraq, Report for Prime Minister's Advisory Committee (PMAC)*, 4 October 2012, p. 43, at: http://pdf.usaid.gov/pdf_docs/pnadz673.pdf

11. World Bank, *Economy Profile: Iraq*, 2013, at: www.doingbusiness.org/~/media/giawb/doing%20business/documents/profiles/country/IRQ.pdf

12. Sheila Crisostomo, 'Iraq eyes hiring of up to 2,000 Pinoy doctors, nurses', *Philippine Star*, 13 November 2012, at: www.abs-cbnnews.com/global-filipino/11/12/12/iraq-eyes-hiring-2000-pinoy-doctors-nurses

13. Bassam Yousif, 'Aspiration and reality in Iraq's post-sanctions economy', *Middle East Report*, 266 (Spring 2013), p. 10.

14. USAID/Tijara, *USAID–Tijara Provincial Economic Growth Program*, p. 43.

15. Richard Posner, 'Too many government workers?', Becker-Posner Blog, 26 September 2011, at: www.becker-posner-blog.com/2011/09/too-many-government-workersposner.html

16. United States Special Inspector General for Iraq Reconstruction (SIGIR), *Quarterly Report to the United States Congress*, 30 April 2011, p. 85, at: http://www.sigir.mil/files/quarterlyreports/April2011/Report_-_April_2011.pdf

17. Nagih al-Obaidi, 'Holidays in Iraq: Too many national vacations dangerous, bad for business', Niqash, 22 December 2011, at: www.niqash.org/articles/?id=2957

18. Interview with the author, January 2013.

19. Patrick Cockburn, 'Ten years on from the war, how the world forgot about Iraq', *Independent*, 3 March 2013.

20. United Nations/World Bank, *Joint Iraq Needs Assessment*, October 2003, p. 28, at: http://siteresources.worldbank.org/INTIRAQ/Overview/20147568/Joint%20Needs%20Assessment.pdf

21. Economist Intelligence Unit, *Iraq Country Profile*, 2004.

22. United States Government Accountability Office (GAO), 'Rebuilding Iraq: Integrated strategic plan needed to help restore Iraq's oil and electricity sectors', 2007, p. 12, at: www.gao.gov/new.items/d07677.pdf

23. SIGIR, *Quarterly Report*, p. 16.

24. All of Iraq's annual state budget laws from 2006 to 2013 are available on parliament's website (www.parliament.iq) and are on file with the author.

25. United States GAO, 'Securing, stabilizing, and rebuilding Iraq – Progress report: Some gains made, updated strategy needed', June 2008, GAO-08-937, p. 53, at: http://www.gao.gov/products/GAO-08-837

26. 'Al-Shahristani blames the ministry of electricity for the deteriorating power supply, and describes his role as setting out strategies', Al-Forat News website, 25 July 2013, at: www.alforatnews.com/index.php?option=com_content&view=article&id=46284&Itemid=53

27. Iraqi ministry of planning and development cooperation, 'Iraq household socio-economic survey 2007', Baghdad, 2008.

28. United States GAO, 'Securing, stabilizing, and rebuilding Iraq – Progress report', p. 52.

29. SIGIR, *Quarterly Report*, p. 4.

30. ibid., p. 16.

31. Ali Abdel Sadah, 'Iraq suffers power crisis as temperatures soar', Al-Monitor Iraq Pulse, 31 July 2013, at: www.al-monitor.com/pulse/originals/2013/07/iraq-frustration-over-ongoing-electricity-crisis.html

32. The televised debate is available at: www.youtube.com/watch?v=XsUU9nll4T0

33. 'Popular movement and demonstrations in southern Iraq demand al-Maliki's resignation and al-Shahristani's dismissal', Aswat al-Iraq, 27 July 2013, at: http://ar.aswataliraq.info/%28S%28zwj5pb45l5e4rw45rxxbylne%29%29/Default1.aspx?page=article_page&id=319492&l=1

34. 'Al-Mutalabi: Basra protesters are militiamen and barbarians', Ur News, 29 July 2013, at: www.uragency.net/index.php/araqiat/2012-03-11-16-33-45/46-2012-04-19-08-09-11/2012-04-19-08-09-17/22327-2013-07-29-10-30-13

35. 'Demonstrations force the minister of the interior to visit Thi Qar, and surround his place of residence in Basra', Iraq al-Qanoon, 2 August 2013, at: www.qanon302.net/news/news.php?action=view&id=26710

36. 'Iraq electricity minister resigns after deadly protests', BBC News, 21 June 2010, at: www.bbc.co.uk/news/10371581

37. James Drummond and Peter Shaw-Smith, 'Iraq forced to wait for universal electricity', *Financial Times*, 14 November 2011, at: www.ft.com/intl/cms/s/0/a3cf4288-0548-11e1-a3d1-00144feabdc0.html

38. 'Kirkuk cuts off electricity from Iraq's other provinces', Agence France Presse, 18 January 2011, at: www.alwasatnews.com/3056/news/read/521958/1.html

39. Maad Fayyadh, 'Kirkuk decides to cut off the national electricity network in protest over shortages', *Asharq Alawsat*, 19 January 2011, at: www.aawsat.com/details.asp?section=4&article=604454&issueno=11740

40. 'Kirkuk buys electricity from Kurdish region', Middle East Online website, 29 June 2011, at: www.middle-east-online.com/english/?id=46991

41. Interview with the author, July 2012.

42. 'Baghdad witnesses rains without precedent and al-Maliki heads a committee to resolve the floods and announces a state of alert', Baghdadia News, 25 December 2012, at: www.albaghdadianews.com/local/item/22217-BiDAD-byomD-ALZAE-inE-LYOBNj%D8%A9-NAkLAkKn-nEaYO-kvl%D8%A9-kLIAkv%D8%A9-AkJnzh AlAb-NnIkl-AkAYOblJAE.html

43. 'Water levels increase in Kirkuk and Mosul, tens of households are destroyed', *Jareeda al-Bayan*, 29 January 2013, at: http://albayaniq.com/?p=3812

44. Iraqi ministry of human rights, 'Annual report on the situation of prisons and detention centres in Iraq', 2008 (in possession of the author).

45. Human Rights Watch, 'The quality of justice: Failings of Iraq's Central Criminal Court', 14 December 2008, at: www.hrw.org/en/reports/2008/12/14/quality-justice-0.

46. US Bureau of Democracy, Human Rights and Labor, '2008 Human Rights Report: Iraq', 25 February 2009, at: www.state.gov/g/drl/rls/hrrpt/2008/nea/119116.htm

47. Amnesty International, *Broken Bodies, Tortured Minds: Abuse and neglect of detainees in Iraq*, February 2011, at: http://www.amnesty.org/en/library/asset/MDE14/001/2011/en/48c3c6e6-9607-4926-abd7-d1da1c51a976/mde140012011en.pdf; see also Human Rights Watch, *At a Crossroads – Human rights in Iraq eight years after the US-led invasion*, February 2011, at: http://www.hrw.org/reports/2011/02/21/crossroads

48. United Nations Office of the High Commissioner for Human Rights, 'Report on human rights in Iraq: January to June 2012', UNAMI Human Rights Office, Baghdad, 2012.

49. See, for example, Human Rights Watch, 'Iraq: Secret jail uncovered in Baghdad', 1 February 2011.

50. See Public Prosecutor Law No. 159 (1979), with all corresponding amendments. An unofficial English language translation is available at: www.gjpi.org/wp-content/uploads/gjpi-pp-1979-v1-eng.doc

51. Interview with the author, July 2010. An Iraqi practising attorney agrees: 'Prosecutors almost never raise any objections to the way in which investigations and trials are conducted.' Interview with the author, January 2011.

52. Daham Mohamed Al-Azawi, *The Christians of Iraq: The plight of the present and fear of the future*, Arab Scientific Publishers, Doha, 2012, p. 24; Suhail Qasha, *The Christians of Iraq*, Alwarrak Publishing Ltd, London, 2009, p. 31.

53. Qasha, *Christians of Iraq*, p. 94.

54. ibid., p. 297.

55. Al-Azawi, *Christians of Iraq*, p. 1.

56. Report dated 20 October 2012, signed by Ali Ghidan Majid, commander of Iraq's ground forces. In the author's possession.

57. 'July deadliest month in Iraq in more than five years', *Al-Akhbar*, 1 August 2013, at: http://english.al-akhbar.com/node/16604

CHAPTER 7: THE RAVAGES OF CORRUPTION: THE SECOND INSURGENCY

1. United States SIGIR, 'Assessing the state of Iraqi corruption', Testimony of Stuart W. Bowen, Jr, House Committee on Oversight and Government Reform, 4 October 2007.
2. Alain Ménargues, *Les Secrets de la guerre du Liban*, Editions Albin Michel, Paris, 2004, p. 213.
3. Interview with the author, February 2012.
4. Interviews with the author, August and September 2012.
5. Interview with the author, August 2012.
6. P. Volcker, R. Goldstone and M. Pieth, *Manipulation of the Oil-for-Food Programme by the Iraqi Regime*, Independent Inquiry Committee into the United Nations Oil-For-Food Programme, 27 October 2005, at: http://www.isn.ethz.ch/Digital-Library/Publications/Detail/?ots591=0c54e3b3-1e9c-be1e-2c24-a6a8c7060233&lng=en&id=13894
7. Paul Harris, 'Emerging wave of Iraq fiction examines America's role in "bullshit war" ', *Guardian*, 3 January 2013, at: www.theguardian.com/world/2013/jan/03/iraq-fiction-us-military-war
8. Office of the SIGIR, 'Development fund for Iraq: Department of Defense needs to improve financial and management controls', SIGIR 10-020, 27 July 2010.
9. For an interesting and entertaining account of US corruption, incompetence and wilful ignorance, see Peter Van Buren, *We Meant Well: How I helped lose the battle for the hearts and minds of the Iraqi people*, Metropolitan Books, New York, 2011.
10. Office of the SIGIR, 'Falluja waste water treatment system: A case study in wartime contracting', SIGIR 12-007, 30 October 2011.
11. Office of the SIGIR, 'Basrah modern slaughterhouse, Basrah, Iraq', SIGIR PA-09-189, 27 April 2010.
12. Rajiv Chandrasekaran, *Imperial Life in the Emerald City: Inside Iraq's Green Zone*, Vintage Books, New York, 2007.
13. CPA Order 55 (2004).
14. After its inception, the integrity commission established several departments covering, among other things, investigations, legal matters, civil society relations and special operations. The last-mentioned department carried out dozens of operations, using secret cameras and other recording equipment. See the integrity commission's 2009 Annual Report, pp. 19–27. With regard to public procurement – a major source of inefficiency and corruption – the commission employs officials to inspect irregularities based on specific complaints. See, Organisation for Economic Co-operation and Development (OECD), *Improving Transparency within Government Procurement Procedures in Iraq*, February 2010, p. 7, at: http://www.oecd.org/countries/iraq/improvingtransparencywithingovernmentprocurementproceduresiniraq.htm
15. Interview with the author, February 2011.
16. Interview with the author, February 2011.
17. Interview with the author, February 2011.
18. In a report on corruption in Iraq, the US embassy in Baghdad wrote: 'Since [the integrity commission] has no real authority to demand or even cajole Ministry officials to provide books, records, documents and witnesses, [it] relies upon the [inspectors general] and the [investigative judges] to provide such evidence. Even where [inspectors general] cooperate, the pervasive atmosphere of corruption, criminal and sectarian violence, and political/tribal partisanship undermine true anti-corruption efforts' (US Embassy Report on Corruption, September 2007).
19. The US embassy in Baghdad wrote that the integrity commission 'is currently a passive rather than a true investigatory agency. Though legally empowered to conduct investigations the combined security situation and the violent character of the criminal elements within the ministries make investigation of corruption too hazardous for all but a tactically robust police force with the support of the Iraqi government. Currently this support is lacking' (US Embassy Report on Corruption, September 2007).

20. In an interview, Judge Radhi said 'they have militias, and they attacked my neighbour-hood with missiles, and these missiles fell very close to my house' (Lisa Myers and Aram Roston, 'Iraqi official: "Corruption has crippled Iraq" ', NBC News, 7 September 2007, at: www.nbcnews.com/id/20040662/ns/nbc_nightly_news_with_brian_williams-nbc_news_investigates/t/iraqi-official-corruption-has-crippled-iraq/#.UixQQj-sI4k). In another interview, he said 'most ministries are involved. Some officials, such as the minister of defence, have been dismissed, but we have about $4 billion in corruption cases there [and] $2 billion in cases involving the Interior Ministry' (Corey Flintoff, 'Iraqi watchdog official alleges high-level corruption', National Public Radio, 7 September 2007, at: www.npr.org/templates/story/story.php?storyId=14245376). Judge Radhi subsequently appeared before the US House of Representatives Oversight Committee on 4 October 2007 and the Senate Committee on Appropriations on 11 March 2008, where he repeated many of the same allegations and also indicated that, of the 3,000 corruption cases his commission had investigated and forwarded to the courts for prosecution, only 241 had been adjudicated (David Corn, 'Judge Radhi testifies on Iraqi corruption', *The Nation*, 5 October 2007, at: http://www.thenation.com/blog/156353/judge-radhi-testifies-iraqi-corruption-gopers-attack-update#); see also Senate Committee on Appropriations#, Testimony of Judge Radhi Hamza al-Radhi, 11 March 2008.

21. In a press interview, Mousa Faraj said: 'The ministry of defence comes top among state institutions with regard to administrative and financial corruption, followed by the ministries of interior, commerce, oil and electricity. The problem here lies in the fact that corruption is rampant among the middle management of ministries starting with general secretaries, their advisers and general directors of institutions and not necessarily the ministers themselves' (Niqash, 17 July 2008).

22. In testimony before the US senate, a former senior US embassy official said: 'The Prime Minister's office has ignored the Iraqi constitution and thrown it into the Tigris River, as they have attempted to seize control over [the integrity commission]'s internal operations, replacing staff and withholding funds' (Senate Democratic Policy Committee Hearing, Testimony of James Mattil, 12 May 2008).

23. Article 2 of Law 6 (1990).

24. United Nations Development Programme, 'Strengthening the working relationship between the Iraqi Council of Representatives and the Board of Supreme Audit', Background paper, 2009, p. 8.

25. Interview with the author, January 2011.

26. Under Law 6 of 1990, the Board of Supreme Audit could refer any criminal matter to the courts, and the relevant minister was required to fire officials who were merely under investigation. This amendment to the 1990 law continues to provide the basis for the board's mandate.

27. Interview with the author, September 2011.

28. See SIGIR, *Quarterly Report and Semiannual Report to the United States Congress*, 30 January 2009, at: http://www.dtic.mil/dtic/tr/fulltext/u2/a493379.pdf

29. CPA Order 57 (5 February 2004) establishes 'independent Offices of Inspectors General to conduct investigations, audits, evaluations, inspections and other reviews in accordance with generally accepted professional standards' (Section 1). It also gives inspectors general the responsibility to audit all ministry records and carry out administrative investigations (Section 5).

30. Interview with the author, October 2009.

31. Interview with the author, October 2009.

32. Interview with the author, October 2009.

33. See Order 19 (2005).

34. Interview with the author, October 2009.

35. In November 2008, it was reported that: 'The government of Prime Minister Nuri Kamal al-Maliki is systematically dismissing Iraqi oversight officials . . . While some

Iraqi officials defended the dismissals, saying there had been no political motivation, others pointed to the secrecy involved as supporting their view that those removed had lost their posts without good cause' (James Glanz and Riyadh Mohammed, 'Premier of Iraq is quietly firing fraud monitors', *New York Times*, 18 November 2008, at: www. nytimes.com/2008/11/18/world/middleeast/18maliki.html?pagewanted=all&_r=0).
36. Interview with the author, February 2011.
37. Interviews with the author, February and March 2011.
38. Article 136(b) of Law 23 (1971) provides in relevant part: 'The transfer of the accused for trial for an offence committed during performance of an official duty, or as a consequence of performance of this duty, is possible only with permission of the minister responsible or his deputy, in accordance with the stipulations of other codes.'
39. The minister's decision not to grant authorization for prosecution is not subject to appeal. The US state department reports: 'Section 136(b) . . . provided immunity to selected government employees and enabled a component of the executive branch to terminate proceedings initiated by the judicial branch. During the year permission was given to arrest only lower-level ministry employees under Section 136(b)' (Bureau of Democracy, Human Rights, and Labor, '2009 Country report on human rights practices – Iraq', 11 March 2010, at: http://www.refworld.org/docid/4b9e52ea6e.html).
40. See the integrity commission's 2008 Annual Report, pp. 35–46, and its 2009 Annual Report, p. 5. According to the latter, a case against a telecommunications ministry official that was withdrawn involved the waste of $15.5 million. Another, against an electricity ministry official, related to the embezzlement of 58 billion Iraqi dinars (approximately $50 million).
41. Abed al-Mehdi Abed al-Munim Hassan, 'The story of the inspector general from the trade ministry who was sent to China under threats', 16 March 2008, Buratha News Agency, at: http://www.burathanews.com/news_article_37762.html
42. Interview with the author, September 2009.
43. 'Integrity commission names most corrupt ministries', AKnews, 7 March 2011, at: www.iraq-businessnews.com/tag/integrity-committee/page/2/
44. 'The Iraqi parliament prepares to impeach the trade minister for corruption . . . Security forces arrest his brother', *Asharq Alawsat*, 11 May 2009, at: www.aawsat. com/details.asp?issueno=10992&article=518708
45. ibid.
46. Transcripts of the impeachment process are available at: www.parliament.iq
47. Sameer N. Yacoob, 'Iraq trade minister resigns amid corruption scandal', Associated Press, 25 May 2009, at: www.huffingtonpost.com/2009/05/25/iraq-trade-minister-resig_n_207297.html
48. Qasem al-Qaabi, 'Resigned Iraq's trade minister appears before a court to face corruption charges. . . and his party requests that he be released on bail', *Asharq Alawsat*, 2 June 2009, at: www.aawsat.com/details.asp?issueno=10992&article=521681; Nada Bakri, 'Iraq's ex-trade minister, Abdul Falah al-Sudani, detained in graft investigation', *Washington Post*, 31 May 2009, at: www.washingtonpost.com/wp-dyn/content/article/2009/05/30/AR2009053001089.html
49. Aram Roston, *The Man Who Pushed America to War*, Nation Books, New York, 2008, pp. 298–301.
50. Interview with the author, October 2011.
51. Interview with the author, June 2011.
52. Interviews with the author, Summer 2011.
53. The law's full text is available at: www.parliament.iq
54. Interview with the author, November 2011.
55. Interview with the author, September 2013.
56. US Embassy, Untitled Report, September 2007, at: www.fas.org/irp/eprint/anticorruption.pdf

57. 'Have Bush administration reconstruction and anti-corruption failures undermined the US mission in Iraq?', Senate Democratic Policy Committee Hearing, Testimony of James Mattil, 12 May 2008.
58. The former integrity commission chief testified: '[T]he cost of corruption that my Commission has uncovered so far across all ministries in Iraq has been estimated to be as high as $18 billion' (Testimony of Judge Radhi Hamza al-Radhi, US Senate Committee on Appropriations, 11 March 2008). The former chief integrity commission investigator agreed: 'Of this $18 billion, I believe at least $4 billion have been lost due to corruption and criminal acts in the Ministry of Defense alone' (Testimony of Salam Adhoob, US Senate Democratic Policy Committee Hearing, 22 September 2008).
59. See the integrity commission's 2008 Annual Report, p. 47. As a result of the February 2008 general amnesty law passed to placate the Sunni Arab community, which claimed that the majority of those jailed were Sunni Arabs, all officials convicted of corruption-related crimes prior to 2007, including electricity and defence ministry officials, were released. Altogether 2,772 officials convicted of corruption-related crimes were released in 2008. See the 2008 Annual Report, p. 2. An additional 498 officials found guilty of having stolen or embezzled close to $200 million were released in 2009. See the integrity commission's 2009 Annual Report, p. 5.
60. The integrity commission referred an investigative file to the courts concerning a case in which it found that more than $100 million had been stolen by a defence ministry official. See the integrity commission's 2010 Annual Report, p. 40. The courts handed down 1,017 convictions in 2010, as compared to 196 in 2007 (ibid., p. 19).
61. In an example of how poor Iraq's procurement process remains, the electricity minister was forced to resign in August 2011 after being accused of having signed multi-billion dollar contracts with a Canadian shell company (a company with a physical address but without assets or operations) and a German firm that had declared bankruptcy. The minister entered into these contracts despite years of supposed government action on corruption.
62. GAO, 'Securing, stabilizing, and rebuilding Iraq'.
63. See the integrity commission's 2008, 2009 and 2010 annual reports; see also SIGIR, *Quarterly Report and Semiannual Report to the United States Congress*, January 2011, p. 77.
64. 'Maliki "seeks $5b arms deal with Russia" ', UPI, 8 October 2012, at: www.upi.com/Business_News/Security-Industry/2012/10/08/Maliki-seeks-5B-arms-deal-with-Russia/UPI-22531349725726/
65. 'Iraq cancels $4.2 bn Russia arms deal over graft concerns', Agence France Presse, 10 November 2012, at: http://english.ahram.org.eg/NewsContent/2/8/57704/World/Region/Iraq-cancels--bn-Russia-arms-deal-over-graft-conce.aspx
66. Igor Popov, 'Behind Russia's $15 billion-plus arms export industry', Russia Beyond the Headlines website, 4 February 2013, http://rbth.ru/politics/2013/02/04/behind_russias_15_billion-plus_arms_export_industry_22487.html
67. Pavel Felgenhauer, 'The payment of kickbacks – a norm in Russia's arms trade', Jamestown Foundation website, at: www.jamestown.org/regions/middleeast/single/?tx_ttnews[tt_news]=40110&tx_ttnews[backPid]=675&cHash=876c360cc50feb30d6784cc6d52b0ec3#.Uf_CG22CDLM
68. Mohamed Tawfeeq and Joe Sterling, 'Iraq cancels new arms deal with Russia', CNN, 10 November 2012, at: http://edition.cnn.com/2012/11/10/world/meast/iraq-russia-arms-deal/index.html
69. See news report aired on al-Hurra in December 2012, available at: www.youtube.com/watch?v=PsRwGvryTiA
70. 'Iraq to renegotiate Russia arms deal: spokesman', Agence France Presse, 12 November 2012, at: http://english.ahram.org.eg/NewsContent/2/8/57887/World/Region/Iraq-to-renegotiate-Russia-arms-deal-spokesman.aspx

71. 'Dabbagh's website suspended', All Iraq News, 21 November 2012, at: www.alliraqnews.com/en/index.php?option=com_content&view=article&id=23111:dabb aghs-website-suspended-&catid=35:political&Itemid=2

72. Najah Mohamed Ali, 'Suspicious Russian arms deal creates controversy within al-Maliki's government', Al-Arabiya, 30 November 2012, at: www.alarabiya.net/articles/2012/11/30/252565.html

73. 'Maliki accepts Dabbagh's resignation', Aswat al-Iraq, 30 November 2012, at: http://en.aswataliraq.info/(S(sn5y1545dg42tmvydbtpt545))/Default1.aspx?page=article_page&id=151594; 'Maliki's spokesman resigns over Russian arms deal scandal', Al-Hayat, 30 November 2012, at: http://alhayat.com/Details/457544; 'Iraq cabinet terminates contract of Ali al-Dabbagh', Alsumaria News, 30 November 2012, at: www.alsumaria.tv/news/67310/iraq-cabinet-terminates-contract-of-ali-al-dabbagh/en

74. Jawdat Kadhim, 'Baghdad: The investigatory committee in the Russian arms deal discovers a large difference in price amounting to around 1 billion dollars', Al-Hayat, 26 December 2012, at: http://alhayat.com/Details/465898

75. The parliamentary report is available at: www.parliament.iq and is also in the author's possession.

CHAPTER 8: THE THIRD INSURGENCY: ENVIRONMENTAL DISASTER

1. 'Dust storm over Iraq and Iran: health hazards', NASA Earth Observatory, undated, at: http://earthobservatory.nasa.gov/NaturalHazards/view.php?id=39403

2. 'The number of dust storms in Iraq may reach 300 a year within the next ten years', Sumaria News, 20 June 2012.

3. 'Dyala river ruins palm and orange groves', Assabah, 20 August 2013, at: www.alsabaah.iq/ArticleShow.aspx?ID=52249

4. Omar al-Shaher, 'Iraq plans to launch satellite to deal with water crisis', Al-Monitor Iraq Pulse, 30 April 2013, at: www.al-monitor.com/pulse/originals/2013/04/iraq-plans-satellite-launch.html

5. Akio Kitoh, Akiyo Yatagai and Pinhas Alpert, 'First super-high-resolution model projection that the ancient Fertile Crescent will disappear in this century', Hydrological Research Letters, 2 (2008), pp. 1–4.

6. Official Website of the Greater Anatolia Project, at: www.gap.gov.tr/english

7. Joost Jongerden, 'Dams and politics in Turkey: Utilizing water, developing conflict', Middle East Policy, 17:1 (2010), p. 137.

8. Adel Mehdi, 'Iraq accuses Syria of storing additional waters that Turkey released from the Euphrates', Al-Hayat, 9 November 2009.

9. 'Iraq accuses Iran of water theft', Al Jazeera English, 23 October 2009, at: www.youtube.com/watch?v=kvimu0a1HtY&feature=player_embedded

10. Muhammed Abdullah, 'Diyala battles water shortage', Niqash, 29 October 2009, at: http://www.niqash.org/articles/?id=2560

11. 'Salim al-Jubouri MP: Wand river is now permanently dry, and the greater danger is that Dyala river as a result of Iran's water policies', Altahreernews, 15 August 2011, at: www.altahreernews.com/inp/view.asp?ID=1208

12. United Nations Environment Programme, Desk study on the environment in Iraq, 2003.

13. 'Iraq's drinking water drying up, sewage pollutes shrinking rivers', Environment News Service, 14 May 2010, at: www.ens-newswire.com/ens/may2010/2010-05-14-01.html

14. Dale Lightfoot, 'Survey of infiltration Karez in Northern Iraq: History and current status of underground aqueducts', UNESCO, September 2009, at: http://unesdoc.unesco.org/images/0018/001850/185057e.pdf

15. Saleem al-Wazzan, 'Salt levels in Shatt al-Arab threaten environmental disaster', Niqash, 2 September 2009, at: www.niqash.org/articles/?id=2517

16. 'Iran comes to Iraq's aid over water problem', Press TV, 11 October 2009, at: www.presstv.ir/detail.aspx?id=108380&sectionid=351020201

17. Wilfred Thesiger, *The Marsh Arabs*, Penguin Classics, London, 2008.

18. Interview with the author, September 2013.

19. Christopher Bellamy, 'Iraqi push to complete strategic "Third River" ', *Independent*, 31 August 1992, at: www.independent.co.uk/news/world/iraqi-push-to-complete-strategic-third-river-1580538.html

20. United Nations High Commission for Refugees, 'Missan Governorate Assessment Report', November 2006, at: http://www.unhcr.org/45db06c42.html

21. United Nations Environment Programme, 'The Mesopotamian marshlands: Demise of an ecosystem', 2001, p. 35, at: http://www.unep.org/Documents.multilingual/Default.asp?DocumentID=307&ArticleID=3866&l=en (my emphasis; references omitted).

22. 'Resurrecting Eden', CBS News, 15 November 2009, at: www.cbsnews.com/video/watch/?id=5658502n

23. United Nations Integrated Water Task Force for Iraq, 'Managing change in the marshlands: Iraq's critical challenge', United Nations White Paper, 2011, p. 20, at: http://iq.one.un.org/documents/Marshlands%20Paper%20-%20published%20final.pdf

24. Steve Lonergan, 'Ecological restoration and peacebuilding: The case of the Iraqi marshes' in D. Jensen and S. Lonergan (eds), *Assessing and Restoring Natural Resources in Post-Conflict Peacebuilding*, Earthscan, London, 2012, p. 228.

25. 'Iraq approves Kuwait oil exploration deal', Middle East Online, 10 January 2013, at: www.middle-east-online.com/english/?id=56372

26. 'Iraq expels Turkish firm from oil exploration deal', Agence France Presse, 7 November 2012, at: http://english.ahram.org.eg/NewsContent/3/12/57440/Business/Economy/Iraq-expels-Turkish-firm-from-oil-exploration-deal.aspx

27. Dunia Frontier Consultants, *2011 Foreign Commercial Activity in Iraq*, 2012, at: http://duniafrontier.com/products-page/iraq-research-reports/2011-foreign-commercial-activity-in-iraq

28. Interview with the author, January 2011.

29. 'Turkey's Erdogan accuses Baghdad of dragging Iraq to civil war', Agence France Presse, 21 November 2012, at: www.dailystar.com.lb/News/Middle-East/2012/Nov-21/195803-turkeys-erdogan-accuses-baghdad-of-dragging-iraq-to-civil-war.ashx

30. 'Iraq wants to open new chapter with Turkey: PM', Agence France Presse, 6 December 2012, at: http://english.ahram.org.eg/NewsContent/2/8/59925/World/Region/Iraq-wants-to-open-new-chapter-with-Turkey-PM.aspx

31. 'Fatah al-Sheikh calls for a boycott of Turkish goods in protest over Erdogan's statements', National Iraqi News Agency, at: www.ninanews.com/arabic/News_Details.asp?ar95_VQ=FLDIHG

32. 'Al-Allaq: Erdogan is sectarian and is planning a conspiracy against Iraq . . . Yassin al-Majid calls for the Turkish Ambassador to Iraq to be expelled in response to Erdogan's interference', *Jareeda Al-Bayan*, 26 December 2012, at: www.albayaniq.com/?p=2576

33. 'Iraqis block Iranian pilgrims in retaliation for cutting off river water', Kuwait News Agency, 18 July 2011, at: www.kuna.net.kw/ArticleDetails.aspx?id=2180777&language=en

34. 'Iraqi farmers block Iran border post', Agence France Presse, 10 July 2011.

35. 'Missan prevents importation of vegetables through crossing point with Iran', Aswat al-Iraq, 6 October 2009.

36. Randy Schnepf, 'Iraq agriculture and food supply: Background and issues', Congressional Research Service, 7 June 2004, at: http://crs.wikileaks-press.org/RL32093.pdf

37. CPA Orders 12 and 54.

38. See Sumaria TV news report, 5 June 2012, at: www.youtube.com/watch?v=
AX3U5RcQics; Al-Fayhaa news report, 30 September 2012, at: www.youtube.com/
watch?v=T7Xo2c7aDew

39. 'Parliamentary economics committee: The delay in implementing the customs and
duties law was done to satisfy the desires of neighboring countries', Al-Baghdadia
News, 26 June 2012, at: www.albaghdadianews.com/economy/item/11785-AkAjb
ZHADn%D8%A9-AkBEkLAln%D8%A9bavnk-bZBnj-jAlNl-AkbIEJ%D8%A9-
AkKLEKn%D8%A9-vAs-kEiB%D8%A9-DNk-AkvNAE.html

40. 'The government decides to postpone the application of the customs and duties law
until the appropriate circumstances for its application emerge', Al-Forat News website,
26 June 2012, at: http://www1.alforattv.net/modules/news/article.php?storyid=76821

41. 'Iran hit by sandstorm pollution', BBC News, 7 July 2009, at: http://news.bbc.co.uk/2/
hi/middle_east/8139007.stm

42. See, for example, Akram Keremat, Behrouz Marivani and Mehdi Samsami, 'Climatic
change, drought and dust crisis in Iran', *World Academy of Science, Engineering and
Technology*, 57 (2011), at: www.waset.org/journals/waset/v57/v57-3.pdf. Kuwait is
also increasingly suffering from dust storms. See Gareth Harvey, 'Weatherwatch: Dust
storms wreak havoc in Kuwait', *Guardian*, 29 March 2011, at: www.theguardian.com/
news/2011/mar/29/weatherwatch-dust-storms-kuwait; and 'Dust storm on the
Arabian peninsula', Nasa Earth Observatory, April 2013, at: http://earthobservatory.
nasa.gov/NaturalHazards/view.php?id=80839

43. 'Iraq must take steps to prevent dust storms: Larijani', *Tehran Times*, 4 November
2009, at: http://news.kodoom.com/en/iran-politics/iraq-must-take-steps-to-prevent/
story/541049/

44. 'Iran, Iraq sign $1.2b deal to bring dust storms under control', *Tehran Times*,
4 October 2011, at: www.tehrantimes.com/politics/3165-iran-iraq-sign-12b-deal-to-
bring-dust-storms-under-control

45. 'Massive dust storms bring Iran to a standstill', *Tehran Times*, 16 April 2011.

46. 'Iran will take all legal measures to tackle issue of dust storms: official', *Tehran
Times*, 27 May 2012, at: http://www.tehrantimes.com/politics/98292-iran-will-take-
all-legal-measures-to-tackle-issue-of-dust-storms-official-; 'Iran Foreign Minister
Salehi meets al-Maliki and Zebari to confirm support for Iraq's security and stability',
Nahrain Net, 11 May 2011, at: www.nahrainnet.net/news/52/ARTICLE/17050/2011-
05-11.html

47. 'Iranian provinces wrestling with dust storms', Radio Zamaneh, 25 June 2012, at:
http://radiozamaneh.com/english/content/iranian-provinces-wrestling-dust-storms

48. 'Iran, Iraq to discuss issue of dust storms', *Tehran Times*, 30 October 2012, at: www.
tehrantimes.com/politics/102901-iran-iraq-to-discuss-issue-of-dust-storms

49. 'Iran criticizes Iraq for inaction about dust storms', Radio Zamaneh, 7 November
2012,at:http://radiozamaneh.com/english/content/iran-criticizes-iraq-inaction-about-
dust-storms

50. Joint Analysis and Policy Unit, 'Sand and dust storm fact sheet', UNIraq, February
2013, at: http://reliefweb.int/sites/reliefweb.int/files/resources/SDS%20Fact%20Sheet.
pdf

51. Fadhel Rashad, 'Najaf: 13 people die during a dust storm', *Al-Hayat*, 17 April 2011.

52. Interviews with physicians in Salah al-Din province. Many of my observations on the
health impact of environmental deterioration are based on research that I carried out
with my wife and with the assistance of colleagues and relatives during the summer
of 2010 in farmland areas in the border area between Salah al-Din and Kirkuk provinces. For more, see Rouba Beydoun, 'Deprioritising people's lives, The response of
the state and international actors to the drought crisis in Salaheddine Governorate,
Iraq after 2003', Summer 2010, unpublished.

53. 'Baghdadis' sufferings double with the dust storms and repeated electricity and water
cuts', Radio Sawa, 18 May 2008, at: www.radiosawa.com/content/article/114569.html

54. N. Vijay Jagannathan, Ahmed Shawky Mohamed and Alexander Krember, 'Water in the Arab world: Management perspectives and innovations', World Bank, 2009, at: http://siteresources.worldbank.org/INTMENA/Resources/water-in-the-arab-world-ch24.pdf
55. Interviews with the author, July 2010.
56. Interview with the author, July 2010.
57. Interviews with the author, Summer 2010.
58. 'Baghdadis' sufferings double with the dust storms and repeated electricity and water cuts', Radio Sawa, 18 May 2008, at: www.radiosawa.com/content/article/114569.html
59. Iraqi National Investment Commission, 'Investment opportunities in agriculture sector', undated, at: www.investpromo.gov.iq/index.php?id=62
60. United Nations Country Team, 'Iraq facts and figures', at: http://iq.one.un.org/Facts-and-Figures

CHAPTER 9: WHAT IS TO BE DONE?

1. In support of that argument, former US diplomat and adviser to senior Kurdish politicians Peter Galbraith, who played a pivotal role in post-2003 Iraq, wrote that 'Iraq was cobbled together by the British at the end of World War I from three different Ottoman valiyets, or provinces: predominantly Kurdish Mosul in the north, mostly Sunni Baghdad at the center, and Shiite Basra in the south', the suggestion being that these three areas had nothing in common, other than that they were occupied by the Ottomans (Galbraith, *End of Iraq*, p. 7).
2. Haddad, *Sectarianism in Iraq*, p. 38.
3. See, for example, 'The Latinobarómetro poll: The democratic routine', *Economist*, 29 October 2011; 'Tunisians disaffected with leaders as conditions worsen', Pew Research Global Attitudes Project, 12 September 2013, at: www.pewglobal.org/2013/09/12/tunisians-disaffected-with-leaders-as-conditions-worsen/
4. Opinion polls consistently show that a majority of Iraqis never go to mosque or church to pray; of those who do most do so only very rarely. See, for example, 'Iraqis' own surge assessment: Few see security gains', ABC News/BBC/NHK Poll: Iraq – Where things stand, 10 September 2007, p. 33, at: http://abcnews.go.com/images/US/1043a1IraqWhereThingsStand.pdf
5. Mahmoud Jabar, 'Al-Maliki calls for the political process to be corrected and for sectarianism to be denounced', *Al-Arab*, 19 January 2009, at: http://www.alarab.com.qa/details.php?docId=69769&issueNo=392&secId=15
6. 'In front of the Iraqi provincial conference, al-Maliki warns of a return to sectarianism', *Al-Arab*, 9 June 2009, at: http://www.alarab.com.qa/details.php?docId=85279&issueNo=533&secId=15
7. Ali al-Saffar, 'Braving Baghdad', British Iraqi Forum website, 22 February 2011, at: http://britishiraqiforum.wordpress.com/2011/02/22/braving-baghdad/
8. Sermon available at: https://www.youtube.com/watch?feature=player_embedded&v=1W4WU6E_qr0
9. Sermon available at the Imam Holy Shrine website, at: http://www.imamhussain.org
10. See for example 'Al-Karbalai describes the closed list system as a failure with many disadvantages', Imam Hussain Holy Shrine website, 12 July 2013, at: http://www.imamhussain.org/fri/51vie.html
11. See, for example, 'Al-Kerbalai condemns the recent terrorist attacks and calls for a law regulating the financing of political parties', 4 October 2013, at: www.imamhussain.org/fri/63vie.html
12. Interview with the author, March 2013.
13. Interview with the author, April 2013.
14. See, for example, International Crisis Group, 'Iraq and the Kurds: Trouble along the trigger line', Middle East Report Number 88, 8 July 2009, at: www.crisisgroup.org/en/regions/middle-east-north-africa/iraq-iran-gulf/iraq/088-iraq-and-the-kurds-trouble-along-the-trigger-line.aspx

BIBLIOGRAPHY

Abdullah, Thabit A.J., *A Short History of Iraq*, Pearson Longman, Harlow, 2003

Aburish, Saïd, *Saddam Hussein: The politics of revenge*, Bloomsbury, London, 2000

Agnew, J., T.W. Gillespie, J. Gonzalez and B. Min, 'Baghdad nights: Evaluating the US military "surge" using nighttime light signatures', *Environment and Planning A* 40:10 (2008), pp. 2285–95

Agresto, John, *Mugged by Reality: The liberation of Iraq and the failure of good intentions*, Encounter Books, New York, 2007

Al-Azawi, Daham Mohamed, *The Christians of Iraq: The plight of the present and fear of the future*, Arab Scientific Publishers, Doha, 2012

Al-Bayati, Hamid, *From Dictatorship to Democracy: An insider's account of the Iraqi opposition to Saddam*, University of Pennsylvania Press, Oxford, 2011

Al-Fahed, Abdel Razzaq Mutlaq, *Iraq's Political Parties and Their Role in the National Movement 1934–1958*, Printing Company for Distribution and Publication, Beirut, 2011

Al-Janabi, Adnan, *The Rentier State and Dictatorship*, Iraqi Studies, Baghdad, 2013

Al-Jezairy, Zuhair, *The Devil You Don't Know*, Saqi, Beirut, 2009

Al-Khalili, James, *Pathfinders: The golden age of Arabic science*, Penguin, London, 2010

Al-Sa'igh, Hanna Razzouqi, *Something from Iraq's History: 40 years in the ministry of finance*, Toronto, Canada, 2008

Allawi, Ali, *The Occupation of Iraq: Winning the war, losing the peace*, Yale University Press, New Haven and London, 2007

Amnesty International, *Broken Bodies, Tortured Minds: Abuse and neglect of detainees in Iraq*, February 2011, at: http://www.amnesty.org/en/library/asset/MDE14/001/2011/en/48c3c6e6-9607-4926-abd7-d1da1c51a976/mde140012011en.pdf

Anderson, Benedict, *Imagined Communities: Reflections on the origin and spread of nationalism*, Verso, London, 2006

Anderson, Jon Lee, *The Fall of Baghdad*, Penguin Press, New York, 2004

Antoon, Sinan, *The Corpse Washer*, Yale University Press, New Haven and London, 2013

Arato, Andrew, *Constitution Making Under Occupation*, Columbia University Press, Chichester, 2009

Bashkin, Orin, *The Other Iraq: Pluralism and culture in Hashemite Iraq*, Stanford University Press, 2008

——, *New Babylonians: A history of Jews in modern Iraq*, Stanford University Press, 2012

Batatu, Hanna, *The Old Social Classes and the Revolutionary Movements of Iraq: A study of Iraq's old landed and commercial classes and of its communists, Ba'thists and Free Officers*, Saqi Books, London, 2012

Bremer, L. Paul, *My Year in Iraq: The struggle to build a future of hope*, Simon & Schuster, New York, 2006

Chandrasekaran, Rajiv, *Imperial Life in the Emerald City: Inside Iraq's Green Zone*, Vintage Books, New York, 2007

Cochrane, Marisa, 'The Battle for Basra', Institute for the Study of War, at: http://www.understandingwar.org/sites/default/files/reports/Iraq%20Report%209.pdf

Cockburn, Patrick, *The Occupation: War and resistance in Iraq*, Verso, London, 2007

——, *Muqtada Al-Sadr and the Fall of Iraq*, Faber and Faber, London, 2008

Conference of the Iraqi Opposition, *Final Report on The Transition to Democracy in Iraq*, November 2002, at: www.iraqfoundation.org/studies/2002/dec/study.pdf

Constitution Project, 'The report on the Constitution Project's Task Force on Detainee Treatment', Washington, DC, 2013, at: http://detaineetaskforce.org/read/

Coughlin, Con, *Saddam: The Secret Life*, Macmillan, London, 2002

Dann, Uriel, *Iraq under Qassem: A political history, 1958–1963*, Praeger, New York, 1969

Davis, Eric, *Memories of State: Politics, History and collective identity in modern Iraq*, University of California Press, London, 2005

Deeks, Ashley and Matthew D. Burton, 'Iraq's constitution: A drafting history', *Cornell International Law Journal*, 40:1 (2007)

Diamond, Larry, *Squandered Victory: The American occupation and the bungled effort to bring democracy to Iraq*, Times Books, New York, 2005

Dodge, Toby, *Inventing Iraq: The failure of nation building and a history denied*, Columbia University Press, New York, 2003

Dunia Frontier Consultants, *2011 Foreign Commercial Activity in Iraq*, 2012, at:http://duniafrontier.com/products-page/iraq-research-reports/2011-foreign-commercial-activity-in-iraq

Eisenstadt, Michael and Ahmed Ali, 'How this ends: Iraq's uncertain path towards national reconciliation', Washington Institute Policywatch 1553, 17 June 2009, at: http://www.washingtoninstitute.org/policy-analysis/view/how-this-ends-iraqs-uncertain-path-toward-national-reconciliation

El-Faragi, Fadel Ali, 'The Iraqi experience in combating desertification and its impacts', Division of Desertification Control, Ministry of Agriculture and Irrigation, 2010

Feldman, Noah, *What We Owe Iraq: War and the ethics of nation building*, Princeton University Press, Oxford, 2004

Feldman, Noah and Roman Martinez, 'Constitutional politics and text in the new Iraq: An experiment in Islamic democracy', *Fordham Law Review*, 75:2 (November 2006)

Galbraith, Peter, *The End of Iraq: How American incompetence created a war without end*, Simon & Schuster, London, 2006

Ghai, Yash and Jill Cottrell, 'A review of the draft constitution of Iraq', 3 October 2005, www.law.wisc.edu/gls/arotcoi.pdf

Ghanim, David, *Iraq's Dysfunctional Democracy*, Praeger, New York, 2012.

Gordon, Michael R., *The Endgame: The inside story of the struggle for Iraq, from George W. Bush to Barack Obama*, Vintage, New York, 2012

Grittings, John, *Beyond the Gulf War: The Middle East and the new world order*, Catholic Institute for International Relations, London, 1991

Haddad, Fanar, *Sectarianism in Iraq*, Columbia University Press, New York, 2011

Halchin, L. Elaine, 'The Coalition Provisional Authority (CPA): Origin, characteristics, and institutional authorities', Congressional Research Service, The Library of Congress, 6 June 2005, www.fas.org/sgp/crs/mideast/RL32370.pdf

Hall, M. Clement, *The History of Iraq, 1990–2012*, Amazon Digital Services, Kindle Edition, 2012

Halliday, Denis J., 'The deadly and illegal consequences of economic sanctions on the people of Iraq', *Brown Journal of World Affairs*, 7:1 (Winter/Spring 2000)

Harris, Shane and Matthew M. Aid, 'Exclusive: CIA files prove America helped Saddam as he gassed Iran', *Foreign Policy*, 26 August 2013, at: www.foreignpolicy.com/articles/2013/08/25/secret_cia_files_prove_america_helped_saddam_as_he_gassed_iran?print=yes&hidecomments=yes&page=full

Haseeb, Khair el-Din, *Planning Iraq's Future: A detailed project to rebuild post-liberation Iraq*, Center for Arab Unity Studies, Beirut, 2006

Hassan, Hamdi, *The Iraqi Invasion of Kuwait: Religion, identity and otherness in the analysis of war and conflict*, Pluto Press, London, 1999

Haysom, Nicholas, 'The United Nations' Office of Constitutional Support, summary and critical review of the draft constitution presented to the TNA on 28 August 2005', 15 September 2005, unpublished

——, 'The Iraqi constitution-making process – critical evaluation', Office of Constitutional Support, United Nations Assistance Mission for Iraq, Unpublished, December 2005

Hiltermann, Joost, *A Poisonous Affair: America, Iraq and the gassing of Halabja*, Cambridge University Press, 2007

Human Rights Watch, 'The quality of justice: Failings of Iraq's Central Criminal Court', 14 December 2008, at: www.hrw.org/en/reports/2008/12/14/quality-justice-0

——, 'Iraq: Secret jail uncovered in Baghdad', 1 February 2011

——, *At a Crossroads – Human rights in Iraq eight years after the US-led invasion*, February 2011, at: http://www.hrw.org/reports/2011/02/21/crossroads

Iman, Mona, 'Draft constitution gained, but an important opportunity was lost', United States Institute of Peace website, October 2005, at: http://www.usip.org/publications/draft-constitution-gained-important-opportunity-was-lost

International Crisis Group, 'After Baker-Hamilton: What to do in Iraq', Middle East Report Number 60, 19 December 2006

——, 'Oil for soil: Toward a grand bargain on Iraq and the Kurds', Middle East Report Number 80, 28 October 2008, at: www.crisisgroup.org/en/regions/middle-east-north-africa/iraq-iran-gulf/iraq/080-oil-for-soil-toward-a-grand-bargain-on-iraq-and-the-kurds.aspx

——, 'Iraq and the Kurds: Trouble along the trigger line', Middle East Report Number 88, 8 July 2009, at: www.crisisgroup.org/en/regions/middle-east-north-africa/iraq-iran-gulf/iraq/088-iraq-and-the-kurds-trouble-along-the-trigger-line.aspx

——, 'Iraq's uncertain future: Elections and beyond', Middle East Report Number 94, 25 February 2010, at: http://www.crisisgroup.org/en/regions/middle-east-north-africa/iraq-iran-gulf/iraq/094-iraqs-uncertain-future-elections-and-beyond.aspx

——, 'Iraq's secular opposition: The rise and decline of al-Iraqiya', Middle East Report Number 127, 31 July 2012, at: www.crisisgroup.org/~/media/Files/Middle%20East%20North%20Africa/Iraq%20Syria%20Lebanon/Iraq/127-iraqs-secular-opposition-the-rise-and-decline-of-al-iraqiya.pdf

Iraqi ministry of human rights, 'Annual report on the situation of prisons and detention centres in Iraq', 2008 (in possession of author)

Iraqi National Investment Commission, 'Investment opportunities in agriculture sector', Undated, at: www.investpromo.gov.iq/index.php?id=62

Ireland, Philip Williard, *Iraq: A study in political development*, Russell and Russell, New York, 1937

Isikoff, Michael, *Hubris: The inside story of spin, scandal, and the selling of the Iraq war*, Crown, New York, 2006

Ismael, Tareq, *The Rise and Fall of the Communist Party of Iraq*, Cambridge University Press, 2007

Jagannathan, N. Vijay, Ahmed Shawky Mohamed and Alexander Krember, 'Water in the Arab world: Management perspectives and innovations', World Bank, 2009, at: http://siteresources.worldbank.org/INTMENA/Resources/water-in-the-arab-world-ch24.pdf

Jaine, Caroline, *A Better Basra: Searching for strategy and sanity in Iraq*, Askance Publishing, Cambridge, 2011

Jongerden, Joost, 'Dams and politics in Turkey: Utilizing water, developing conflict', *Middle East Policy*, 17:1 (2010), pp. 137–43

Kadhim, Abbas, *Reclaiming Iraq: The 1920 revolution and the founding of the modern state*, University of Texas Press, Austin, 2012

Keremat, A., B. Marivani and M. Samsami, 'Climatic change, drought and dust crisis in Iran', *World Academy of Science, Engineering and Technology*, 57 (2011), at: www.waset.org/journals/waset/v57/v57-3.pdf

Khadduri, Imad, *Iraq's Nuclear Mirage: Memoirs and delusions*, Springhead Publishers, Ontario, 2003

Khadduri, Majid, *Independent Iraq*, Oxford University Press, London, 1951

Kilfoyle, Peter, *Lies, Damned Lies and Iraq: An in-depth investigation into the case for war and how it was misrepresented*, Harriman House Ltd, Hampshire, 2007

Kitoh, A., A. Yatagai and P. Alpert, 'First super-high-resolution model projection that the ancient Fertile Crescent will disappear in this century', *Hydrological Research Letters*, 2 (2008), pp. 1–4

Lightfoot, Dale, 'Survey of infiltration Karez in Northern Iraq: History and current status of underground aqueducts', UNESCO, September 2009, at: http://unesdoc.unesco.org/images/0018/001850/185057e.pdf

Lonergan, Steve, 'Ecological restoration and peacebuilding: The case of the Iraqi marshes' in D. Jensen and S. Lonergan (eds), *Assessing and Restoring Natural Resources in Post-Conflict Peacebuilding*, Earthscan, London, 2012

Main, Ernest, *Iraq from mandate to independence*, G. Allen & Unwin Ltd, London, 1935

Makiya, Kanan, *Republic of Fear: The politics of modern Iraq*, University of California Press, Berkeley, 1998

McDowall, David, *A Modern History of the Kurds*, I.B.Tauris, New York, 2005

Ménargues, Alain, *Les Secrets de la guerre du Liban*, Editions Albin Michel, Paris, 2004

Mofid, Kamran, *The Economic Consequences of the Gulf War*, Routledge, London, 1990

Morrow, Jonathan, 'Iraq's constitutional process II: An opportunity lost', United States Institute of Peace, November 2005, at: http://www.usip.org/publications/iraqs-constitutional-process-ii-opportunity-lost-arabic-edition

Muttitt, Greg, *Fuel on the Fire: Oil and politics in occupied Iraq*, Vintage, London, 2012

Nakash, Yitzhak, *The Shi'is of Iraq*, Princeton University Press, Oxford, 2003

Norwegian Institute of International Affairs (NUPI), *More than 'Shiites' and 'Sunnis': How a post-sectarian strategy can change the logic and facilitate sustainable political reform in Iraq*, Oslo, 2009

O'Leary, Brendan, *How to Get Out of Iraq with Integrity*, University of Pennsylvania Press, Philadelphia, 2009

Organisation for Economic Co-operation and Development (OECD), *Improving Transparency within Government Procurement Procedures in Iraq*, February 2010, at: http://www.oecd.org/countries/iraq/improvingtransparencywithingovernmentprocure-mentproceduresiniraq.htm

Parker Ned and Raheem Salman, 'Notes from the underground: The rise of Nouri al-Maliki', World Policy Institute, 2013, at: www.worldpolicy.org/journal/spring2013/maliki

Pax, Salam, *The Baghdad Blog*, Atlantic Books, London, 2003

Phillips, David L., *Losing Iraq: Inside the postwar reconstruction fiasco*, Westview Press, New York, 2005

Powell, Colin, *It Worked for Me: In life and leadership*, Harper, New York, 2012

Qasha, Suhail, *The Christians of Iraq*, Alwarrak Publishing Ltd, London, 2009

Rawaf, Salman, 'The 2003 Iraq war and avoidable death toll', *PLOS Medicine*, 10:10 (2013), at: http://www.plosmedicine.org/article/info%3Adoi%2F10.1371%2Fjournal.pmed.1001532

Ricks, Thomas E., *Fiasco: The American military adventure in Iraq*, Penguin, New York, 2007

Robinson, Linda, *Tell Me How This Ends: General Petraeus and the search for a way out of Iraq*, PublicAffairs, New York, 2009

Roston, Aram, *The Man Who Pushed America to War: The extraordinary life, adventures, and obsessions*, Nation Books, New York, 2008

Saghieh, Hazem, *The Iraqi Baath*, Saqi, London, 2004

Said, Edward W., *From Oslo to Iraq*, Pantheon Books, New York, 2004

Salucci, Ilario, *A People's History of Iraq: The Iraqi communist party, workers' movements, and the left 1924–2004*, Haymarket Books, Chicago, 2005

Sassoon, Joseph, *The Iraqi Refugees: The new crisis in the Middle East*, I.B. Tauris, New York, 2011

——, *Saddam Hussein's Ba'th Party: Inside an authoritarian regime*, Cambridge University Press, 2012

Schnepf, Randy, 'Iraq agriculture and food supply: Background and issues', Congressional Research Service, 7 June 2004, at: http://crs.wikileaks-press.org/RL32093.pdf

Shaaban, Abdel Hussein, *The Roots of Iraq's Democratic Movement*, Bissan Publishers, Beirut, 2007

——, *Civil Society*, Atlas Press, Beirut, 2012

Shadid, Anthony, *Night Draws Near: Iraq's people in the shadow of America's war*, Picador, New York, 2006

Simon, Reeva Spector, *Iraq Between the Two Wars: The militaristic origins of tyranny*, Columbia University Press, New York, 2012

Sissons, Miranda and Abdulrazzaq al-Saiedi, 'A bitter legacy: Lessons of de-Baathification in Iraq', International Center for Transitional Justice, March 2013, at: http://ictj.org/sites/default/files/ICTJ-Report-Iraq-De-Baathification-2013-ENG.pdf

Synnott, Hilary, *Bad Days in Basra: My turbulent time as Britain's man in southern Iraq*, I.B. Tauris, London, 2008

Thesiger, Wilfred, *The Marsh Arabs*, Penguin Classics, London, 2008

Tomkins, Adam, *The Constitution after Scott: Government unwrapped*, Clarendon Press, Oxford, 1998

United Kingdom Government, *Iraq's Weapons of Mass Destruction: The assessment of the British government*, at http://news.bbc.co.uk/nol/shared/spl/hi/middle_east/02/uk_dossier_on_iraq/pdf/iraqdossier.pdf

United Nations Assistance Mission for Iraq, 'History of the Iraqi constitution-making process', December 2005, unpublished

United Nations Country Team, 'Iraq facts and figures', at: http://iq.one.un.org/Facts-and-Figures

United Nations Development Programme, 'Strengthening the working relationship between the Iraqi Council of Representatives and the Board of Supreme Audit', Background paper, 2009

United Nations Environment Programme, 'The Mesopotamian marshlands: Demise of an ecosystem', 2001, at: http://www.unep.org/Documents.multilingual/Default.asp?DocumentID=307&ArticleID=3866&l=en

——, Desk study on the environment in Iraq, 2003

United Nations High Commission for Refugees, 'Missan governorate assessment report', November 2006, at: http://www.unhcr.org/45db06c42.html

United Nations Integrated Water Task Force for Iraq, 'Managing change in the marshlands: Iraq's critical challenge', United Nations White Paper, 2011, at: http://iq.one.un.org/documents/Marshlands%20Paper%20-%20published%20final.pdf

United Nations Joint Analysis and Policy Unit, 'Sand and dust storm fact sheet', UNIraq, February 2013, at: http://reliefweb.int/sites/reliefweb.int/files/resources/SDS%20Fact%20Sheet.pdf

United Nations Office of the High Commissioner for Human Rights, 'Report on human rights in Iraq: January to June 2012', UNAMI Human Rights Office, Baghdad, October 2012

United Nations/World Bank, *Joint Iraq Needs Assessment*, October 2003, at: http://siter-esources.worldbank.org/INTIRAQ/Overview/20147568/Joint%20Needs%20 Assessment.pdf

United States Bureau of Democracy, Human Rights, and Labor, '2008 Human Rights Report: Iraq', 25 February 2009, at: www.state.gov/g/drl/rls/hrrpt/2008/nea/119116. htm

——, '2009 country report on human rights practices – Iraq', 11 March 2010, at: http:// www.refworld.org/docid/4b9e52ea6e.html

United States Committee on International Relations House of Representatives, 'US policy toward Iraq', Hearing, One Hundred Seventh Congress, Second Session, 19 September 2002, Serial No. 107–115, www.house.gov/international_relations/81813.pdf

United States Department of Defense, 'Measuring stability and security in Iraq', March 2009

United States Department of State and the Broadcasting Board of Governors, Office of Inspector General, 'Review of awards to Iraqi National Congress Support Foundation', Report Number 01-FMA-R-092, September 2011

United States Embassy Report on Corruption, September 2007

United States Government Accountability Office, 'Rebuilding Iraq: Integrated strategic plan needed to help restore Iraq's oil and electricity sectors', 2007, GAO-07-677, at: www.gao.gov/new.items/d07677.pdf

——, 'Iraq reconstruction – better data needed to assess Iraq's budget execution', January 2008, GAO-08-153, at: www.gao.gov/new.items/d08153.pdf

——, 'Securing, stabilizing, and rebuilding Iraq – Progress report: Some gains made, updated strategy needed', June 2008, GAO-08-837, at: http://www.gao.gov/products/ GAO-08-837

——, 'Stabilizing and rebuilding Iraq – Iraqi revenues, expenditures and surplus', August 2008, GAO-08-1031, at: www.gao.gov/new.items/d081031.pdf

United States Office of the Special Inspector General for Iraq Reconstruction, *Quarterly Report and Semiannual Report to the United States Congress*, 30 January 2009, at: http://www.dtic.mil/dtic/tr/fulltext/u2/a493379.pdf

——, 'Basrah modern slaughterhouse, Basrah, Iraq', SIGIR PA-09-189, 27 April 2010

——, 'Development fund for Iraq: Department of Defense needs to improve financial and management controls', SIGIR 10-020, 27 July 2010

——, *Quarterly Report and Semiannual Report to the United States Congress*, January 2011, at: http://www.sigir.mil/files/quarterlyreports/January2011/Report_-_January_ 2011.pdf

——, *Quarterly Report to the United States Congress*, 30 April 2011, at: http://www.sigir. mil/files/quarterlyreports/April2011/Report_-_April_2011.pdf

——, 'Falluja waste water treatment system: A case study in wartime contracting', SIGIR 12-007, 30 October 2011

United States Senate Democratic Policy Committee Hearing, 'Have Bush administration reconstruction and anti-corruption failures undermined the US mission in Iraq?', Testimony of James Mattil, 12 May 2008

——, Testimony of Salam Adhoob, 22 September 2008

United States Special Inspector General for Iraq Reconstruction, 'Assessing the state of Iraqi corruption', Testimony of Stuart W. Bowen, Jr, House Committee on Oversight and Government Reform, 4 October 2007

USAID/Tijara, *USAID–Tijara Provincial Economic Growth Program: Assessment of current and anticipated economic priorities in Iraq, Report for Prime Minister's Advisory Committee (PMAC)*, 4 October 2012, at: http://pdf.usaid.gov/pdf_docs/ pnadz673.pdf

Van Buren, Peter, *We Meant Well: How I helped lose the battle for the hearts and minds of the Iraqi people*, Metropolitan Books, New York, 2011

Visser, Reidar, 'Shi'a perspectives on a federal Iraq: Territory, community and ideology in conceptions of a new polity' in Daniel Heradstveit and Helge Hveem (eds), *Oil in the Gulf: Obstacles to democracy and development*, Ashgate, Aldershot, 2004

——, *Basra, the Failed Gulf State: Separatism and nationalism in southern Iraq*, Lit Verlag, Münster, 2005

——, 'Historical myths of a divided Iraq', *Survival*, 50:2 (April–May 2008)

Volcker, P., R. Goldstone and M. Pieth, *Manipulation of the Oil-for-Food Programme by the Iraqi Regime*, Independent Inquiry Committee into the United Nations Oil-For-Food Programme, 27 October 2005, at: http://www.isn.ethz.ch/Digital-Library/Publications/Detail/?ots591=0c54e3b3-1e9c-be1e-2c24-a6a8c7060233&lng=en&id=13894

Von Sponeck, H.C., *A Different Kind of War: The UN sanctions regime in Iraq*, Berghahn Books, New York, 2006

Whiteley, Jason, *Father of Money: Buying peace in Baghdad*, Potomac Books, Washington, DC, 2011

Woodward, Bob, *Obama's Wars*, Simon & Schuster, New York, 2010

World Bank, *The Economic Development of Iraq: Report of a mission organized by the International Bank for Reconstruction and Development at the request of the government of Iraq*, Johns Hopkins Press, Baltimore, 1952

World Bank, *Economy Profile: Iraq*, 2013, at: www.doingbusiness.org/~/media/giawb/doing%20business/documents/profiles/country/IRQ.pdf

Yergin, Daniel, *The Prize*, Free Press, New York, 1991 (reissued 2011)

Yousif, Bassam, 'Aspiration and reality in Iraq's post-sanctions economy', *Middle East Report*, 266 (Spring 2013)

Index

Accountability and Justice Commission (AJC) 68, 126
Advanced Detection Equipment (ADE) 1–5, 190
Agresto, John 65
agriculture, and the environmental disaster 230–5, 238–41
Ahmadinejad, Mahmoud 236
Allawi, Ali 51, 55, 261n22
Allawi, Ayad 123
  2010 election 128
  on al-Maliki's second government 129
  assassination attempt on 58
  on exiles in government 51, 55
  Governing Council 49
  as interim prime minister 81–2
  in opposition 156–7
  and Wifaq 42
Allawi, Mohamed 152–4
al-Amidi, Abdul Mehdi 228
Amman meeting (2007) 210–11
Amnesty International 182
Anbar province 83, 132
  demonstrations in 138, 157
  federalism movement 143
  flood 179
  oil investment 166
Anfal campaign 31, 35
anti-desertification 110, 234–5, 237
anti-terrorism laws 182
Arab League, 2011 summit 155
Arab Spring 135, 233, 256
Article 61(c) of the constitution 81

ATSC Limited 1, 2
Atta, Qassem 66, 71
Attiyah, Khaled 204

Baath party 26, 27–37, 56, 58
  de-Baathification 68–9, 106–7, 125–6, 130, 133, 164, 206–7, 254
Badr Corps 103, 105
al-Badri, Abdul Aziz 217
Baghdad
  history 17–18
  al-Muttalabi on 139
  occupation 7, 71–3, 103, 118
  quality of life 249
  services 171–4, 177, 179
  violence 5–6, 66, 103–9, 115, 136, 185–7, 207, 247
  see also decentralisation
al-Bakr, Ahmed Hassan 28, 31
Barzani, Masoud 128
Basra 18, 143
  budget 150
  Charge of Knights 123
  demonstrations in 136–7, 229
  environmental disaster 224–5
  Turkish investment 228–9
BBC 2–3
biography of author 6–9
Board of Supreme Audit 72–3, 198–9, 201, 208
al-Bolani, Jawad 266n11
borders, Iraq's 17, 18, 244
Bowen, Stuart 189

Bremer, L. Paul, III 59, 62, 68, 69–71, 80
bribery 68, 215
Britain *see* United Kingdom
budgets, annual state 72–3, 110, 152, 179,
    190, 193
Bush, George W. 46, 69–70, 260n13

al-Chalabi, Ahmed 42–3, 68–9, 125–6,
    206–7, 260n21, 263n18
Charge of the Knights 123
Chevron (oil company) 166
Christian community 184–7, 246
civil conflict 103–11, 114–16, 161, 255
    and security forces 116, 136, 141, 144, 146
climate 172–3
    change 213, 221, 222–5
    see also environment
Coalition Provisional Authority (CPA) 62,
    65, 68–73, 209–11
    and the constitution 75–8
    'trade liberalization policy' 231
Communist party 25, 27, 30, 32, 191
constitution 14, 84–102, 251–6
    Article 61(c) 81
    and the CPA 75–8
    and decentralisation 149–51
    drafting of 84–98
    and Islam 91–3
    and federalism 94–5, 142–5
    and the judiciary 132–3
    and the military 97–8, 127, 131–2
    and oil and gas 95–6, 164–5
    and parliament 130–1, 146–51
    repugnancy clause 91
    rules of procedure 134
    and the separation of powers 96–8,
        148–9
    and women 93–4
corruption 9, 51, 53, 55, 121, 249, 252
    anti-corruption law 196
    and the CPA 194–9
    impact of 214–17
    and al-Maliki 155
    and parliament 201–6
    prior to 2003 190–4
    and violence 107
criminal gangs 72–3
'current fields' 96, 164
customs and duty 231–5

al-Dabbagh, Ali 216–17
dams 223–4
date palms 230–1, 233
Dawa Party 27, 43, 49, 122

and the constitution 100
    and al-Jaafari 43, 111
    and al-Maliki 54, 111
de-Baathification process 68–9, 106–7,
    125–6, 130, 133, 164, 206–7, 254
decentralization 30, 142, 147, 253
    2013 law 149–51
defence, ministry of 214–17
democratization 251
department of defense (US) 195
depleted uranium 221
desertification 221–2, 234, 238–9
    anti- 110, 234–5, 237
Development Fund for Iraq (DFI) 194–6
disease 238
Dora district 66, 185–6
al-Dulaimi, Adnan 114–15
al-Dulaimi, Saadoun 132, 216
dust storms 219–22, 227, 235, 237–8
duty, on imports 231–5
Dyala province 121, 132, 144, 147, 224,
    239

economic conditions 23–4, 232–5, 240
education 172, 179
Egypt 233
elections 158–60, 247–8
    1980 34
    2005 82–4
    2009 122, 123, 144, 202
    2010 125–9, 159, 160
    2013 139, 160
    2018 255
    campaign issues 248–9
electricity 171–8, 179, 214, 224, 233, 237
elites, exiles becoming 51–61
embezzlement 215
employment/unemployment 161, 168–71,
    193, 240, 249, 254
environment 213
    agriculture 230–5, 238–41
    dust storms 219–22, 227, 235, 237–8
    government agreement with Iran 235–7
    impact of environmental disaster
        237–41
    water resources 222–30
Erbil 96, 167, 228, 229, 250
Erbil agreement 128–30, 134, 147
exiles, transition to political elites 51–61
Exxon (oil company) 166

Fadhila (Virtue) party 123, 204
Faisal bin Hussein, King 19–22, 63
Faisal II 22, 25

Fallujah 103, 136, 156, 195
Faraj, Mousa 198
Federal Supreme Court 112, 128, 132–3,
    147, 266n11, 267n15
federalism 50–1, 64, 80–1, 94–6, 100–1,
    142–4, 147, 157
fibre-optics 153
finance, political 159
food rationing system 154, 202–4
foreign policy 24, 94, 95, 193, 232
Future of Iraq Project 49–51, 80

Galbraith, Peter 279n1
gas sector *see* oil and gas sector
Ghai, Yash 99
Gorran Movement 128–9
Governing Council 77, 80–2
    and Allawi 49, 50
    Article 61(c) of the constitution 81
    and the TAL 79, 91–2
    and Tawafuq 114
government
    and corruption 199–201, 206–9
    customs law 233–5
    and the environmental disaster 228–30,
        235–7
    of national unity 110–12, 128, 131–2,
        146, 205
    roles of 148
    see also al-Maliki
Government Accountability Office (US) 110
governments of national unity 110–12,
    128, 131–2, 146, 205
graft 189, 194–6
Great Iraqi Revolution 19
Green Zone 135, 136, 155, 210
guns 79

Haddad, Fanar 63–4, 245
al-Hakim, Abdel Aziz 41, 263n18
Halliday, Denis 36
Hamid, Alaa Jawad 208–9
al-Hamoudi, Humam 85, 87, 263n18
Hamza, Khidhir 46
Harris, Arthur 21–2
al-Hashimi, Tariq 138, 156, 229
Haysom, Nicholas 100, 262n12
health services 172, 179, 238
Higher Judicial Council 147
HIV/Aids program 213–14
holidays, official 170–1
human rights 161, 180–7
Hussein, Saddam 56
    assassination attempt 43

and Baath party 31, 33–7
and corruption prior to 2003 190–4
and desertification 221
invasion of Iran 225
and the military 57–8
Hussein, Safa al-Sheikh 36

incompetence, of internationals 209–14
Independent Electoral Commission of
    Iraq (IECI) 82–4, 159, 207
Independent High Electoral Commission
    see Independent Electoral
    Commission of Iraq
Independents 122
'information crimes' bill 147
integrity commission 133–4, 137, 147, 154,
    197–9, 203, 207–8, 210, 212, 252
    al-Ugaili, Rahim 134, 137, 198, 207–8
interim government 89–90
International Atomic Energy Agency
    (IAEA) 46
International Monetary Fund (IMF) 232
Iran
    environmental agreement with 235–7
    revolution 34
    and SCIRI 41
    war with 34–5
    water resources 223–4, 225, 227
Iraq Petroleum Company 33
Iraqi Islamic Party (IIP) 43–4, 49, 104, 120,
    124, 202
    and the constitution 90, 100
Iraqi National Accord (Wifaq) 42, 49
Iraqi National Congress (INC) 42–3, 49
Iraqiya alliance 85, 100, 123–4, 126,
    127–9, 146, 156–7, 229
Islam, and the constitution 87, 91–3
Islamic Supreme Council of Iraq (ISCI)
    see SCIRI
Israel 191
al-Issawi, Rafi 138, 229

al-Jaafari, Ibrahim 43, 111, 196
al-Jabiri, Jihad 3
al-Janabi, Abdul Nasser 116–18
Jeffrey, James F. 128
Jihaz al-Amn al-Khaass (Special Security
    Organization) 31
al-Jubouri, Salim Abdullah 267n11
al-Jubouri, Withab Shaker 113
judiciary 132–4
    Higher Judicial Council 147
    and human rights 183–4
    see also Federal Supreme Court

Kana', Yonadam 246
Karbala province 18, 179, 228, 234, 255
Kirkuk province 29, 42, 80, 141, 178, 179,
    229, 239
Kufa 185
Kurdish alliance 41–2, 55, 59–60, 85, 122,
    157–8
Kurdistan Democratic Party (KDP) 29,
    41–2, 49–50
Kurdistan regional government (KRG) 80,
    96, 164–7, 214
Kurds/Kurdistan region 35–6, 243, 250–1
    after 2003 war 55–6, 63–5
    and the constitution 87–90,
        100, 101
    during monarchy 21–22
    electricity supply 178
    expulsion to Iran 32
    and Iranians 35
    Kurdish alliance 41–2, 55, 59–60, 85,
        122, 157–8
    Kurdistan Democratic Party (KDP) 29,
        41–2, 49–50
    and the new parliament 59–60
    oil and gas in 96, 164–7
    regional government (KRG) 80, 96,
        164–7, 214
    and the TAL 79–81
    water shortage 224
Kuwait, invasion of 35

al-Lami, Ali Faisal 207
land reform 25–6
language 209
    of the constitution 213
    English 169
    and the exiles 52
    Kurdish 29–30
    and the new government 63
Latifiyah 119
leadership council 87–93, 95–6, 98–9, 100,
    164
Lebanon 1, 111, 159, 178, 191
looting 61–2

McCormick, James (Jim) 1, 3
al-Mahdi, Adel Abed 212
Mahdi Army 44, 104, 105
    and the Charge of the Knights 123
    professor's kidnapping 109
al-Mahdi, Hadi 136–7
al-Mahmoud, Medhat 132–3
Majid, Ali Ghidan 186
al-Majid, Ali Hassan 31

al-Maliki, Nouri 12–13, 43, 53–4, 104, 111
    2010 election 126–7, 246–7
    and the ADE 3–5
    Charge of the Knights 123
    on civil conflict 117
    and corruption 212
    and exile 53–4
    and the integrity commission 208
    and the military 58, 131, 141
    and the militias 115–16, 123, 141
    and parliament 205–6
    and public services 174–6
    second government 129, 129–46
    and Turkey 229–30
marshlands 225–7
al-Mashhadani, Mahmoud 117, 202
Maysan province 226, 230
military 57–8
    budget 179–80
    and the constitution 97–8, 127, 251–2
    disbanding after 2003 war 66–8,
        69–73
    al-Maliki takes control 131
    procurement 215–17
    restoration of the 118–19
    US occupation forces 66–8
militias 103–8, 144–5, 155–6, 159
    Badr Corps 103, 105
    Lebanese 191
    Mahdi Army 44, 103, 104, 105
monarchy period 19–24
Mosul 17, 18, 185, 186
Mousa, Hamid Majid 77
al-Moussawi, Ali 216
Mukhabarat 32, 33, 52, 58, 192
Mustafa, Abdel Rahman 178
al-Mutlaq, Salih 126, 157, 229
al-Muttalabi, Saad 138–9

Najaf province 18, 103, 119–20, 154, 156,
    237, 255
Nasariya 241
Nasser, Abdul Gamal 24
National Dialogue Front 126
nationalism 249
Nationalist Progressive Front 30–1
natural resources 10, 25, 34, 45, 95–6, 145,
    162, 252–3
nepotism 214–15, 249
nerve-gas attacks 45–6
Ninewa 121, 132, 179, 186, 222, 228, 239
nuclear weapons 46
al-Nujaifi, Ayatollah 154
al-Nujaifi, Usama 129, 157

Obama, Barack 145–6
Oil for Food Programme 37, 193, 194
oil and gas sector 33–4, 162–7, 170, 254
    and 2003 war 46
    and the constitution 95–6
    corruption in 107
    ministry 62, 171, 228
    mismanagement 154
    Oil for Food Programme 37
    prices 232
    prior to 2003 war 193–4
Organization of the Petroleum Exporting
    Countries (OPEC) 35
Osman, Hiwa 138–9
Ottoman Empire 17–18
oversight system 201, 202, 205, 212

parliament
    and the constitution 146–51
    and corruption 199–206
    debate on civil conflict 116–17
    during monarchy 20
    during occupation 59–60, 70
parties/entities (political) 40, 49–51, 83–4,
    255
    Communist 25, 27, 30, 32, 191
    and corruption 200–1
    Dawa 27, 43, 122
    Fadhila (Virtue) 123, 204
    financing of 159, 248, 252
    Gorran Movement 128–9
    Independents 122
    Iraqi National Accord (Wifaq) 42
    Iraqi National Congress (INC) 42–3, 49
    Iraqiya alliance 85, 100, 123, 126–30,
        132, 138, 144, 146, 155–7, 229
    Kurdistan Democratic Party (KDP) 29,
        41–2, 49–50
    National Dialogue Front 126
    Nationalist Progressive Front 30–1
    Patriotic Union of Kurdistan (PUK)
        41–2, 49–50, 128
    Shia Islamic Supreme Council of Iraq
        120
    State of Law alliance 122, 123, 126–7,
        128, 147, 159, 202, 207
    Sunni Iraqi Islamic Party 120
    Supreme Council for the Islamic
        Revolution in Iraq (SCIRI) 40–1, 49,
        85, 101, 122
    Tawafuq alliance 114–15, 202
    United Iraqi Alliance (UIA) 85, 87, 122
    see also Baath party; Iraqi Islamic Party
        (IIP); Iraqiya alliance

Patriotic Union of Kurdistan (PUK) 41–2,
    49–50, 128
pollution 35, 221, 224, 226, 235, 236
Powell, Colin 67, 69
pre-war planning (2002) 49–51
prime ministers see Allawi, Ayad;
        al-Jaafari, Ibrahim; al-Maliki, Nouri
private sector 169–70
pro-poor laws 25
protests
    civilian 135–7, 141, 176, 255
    see also violence
public sector 168–71
public services 161, 171–80
PUK (Patriotic Union of Kurdistan) 41–2,
    49–50

al-Qaida 113, 114, 119
al-Qaisi, Majid 217
Qasim, Abed al-Karim 24–8
Qatar 146, 236

al-Radhi, Radhi Hamza 197
rationing system, food 154, 202–4
RCC (revolutionary command council)
    27–9
reconciliation process 112–14, 120
referendum, on the constitution 10, 18,
    86–7, 90, 99, 101
refugees 108–9
religion, under Saddam Hussein 193
republican period 24–8
repugnancy clause 91
revolution
    against monarchy 25–8
    Arab Spring 135, 233, 256
    Iran 34
revolutionary command council (RCC)
    27–9
revolutions, Middle East/North Africa 135
al-Rifa'i, Abdel Karim 239
Rumaila oilfield 228

al-Saadi, Sabah 204
al-Sadr, Mohamed Baqr 27
al-Sadr, Moqtada 44, 100
Sadrist movement 44, 157–8, 160
    and the constitution 100
    and Mahdi Army 103
al-Safi, Sayyed Ahmed 247–8
Salah al-Din 120–1, 132, 143–4, 147, 166,
    190, 238, 239
Samara 121
al-Samarai, Abdel Khaleq 31

al-Samarai, Ayad 202, 235
sanctions 36–7, 48, 231
sandstorms 220
SCIRI (Supreme Council for the Islamic
    Revolution in Iraq) 40–1, 49, 85, 101,
    122
    Badr Corps 103–4
'second insurgency' 189
secret police 32, 33, 52, 58, 192
'secret prisons' 182
sectarianism 63–5, 70, 137–42, 249
secularism 245–6
security forces 136, 145, 180–1, 197,
    240–1, 249
    and the ADE 2, 190
    and civil conflict 116, 136, 141, 144, 146
    human rights 181–2
    and intimidation 132–3
services, delivery of 11, 13, 136, 214
    see also electricity; water
sewers 178–9
al-Shahristani, Hussein 5, 87, 174, 176
Shalal, Raad 177
Sharia law 91, 93
shawkasham 234
Shia Arabs 62, 243, 247, 253
    and the constitution 76, 81, 84–5, 90,
        92, 100, 101
    counselling against violence 103
    and the military 70–1
    and the Sadrists 158
    violence against 114
    see also Badr Corps
Shia Islamists 63, 122
    Shia Islamic Supreme Council of Iraq
        120
    Supreme Council for the Islamic
        Revolution in Iraq (SCIRI) 40–1
single electoral constituency 82–3
al-Sistani, Ali 62, 76–7, 84, 98, 106
Slocombe, Walt 70
Somers, Daniel 260n16
Special Security Organization (Jihaz
    al-Amn al-Khaass) 31
state department (US) 215
State of Law alliance 122, 123, 126–7, 128,
    147, 159, 202, 207
al-Sudani, Faleh 202–5, 206
al-Sudani, Sabah 203
Sunni Arabs 70, 243
    and the constitution 90, 92, 101
    discrimination against 116
    targeted by al-Qaida 113
    and the TNA 85

violence against 114–15
    see also Iraqi Islamic Party (IIP)
Sunni Islamists 93, 104
    Sunni Iraqi Islamic Party 120, 124
Supreme Council for the Islamic
    Revolution in Iraq (SCIRI) 40–1, 49,
    85, 101
    Badr Corps 103, 104
'surge', US military 118
Syria
    and Iraqi refugees 109
    and water 223

TAL (transitional administrative law)
    78–81, 86–94, 98
Tamim province 121
Tawafuq alliance 114–15, 202
terrorism 249
    laws against 182
    al-Qaida 113, 114, 119
    see also civil conflict; violence
Thesiger, Wilfred 225
Thi-Qar 5
Tigris and Euphrates 222–3
Tikrit 31, 119–21, 190, 238
al-Tikriti, Anas 138–9
TNA (transitional national assembly)
    81–9
Torhan, Hassan 178
torture 48, 181–2
Total (oil company) 166
trade 231–4, 240
    ministry of 202–3
'trade liberalization policy' 231
transitional administrative law (TAL)
    78–81, 98
transitional national assembly (TNA)
    81–9
Transparency International 189
tribes 53, 109, 120
al-Tufayli, Salah 140
Tunisia 233
Turkey 146, 223, 228–30, 236
Twelver Ja'fari school 264n25

al-Ubaidi, Harith 204
al-Ugaili, Rahim 134, 137, 198, 207–8
unemployment/employment 161, 168–71,
    193, 240, 249, 254
United Iraqi Alliance (UIA) 85, 87, 122
United Kingdom
    2003 war 38
    and allies in Iraq 39–44
    Iraq Petroleum Company 33

and Iraq's monarchy period 19–22
occupation after 2003 war 45–9
United Nations 209, 212–14
  and constitution drafting process 82,
     87, 88, 99, 100
  Convention to Combat Desertification
     237
  Environmental Programme 226
  on Iraq's unemployment 240
  sanctions 36–7, 48
  Security Council Resolution 1483 194
United States
  2003 war 11, 37–8
  and allies in Iraq 39–44
  bombing campaign 35
  and the constitution 87–9, 95
  department of defense 195
  embassy 209, 211, 272n18, 19
  investment in Iraq 173
  and Iraq's agriculture 240
  and looting 61–2
  and al-Maliki 145
  military 'surge' 118
  occupation after 2003 war 45–9, 53, 59,
     61–73, 103–11
  state department 215
  and torture 48

al-Uzri, Hussein 207

vilayets 18
violence 12, 103–24
  and the ADE 2, 4
  against Christians 186–7
visas 166

Wahid, Karim 176
Wand River 223, 224
war
  2003 37–8, 49–51
  with Iran 34–5
water resource 222–30, 238,
     250–1
weapons
  guns 79
  of mass destruction 35, 45–7
weather 172–3
Wifaq (Iraqi National Accord) 42, 49
WMD 35, 45–7
women 26, 85
World Bank 23–4, 169

al-Yasiri, Hiyam 153–4

Zawbai, Talal 217